The second edition of *The Australian Editing Handbook* gave editors a clear overview of the publishing industry. With its compact form, clear diagrams and clear layout, this new and equally readable edition will be the practical manual of choice for new editors and proofreaders, and students in Australian editing and publishing courses. More experienced editors who are familiar with the second edition will find the book valuable for its wealth of tips, from simple but hard-to-find reminders about the sequence of marks to use in cases of infrequent footnotes (*, †, ‡, §, ‖ and ¶) to new information about editing ebooks—material that by itself justifies acquisition of the new edition.

~ **Trischa Mann**, President, Editors Victoria

The Australian Editing Handbook has always distinguished itself as a thoroughly helpful compendium on copy-editing practice—like Butcher's *Copy-Editing for British Editors*. This fresh edition updates almost everything, and foregrounds onscreen editing as the norm for practising editors. In four sequenced chapters the handbook takes novice editors (working in either Windows or the Mac environment) through the essentials of copy-editing a MS, and helps proofreaders in using Adobe Reader notes to signal corrections needed in the final stages. The section on ebooks has grown from two pages in the second edition to a twenty-page chapter in this third edition, with both strategic and practical advice on use of the common EPUB format and its relationship to Kindle. There's much value in here for editors transitioning to electronic publishing, apart from its solid coverage of the core editing skills essential in any medium. Editors seeking accreditation with the Australian Institute of Professional Editors should make the most of this new edition.

~ **Pam Peters** DE, President, Society of Editors (NSW) Inc 2008–12

This new edition is a fund of information and guidance on all aspects of editing in Australia. And it includes a wealth of up-to-date help for editors struggling to come to grips with e-editing—all in a highly readable style.

~ **Canberra Society of Editors**

T0385514

The
Australian
Editing
Handbook

Third Edition

The Australian Editing Handbook

Third Edition

Elizabeth Flann
Beryl Hill
Lan Wang

WILEY

This edition published in 2014 by John Wiley & Sons Australia, Ltd
42 McDougall St, Milton Qld 4064

Office also in Melbourne

Typeset in 9.5/12.5 pt Impressum Std

© Elizabeth Flann, Beryl Hill, Hui-chang Wang 2014

First published 1994
Reprinted 2001, 2003 (1st edn), reprinted with revisions 2004, 2008, 2009 (2nd edn), 2011, 2012

© Elizabeth Flann and Beryl Hill 1994, 2001, 2003, 2004, 2008

The moral rights of the authors have been asserted

National Library of Australia Cataloguing-in-Publication data:

Author:	Flann, Elizabeth, author.
Title:	The Australian editing handbook / Elizabeth Flann, Beryl Hill, Lan Wang.
Edition:	3rd ed.
ISBN:	9781118635957 (pbk)
	9781118635988 (ebook)
Notes:	Includes index.
Subjects:	Editing—Handbooks, manuals, etc.
	Publishers and publishing—Australia—Handbooks, manuals, etc.
Other Authors/Contributors:	Hill, Beryl, author.
	Wang, Lan, author.
Dewey Number:	808.027

Cover design by Wiley

Cover image © iStock.com/Qweek

Printed in Singapore by C.O.S. Printers Pte Ltd

10 9 8 7 6 5 4 3 2 1

Disclaimer
The material in this publication is of the nature of general comment only, and does not represent professional advice. It is not intended to provide specific guidance for particular circumstances and it should not be relied on as the basis for any decision to take action or not take action on any matter which it covers. Readers should obtain professional advice where appropriate, before making any such decision. To the maximum extent permitted by law, the author and publisher disclaim all responsibility and liability to any person, arising directly or indirectly from any person taking or not taking action based on the information in this publication.

Foreword

Readers of earlier editions of Elizabeth Flann's and Beryl Hill's *The Australian Editing Handbook* will be delighted to see the publication of this new updated edition.

In the 20 years since the first edition was written—and indeed in the 10 years since the publication of the second edition—the publishing industry, and consequently the editing profession, has undergone profound changes. Editors are now more likely to be employed on a freelance or contract basis than be employed in-house by publishers. A large proportion of their work is as likely to come from the corporate world or government departments as from publishers of books. But the greatest change has been in the delivery of content. Companies that were once proudly known as book publishers now refer to themselves as technology companies as they and the rest of the world deliver their publications in a wide variety of print and digital formats across numerous channels.

As a result of these changes the role of the editor has expanded well beyond traditional areas. Job descriptions for editors are many and varied, ranging from straightforward proofreading to comprehensive project management and facilitation of the whole publishing process (including a knowledge of the technology that supports this).

Despite all these changes, despite the ready availability of self-publishing channels, the basic principles that underlie the editor's role remain as important and unchanged as ever—their role is to improve the quality of the finished product in whatever part of the process they have been employed to work.

There are no better models for beginning editors, or indeed more experienced editors, than the authors of this book, who have stayed true to their original purpose but have updated the work to integrate the processes for all formats. This third edition has been substantially revised to incorporate new technologies and the editor's expanding roles and responsibilities. Flann and Hill have ensured the book's relevance by bringing digital expert and accredited editor Lan Wang into the author team to completely update and expand on all aspects of the book. These authors understand editors and the diversity of their responsibilities.

Between them, they have many years of experience in writing, editing and lecturing. All three have personally helped me to hone my craft and to develop a passion for getting it right.

Readers can be assured of finding between the covers the most comprehensive, accessible and up-to-date guide to all aspects of editing. In the future we will see even more rapid change in the way we deliver written content, but this edition of *The Australian Editing Handbook* will remain a must-have reference for editors everywhere.

Rosemary Noble

Project Manager, Institute of Professional Editors (IPEd) Transition Project

Former IPEd council chair and Victorian council representative

Honorary Life Member, Editors Victoria

Contents

About the authors

Elizabeth Flann has worked in children's publishing, as a commissioning editor and publisher; in general and educational publishing, as a senior editor and training editor; as a project manager for major government publications; and as a freelance general, technical and script editor. She has lectured in editing and scriptwriting at Deakin University, the University of Melbourne and the Victorian College of the Arts, and has a PhD in literary and communication studies. She is the author of a number of primary and secondary textbooks, and currently spends her time as a writer, environmental advocate and occasional guest lecturer.

Beryl Hill was trained as an editor by the legendary Barbara Ramsden at Melbourne University Press, and in turn has introduced many editorial trainees to the intricacies of copy editing. She is the author of a number of style guides and has edited all kinds of publications—from academic and educational textbooks to illustrated books for children; from formal government publications to books of humour and a magazine for rock climbers; from cookery and gardening books to websites. She is also the author of the history of the CSIR Ski Club. She has held senior editorial positions with many publishers, including Melbourne University Press, Penguin Books, Oxford University Press, Lothian Books and Deakin University, and has had extensive experience as a freelance editor and guest lecturer at RMIT University and Monash University.

Beryl and Elizabeth each received the Distinguished Editor Award (an honorary award from IPEd, the Institute of Professional Editors) and are honorary life members of Editors Victoria, where they were members of the committee of management and conducted a number of training sessions. They both served on the inaugural panel of assessors for developing the accreditation process for IPEd, and Beryl was an invigilator for the initial IPEd examinations in Melbourne.

Lan Wang is the publishing manager at the Australian Institute of Family Studies and an IPEd Accredited Editor. She specialises in maximising the use of technology to ensure that the publication process, from manuscript to print and electronic output, is as smooth as possible. She has worked in a wide range of publishing environments, including trade publishers, government agencies, academic centres and non-government organisations, as both an in-house and freelance editor, typesetter and project manager. She has been a guest lecturer at RMIT University and the University of Melbourne, and presented training workshops on ebooks and on freelancing for Editors Victoria and IPEd. She has also been active in supporting the professional activities of Editors Victoria and has assisted in developing and marking the IPEd Accreditation Exam. She was the convenor of the 2nd National Editors Conference held in Melbourne in 2005.

List of figures and tables

Figures

Tables

How to use this book

Editors play a central role in the publishing process, in terms of both management and quality control. At a broader level, editors may oversee a publishing project from start to finish, or manage teams of editors, designers, proofreaders and other professionals to ensure that the required elements of the publication are produced to a high standard, on time and on budget. At a more detailed level, editors may tackle the editing, proofreading or indexing tasks themselves, delving into the publication to ensure that the content is logical and complete, the words are clear and free of errors, the language is appropriate for the audience, and the manuscript is appropriately prepared for production. The wide range of these tasks makes the editing profession both challenging and rewarding.

This book is intended for beginning editors, students of editing and publishing, or any editor who may wish to learn more about a specific aspect of editing, such as the relatively new landscape of ebooks.

The book is broken up into three major parts, covering:

- the broader aspects of editing and publishing

- the principles and techniques of editing

- the production side of the publishing process.

Where appropriate, we have included figures and tables to illustrate and illuminate the text. When these illustrations relate to more than one area of text, as in the first section of this book, or are likely to be referred to frequently, such as proofreading symbols, they have been placed in the appendixes section for easier reference.

All of these areas are addressed from the perspective of an editor, whether in-house or freelance. We have chosen to focus on book publishing rather than broader areas of publishing such as newspapers, magazines or general websites, as we believe that the principles learned here can be applied and extended across other areas of publishing and will give beginning editors an excellent start on their long journey towards finding their own niche in this fascinating profession.

Acknowledgements

I would like to thank those who have generously provided valuable feedback on the manuscript. My particular gratitude of course goes to my co-authors, Elizabeth and Beryl, for their wise support and encouragement. Special thanks to Liz Steele for volunteering her rare spare time to read and review the entire manuscript, and to Sarah Hazelton, Penny Johnston and Max McMaster, who provided excellent comments on specific chapters of the book.

Most importantly, I am grateful to my wonderful partner, Jane, for forgiving the many lost evenings and weekends spent devoted to this book.

Lan Wang

PART A

Introduction to publishing

Publishing is a complex process that involves the application of numerous roles and skills, including commissioning the material, managing the publishing process, substantive and copy editing, designing, typesetting, proofreading, indexing, printing, marketing and distribution. Some people may fill a number of these roles, while others will focus on one specific task, depending on the size of the publishing organisation and the nature of the project and personnel involved. Part A of this book provides a broad overview of these roles and how the entire publishing process is managed from start to finish.

Publishing roles and responsibilities

With the increase in complexity and accessibility of digital media, publishing is no longer mainly the domain of traditional publishing houses and government or corporate departments. Editors may find themselves working on a diverse range of publications, both print and electronic, from standard trade paperbacks, manuals, technical reports and journals to family histories, newsletters or digital publications such as websites, ebooks, social media content or ebook applications.

Terminology and coverage

Publishing and editing roles and products vary greatly, and this book cannot cover all possibilities and variations. Therefore the focus is mainly on book products published in print or electronically, using the following terminology:

- The term *publication* is used to refer generically to any written work (such as a printed report, an issue of an academic journal or an ebook), no matter the content or format in which it has been published.

- *Book* refers to a stand-alone work of fiction or non-fiction (such as a printed volume of poetry, an online technical report or a fiction ebook) published in print or digitally, but does not include serial works (such as a journal) or more open-ended works (such as a company website or a blog). Particular types of books will be specified where relevant.

ebook application
stand-alone book application software, usually multimedia, that is not necessarily based on a particular standard and may run on only some devices

format (book)
the size, style, margins etc. for a publication; the trimmed page size; the medium of production, such as print, ebook or website

(continued)

Terminology and coverage *(cont'd)*

EPUB
a free and open ebook standard developed by the International Digital Publishing Forum

PDF (Portable Document Format)
an Adobe file format commonly used in print and ebook production to view, proofread and print the exact typeset layout of a book without having to have the software that created it

- An *ebook* is an electronic version of a publication, such as an EPUB, a PDF, an ebook app or a website, whether or not there is a printed version of the publication.

- The term *publisher* is used here when referring to an individual or organisation that is responsible for producing and releasing a publication (such as a trade publisher, a government department or a charity).

For the sake of brevity and readability, this book does not include discussion of editing and production for newspapers, magazines and general websites, although many of the same principles would apply in those areas.

manuscript (MS, pl. MSS, typescript)
originally handwritten copy, now used to describe an author's unpublished copy, whether in hard copy or electronic format

In most cases the publishing process still follows a conventional sequence, starting with the initial manuscript, proceeding through the editing and production stages, and culminating in a book, report, manual or other publication, whether in print or electronic format. We will take this as the standard model throughout this book and variations from this model will be dealt with where relevant.

The production of a finished publication from a raw manuscript or an author's or publisher's idea is a multistage process in which the editor plays a key role. Creating a printed or electronic publication requires ongoing cooperation between individuals and departments, and with companies outside the publishing organisation. Editors may manage all aspects or only parts of a publishing project to ensure that the required elements of the publication are produced to a high standard, on time and on budget. They may also tackle one or more of the editing, proofreading or indexing tasks themselves, delving into the publication to ensure that the content is logical and complete, the words are clear and free of errors, the language is appropriate to the audience, and the manuscript is appropriately prepared for production.

proofreading
checking typeset pages to ensure that they are free of errors, well laid out, accurate and complete

The editor, therefore, must be competent in liaising with others and in organising materials, people and processes. As well as being an arbiter of sense, structure, style and taste, an editor must also be a tactful yet firm adviser, and a watchdog on schedules and costs. A strong overall knowledge of the publishing process and the role of the individuals involved is also an essential part of the editor's toolkit.

A multinational publishing company or large government department may employ dozens or even hundreds of people in clearly defined groups or departments, each with specific roles and tasks. In contrast, a small publishing company or community group may employ only two or three publishing staff, each of whom has a wide range of responsibilities. Where necessary, publishers commission external assistance from editors, designers, illustrators, ebook developers, animators, sound recorders, proofreaders, indexers and publicists, among others.

No matter what the size of the organisation, the overall progression of a publication remains the same. This chapter provides an overview of general publishing processes and the various roles and tasks involved. Many aspects of these are then dealt with in more detail in the remaining chapters of the book.

INTERRELATIONSHIPS IN PUBLISHING

This section describes the individuals and teams who may be involved in the publishing process, the tasks they undertake and how they work with each other. There are wide variations between different publishing organisations, not only in staffing levels but also in the way in which they deal with the stages of production. In some organisations each role might be undertaken by several dedicated staff, while in others one person may handle several of the roles. Other organisations outsource the majority of the functions. Role titles also vary considerably; for example, copy editors, production editors, editorial coordinators and assistant editors may all undertake some aspects of editing but may also have other roles and responsibilities. Some instances of these variations are covered here, but the following should be taken as an overall guide to the different functions, recognising that every publishing organisation will be different.

Figure 1.1 (overleaf) shows an example of the individuals and responsibilities within a medium-sized publishing company and the way in which they work with each other throughout the publishing process. This illustrates the degree to which the roles and tasks need to be coordinated and individuals need to collaborate with each other in order to successfully publish a work.

copy editing
examining and correcting a written work according to an established editorial style; usually also involves electronic styling of a document in preparation for typesetting

substantive (structural) editing
examination and correction of a written work to ensure that its structure is sound, its order logical, its content complete, and the language clear and appropriate for its audience

prepress
preparation by a commercial printer of a digital file, such as a PDF or InDesign document, so that it is suitable for printing on specific equipment

proof
a trial reproduction of a typeset document or artwork for the purpose of checking and correction

Figure 1.1: example of interrelationships in a publishing company

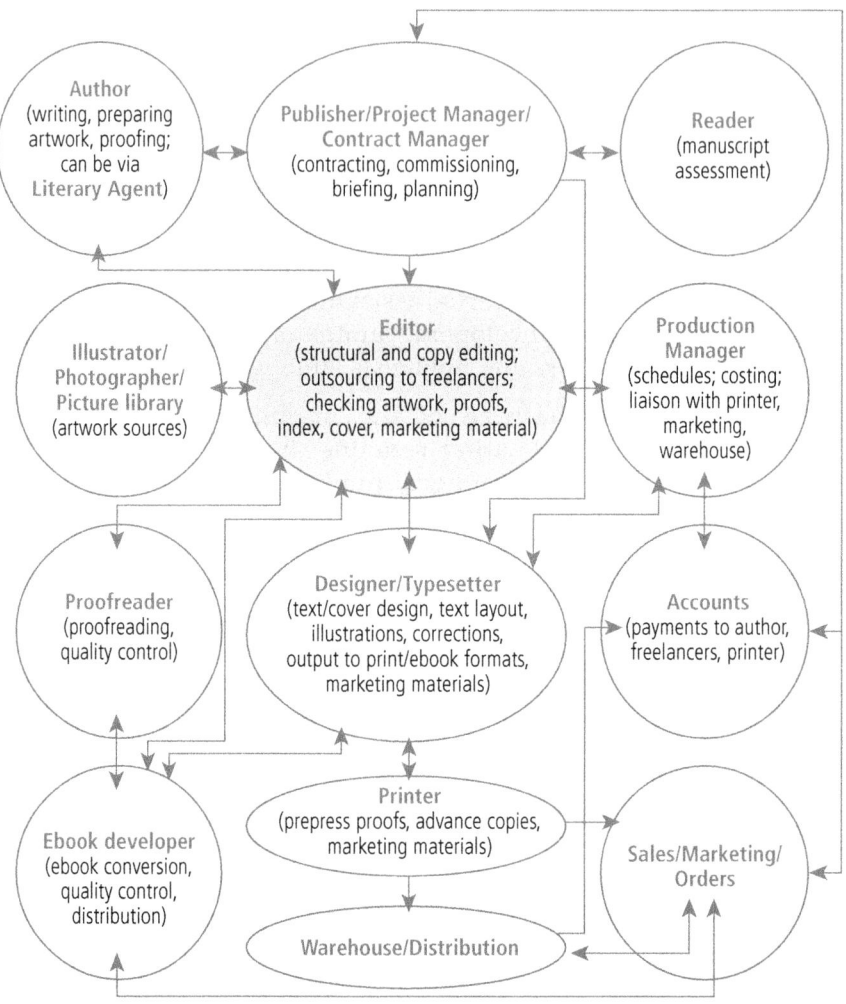

ROLES AND RESPONSIBILITIES

The author

The author may have approached one or more publishers with a proposal, a draft or the finished manuscript of a written work. Alternatively, a publisher, publication manager or commissioning editor may have sought out an appropriately qualified or skilled person to write on a particular topic or to edit or compile, say, a collection of academic papers or commentaries on current events, or may have commissioned one or more writers for a series, such as reading books for primary school students.

Once a proposal has been discussed and accepted and the publication contracted, the author works with the publisher and editor to produce an acceptable manuscript, together with whatever artwork or other materials are required.

After consultation with the publisher and/or editor, the author is responsible for:

- delivering, on time, an acceptable manuscript (complete, clearly presented, factually accurate and to the length specified in the contract), usually in electronic format

- supplying suitable artwork, or acceptable roughs for an illustrator to follow

- providing appropriate acknowledgements

- ensuring that no plagiarised, libellous or defamatory material is included

- checking publication proofs

- preparing an index if one is required and the author is able and willing to do so

- discussing with the marketing/publicity department any advance publicity channels for the book (e.g. media interviews, recommendations for review or complimentary copies, public appearances, readings, social media) and helping to prepare a marketing plan.

The author may also be responsible for seeking permission to reproduce copyrighted material from other sources (e.g. text extracts from other publications, such as books, newspapers or journals, websites, blogs or poetry; or tables, graphs, maps, photographs or other artwork), though this is also sometimes the responsibility of staff of the publishing organisation.

If there is more than one author, which is quite common for educational textbooks and other non-fiction publications, one of them is usually designated as the key author with whom the publishing staff liaise for the duration of the project, to simplify communication.

The publisher

In trade book publishing the publisher is principally concerned with planning and carrying through a successful and innovative

artwork
graphic material, such as photographs, drawings or charts, prepared for reproduction

rough
an artist's or author's sketch or layout to be used as a guide for the illustrator or designer

index
an alphabetical list of entries identifying where in a book significant topics, concepts, people and places are mentioned

permissions
agreement(s) obtained from the copyright owner to reproduce part or all of a copyrighted text or artwork in a publication

publishing program, with a forward list to cover the next two to three years, sometimes longer for extended projects.

The publisher will:

- commission new books from known, reputable or promising authors, or offer contracts to literary agents to win highly sought-after works

- negotiate the acquisition of other suitable books (such as a takeover edition of a book previously released by another publisher)

- explore new areas of publishing in developing or previously neglected areas

- accurately assess the prospects of reprints, new editions or repackaged works of existing titles in the organisation's backlist.

reprint
printing more copies of a publication, in exactly the same format or with only very minor corrections

Each of these projects must be shown to be a financially viable proposition for the organisation and one that will further its reputation in its particular fields.

The publisher must take many factors into account, including:

edition
a new publication; a changed and/or reset reprint; a publication produced in a different format (e.g. paperback or ebook)

- the size of the target market

- the existing or potential competition

- the possibility that a book will become prescribed reading for, say, Year 12 students in English literature

backlist
books already published by a company and kept in print

- a book's chances of becoming a best-selling novel or non-fiction book

- the potential for converting a book into ebook formats.

ebook
a digital version of a book, designed to be read using a device such as a personal computer, tablet or dedicated ebook reader

The publisher must be a competent negotiator capable of convincing authors to take on proposed projects, and must also be the first to identify and contract likely authors—competition from other publishers can be keen! The publisher must be alert to all possible sources of books with potential for the organisation's list, and should be able to recognise seemingly unpublishable work that could be reworked by a skilled editor into a viable publishing proposition. Increasingly, this includes identifying works that have already been self-published, including those published on the internet, that could be re-issued successfully through more formal channels.

The publisher looks for quality and originality of ideas and writing; the historical, social, cultural or educational value of a topic; and an innovative presentation. Other people in the editorial and marketing departments are often asked to read and comment on the initial manuscript or idea to assess whether it will sell widely and quickly or only to a specialist market, or whether it might perform well on the company's backlist (that is, sell steadily in good numbers for many years, with potential for reprints and new editions).

Authors and agents may choose to make submissions to several publishers simultaneously, and sometimes agents put up manuscripts for bids. Publishers should be advised by the author/ agent if they are competing against others for the rights to the book, and must be aware of time limits, auction details or other requirements.

Assessment time varies. Manuscripts that are obviously unsuitable for the publisher's list can be rejected almost immediately. Others may take some weeks to assess properly, especially if the publisher commissions a reader's report (a modest fee is usually paid for this service), for example, for technical or educational subjects, current affairs or literary works. The publisher may also seek a legal opinion at this stage to ensure that the work presents no potential legal problems.

Book proposals are usually discussed at acquisitions meetings, where the publisher meets with representatives from other sections of the organisation, such as senior editors, sales and marketing staff, the production manager and accounting staff. All aspects of the book are reviewed to ensure that it will be financially viable or, if not, to decide whether there is a strong case for publishing anyway (for example, to ensure completeness of a series or to embark on a new area of publishing). If the committee agrees to proceed with a particular book, a contract is drawn up and signed by both publisher and author. The author is then given general guidelines to follow in preparing the final manuscript.

The publisher remains in regular or occasional personal contact with the author during the subsequent progress of the work. At either the editor's or the author's request, the publisher will try to resolve any difficulties arising between the author and members of the publishing organisation at any stage of negotiation or production.

The publisher, often in consultation with the sales department, decides on the most appropriate publishing date, and briefs the

extent
the length of a book:
the number of pages
or the number of words

production manager and editor accordingly. The publisher must also brief the editor on the proposed extent and style of the book, the number of illustrations and their reproduction (whether in colour or black and white), the format(s) in which the book is to be published (e.g. print, EPUB or ebook application) and other publication details. The publisher will indicate the target market, the main theme of the book, the appropriate language level and level of editing, and may give the editor an indication of whether the author is likely to be cooperative or difficult, or is about to go on safari in Africa.

Large publishing companies may also employ commissioning editors, who are responsible for generating and commissioning new titles and finding new authors. In smaller organisations, tasks may be collapsed, so that a publisher or commissioning editor may also supervise or edit the manuscript.

A sample
publisher's
brief is given in
appendix 1.

In corporate and government organisations, publications are normally commissioned and written by in-house staff or by consultants employed by the organisation, under the oversight of a publication manager. Government publications often have to follow strict guidelines, and it is the publication manager's responsibility to ensure that authors, editors and designers associated with the project are fully briefed on requirements and formats.

The project management team

The project manager

Project managers may be staff members, such as in-house editors, or they may be external editorial or publishing consultants contracted to take on the management of a particular publishing project. In either case they may employ in-house, contract or freelance consultants, and will be answerable to a senior member of the organisation, such as a publisher, publication manager or company manager. They will usually have extensive experience in the relevant field of publishing, as editors or designers, or as production managers or controllers. Senior editors working in-house have a number of similar responsibilities within the company structure.

When commencing work on a publishing project, the project manager will need to know:

• the management plan

• the contract conditions, if applicable

- the staffing policy

- the budget

- the time frame

- the requirements or specifications of the project (audience, extent, style, formats etc.)

- a schedule for meetings and preparation of updated progress reports.

Project management is discussed in more detail in chapter 2.

The contracts manager

Large organisations often employ a contracts or rights and permissions manager. In other cases, contract issues may be the responsibility of the publisher, the publication manager or the organisation's legal advisers.

Once the decision to publish is made, a contract is drawn up by the contracts manager or publisher for approval and acceptance by the author (or copyright owner). The contract is a legally binding agreement between the author and the publishing organisation, in which the author (the owner of the copyright) leases to the publishing organisation the right to develop and publish the work on the author's behalf under a number of agreed conditions. To avoid any later difficulties, this contract should be signed by both parties before any substantial editorial or design work is begun.

The contract will establish:

- the rights and obligations of each party (including a literary agent, if one is involved)

- any advance payments (on signing the contract, on receipt of the final manuscript or on publication)

- the royalty rate and when royalties will be paid (usually twice a year)

- the ownership of copyright

- the type(s) of licence granted by the author to publish the work (including exclusive rights and territorial rights).

The author gives a guarantee that no one else's copyright (on text, quotations or artwork) has been infringed upon; that no formula, instruction, activity or recipe included in the work contains directions likely to cause injury; and that permission to use copyright material has been (or will be) sought and received. The contract also stipulates who is responsible for providing the artwork, paying permissions fees (the author or the publisher, or both) and the amount, if any, to be paid by the publisher; anthologies, in particular, usually involve substantial permissions fees, as do many educational books and websites.

The contract also defines any subsequent rights for further reproduction of all or any part of the work as extracts or translations, or in electronic media, and any options for television or film rights or merchandising, plus any requirements for new editions and reprints. It may specify options on future work by the author, and define the publisher's obligation to advise the author if the work goes out of print. The contract will also specify how other income; for example, Copyright Agency Limited (CAL) distributions, and fees for future permissions to use the author's work — is to be divided between the author and the publisher.

Copyright Agency Limited (CAL) a non-profit organisation representing artists and other content creators that provides information and advice on copyright issues

A date for delivery of the manuscript is specified, together with the approximate extent of the manuscript and the amount of illustrative or other material allowed for. The number of complimentary copies to be given to the author on publication will also be specified in the contract.

It may be helpful for the editor to read the contract (if available) before starting work on the manuscript, but remember that all the details of the contract are confidential. No separate contract is required for authors who are writing as government or corporate employees; their rights and responsibilities are covered by their contract of employment. Freelance editors and consultants may also be required to sign a formal contract for each project.

The editor

The editor's role can range from the very broad to the specific, but essentially involves working directly with an author's manuscript to ensure that the work is as polished as possible at publication.

In larger companies where several editors are employed, a managing (or senior) editor may supervise a team of editors and editorial assistants, and oversee outsourcing work to freelance editors. Experienced editors give valuable on-the-spot training, advice and guidance to trainee editors, and help to resolve any difficulties that may arise. Smaller organisations may employ only one editor.

The editor may be responsible for liaison with a number of other people on a range of issues, including:

- the *publisher*—participating in preliminary discussions to provide structural guidance to the author before the contract is signed; reporting on the progress of all contracted publications, including any possible legal issues, difficulties with the production or budget problems

- the *author*—discussing the development of the manuscript and any proposed structural reorganisation; advising on house style, and preparation and editing of the manuscript; ensuring that artwork, permissions and indexing are provided where required; obtaining approval of the proposed design and cover blurb; checking proofs

- a *freelance editor* and/or *proofreader*—organising contracts; briefing them regarding the nature and scope of the work; liaising on any editing or proof stages that are not being carried out in-house; ensuring that editorial standards have been met; checking and approving invoices for payment

- the *indexer*—organising contracts; briefing regarding the scope of the work; checking that the work meets requirements; checking and approving invoices for payment

- the *production manager* or *production assistant*—estimating the extent of the manuscript; making decisions on format(s) and paper stock to be used; obtaining estimates of printing costs; preparing a blad for marketing purposes; outlining budget restrictions; planning an appropriate and realistic schedule for the production of each publication; planning the movement of material between editor, designer, typesetter, printer, ebook developer and others involved in the publication

- the *designer* or *illustrator*—preparing the necessary briefs

- the *designer* or *typesetter*—briefing and liaising on the text and cover design; proofreading and making corrections

- the *printer*—checking printer's proofs, unbound or folded sheets, advance copies, covers, jackets and run-ons for marketing material

- the *ebook developer*—proofreading and making corrections; checking functionality and linking

house style
a publisher's guide to preferred spellings, punctuation, word usage, formatting and preparation of electronic files

blurb
a description of the book to appear on the jacket or back cover, or in publicity material

stock
paper or other material (e.g. cloth, plastic) used for printing or binding

blad
a version of a publication created for marketing purposes, containing sample chapters or sections and enclosed in a proof of the cover

A sample page design brief is provided in appendix 2.

copy
all material that is
to be set in type

- the *marketing/publicity department*—providing information
  on the author and blurbs, and copy for advertisements,
  catalogues and marketing material; proofreading cover blurbs.

Remember that the author is responsible for the content (the
facts, the argument or analysis, the originality of ideas or story),
and the editor for professional advice on the form (the shape,
the organisation and 'packaging'). Flexibility of approach and
constant communication of ideas and information between editor
and author are essential.

The editor must be aware of all the information in the relevant
editorial files, of which version of the manuscript to use and of
decisions made on preferred style, spelling, what artwork or
other materials are still to come, biographical notes, the author
photograph, the list of agreed artwork, copyright information
and permissions, readers' reports, and so on. Copies of email
correspondence should also be filed so that discussions and
decisions on any changes are recorded. The editor is responsible
for the efficient and secure management of all relevant files
throughout the publication process, including all versions of the
manuscript, artwork, cover concepts and blurbs, and any other
relevant material, all of which should be clearly identified with
the author's name and the publication's title. Normally such files
are stored electronically on a secure server managed by the
publishing organisation.

file
a set of digital
information with a
unique name and
location in a computer
system or external
storage medium
(such as a hard disk
or file server)

Division of editing tasks

Editors are required to perform different tasks at different stages
of a manuscript's development, according to the requirements of
the particular manuscript. Sometimes the editing tasks are divided
among several editors. The management of the editing process may
be the responsibility of a managing editor, a project manager or a
production controller, but is often the responsibility of a copy editor.
A complex manuscript may require the attention of a substantive
(structural) editor. The copy editor may also be responsible for
proofreading, indexing or supervising freelance proofreaders.

In a complex manuscript where the tasks are undertaken by a
number of different editors, the job divisions can be summarised
as follows.

A *managing editor:*

- liaises with the author and publisher, and with the design,
  production, marketing and publicity departments

- checks that any requirements for specific structure, formats and styles are adhered to

- ensures that editorial standards are met

- ensures that legal requirements such as the use of government symbols or the provision of a letter of transmittal are met

- ensures that schedules are maintained (especially if publication is tied to a specific event or date)

- supervises the allocation of work and other staff involved in the project

- commissions and contracts additional staff as required (freelance editors, proofreaders, indexers, designers, picture researchers, illustrators, cartoonists, photographers, stylists, typesetters) and oversees their work.

A *substantive (structural) editor*:

- establishes the structure and sequence of the manuscript

- ensures that all material is clear and unambiguous, logically organised and comprehensive

- suggests improvements in style, structure, factual content and illustration

- assists with the development of characters, plot and setting in fiction works

- tailors the language to suit the target market or to reduce sexist, racist or other bias

- suggests appropriate artwork.

A *copy editor*:

- corrects editorial and linguistic errors (grammar, spelling, punctuation, paragraphing, inaccuracies, omissions, repetitions, ambiguities, language level)

- applies electronic styling to the manuscript to reflect the structure of the content

- prepares and maintains an editorial style sheet and a list of design styles

- watches for potential libel, obscenity, plagiarism or breach of copyright

letter of transmittal
a signed letter from the head of a reporting body to the responsible government minister, authority or client

electronic styling
identifying the semantic role of paragraphs or characters in a text, which can then be used to control the consistent appearance (formatting) of all text during typesetting (not to be confused with editorial style)

editorial style
editorial decisions made about the grammar, punctuation, usage and spelling of text

15

prelims
(preliminary pages)
all pages preceding the
main text of a work,
such as the title page,
imprint page, preface
and contents page

endmatter
all material that follows
the main text, such
as appendixes, notes,
bibliography and index

sample setting
a page design showing
where and how text
and graphic elements
are to be presented

For a sample
artwork and
permissions brief,
see appendix 3.

For a sample
illustration brief,
see appendix 4.

- checks the progress of copyright permissions with the author or permissions assistant

- prepares preliminary pages (prelims), and edits endmatter such as notes, appendixes, bibliography, glossary and index

- checks all artwork and its labelling and placement

- ensures that all artwork is inserted, and prepares and follows up checklists of artwork at various stages

- prepares a brief for an illustrator if necessary

- selects material for a sample setting

- prepares the final version of the manuscript for the designer or typesetter

- prepares a brief for the designer listing the types of headings, the number and types of artwork, what sort of quoted material is included (text, poetry etc.) and other requirements for fonts (for foreign languages, mathematics etc.), and transmits clearly the author's and publisher's preferences and requirements

- writes cover blurbs and marketing material

- checks printer's proofs

- checks advance covers and advance copies

- maintains a record of corrections for future reprints or new editions.

A *freelance editor*:

- carries out all the basic tasks of a copy editor

- may be contracted for a specific task, such as substantive or scientific editing

- may be required to organise artwork and permissions or picture research, and compile an artwork and permissions brief.

A *proofreader*:

- checks proofs or ebook versions at every production stage

- checks that all artwork has been correctly placed.

In many cases, however, all these tasks will be the responsibility of the in-house or freelance copy editor.

The freelance editor

A freelance editor is employed by an organisation or an individual on a contract basis to work, usually from home, on a specific project or a series of complementary projects.

The main difference between a freelance and an in-house editor is that the freelance editor works in relative isolation, without the support network available to an in-house editor. Freelance editors therefore need a clear understanding of what should be done and what information is needed to do it. Publishers, managing editors and project managers do not want to send out a manuscript to an editor and then find there is a week's work still to be done on it when it is returned. For this reason, they will usually seek freelance editors who have previously worked as in-house editors and are experienced in all aspects of the publishing process.

Most publishing organisations send a brief with the manuscript outlining what they expect the freelance editor to do. If no written brief is provided, or problems not identified in the brief appear during editing, it is important for freelance editors to seek clarification of the project from the person who is commissioning the work and take notes, including dates, of all discussions. It is also a good idea to send the organisation a copy of these notes, and to keep on file copies of all emails and notes of telephone conversations in case of future disagreements.

Freelance editors rely heavily on liaison with in-house personnel. It is important for a freelance editor to know the complete schedule for the manuscript and the full extent of their involvement in the production. For example, if they are required to both edit and proofread the book, or edit and proofread the index, they will need notification of the estimated timing of these stages so the tasks can be fitted into their own schedule. Otherwise, these jobs may need to be split up and passed on to another person. It is essential to have good, regular communication between freelance and in-house editors and for freelance editors to have strong time-management skills to ensure that schedules can be managed appropriately.

It is equally important for a freelance editor working for a publishing organisation to ensure that the terms of any contract make clear such questions as whether the budget is fixed or can be negotiated, and what steps to take if work on the manuscript exceeds the schedule or budget.

Freelance editors are often employed for the copy-editing process only, while other (often cheaper and less experienced) freelance proofreaders may be used for the later stages. Most freelance editors prefer to at least oversee the later stages of a manuscript they have edited. It is frustrating for a meticulous editor to see a project appear in print full of typographical errors because of careless proofreading. It is particularly galling if the publication is then unfavourably reviewed for 'sloppy editing'.

typography
arranging type to form a pleasing design and assist in communicating its content and meaning

The availability of desktop publishing systems and the ease of publishing works as ebooks has created a boom in self-publishing, particularly in romance, crime and popular fiction. This has led to an increasing trend for authors to seek the services of freelance editors to help them prepare their work for publication. Before editors agree to work with a self-publishing author, a contract should be developed that states either an hourly rate or a quote for the whole job, and spells out clearly what services will be included. For example:

- Will the work include substantive (structural) editing and electronic styling, or basic copy editing only?

- Who will be responsible for doing corrections and formatting?

- Will proofreading of the final page proofs be part of the job?

- Should the editor offer design advice?

For more details about contracts and other management issues, see chapter 2.

- Who will organise permissions requests for photographs or other material used?

- Who will be responsible for checking factual data?

The production team

The production manager

In large companies and organisations, production of a publication normally falls under the direction of a production manager, production controller or production assistant, who manages and records all the physical stages of production. In smaller organisations, the production manager's role may be undertaken by the publisher, publication manager or editor.

typesetting or desktop publishing (DTP)
the use of specialist software, such as Adobe InDesign or QuarkXPress, to produce a print-ready and/or electronic copy of a publication

The production manager is responsible for:

- working with the publisher, editor and other staff to establish or confirm schedules for editing, design, typesetting, printing and the development of electronic publications

- organising competitive quotes from external suppliers such as designers, typesetters, printers and electronic product developers, as required

- commissioning and contracting freelance staff, as required (unless this is done by a managing editor)

- costing each publication and maintaining budget control

- maintaining progress reports on each publication for discussion at publishing meetings

- liaising with editors, designers, illustrators, typesetters, ebook developers, multimedia specialists, animators, sound recorders, printers, warehouses, and shipping and customs agents, as required

- together with the editor, designer and publisher, ensuring that the publication is produced on time, to the highest quality within the available budget

- confirming the final details and approving the printed and/or electronic versions of the publication

- organising delivery of printed sales materials and finished stock

- organising the upload of ebook publications to online sales portals

- at a later date, organising and checking any reprints that are required.

The designer

The designer, who may be employed either freelance or in-house, is responsible for:

- interpreting and following the brief from the editor (including recommendations from the publisher)

- commissioning illustrators, in consultation with the editor and picture researcher (if there is one)

- designing the cover and all aspects of the text (the type and the size of the page, line lengths, chapter and page drops, styles of headings and ancillary material such as appendixes and other text elements, layout of artwork)

drop
the distance between elements on a page, such as from the top of the page or the baseline of the running head to the baseline of the first line of the type area

- ensuring that reports, manuals and so on adhere to any pre-existing guidelines regarding format and design

- formatting the text using a desktop publishing system (this task may be given to a typesetter or editor to follow the designer's instructions), and checking that pages have been consistently prepared according to the design specifications

- checking proofs of all colour and black-and-white artwork, and colour proofs of covers

- designing marketing material, and packaging (such as slip cases) and ancillary material.

If pages are to be prepared by a separate typesetter, the designer will be responsible for providing specifications for styles or a page template, using the appropriate software program.

Both the designer and editor check that the final artwork is complete and correctly inserted and scaled. They later check the final print or electronic proofs to ensure that all the pages have been produced correctly.

The typesetter

Typesetting may be carried out by an editor, a designer or a specialist typesetter. In this book, for clarity, the person who is doing the typesetting is referred to as a typesetter, even if they also perform other roles.

Typesetters use desktop publishing software to format and lay out manuscripts into pages according to design guidelines, and integrate graphics and other design elements as required. They may work with editors, the production manager and the designer to ensure all elements of the publication are accurately composed according to the brief. The resulting files are then delivered to a printer or to an ebook developer, for production of a print or electronic publication, respectively. Some typesetters may also provide conversion services to create electronic versions of the publication.

Government and corporate organisations and smaller trade publishers may employ in-house or freelance typesetters, while larger publishing companies often use offshore (overseas) typesetting services.

Editors are increasingly involved in typesetting, with tasks ranging from more traditional proofing and checking, to taking in corrections electronically—to both the manuscript and the page proofs—and undertaking the entire typesetting process themselves.

The printer

Local or offshore printing companies are contracted by publishing organisations to print and bind a publication (and other supporting material).

The printer is responsible for:

- providing quotes for printing according to the publication's specifications

- supplying sample paper stock or a dummy if required

- undertaking prepress work to prepare the publication's files for printing

- preparing and supplying final hard-copy or soft-copy proofs of the complete publication for checking by the production manager, designer, editor and/or publisher

- printing the publication; collating, sewing or binding, trimming, adding covers, and packing and delivering the finished product (this work may be done by a separate company specialising in binding)

- replicating (producing in quantity) any associated materials, such as map inserts, and packaging, or subcontracting this work.

If required, the printer can supply printed sheets or unbound copies so the publishing company can check that all sections are in sequence, and that the paper stock is the one specified. The printer will also send any requested advance copies of the publication. Advance copies are checked and approved by the editor, the designer, the production manager and/or the publisher, and sometimes also by the author. The specified number of acceptable finished copies must then be delivered by the scheduled date.

dummy
a set of blank pages made up to the specified size and format of a printed book

hard copy
copy produced as a printout from a word processor or typesetting program; any computer printout

soft copy
copy produced as a digital version of a word processor or typesetting file

trimming (printing)
cutting the edges of printed pages after they are bound to create a smooth edge

section
a printed sheet folded in multiples of four, usually consisting of 8, 16, 32 or 48 pages

Ebook developers

Ebook developers are responsible for producing an electronic version of the publication, such as an EPUB, website or separate ebook application. Their tasks may involve the following:

- designing the look and feel of the product (in line with the look and feel of the print product, if there is one)

- for ebook applications, designing and programming the elements, structure, navigation and interactivity

- creating any related interactive material, such as videos, audio or animations

- programming software to manage complex conversion projects

An overview of ebooks, and ebook editing and proofreading, is provided in chapter 15.

- outputting ebooks from the typeset files used for print publications

- scanning and digitising backlist print publications

- proofing and checking the product, in liaison with the editor, designer, production manager and/or publisher

- submitting ebook publications to online sales portals on behalf of the publisher.

The sales and marketing teams

During the production period the publisher and editor brief the sales and marketing teams on the significance of the publication as a whole, and on any special features that will help them in selling it to the target market. The editor is frequently required to prepare and present proposals to sales conferences, often illustrated with cover roughs and other material, for potential publications or publications in production.

The editor then keeps the sales and marketing staff informed of progress or delays with production. The editor also prepares appropriate copy and artwork, such as cover roughs and blurbs, to be included in the organisation's promotional catalogues or other marketing material.

Project and production management

Effective project management in a publishing organisation is central to ensuring that a publication is written, edited and produced to the highest standards possible within the available budget and schedule. While even the most self-contained project requires good management, many publishing companies and publishing departments in corporate and government organisations outsource their publishing work to contractors and freelancers, and in these cases the role of the project manager becomes even more important.

PROJECT MANAGEMENT

The management plan

The publisher provides the project manager with details of the aims, scope, audience, budget and time frame for the publication.

The first thing the project manager needs to do is to draw up a management plan. This plan will include information on:

- whether the manuscript is complete or some material is still to be supplied

- the scope of the project, such as audience, format, extent

- the available budget for the project

- the contract conditions for the author(s)

- the personnel required to complete the project, and a recruitment policy, if necessary

- an overall schedule for the project

- a detailed schedule for each member of the team

- protocols for accountability for each member of the team

- a system of file management for securely storing and sorting the manuscript, artwork and other documents.

The project manager will have ultimate responsibility for all these matters, but may be assisted by a publications assistant or production controller in keeping track of the various stages of production and in maintaining records.

Personnel and contracts

Some or all project management work, including that of project managers themselves, may be outsourced to contractors or freelancers. The publisher or a senior in-house editor may contract an external project manager if required. Identifying and contracting any other external personnel for the project may then be the responsibility of the project manager. However, often the entire project is managed in-house using the organisation's existing staff resources.

Contracting a project manager

If the project manager is not working in-house, a contract, signed by both the publishing organisation and the project manager, should set out clearly each party's rights and obligations. Matters that may need to be negotiated include the following:

- Is it a fixed contract or can changes be made if the project runs over budget or over time?

- Are there penalties for exceeding the budget or going over time?

- Who is responsible for paying contractors and freelancers — the organisation or the project manager?

- Is there provision for compensation or rescheduling if the project is delayed by an external party (such as the author or printer)?

- When will payments to the project manager be made?

- Can the project manager claim for out-of-pocket expenses?

- Is there a clause covering professional liability? This is included in some contracts, particularly those involving government departments, universities and similar organisations, and may require the contractor to take out costly insurance.

Most contracts will provide a payment (normally one-third or one-half of the budget) at commencement of the work and another on completion. However, when projects have a very long time frame, sometimes up to 12 months, there should be provision for payments at regular intervals, ideally every few weeks, over the duration of the project.

Establishing and managing the project team

External project managers are usually expected to assemble their own team for the project. In some cases they may be required to provide a complete service package, and their contract and remuneration will include provision for payment of contractors and freelancers. In other cases the project manager will be responsible for recruitment of personnel and for keeping costs within budget, but actual payment of contractors and freelancers will be made by the organisation.

Although the organisation may have used a tendering system to appoint the project manager, such an approach is not commonly used in choosing other members of the team. The project manager will probably have a list of experienced and reliable people to call on, and the organisation may also know of people with experience in the particular area. For a large project in a specialist area it may be necessary to advertise for expressions of interest. Professional societies often produce directories where members list information about their skills, specialties and experience; professional colleagues can also provide word-of-mouth recommendations.

Members of a project team can include editors, proofreaders, indexers, designers, illustrators, typesetters, production managers, printers, warehouse/distribution services and ebook developers. When the manager is choosing among candidates, it is vital that all are given exactly the same brief and that the brief is as detailed as possible.

The aspects of the contracts to be negotiated between the project manager and each external supplier include:

- details of the scope and type of work required

- the schedule for completion of the work

- the total fee or payment rate for the project

- the schedule of payment, if the project is lengthy or complex

- any penalties for delays or work that is below standard

- whether there is potential for renegotiation should unforeseen events arise for either party

- any intellectual property issues

- security, confidentiality and document management responsibilities

- any liability insurance required.

The most important tasks of the project manager are to monitor team members' adherence to the budget, schedule and specifications of the project.

The budget

Project managers usually have to work within a fixed budget, but they may have some leeway in deciding how to allocate their resources. When deciding between competing quotes, for example, the cheapest option is not always the most cost-effective. An experienced freelance editor with a higher hourly rate is likely to work efficiently and to time; would be expected to have more advanced editorial skills; is more likely to know how to present copy for designers, typesetters and printers; and will often be able to detect and deal with potential problems before they cause disruption to the budget and schedule. These advantages may make this editor a better choice for a complex project than a less experienced editor whose hourly rate is lower but who may prove to be more costly in both time and money. On a simple, straightforward publication, however, the decision might be different.

The project manager needs to keep meticulous records so they are aware of the progress of the budget at each stage of the publication. If any problems are likely to affect the budget (such as the addition of new material; time delays due to rewriting, printing or other setbacks; or staffing difficulties), it is important to have contingency plans prepared and to advise the publishing organisation if the changes are likely to require renegotiation of any of the terms of the contract.

The schedule

Since the publication date is likely to be fixed, often to meet a deadline such as an international conference, a parliamentary meeting, an anniversary such as Mother's Day, or the date when schools or universities make purchasing decisions for the following year, the longer the time allowed between commencement of the project and the estimated publication date, the easier it will be for the project manager. Some projects may commence one or more years in advance, at the stage of briefing the author(s) before the text is actually written. Others, such as reports to a committee, arise in response to specific events and may have a much shorter time frame—sometimes as little as a few weeks—so that writing, editing, design and formatting may all be occurring simultaneously.

The project manager must ensure that all members of the team are aware of the timing for their particular contribution and monitor each person's progress so that the schedule follows the management plan. Any delays must be dealt with promptly so that they do not adversely affect the work of the rest of the project team. The manager must stay in regular touch with the team members and also keep relevant staff in the publishing organisation informed on the progress of the project.

The requirements or specifications of the project

The publishing organisation will have briefed the project manager on the anticipated readership, form and scope of the publication. The project manager must then ensure that not only the author(s), but also the editor and designer and anyone else working on the text, are given detailed specifications of the extent, language level, writing style (formal or informal, specialised or general), house style requirements and any special issues, such as accessibility for people with disabilities.

accessibility
making electronic documents available in alternative publication formats to increase the ability of people with disabilities to view, listen to and/or understand the content

If the project includes ancillary materials, such as CD-ROMs or web content, it is important that the project team ensures that they are compatible in style and language level with the publication, and that any specific needs related to the particular medium are also addressed.

CD-ROM (compact disc read-only memory)
a compact disc used for storing digital data that can be read optically and processed by a computer

The project manager must also ensure that the team produces work that is of a suitable standard and that meets the requirements of the project. For example, a designer or typesetter might be required not only to lay out a document as a print publication, but also to set the file up for efficient conversion to an ebook format. Failure to do so properly may cause major technical problems later in the production process.

PRODUCTION MANAGEMENT

Production management is a subset of project management and involves the management of all the elements that go towards the editing, design, typesetting, printing and conversion to electronic format of the publication. The three most important aspects of the production process are: the format(s) of the publication, the costs associated with its production (and hence its profitability and viability), and the time taken to produce it. The editor's role in ensuring the smooth passage of the publication through the various production stages is discussed in the following sections.

Figure 2.1 provides an overview of the typical roles involved in the production of a publication that is released both in print and as an ebook. The roles and workflows will vary between different kinds of publishing organisations, especially in the division of responsibilities, and depending on the specific requirements of the final publication format, but many of the basic editing tasks remain the same across most projects.

Figure 2.1: typical production roles and workflow of a publication in print and electronic formats

Stage	Production roles
Writing	Editor: structural advice, permissions, project management
Editing	Editor: structural and copy editing, electronic styling, managing artwork, liaising with designer/typesetter
Design/typesetting	Designer/typesetter and illustrator: design and layout of text and artwork
Proofreading	Proofreader/editor: line-by-line checking of page proofs Typesetter: corrections to page proofs
Indexing	Author/indexer: create and supply index Editor: check index before and after typesetting Typesetter: typeset index
Checking final pages	Editor/typesetter: check and make final corrections Designer/typesetter: check and create PDF for printer
Printing and ebook creation	Editor/designer/production department: check prepress proofs and approve final version for printing Editor: check ebook for conversion issues

Briefing the author

The production process begins when an author's work is commissioned or contracted. For best results, and to avoid misunderstanding, any face-to-face or telephone briefing, and any verbal agreements made with an author, usually by the publisher or a senior editor, should be confirmed in writing as soon as possible. Copies of all letters, notes and emails should be kept on file as a record of discussions.

Many publishing companies will ask the author to complete an author's questionnaire, which provides more details about the author, the book, the expected audience and other information that would assist with the book's marketing and sale.

For an example of an author's questionnaire for an educational publishing house, see appendix 7.

Project managers and editors must remind the author of the contractual commitment for a specified manuscript length, and of the need to meet other requirements specified in the contract, such as adhering to a particular template, obtaining permissions or providing artwork.

The author must also agree to deliver a satisfactory manuscript by a stipulated date in order to fit in with the forward publishing program, for which an estimate of expected income is built into the budget for that year. The author must notify the publisher or editor without delay if the agreed date cannot be met.

Artwork and permissions brief

Authors often wish to include in their work extracts, illustrations, photos or other material created by someone else. In these cases, permission must be sought from the copyright owner (and a fee paid, if necessary) before they can be reproduced.

For a sample artwork and permissions brief, see appendix 3.

It is particularly important that the author is briefed to start the permission-seeking process at the earliest opportunity. Copyright permissions must be cleared before too much work is done, in case permission to use the desired extracts or artwork is denied or the fee required is excessive.

The whole procedure needs very careful record-keeping from the start, and prompt follow-up. The sooner the author (or permissions assistant) can start this work, the more likely it is that the scheduled publication date can be met.

For a more detailed description of copyright and permissions procedures, see chapter 5.

Illustration briefs

There are two types of illustration briefs. The publisher and editor may brief the author, to provide guidance on how the author should illustrate or research artwork for a particular book.

Alternatively, the author may supply an illustration brief, together with roughs—drawings or outlines for the editor, designer and illustrator to work from.

Complex artwork, such as maps, graphs and diagrams, takes time to commission and produce. It must be carefully checked by the author and editor for accuracy and consistency of presentation, especially with regard to labels and captions (for example, for spelling and use of consistent font style), before the pages are laid out.

Sometimes an author's rough or instructions will be so inadequate that the artist may have difficulty in interpreting what is required. It is important for the editor to understand the author's intentions, and to translate these into instructions that the artist and designer can follow with minimum effort.

The number of illustrations required by the author should also be monitored closely, as including even one or two more in each chapter could have a disastrous effect on the estimated profit margin for the publication. The editor must always consult the publisher and the production manager if faced with this situation.

For a sample
illustration brief,
see appendixes
3 and 4.

Careful and early preparation is essential to avoid delays and escalating costs, and to enable substitutions if the first-choice artwork is not available or proves too expensive.

Briefing the designer and typesetter

Cover design brief and copy

Most publishing organisations prepare the cover design and copy at the earliest opportunity so that publicity and early sales from preprinted advance covers can begin.

Preparing cover briefs at an early stage allows adequate time for choosing the most appropriate design, or for reworking a design if part or all of it needs to be changed for any reason. The cover copy and blurb have to be approved, usually by the publisher (or publishing committee), the editor, the author and the marketing manager. Sometimes the author provides acceptable copy for the blurb, but more usually the editor rewrites the author's draft blurb to present information in a way that will draw and hold the reader's interest and promote sales of the book.

For more
information
on preparing
cover copy, see
chapter 8.

The cover design should be in sympathy with the page design. The designer usually provides a specified number of draft versions of cover concepts (roughs) for consideration and final approval by the publisher, author, project manager and marketing manager.

For government and corporate publications the editor should check that requirements regarding size, colour and layout are followed, and that all the required information, such as company or department titles and logos, together with other corporate style specifications (colours and design elements), has been included.

Page design brief

The project manager or editor must supply a page design brief before the designer or typesetter can begin work. The brief must give a clear idea of the publisher's and author's intentions, which must then be translated into a suitable type design and layout. The design brief enables the designer to organise a sample setting of the page design using material selected by the editor (such as examples of straight text, tables, references, long quotes, captions and notes) and ensures that there will be minimal delay in typesetting the manuscript.

The page design brief gives details of:

- presentation (including house style)

- the order of the book

- the layout of artwork, and whether any illustrations have to be commissioned

- the number and weights of headings, and details of ancillary material, such as appendixes and other text elements

- notes, captions, labels and footnotes

- any special characters required (such as mathematical symbols, foreign language diacritics, currency symbols and fractions)

- estimated extent.

Where the typesetter is not also the designer, a separate brief may be required for the typesetter. This brief is based on the approved sample setting, and indicates type styles, headings, chapter drops, space for artwork and position of captions; layout of tables, graphs and diagrams; and formatting instructions for the text, prelims, endmatter and cover copy. Often, the designer provides the typesetter with a template that has most or all of these instructions and styles embedded in the electronic file.

layout (design)
a plan of a publication page, specifying the typeface and font styles and size, area of the text block, treatment of headings and other text elements, and position of illustrations

references
a detailed listing of books and articles that are referred to in a publication; related sources that are not mentioned in the text are not included

note
a supporting comment or citation added to the text either at the bottom of the relevant page (footnote) or at the end of a chapter, section or the work (endnote); usually indicated in the text with a superscript symbol, number or letter

diacritic
a typographic mark combined with a letter to indicate a change in pronunciation (e.g. à, ç, ñ)

For a sample page design brief, see appendix 2.

Typesetting and layout

layout (typesetting)
assembly of all the
elements (text and
artwork) to make up
a page

Simpler publications, such as unillustrated non-fiction or fiction books that are to be set to a standard template, with appropriate running heads and folios added where necessary, will be paged by a typesetter. More complex publications, such as educational textbooks featuring numerous illustrations, tables and photographs, are usually paged by a designer.

running head,
running foot
a title or brief
descriptive heading
printed at the head
(top) or foot (bottom)
of each page

The final edited text and artwork for typesetting and layout will be supplied by the editor or project manager, along with instructions for the appropriate placement and setting of elements such as illustrations and tables.

folio
a single leaf of a
manuscript; a printed
page number

The typesetter or designer will submit draft pages (page proofs) for checking, usually by chapter or section, depending on the length of the publication or the requirements of the project manager.

It is the editor's and author's responsibility to check the page proofs, as copy and artwork can sometimes be accidentally placed out of order or omitted. At this stage, too, the editor or proofreader and the author read the text carefully to identify any errors that were missed in the initial edit or were introduced during typesetting. The editor compiles all proofreader and author corrections into a master proof for the typesetter to work from. Corrections to the page proofs should also be checked by the editor. This cycle may be repeated a few times, depending on the budget and schedule. Alterations at the final stage must be kept to an absolute minimum to avoid additional costs, unnecessary delays or hurried changes that can cause further mistakes.

author corrections
changes made to
proofs by the author(s)

The author or indexer then prepares the index from the corrected page proofs. Even at this late stage, previously unnoticed errors may be discovered. Editorial discretion must be used in deciding how many of these last-minute corrections are essential.

Page proofs and indexes should be turned around as quickly as possible, particularly if the publication is running behind schedule.

Printed publications

imposition
arrangement of typeset
page spreads on a large
sheet to ensure pages
appear in the proper
sequence while
maximising printing
efficiency

Final page proofs

The electronic files of final page proofs are usually transmitted as PDF (Portable Document Format) files to the printer for imposition in the sequence that will enable the publication to be printed, collated and bound in the correct order.

The *Style Manual for Authors, Editors and Printers*, 6th edition (referred to in this book as the *Style Manual*), is a good reference for details of imposition schemes.

The printer will send the files to prepress to ensure that they are set up appropriately for the specifications of the job and for imposition. A printout of these files (or, increasingly, a PDF of the pages) will then be sent to the publisher to confirm that all the content has been correctly transmitted. These final printer's proofs are checked by the designer, production manager, editor and publisher to ensure that the imposition is correct and that pages are in the proper sequence, fonts have not been substituted, colours (if any) appear in the correct places, and so on.

Only absolutely crucial corrections should be considered at this point, as they are costly and time-consuming.

For a more detailed list of what to check in printer's proofs, see chapter 14.

Advance copies and delivery of stock

Sometimes advance copies of the publication are requested, usually for marketing purposes. This presents another opportunity for checking that the final instructions and corrections have been carried out correctly. If the advance copies are unsatisfactory because of any major error on the part of the printer—wrong paper stock used, pages misbound, colour separations reversed or out of register, sections missing or repeated—the printer will be obliged to reprint all or part of the publication. Further advance copies will then be required to check that the faults have been corrected. If, however, the faults are relatively minor, the publisher may negotiate with the printer for compensation, perhaps in the form of a deduction from the cost of printing.

registration (printing) aligning pages when they are printed offset in two or more colours (requiring two or more passes through the press); if the pages are misaligned (out of registration), the printing will be blurred

If the publication is printed locally, bulk stock will usually be delivered in one instalment, unless a substantial number of advance copies are requested.

Time frame

Writing a book may take several years if the author has to undertake detailed or extensive research. On the other hand, a fast-track book, commissioned from a professional journalist on a current event, can be written in two or three weeks. If priority is given to a book at every stage, books can be delivered to the warehouse within four to six weeks. The usual time frame for producing an average-length book of 224 pages with some artwork, requiring a certain amount of structural revision and detailed copy editing, is for the finished manuscript to proceed through the various stages of production in three to twelve months.

Government and corporate publications — such as annual reports, white papers and committee reports — are often required to meet strict deadlines, and production schedules must be planned with this in mind. Government annual reports, for example, typically must be written, edited, approved, indexed, printed and tabled in Parliament within four months.

Ebooks

Ebook versions of printed publications are generally produced once the typeset document has been finalised. They can be converted from desktop publishing programs, such as InDesign, or generated from databases in the case of certain types of reference works. Ebooks may also be developed into a stand-alone multimedia ebook application. Self-published authors may even generate an ebook from a final word-processing document.

In all cases, the ebooks generated need to be thoroughly checked to ensure that the elements have been converted correctly, no new errors have been introduced and the publication will meet the technical requirements of the online stores to which they will be uploaded. Decisions also need to be made about any exclusions or changes to the layout or order of some elements that might be necessitated by the different format. For example, the imprint page may be moved to the end of the publication to make it easier for the reader to find the beginning of the text. In addition, some elements, such as animations and videos, may be added to the ebook version.

The editor is responsible for ensuring that the publication has been successfully and accurately converted to the new format. In the case of ebook applications, the author may also be involved in ensuring that the ebook has been successfully converted. Again, this may require more than one round of corrections, and the editor may need to weigh up the benefits of making the corrections against the implications for costs and production time.

The production of the electronic version of a publication usually takes place while the hard-copy version is being printed. Any errors that need to be corrected during the printing stage will also need to be corrected separately in the electronic version, so it is very important to keep this sort of double-handling to an absolute minimum.

imprint page bibliographic, copyright and other publishing information printed in a work, usually on the reverse of the title page

An overview of ebooks and ebook editing and proofreading is provided in chapter 15.

The production schedule

Everyone involved in the production of a publication will be given a schedule to follow, which will include the estimated dates for the completion of each stage and any related comments. As the production process progresses, the schedule should be updated with the actual dates of completion. This helps project managers to keep track of the process, as well as being useful for planning similar projects in the future.

The elements that should be part of a production schedule include:

- *Publication details*. The basic details about the publication:

  — title and author

  — format (print and/or electronic)

  — page size and extent (number of pages)

  — number of copies to be printed and type of binding

  — publication date

  — ISBN(s) and price(s).

- *Editing*. The dates when the manuscript is to go to the editor and then to the typesetter.

- *Production costings*. When quotes for design, typesetting, illustration, printing and so on should be requested and the costings completed.

- *Cover design*. When the brief is to be prepared, the roughs designed and approved, and the final artwork delivered.

- *Page design*. The dates when the brief is to be prepared, and the sample setting is to be designed and approved.

- *Illustrations*. The dates when:

  — the author's briefs to the illustrator are due

  — the illustrator completes the artwork

  — the editor checks and edits the artwork

  — the illustrator corrects the artwork

  — the typesetter sets the artwork in the pages.

ISBN (International Standard Book Number)
an international book numbering system that identifies each publication, whether in book or electronic form, by a unique number

- *Proofs*. The dates when the first and subsequent page proofs are completed and sent to the editor and author for checking and proofreading. Depending on the time and budget available, there may be two or three rounds of proofing, sometimes more, but the exact number should be specified at the commencement of the project.

- *Indexing*. The dates when the indexer receives the near-to-final page proofs for indexing, the editor receives the index for checking and the typesetter receives the index for layout. Again, this will need to be repeated to allow for checking and proofreading.

- *Final pages*. The dates when the final page proofs are to be ready for approval by the author, editor, publisher and designer. When all approvals have been granted, the date that the files go to the printer.

- *Prepress proofs*. The dates when the prepress proofs are prepared and approved by the editor, publisher, designer and production manager.

- *Printing*. The dates when the publication goes to the printer, and advance copies and bulk stock are due for delivery at the warehouse and distribution to stores begins.

- *Ebook conversion*. The dates when:

  — the final versions of the text and graphics are extracted from the typeset file (or other source) and sent for conversion to an ebook

  — the ebook is to be checked and proofread by the editor

  — corrections to the ebook are to be made and the final version created

  — the ebook is to be released through the relevant sales portals.

If an unexpected problem occurs that will delay the editing, or if it becomes clear that the schedule is unrealistic in view of the amount of research or rewriting required of the author or the extent of structural or detailed copy editing to be done, the editor should immediately inform the publisher and the production manager so that an alternative schedule can be prepared. In some cases a book may be put on hold until the author deals with major problems, such as restructuring the manuscript, incorporating more up-to-date material, or obtaining permissions or further illustrations. Other issues may arise during the typesetting, printing or electronic conversion phases; again, the relevant staff should alert the publisher and production manager as soon as possible so that the schedule can be revised.

An editorial schedule and checklist

Editors normally work on a number of projects at the same time, often with each one at a different stage of production, so it can require quite a juggling act to keep them all running smoothly. Maintaining careful records of schedules, as well as using checklists for every stage of the process, will help in managing the unexpected during the production of a publication.

An invaluable tool for keeping track is an editorial schedule and checklist. A detailed checklist is useful for all editors. It will be kept by most experienced in-house editors and is a necessity for freelance editors. In the checklist editors can record what has been sent to them and when, who it has been passed on to and when, and what is due to come to them and when.

For a sample editorial schedule and checklist, see appendix 5.

PART B

The basics of editing

Quality control is the editor's core task in publishing. The skills required to perform this role include understanding the conventions used in publishing; analysing the logic and structure of the text; judging the suitability of the language used; applying appropriate editorial styles and rules of grammar, punctuation and spelling; and preparing the document for typesetting by editing onscreen and applying electronic styling. Editors must also know how to handle artwork, understand legal issues and work with different types of publications. Part B addresses each of these areas of editorial work, with detailed discussion of techniques that will save time and effort so that editors can focus on ensuring the content reaches the highest quality possible within the given budget and schedule.

3

Getting ready for editing

Editors' duties extend well beyond copy editing text. In some organisations the editor may even be encouraged to put forward ideas for future projects or to identify suitable authors for the publisher to contact. The breadth and depth of the tasks an editor performs contributes to ensuring that an author's work reaches its audience in the most acceptable form.

This chapter looks at how the editor prepares for each editing job, from ensuring that all the relevant resources are at hand to making contact with the author. A checklist of questions to ask at the start of a job is included at the end of the chapter.

SETTING UP THE WORKSPACE

Before beginning, editors should make sure that they have everything they will need conveniently to hand, that their computer and printer are in good working order, and that they are well supplied with coffee or tea (preferably on a separate work surface).

It is important to ensure that the workspace is comfortable, well lit and ergonomically sound, and that there is access to a telephone and email.

In-house editors will need to work with the equipment and workspace provided by their organisation. Freelance editors may have a little more leeway, depending on their financial and physical resources. In any case, the best results are usually achieved by using the latest software and hardware and the most comfortable furniture available. Almost all editors use a recent version of the word processing program Microsoft Word for editing, mainly due to its strong reviewing features (also known as *Track Changes*) and

For further discussion about the technological requirements for onscreen editing, see chapter 6.

Track Changes
a system used in Microsoft Word for electronically recording changes in word processing documents

ubiquity in the industry. This is the software program that this book will refer to the most.

Editing resources

The editor should assemble appropriate reference books or ensure that they are accessible, perhaps through the local library or online. Apart from any specialist references relating to a particular manuscript or in-house style guides provided by the publisher, there are certain resources most experienced editors would not be without. For a new or trainee editor they will prove invaluable.

Essential reference books include:

- a good up-to-date dictionary, preferably the latest edition of the *Macquarie Dictionary* or *The Australian Concise Oxford Dictionary* (or the older but more comprehensive *The Australian Oxford Dictionary*)—if you work for a company or organisation that has a house style, it will normally specify one of these dictionaries; many editors use more than one

- the most recent Australian *Style Manual for Authors, Editors and Printers* (the *Style Manual*) or any other style guide that is required for the publication (such as *The Australian Guide to Legal Citation*, *The Chicago Manual of Style*)

- *Roget's International Thesaurus*.

Other references we recommend are:

- Writing and style

    — *The Little, Brown Handbook*

    — *The Handbook of Nonsexist Writing for Writers, Editors and Speakers*

    — *New Oxford Style Manual*

    — *The Elements of Style* (Strunk & White)

- English-language usage

    — *The Cambridge Guide to Australian English Usage*

    — *The New Fowler's Modern English Usage*

- English grammar

    — *Rediscover Grammar*

    — *Penguin Dictionary of English Grammar*.

Details of recommended references are listed in appendix 11.

Editors may also need specialist dictionaries (for example, of medical, biological or computer terminology), foreign language dictionaries, a biographical dictionary, or access to a reputable encyclopaedia.

Increasingly, editors are supplementing or replacing printed references with web reference sources such as the Macquarie Dictionary Online, which offers subscription-only access to its dictionary and thesaurus; the online Oxford Dictionaries, which includes free access to both dictionary and thesaurus, and subscription access to additional resources such as style and usage guides; and Bartleby.com, which offers free access to older editions of dictionaries, thesauruses, encyclopaedias, style guides and related reference materials. Care must be taken to ensure that any online sources used are reputable and of high quality. The vast majority are American or British and therefore must be used with appropriate caution in the Australian context.

Editors also have access to dictionaries and thesauruses that are built in to some software programs and operating systems. All versions of Word include a built-in dictionary, and all Macintosh computers come with a searchable version of the *Oxford Dictionary of English* and *Oxford Thesaurus of English*.

Professional editing standards

The nationally agreed *Australian Standards of Editing Practice*, 2nd edition, provides a framework for the skills and knowledge that editors should possess for the effective execution of their craft. It was prepared by the Institute of Professional Editors (IPEd), the peak body for Australian editing societies. The standards are available from the IPEd website: www.iped-editors.org/Editing_standards.aspx.

See appendix 10 for a list of useful editing organisations.

Workplace health

Although editing would not normally feature in a list of dangerous occupations, some health issues are worth taking care about. There are three important steps editors can take to avoid physical problems associated with long periods spent hunched over a computer keyboard:

- Ensure that the workstation is ergonomically designed to suit both user and task.

- Take regular breaks to rest their eyes.

- Incorporate some form of load-bearing and stretching exercises into their work break.

An ergonomically sound workstation, particularly the desk and chair, needs to be designed to suit the user. If problems arise, especially with back, neck or shoulder pain, editors should seek advice from their workplace health and safety officer, contact the chair manufacturer or, if necessary, consult a health professional or occupational therapist.

Editors frequently suffer from eye problems caused by spending too long in front of a computer screen or too much unbroken time poring over text in small type sizes on white pages; for example, while proofreading. The best way to avoid problems is to build regular breaks into each working day. To avoid becoming too engrossed in work to remember to take breaks, it may help to set a timer as a reminder until taking breaks becomes a habit, or use workplace safety computer software. Any health or safety problem in the workplace should be reported immediately. It is in employers' as well as employees' interests for problems to be dealt with before they become more serious.

Machines such as photocopiers and printers that produce chemical fumes should be used only in open, well-ventilated locations. Again, it is important to schedule regular breaks when working in an environment where fumes may be a problem.

Freelance editors may think they cannot afford the time to take exercise and eye breaks, but they will find that such breaks actually increase productivity by helping to maintain alertness and preventing back, neck and eye problems. Similarly, purchasing an ergonomically designed desk and chair is worth the investment if it prevents short- or long-term physical problems and improves productivity.

Security and document management

Throughout the editorial and production process, the editor may handle numerous electronic files and printed documents and have regular email, telephone or face-to-face contact with the author and many, if not all, of the personnel involved in the publication. Until the publication is released to its intended audience, all of this material is essentially commercial-in-confidence or of a sensitive nature, and editors are responsible for both the security and integrity of this material while it is in their hands.

It is therefore important for editors to establish procedures for securely and efficiently filing, storing and transmitting the information and materials with which they are working, as well as to simply avoid disclosing any potentially confidential knowledge. In addition to maintaining security, this also helps to avoid loss of work; there is nothing worse, for example, than spending an entire day editing a manuscript only to find that the file has accidentally become corrupted and no backup versions are available.

Editors should be well aware of the relative security requirements of various document and information management systems, including the potential threats of fire, theft or accidental damage. In-house editors should ensure that they are schooled in the standard security procedures of their organisation (or, if there are none, should assist in instituting them). Freelance editors, however, do not have similar organisational resources providing backups and other security for their work and should therefore take their own steps to ensure that they are covered.

Some of the security measures editors and their organisations should consider include:

- having business insurance to cover the loss of equipment and documents in case of fire, theft or damage

- making regular (preferably automatically scheduled) backups of all computer data, both onsite and offsite

- having procedures and protocols for storing sensitive printed documents securely, such as in a locked cupboard or office

- keeping working documents and equipment away from potential fire and water hazards

- using secure, non-guessable passwords

- adopting secure electronic file management practices, such as always working on a copy of the original file

- keeping computer hardware and software updated, especially anti-virus software

- installing an alarm or other security system for the premises

- for freelancers, following any security procedures specified by the contracting organisation.

Good file-management practices are discussed in chapter 7.

Many organisations require freelance editors to sign a contract specifying their security responsibilities, and increasingly require them to have professional indemnity and public liability insurance.

HOW MUCH AND WHAT TYPE OF EDITING IS NEEDED?

Now, workplace organised, coffee or tea to hand, manuscript front and centre, it's time to start. How does the editor develop the confidence to make judgements about the language, structure and content of manuscripts that might vary from a software manual to a critical anthology of Australian literature?

It is important to look at each manuscript in context and ask these questions:

- What is the purpose of the proposed publication?

- Why was it commissioned or accepted?

- Who is going to read or use it?

- How much are they likely to know already?

- What will their expectations be?

- What is the publisher's brief?

- Are there guidelines already laid down for the publication?

- In what formats will it be published (e.g. print or ebook) and will there be any accompanying material (e.g. a website or additional multimedia elements)?

For more questions to ask about a publication, see the checklist at the end of this chapter.

The answers to these questions, along with a full knowledge of budget and time limitations, will be invaluable in helping the editor to decide what kind of editing the manuscript needs.

For a short TAFE-level textbook on a subject that is constantly changing, the editor might be asked for 'a light edit with the absolute minimum number of changes'. The autobiography of a highly respected public figure, on the other hand, might call for lengthy and detailed editing, because a book of this nature relies for its success on the quality of presentation and the accuracy and readability of the text. In making these decisions, the publisher will have weighed the importance of presenting the highest quality publication against three critical factors—the budget, the schedule and the intended audience.

No matter how committed organisations or publishers may be to the idea of quality in publishing, they are running businesses that have to make money to survive. The budget is therefore of primary importance in determining how much time and resources can be allocated to each publication.

In the case of the TAFE book, the market is small and short term, with readers likely to be more interested in content than style. Extra time and money spent on editing would be unlikely to add to the book's profitability or to the satisfaction of the audience, so would not be justifiable. The autobiography, however, would depend very heavily on critical acclaim, could command a relatively high price, and would be likely to go into a reprint, paperback or ebook editions, and keep selling for years. Cost-cutting in the preparation of such a book could prejudice its chances of success, so the publisher would expect the editor to put every effort into making it as polished and well-produced as possible, even if this meant spending extra time and money, or adding photographs, glossaries or appendixes to enhance its appeal to the potential audience.

The publisher's brief (see appendix 1), developed with these considerations in mind, will usually be circulated to the editor along with the manuscript, and it is essential for the editor when making judgements about how much editing to do.

All manuscripts will require basic copy editing; that is, correcting spelling and grammar, and checking for literals, inconsistencies and awkward expression. Major structural faults must also be corrected in all manuscripts. It is in the areas of minor structural defects and suitability of language that, in the absence of detailed instructions from the publisher, the editor's judgement will be called into play. The degree of structural editing that can be justified will usually depend mainly on budgetary and time constraints, but the question of language depends very much on the nature of the anticipated audience.

literal or **typo**
a misprint, such as the omission of letters, incorrect punctuation or the inclusion of incorrect letters in words

AUTHOR CONTACT

The ideal time to make first contact with the author is when the manuscript is still in the planning stages, so the author can be fully briefed; that is, given detailed instructions on house style, general guidelines on how the publisher wants the manuscript prepared (e.g. formatting or templates that must be followed), any substantive changes required, the type of artwork to accompany the text, and a general idea of the layout and cover requirements. The author should also be given a checklist of material to be supplied, and an idea of when it will be required, the proposed schedule for proofs and the publication date.

formatting (text)
marking up text visually, often to express semantic meaning, such as by applying bold, italic, spacing and different typefaces

If the manuscript has already been written, author–editor liaison should be initiated before copy editing begins, especially if there are problems with the manuscript that must be dealt with first. However, even if all seems straightforward, it is important to establish lines of communication early. A pleasant start to the author–editor relationship can make the interaction much easier if problems develop later.

If it is possible to meet personally for a chat, it is a good idea to do this. However, if the author is based some distance away, or if the company does not encourage direct contact (which is frequently the case for freelance editors), a phone call, letter or email will normally be the first introduction.

After studying all the information available from the publisher and the files, the editor will have an idea of what changes will need to be made. If major structural changes or rewriting by the author are necessary, the editor should follow the initial conversation with a written confirmation of exactly what is required and an estimated schedule for delivery of the new material. It is very important that the author be available at the scheduled times, so the editor will need information about any travel plans or work commitments that might cause delays.

The author should be asked to send one or two redrafted chapters before proceeding too far with any rewriting or restructuring, so that the editor and publisher can check that the author has understood and followed the agreed guidelines. It is especially important to recheck the language level of a publication aimed at a specific target audience.

For further
discussion about
onscreen editing,
see chapter 6.

If the changes that will need to be made are relatively minor, editors provide authors with a Word document showing their suggested edits using the *Track Changes* facility. In this way, authors can see where changes have been made and they may have the opportunity to reject those with which they do not agree (for example, if the suggested edit alters the author's intended meaning). In some instances, such as when working with annual reports, authors may not be consulted at all regarding minor editing changes.

In all cases, it is important to be diplomatic when dealing with authors. The basic rules are as follows:

- Be positive about the manuscript's merits.

- Be optimistic about achieving any necessary changes.

- Explain why changes are needed; if they cannot be justified to the author, they may be unjustifiable.

- Give specific reasons for the changes, for example:

  — some of the language is too difficult for the target audience

  — the publication is part of a series and must conform to a house style

  — gender or racial bias in the examples would alienate part of the intended audience.

First questions — a checklist

What do you have?

- What material has been supplied?

- What is still to come?

- Has the author supplied the material electronically?

- Are the supplied files compatible with the editor's computer system?

- Is the manuscript structured and formatted according to the brief?

- Have backup copies of the material been made?

  Who to ask: publisher or publication manager, author, publisher's assistant or personal assistant

Where has the manuscript come from?

- What is the brief from the publisher?

- Does the manuscript meet the conditions of the contract? Are there any special clauses in the contract that the editor needs to be aware of? Is the author to receive an advance?

- What is the background to the work? How much more information can the publisher give the editor (e.g. from verbal communication with the author not recorded on file)?

- Has the publisher read the manuscript?

- Should the manuscript be sent to an external reader for a professional assessment? Who arranges this? Who chooses the reader? Has a reader been approached already? By whom? What fee is to be offered? When does the assessment need to be submitted?

  Who to ask: publisher or publication manager, contracts manager

(continued)

First questions—a checklist *(cont'd)*

What sort of publication will it be?

- What market is it aimed at—academic, general, educational (primary/secondary/tertiary/TAFE), fiction, biography, current events, subject-oriented (sports/craft/medical)?

- Who will read it? Adults or children? The general public, teachers, academics or hobbyists?

- Will it be a print-only publication or an electronic publication, such as an ebook? What is the proposed format (e.g. printed hardback, paperback, spiral-bound limp; or ebook, website)?

- Will it be simultaneously, or sequentially, released in print and electronic form?

- Will it be produced in colour (two or more), or in black and white only?

- Will there be diagrams, maps, tables, cartoons, sketches or photographs?

- Will it have an index, notes, bibliography, appendixes, exercises, reproducible pages, resource lists, or multimedia components?

- Have copies of the manuscript been given to the production department for estimates of extent, costing and preparation of a schedule?

- Is there a companion publication (earlier volume, or teacher's or student's guide)? Is it part of a series?

- Is it an entirely new approach to a subject? Or are there similar works already on the market? Does the editor have a copy of these? How will this one be different?

- Is the title firm or tentative? Who decides?

- What is the proposed print run and price?

- If the work has been previously published (by your organisation or by another), is it to be a straight reprint with no corrections? Will it include revisions or additions? Is it to be a new edition? Will there be any new artwork, tables etc.? If a new edition is required, is it to be by the same author?

- Has there been a production meeting to discuss planning?

  Who to ask: publisher or publication manager, production manager or controller, designer, marketing manager.

hardback
a book bound with stiff or rigid covers, usually cardboard covered with cloth or other material and often covered by a dust jacket; the spine is usually sewn rather than glued

paperback
a book bound with flexible covers, usually heavy paper or thin cardboard; the spine is usually glued rather than sewn, and the cover printed directly with ink

print run
the number of copies of a work to be printed

50

Who is the author?

- Has the author published before? With which organisation? Was it a happy relationship? Is the author/editor/compiler approachable or difficult?

- Will the author be available for consultation? Does the author live locally, interstate or overseas? What are the author's contact details? What is the preferred method of communication, and what is the best time of the day or week to make direct contact?

- If there are two or more authors, who is the contact author?

- Who will read the author's proofs if the author is not available?

   Who to ask: publisher or publication manager, author.

What is the time frame for the publication?

- Is the publication date firm or yet to be set?

- Is production to be fast-tracked or tied to a special event, such as a conference, Anzac Day, Children's Book Week?

- Has a schedule been set?

- How much time has been allocated to each stage of the editing and production process?

   Who to ask: publisher or publication manager, production manager or controller, marketing manager.

Whose responsibility is it?

- Who is involved in costing the project and setting the budget?

- Is the author to secure all the copyright clearances, or is this an in-house service?

- Has the author provided all the necessary details?

- Has a designer been commissioned?

- Who will provide the artwork? Will it be roughs or finished art? Does the editor have to commission any of the artwork?

- Who will make corrections—the author, the editor, the designer or the typesetter?

- Will the author compile the index, if there is one? If not, who will commission an indexer?

   Who to ask: publisher or publication manager, contracts manager.

(continued)

First questions—a checklist *(cont'd)*

Has the book been test-driven?

- Is the editor familiar with the subject, or will it be a new challenge? (The editor should assume the role of an ordinary reader with no specialised background and read the first 20 pages to get a taste of the whole work.)

- Will the book need substantive (structural) editing or specialised editing?

- Is it easy to read?

- If it is a work of fiction, do plot and characterisation stand up?

- Can the editor easily identify its content, scope, level, organisation, accuracy and clarity, and any legal problems?

How will the publication be produced?

- For a printed book or ebook, will it be printed or converted locally or offshore? Has the publisher worked with these suppliers before?

- Are the suppliers familiar with the technical requirements?

- Will there be special requirements, such as die-cuts, embossing, multimedia elements or interactivity?

- For a printed publication produced offshore, how long will it take to ship the printed copies to Australia? When will advance copies be available?

- Have copies been sent to the marketing and publicity departments?

  Who to ask: production manager or controller, marketing manager

forme (die) cutting cutting or punching out paper or board to a required shape, such as to produce a book with rounded corners or with a hole in the middle

Parts of a book

It is important that the editor understands the parts of the book and the different ways in which they need to be edited and prepared for publication. This chapter describes the many parts of a typical print or electronic book. The specific editorial treatment for the different formats is discussed in chapter 7.

A traditional printed book or other publication may be divided into three main sections: the preliminary pages (prelims), the main text and the endmatter. For the most part, these divisions still hold for ebooks, as this makes it easier for readers who are used to printed books to make the transition to electronic versions. However, there are some aspects of the arrangement of the content of printed books that do not necessarily work as well for ebooks, and these are noted in this chapter. Publishers are also gradually working out new ways to present information that might better suit the electronic medium, so no doubt further changes will come.

Ebooks and printing conventions

Depending on the type of ebook, some of the conventions of print publishing do not apply. While ebooks published in portable document format (PDF) or produced as apps may closely resemble a printed book, most ebooks in EPUB, Kindle or website formats are reflowable, meaning that the pagination is dependent on the reading software and the font size and typeface chosen by the reader.

Kindle
an ebook format, device and distribution service developed by Amazon.com Inc.

reflow (ebooks)
technologies that allow ebook content to rearrange and resize elements according to user and device settings

(continued)

verso
the 'back' of a leaf
of paper in a book,
usually a left-hand
(even-numbered) page

recto
the 'front' of a leaf
of paper in a book,
usually a right-hand
(odd-numbered) page

For more
information about
the publication
of ebooks, see
chapter 15.

Ebooks and printing conventions *(cont'd)*

In reflowable EPUB and Kindle ebooks, the individual components and chapters of the book can be forced to begin on a new page, but otherwise the page numbering is controlled by the software used to read the publication. If they are being viewed with two pages side by side, the new page may start either on the left (verso) or right (recto)—and may change if the font size is altered. To complicate matters, the reading software will also allow the pages to be viewed as single pages, in which case recto and verso pages won't exist at all. Publishers also have minimal control over running heads and feet (which are generated by the software), and only limited control over where page breaks in the text will occur.

PRELIMS

As the name suggests, the prelims are the pages containing preliminary material that precedes the main text. In a simple publication, the prelims may consist of:

- a half-title recto page (optional)
- half-title verso page (if a half-title is included)
- a title recto page
- a title verso (imprint) page
- a table of contents.

In a more complex publication the prelims may also include some of the following:

- a frontispiece (sometimes with a tipped-in illustration)
- a dedication
- an epigraph
- a foreword
- lists of illustrations, figures, tables, maps
- a preface
- a letter of transmittal
- acknowledgements
- lists of contributors
- a list of abbreviations.

The prelim pages are usually numbered separately from the text, using lowercase roman numerals. Half-title, title, imprint and blank prelim pages do not carry folios (printed page numbers), although they are taken into account in the pagination (the page numbering sequence). If space is not a problem, the foreword, table of contents and preface will normally begin on a recto page. However, when space or budget is limited this convention need not be strictly adhered to.

In ebooks, publishers are increasingly moving many of the components of traditional prelims towards the back of the book. This is because it is often easier to quickly skip through the prelims to the beginning of the text in a printed book than it is in an ebook, so keeping the prelims short in an ebook helps readers find their way to the start of the text more easily.

lowercase
small letters, as distinct from uppercase (capital) letters

roman (numerals) numbers based on the ancient Roman system of letters (e.g. i, v, x or I, V, X, L, C, D, M)

Half-title recto and verso pages

The half-title recto page has the main title of the book only; subtitle, author names and publisher details are not included. It is common to make the first recto the half-title page, although some publications dispense with this, beginning with the title page. Some paperback books put a short biography of the author or promotional reviews on this page.

In a simple publication, the half-title verso (which faces the title page) will remain blank. However, a number of items may be placed here. If there is a frontispiece or tipped-in artwork, it should appear on the half-title verso. Fiction and non-fiction paperbacks often include a list of the author's previous publications, and if a publication is part of a series, details of the other publications in the series may be listed here.

frontispiece
an illustration facing the title page

The inclusion or exclusion of a half-title page in a printed book is usually dictated by page extent. Because pages are usually printed in multiples of four, it may be preferable to include half-title pages at the beginning of the book rather than leave two pages blank at the end. In ebooks, where page extent is not an issue, it is preferable not to include half-title pages at all because this unnecessarily adds to the number of pages.

Title page

The title page, always a recto, carries the full title, including any subtitle, the names of all authors, coordinating editors and translators, the edition (if applicable), and the publisher's name and logo. Sometimes the title page will include the author's qualifications or titles, and the date and place of publication.

Government and corporate publications may include the name of the relevant department or sponsoring body in place of or in addition to the author names.

Imprint page

The title verso, usually known as the imprint page, contains the publication details, the copyright line and statement, and the cataloguing-in-publication (CiP) data. This information is sometimes moved to the end in ebooks.

CiP (cataloguing-in-publication) data
bibliographic description of a publication, obtained from the National Library of Australia

Letter of transmittal

In some government publications, primarily annual reports, a letter of transmittal from the head of the relevant department to the responsible minister must be included before the foreword (unless the departmental format requires a different location). It should be printed without changes and accompanied by the author's signature and the date of submission.

Foreword

A foreword is written by someone other than the author, often an authority in the field, who commends the publication to the reader or writes in support of its aims. It is placed before the contents page. It should be headed *Foreword* (not *Forward*), and the name and title (or position) of the writer, if appropriate, should be given at the end, often under a facsimile of the writer's signature. Sometimes the date of writing is included, but this risks dating the publication if the book remains available for several years.

Contents

The contents page should be easy to read and not too long, so it is often limited to the chapter headings and, if necessary, one level of subheading. It should be headed *Contents* (rather than *Table of Contents*), and should include entries for the foreword and any prelims that follow the contents page (e.g. lists of illustrations, figures, tables and maps; preface; acknowledgements; lists of contributors; list of abbreviations; and short sections such as *About this book*) with the appropriate roman page numbers. If the publication is divided into parts or sections, these should be included in the contents in the same form as that used in the text (e.g. Part III, Section 4).

Some tertiary and reference publications have an abbreviated contents page of part and chapter titles only, followed by a separate, more detailed contents, with two or three levels of subheading. This may also include names of contributors.

There is no need for a contents page in fiction books if there are no chapter titles, although some children's books include them, especially picture storybooks for younger readers.

In ebooks the contents list is usually hyperlinked to the relevant parts of the book. In EPUBs there are usually no fixed page numbers, so the contents will normally be generated in a separate navigational pane or page and embedded in the ebook metadata. The navigation pane is easily accessed from anywhere in the EPUB. In these cases there may also be a version of the contents replicating the one in the printed book (which may also be hyperlinked; see figure 4.1), although publishers may decide to remove this in order to avoid duplication and to reduce the length of the prelims. Alternatively, the contents list in the prelims may be in a different form to that provided in the navigation pane.

metadata
information about content (e.g. a book, ebook or photograph), such as descriptions of its subject, authorship, ownership and structure, that is not immediately visible in that content but can be used to identify, search and navigate it

Figure 4.1: the contents list of an EPUB as embedded navigation metadata (left), and as separate linked text in the book prelims (right)

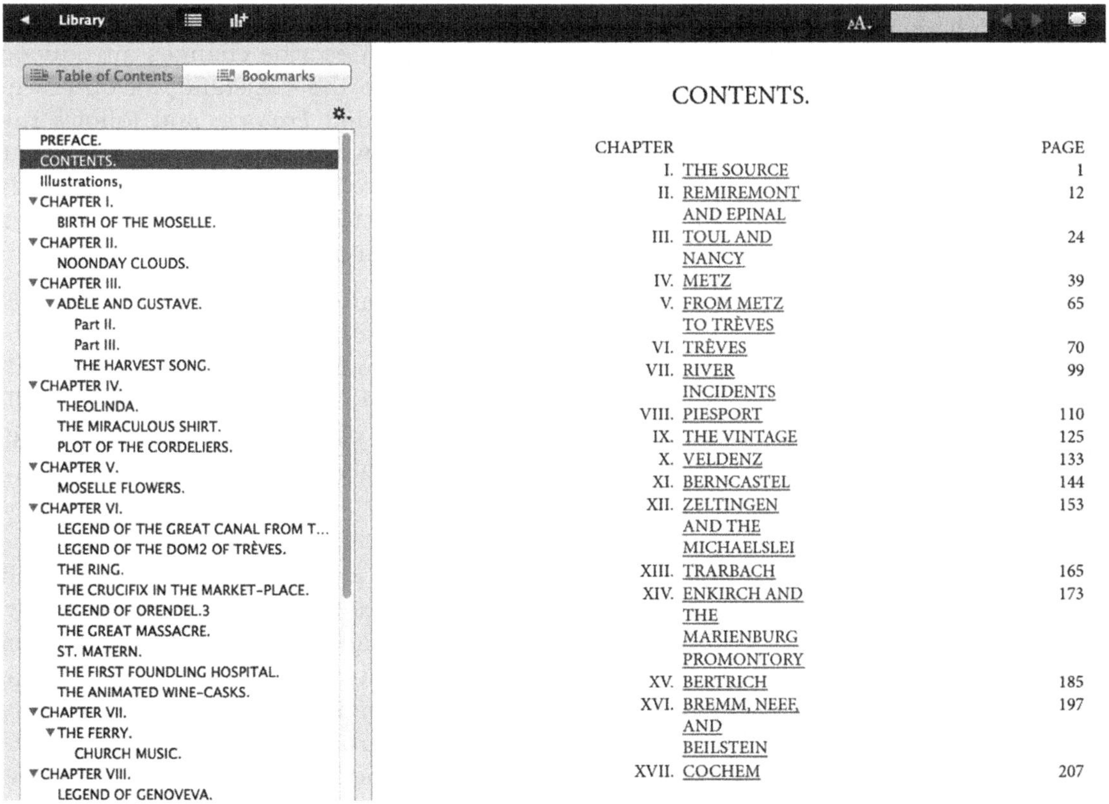

List of artwork and tables

Artwork that is purely decorative is not listed in the prelims, but where artwork is referred to separately, perhaps in a reference book or textbook, it is usually listed with the relevant page numbers. Tables may also be listed. Sometimes the artwork list is divided into separate lists of, say, plates, figures and maps; in such a case the order of presentation should be plates, figures, diagrams, tables, maps.

If the copyright and source information does not appear with the artwork in the text, this may be included below each listed illustration, usually in a smaller typeface on the next line. Alternatively, this information can be included on a separate page, often along with the acknowledgements or in the endmatter.

typeface
a complete set of all the fonts sharing the same design features; also called a font family

In ebooks, these lists may be hyperlinked to the relevant artwork or table in the text, and any page numbers are removed.

Preface

The preface, written by the author(s), may explain why or how the publication came to be written, describe changes introduced in a new edition, and acknowledge the assistance of others in its preparation. It is normally headed *Preface*, and follows the contents page. In educational texts, where it may give the teacher or student directions on how to approach the text, it is sometimes headed *How to use this book*. Occasionally, both a preface and a *How to use this book* section will be included.

The names of all authors of the preface should appear at the end, sometimes following facsimile signatures. The signatures may be followed by the place and date of completion of the manuscript, but this information may be omitted if it is decided that this will date the publication or if some of the original authors (particularly in a new edition of a multi-author work) are unavailable.

Introduction

Arabic numerals
the numbers 0 to 9

The introduction normally forms part of the main text and accordingly is paginated using Arabic numerals. Occasionally, however, the author will write a preface as well as an introduction that does not form part of the main text. In this case, the preface usually becomes the place to thank colleagues and others for their assistance, while the introduction explains how the publication came to be written and may include an overview of the book. It is preferable to combine the two, particularly if there is also an introduction in the main text. If they are to be separate, the introduction in the prelims should follow the preface and be paginated using lowercase roman numerals, and the introduction in the main text should have an expanded title (not just Introduction).

Acknowledgements

Although personal acknowledgements are often included in the preface, they may be set separately under the heading *Acknowledgements*. Source acknowledgements for quotations, illustrations and photographs may be listed in the prelims, beneath the authors' personal acknowledgements or, if extensive, in the endmatter. Personal acknowledgements may also be included in the endmatter. If space permits, the best solution is often to list the personal acknowledgements in the prelims under the heading *Acknowledgements*, and list the source acknowledgements, which may not be finalised until final page proof stage, in the endmatter under a heading such as *Sources*.

Advice on compiling acknowledgements is given in the section on endmatter later in this chapter.

Dedication

An author's dedication, if used, is often very short, and may cause problems of placement if space is limited. Authors usually prefer a full page for the dedication, but this may not always be possible. A dedication can be combined with acknowledgements or an epigraph, or placed on the imprint page. In such cases, the dedication should always be placed at the top of the page and separated from what follows by as much space as possible. The text for a dedication is usually centred on the page.

epigraph
a quotation that appears in the prelims or at the beginning of a part or chapter

Other material

Prelims may also include a list of contributors to a multi-author publication or a collection of conference papers; a list of abbreviations used; or a key to symbols (in, say, a statistics textbook); and sometimes author or contributor biographies. These should follow the rest of the prelims in whatever order seems most logical. Information that is likely to be referred to frequently by the reader, such as a list of symbols or abbreviations, is best placed on a verso as it is easier to flip to a verso page. Alternatively, this type of material may be placed in the endmatter.

In ebooks, special terms, abbreviations, acronyms and symbols may have each instance in the text hyperlinked to bring up an appropriate description or definition. However, some effort is required to set this up during production and therefore it may be an uneconomical option.

MAIN TEXT

The main text is, of course, the core of the book, but in terms of parts is generally structured quite simply. The first text page always starts on a recto with the page number being an Arabic numeral 1.

Parts or sections

Longer or more complex publications may be broken up into broad parts or sections that correspond to different topics, time periods, geographic regions or other organisational devices. Parts may be numbered or have a title. For example, an analysis of world political systems might be divided into *Part A: Europe*, *Part B: Asia*, *Part C: Oceania*, and so on. The numbering system may use Arabic numerals, letters or roman numerals, but should be distinct from the numbering used for the chapters.

Parts often begin with their own opening page (usually a recto). The opening page may simply have the part number and title or it may also include a list of its chapters.

Chapters

Chapters are the main device used for dividing the text in most books. Each chapter usually contains a coherent body of information or narrative that is logically distinct from the other chapters.

page spread
two facing (verso and recto) pages of a book, presented on one sheet

The first chapter always begins on a recto. Subsequent chapters preferably also start on a recto, but may start on a verso if page extent is a problem. In some types of publications, such as textbooks, chapters may begin on an opening recto or verso page (or a double-page spread) that includes an introduction, a short summary or the aims of the chapter.

For more discussion about the treatment of the components of the main text, see chapter 7.

Each chapter is usually consecutively numbered (even if chapters are grouped into parts) using Arabic numerals, but can also use letters or roman numerals. Most non-fiction works have chapter titles, while fiction more often uses only chapter numbers.

call-out, pull-out or **pull quote**
a short piece of text that is highlighted by placing it in the margin or setting it apart in a box or using a different design

Apart from standard paragraphs, the main text may contain figures, tables, boxed text, call-out text, footnotes, quotations, poems and other elements that are treated differently in the text design.

ENDMATTER

Everything that follows the main text is known as the endmatter, including appendixes, glossaries, endnotes, bibliographies and indexes. Some items, such as the source acknowledgements, lists of contributors, lists of useful addresses or advertisements for other publications, may be placed in the prelims but are more usually placed in the endmatter.

It is often the editor's responsibility to decide, based on considerations of space and convenience, on the most appropriate order of the endmatter for a particular publication. Consideration should be given to what readers are most likely to need to read before they tackle the main text, and what is better left to the end, such as supplementary material that is referred to from the main text and additional information that is not essential to the publication.

The order normally followed for endmatter is:

- list of abbreviations and acronyms

- appendixes

- glossary or chronology

- endnotes

- bibliography and/or references

- other lists

- acknowledgements

- index

- advertisements

- additional material (such as booklets, CDs or maps) in a back pocket.

Any additional elements should be placed between the bibliography and the index. If space permits, each item of endmatter should start on a new page. Some paperback books include advertisements, which are placed after the index or, in fiction books, after the end of the last chapter.

Page numbers in the endmatter usually run on from the main text. Advertisement pages are not numbered, but are included as blind folios in working out the page extent.

List of abbreviations and acronyms

Abbreviations and acronyms must be explained in all publications. If there are only a few, these can simply be included in the text as they arise. However, if there are many it may be necessary to provide a separate listing, either in the prelims (if they are essential for the reader to understand the text) or in the endmatter. Unless the list is extensive, both abbreviations and acronyms can be included in the one list, with an appropriate heading.

Appendixes

Appendixes contain material that is supplementary to, rather than part of, the main text. They are used to present relevant or associated documents, such as letters, reports, lists, facsimile material, tables and chronological sequences, that would obstruct the flow of the text if included in the main body of the text, or that are too substantial for inclusion as notes.

If the material submitted as an appendix is very short, it could be incorporated into the text at an appropriate point, or treated as illustrative material, perhaps by setting it in a box or otherwise highlighting it. It is a good idea to consult the author, and ask the designer for help in deciding how to treat such material.

If the publication is organised in parts, with part titles, the appendixes should form a separate part. They may have their own opening page (on a recto), titled *Appendixes*, and a list of the appendix titles.

The first appendix usually commences on a recto, and subsequent appendixes on a new page, either recto or verso. If there are several appendixes and space is limited, they may follow straight on from each other, in which case a reasonable space (usually several line spaces) between each should be allowed.

Glossary or chronology

Glossaries list and define technical or specialist terms used in a particular subject area or text. They may also list and translate foreign words or phrases, or expand on political, historical or sociological references. The words defined are called keywords, and may be set in italics, bold or small caps.

Glossaries covering different types of information may be grouped separately; for example, a history of medical discoveries may have one glossary listing medical terms and another listing significant historical figures in medicine.

Chronologies are commonly included in historical or biographical works, and are treated very much like glossaries, with the dates as the keywords. The dates may appear in chronological or reverse order, depending on the purpose of the listing. A chronology may

---

italic
sloping type, often used to denote emphasis, foreign words, defined terms, titles of books and journals and special uses such as statistical abbreviations

bold/boldface
a heavy typeface used for contrast or emphasis; commonly used in headings

small caps (small capital letters)
uppercase characters set at the x-height of the lowercase letters surrounding them (e.g. BCE and CE)

appear in place of or following the glossary, or may be placed in the prelims.

Endnotes

Endnotes, like footnotes, may be used to provide reference sources for the text, and additional information that is incidental and would otherwise unnecessarily interrupt the flow of the text.

Endnotes are indicated in the main text by superscript figures, which may either be numbered consecutively through the whole publication or restarted with each chapter. If individual chapters are self-contained (e.g. if they are to be made available separately or have been written by different authors), the endnotes must restart their numbering and appear at the end of the relevant chapter. However, the most economical placement of endnotes is in the endmatter, following any appendixes and glossaries.

Endnotes should be headed *Notes* and, if extensive, should be divided by chapter and listed under the chapter title. Where possible the endnotes should begin on a recto, but they can then run on without starting a new page for each chapter division.

In ebooks, endnotes (and footnotes) can be hyperlinked to and from the superscript figure in the text and the note itself.

run on
to make sentences follow each other without starting a new paragraph; to start a new section, chapter or other text on the same page as the end of the last one, rather than on a fresh page

Bibliography and references

A bibliography or list of references should be placed after the appendixes, glossaries and endnotes. A bibliography includes works used or consulted in the preparation of the main text, including those that have not been specifically cited. Some bibliographies are annotated (that is, each entry is followed by an explanatory note or comment). A list of references includes only works directly cited in the main text. If recommended further reading is also to be included, it may be useful to divide the citations under the subheadings *References* and *Suggested further reading*.

Bibliographical entries are listed in alphabetical order without numbers. If the list is further subdivided (for example, by chapter or subject), entries within each section are also listed alphabetically.

Other lists

Other resources that may be in the endmatter include lists of relevant organisations and their contact details, supplementary material (such as videos, websites, software applications or ephemera such as pamphlets or posters) or suppliers.

In ebooks, website and email addresses can be hyperlinked so that selecting them takes the reader to the address in a browser or email program, as appropriate.

Acknowledgements

Acknowledgements may appear in the prelims (as a separate element or combined with the preface, dedication or imprint) or, if space permits, in the endmatter. Long lists of source acknowledgements (e.g. for an extensively illustrated book or anthology) are generally positioned in the endmatter. These should state who owns the copyright to each work or the person or organisation giving permission for its use, preceded or followed by the page number on which the work appears. Sources may be listed alphabetically by source or in the order in which they appear.

Index

Although it is not normally the editor's responsibility to compile the index, it is important to establish at the outset if there is to be an index, how long and extensive it will be and who will compile it.

Unless it is to be referenced to paragraph or section numbers rather than page numbers, the index cannot be compiled until all the pages are finalised. At the copy editing stage a page should be added at the end of the manuscript with the note 'Index—to come'. It is also important to list the index in the page design brief, so that allowance can be made when the extent is calculated.

For details on editing an index, see chapter 13.

In ebooks, an index created for a printed book may be removed altogether because the page numbers are not applicable. It is possible to generate a linked index using programs such as InDesign, and this is becoming an increasingly viable option.

Advertisements

Advertisements for related publications or websites produced by the publishing organisation may be included at the end of a book (most commonly in fiction books). They may appear on both recto and verso pages, or only on rectos, depending on the number of blank pages in the last section.

Marketing information for each publication advertised should include the author's name, the title and subtitle, the ISBN, a short blurb, and brief (attributed) extracts from reviews.

Structural and copy editing principles

Editing tasks may involve any or all of the following:

- structural editing (also known as substantive editing), including:

  — ensuring the text is logical in structure

  — checking there are no missing or inadequately treated topics.

- content editing, including:

  — ensuring factual accuracy and consistency

  — ensuring that the text is free from discriminatory or defamatory material

  — checking any legal issues that might arise.

- copy editing, including:

  — correcting grammar, spelling and punctuation

  — ensuring the appropriate level of formality and language use for the target audience

  — imposing a house style.

- preparing the manuscript for publication, including:

  — applying electronic styling to the author's manuscript file

  — editing and taking in corrections using *Track Changes*

— checking and editing artwork and other non-textual materials

— ensuring that corrections by the typesetter have been taken in correctly.

digital proof
a proof generated directly from electronic files and output on a laser printer or similar device

• proofreading page proofs (hard copy or digital).

Depending on the nature of the publication, editors may perform all or only a few of these tasks, and at different levels of complexity. The following chapters focus mainly on editing general non-fiction books, but many of the processes and techniques described can be used when working with a variety of publication types. Chapter 10 also describes some other types of works, such as fiction, academic and children's books, and the different editorial tasks that might be involved. The range of work required of an editor can be quite broad, so it is important for editors to remain flexible and ensure that they are carefully briefed on whatever project they tackle.

The task of editing text can be divided into three broad areas—structure, content and style—which are considered in detail in this chapter.

QUESTIONS OF STRUCTURE

A well-structured manuscript will convey the author's meaning clearly to the reader and will flow logically from sentence to sentence, paragraph to paragraph, chapter to chapter.

The most common structural problems are illogical arrangement of chapters or sections, and unbalanced treatment of different aspects of the subject. Straightforward problems of structure and flow can often be dealt with by a rearrangement of the manuscript by the editor, once the author's agreement is obtained.

How to identify structural problems

The contents page of the manuscript will often provide a listing of the major headings and subheadings in the publication. If there is no contents page, or it lists only the chapter headings, go through the manuscript and identify all the headings used, with their level. Traditionally, heading levels were marked up on paper using letters; for example, A = major heading, B = subheading, C = subsubheading, and so on. However, when using electronic styling, the heading levels may be called almost anything, as long as the hierarchical order is clear (e.g. *Heading 1*, *Heading 2*, or *H1*,

For details on how to use electronic styles, see chapter 6.

H2, to the number of heads needed). Once the headings have been styled in Microsoft Word, the heading structure can be examined in Word using the Outline view or by generating an automated table of contents.

For all but the simplest manuscripts, examining the hierarchy of headings (see figure 5.1) is a good place to start when assessing the structure of a work, particularly in non-fiction books, such as reference works, technical reports and textbooks. The heading structure of a publication provides the reader with an idea of its overall content and coverage, the relative importance of the subtopics within, and the logical structure of the work.

hierarchy of headings the arrangement of headings and subheadings according to their relative importance and place within a logical sequence

Figure 5.1: hierarchy of headings in Word Outline View (left), and in a Word-generated table of contents (right)

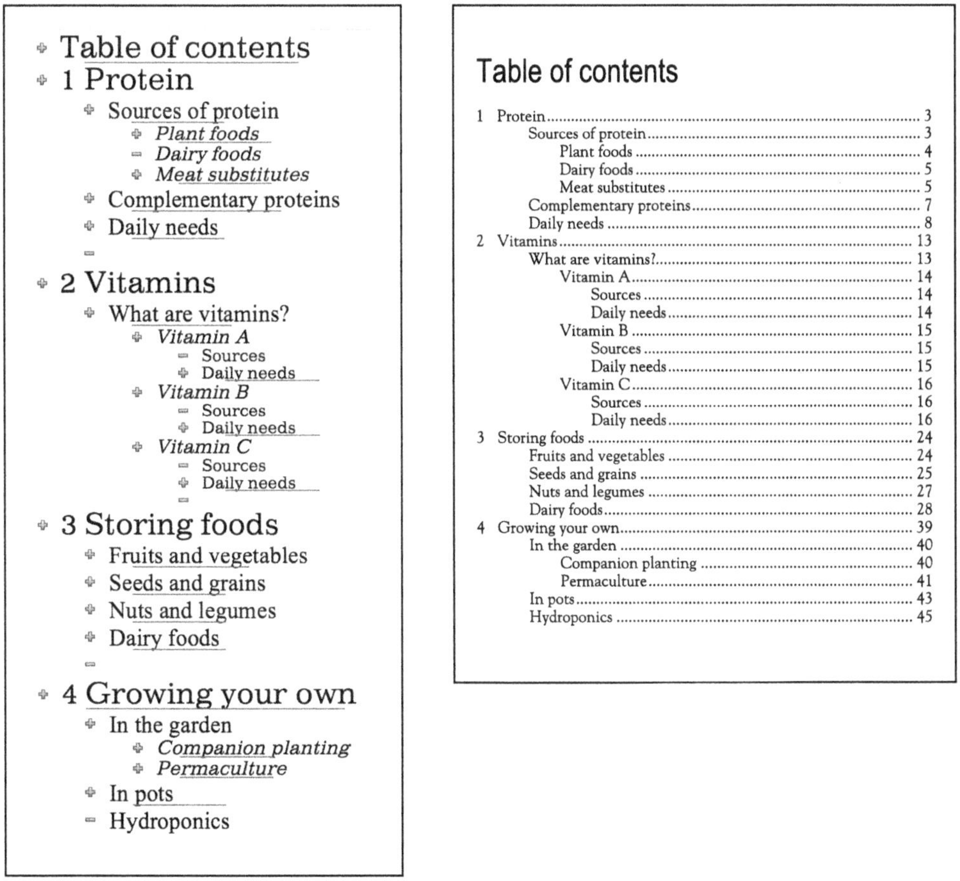

Table of contents
1 Protein
Sources of protein
Plant foods
Dairy foods
Meat substitutes
Complementary proteins
Daily needs
2 Vitamins
What are vitamins?
Vitamin A
Sources
Daily needs
Vitamin B
Sources
Daily needs
Vitamin C
Sources
Daily needs
3 Storing foods
Fruits and vegetables
Seeds and grains
Nuts and legumes
Dairy foods
4 Growing your own
In the garden
Companion planting
Permaculture
In pots
Hydroponics

Table of contents

1 Protein 3
Sources of protein 3
Plant foods 4
Dairy foods 5
Meat substitutes 5
Complementary proteins 7
Daily needs 8
2 Vitamins 13
What are vitamins? 13
Vitamin A 14
Sources 14
Daily needs 14
Vitamin B 15
Sources 15
Daily needs 15
Vitamin C 16
Sources 16
Daily needs 16
3 Storing foods 24
Fruits and vegetables 24
Seeds and grains 25
Nuts and legumes 27
Dairy foods 28
4 Growing your own 39
In the garden 40
Companion planting 40
Permaculture 41
In pots 43
Hydroponics 45

Examine the headings to ensure that they follow one another logically. Do the headings give a clear sense of what each chapter contains? If not, this could indicate structural problems. Misleading, uninformative, overly short or overly long headings should be discussed with the author if they risk impeding the flow of information.

A hierarchy of headings is also useful when looking for imbalance in the treatment of information in the text. For example, a book about Australian wildlife that includes a detailed chapter on wedge-tailed eagles and then crams all other birds into one chapter would require significant restructuring, as would a book on physiology that did not include the digestive system in the headings. It is also a good idea to check for levels represented by only one heading, which could confuse readers and indicate structural problems.

Authors may have their own personal biases within their subject of expertise, so an important aspect of structural editing is to make sure each topic is covered in appropriate detail for the target audience.

Checking the length of each chapter also helps to assess whether the book is balanced. If one chapter is three times as long as each of the other chapters, this should alert the editor to potential structural problems.

When considering a book's structure, here are some questions to ask about the headings:

- Are they all really necessary?

- Do they follow in a logical sequence?

- Do they accurately describe the text that follows?

- Are they brief and well worded?

- Are they consistent in length and style?

- Should there be more, or fewer, or none?

- Are there any isolated subheadings?

For further information on editing fiction works, see chapter 10.

Of course, it is not always possible to assess the structure of a book through an analysis of the heading structure. Most fiction books, for example, have no more than numbered chapter breaks to demarcate the text, and shorter works may have few if any headings. Nevertheless, in these cases the same principles for assessing structure apply. The editor must assess whether any chapters reflect inappropriate breaks in the content and structure of the overall manuscript, whether there is unintentionally uneven or missing treatment of the parts of the content, or whether the text is inadvertently illogical.

Structural problems usually require input by the author, particularly if important areas of the subject of the manuscript have been omitted or treated inadequately. For structural rewriting the editor should give the author detailed guidelines about what is required, and if necessary offer to review the first chapter or section to make sure they are on the right track.

Multi-author books

When more than one author is involved in writing a book, it is very important to know who is the coordinating (contact) author to refer to for decisions. If possible, the editor should discuss the planned style, structure and content of the manuscript with the contact author before writing commences, and ensure that all the authors involved are fully briefed.

Structural problems that can arise in multi-author books include:

- variation in the depth of treatment of sections of the text, often signalled by widely differing chapter lengths, heading styles or divisions within the text

- different formats within chapters (e.g. some authors including student activities or bibliographies, and some not)

- inadequate division of responsibility, leading to unnecessary repetitions, or to omission of important information

- variation in language level and writing style (voice or tone).

voice (grammar) the relationship between the verb and the subject to indicate whether the subject is the doer (active voice) or the receiver (passive voice) of the action

Most of these problems can be avoided by thoroughly briefing authors, but if this has not been possible, and the manuscript has been written to different language levels and in varying styles, some difficult editorial decisions have to be made. If, for example, four chapters of an eight-chapter book are written in an attractive, breezy style that helps make an otherwise starchy subject accessible, the editor and the contact author might decide to ask the other authors to rewrite their chapters to match this style. However, if they are part of a 20-chapter book, this may not be feasible.

tone (writing) the attitude that the author implies in a text about the content and the intended reader

Since such changes almost always require rewriting by the authors, entailing potentially costly delays, it is obviously important to try to avoid such situations by briefing all authors early on—and supplying structural templates for each chapter. If problems of variation of style, content or format do arise, however, the most practical solution (although not always the ideal one) is usually to make changes to the least prevalent style to bring it into line with the majority.

Normally, the editor should discuss any problems directly with the contact author, who will then consult with the relevant co-author(s). If it is decided that the editor should deal directly with the other authors, the contact author must be advised about decisions made and any delays, disagreements or unresolved problems, usually by copying them into all communications.

QUESTIONS OF CONTENT

The editor must make sure that the text is accurate, does not break copyright laws, contains no defamatory or dangerous material, does not include discriminatory material, and avoids or explains parochial references or specialist terms that are likely to be unfamiliar to many of the audience.

Accuracy

Where possible, every date, name, factual statement and table should be checked for accuracy and consistency, whether the work is fiction or non-fiction. If there are simply too many such items for this to be feasible, a spot-check of, say, every tenth item will soon give an idea of how careful the author has been. Accuracy is the author's responsibility, so if the editor finds numerous errors, the manuscript should be returned to the author for detailed checking.

In shorter or less detailed manuscripts, the editor should check any item that can be easily verified; for example, the spelling of names or places, dates of historical events, anachronisms, and simple mathematics, including all additions and percentages in columns of tables. Any inconsistencies or areas where there is some reason to doubt the text must be referred to the author with other editorial queries.

Editors should also be acutely aware of the types of facts that are beyond their expertise to check. The author is the specialist in the field, and the editor should not be expected to check the accuracy of items that are outside the realm of general knowledge.

Copyright and permissions

Obtaining permission to use copyright material is often the author's responsibility, but the editor must be alert for any copyright material (particularly artwork) for which the author may not have sought permission.

Freelance editors are often required by the publishing organisation to put together an artwork and permissions brief that contains details of all material that is or potentially could be subject to copyright. This brief should include a description and the source of the material, the location in the text, whether the author has obtained permission already, and any other information that might assist in obtaining permission for reproducing the material. It is important to know if there are any costs involved, particularly if the fee requires an annual payment or varies depending on usage.

Some general guidelines on how and when to seek permission are given below.

For an example of an artwork and permissions brief, see appendix 3.

Term of copyright

Copyright in Australia generally extends until 70 years after the death of the author or the publication of the work for non-government material, and until 50 years after publication for government material. However, copyright law is complex, and was arguably further complicated by changes in 2005 that aligned Australia's copyright system more closely to that of the United States. It is important, therefore, to check what the current situation is when dealing with any copyright material. If in doubt, visit the Australian Copyright Council's website (www.copyright. org.au), which provides a comprehensive range of useful copyright-related information sheets.

When should permission be sought?

Whenever authors propose to use copyright material other than their own, the author, the editor or the publisher must seek permission from the copyright holder. Copyright material may include text from books, anthologies or volumes of poetry, articles, newspapers, correspondence, recorded interviews, tables, photographs, diagrams, graphs, maps, sketches, cartoons, stills from films and television programs, transcripts of broadcasts, website content, software programs, video clips and audio recordings.

In academic works permission is not generally sought for quoted material used for the purposes of comment, review or criticism. If there is doubt about whether permission should be sought, the editor should contact the Copyright Council.

Permission must be sought for *all* poetry and song lyrics, even if only one or two lines are used, unless they are out of copyright.

Works of art, including paintings, photographs, sketches and cartoons, present a slightly different problem. If the work is held by a collector or an art gallery, it is important to establish whether they or the creator own copyright in the work, as it could be either or both. Fees to galleries for permission (and provision of a photographic reproduction) can be high, which is one of the reasons art books are so expensive.

Finding the copyright owner

Finding the copyright owner can be a complicated and long-drawn-out procedure. If the author plans to use poems or extracts from a previous anthology, the details provided in that publication may be sketchy or nonexistent, and tracking down the copyright owner may involve writing letters to publishers, agents, authors or their descendants.

A sample letter of request for text permission is given in appendix 6. The letter or email should provide the following details:

- the title and author of the book

- the intended audience and market

- the print run and format of publication (e.g. print, ebook)

- date of publication

- retail price(s)

- the exact text for which permission is being sought

- a form for the copyright owner to sign and return if permission is granted.

It may also be necessary to specify in which geographic market(s) the book is to be published; copyright owners may wish to charge higher fees for using their work in a book that will be made available worldwide, for example. Requests for artwork permissions are similar, but also include information on the form in which the artwork should be supplied (e.g. as an Adobe Illustrator file, a scanned image or a photographic reproduction).

If copyright owners cannot be traced even after several letters and conscientious efforts to track them down, the editor has two options: to drop or replace the item in question, or include it with a disclaimer such as:

> Every effort has been made to trace the original source material contained in this book. Where the attempt has been unsuccessful, the publishers would be pleased to hear from the author or publisher to rectify any omission.

However, a disclaimer does not necessarily provide protection if the copyright owner decides to take legal action after the item is published. While it is essential that the editor record on file any attempts that have been made to obtain copyright permission—a minimum of two reminder letters should establish the intention of seeking permission—such evidence is not recognised as a defence in law, and most publishers would be wary of publishing an item under these circumstances.

On no account should the author's word be taken that the copyright owner has 'said it would be OK'. The author should always seek permission in writing and provide a copy to the editor or publisher.

Accurate record-keeping is essential. A large publishing organisation or academic institution producing mainly educational material may employ one or several copyright officers or permissions assistants to handle permissions. Editors need to monitor the author's progress, or maintain their own records of the permission-seeking process.

Fees

As well as granting permission, a copyright holder may ask for a fee for the use of the material, or may specify limitations on how many times the publication may be reprinted before permission has to be renewed, or even specify in which markets or what formats the publication may be made available. Record all these details carefully, and advise the production manager at the time if there are any repeat fees for reprints or new editions, or additional fees for publishing in a different format or to other markets.

Permissions fees for an anthology represent a substantial part of the total budget of the publication. The contract with the author will specify whether the fees are to be paid by the author or the publishing organisation, or shared in some proportion between the parties.

The Australian Society of Authors can provide information on the scale of fees usually charged by Australian authors, such as a fee per line of poetry or per thousand words for text, tied to the number of copies of the publication to be printed or whether it is to be published online (which generally makes the material available worldwide).

If the permissions fees demanded are excessive or threaten to blow out the budget (as can happen with an anthology or a highly illustrated work, when thousands of dollars are involved), the editor should suggest that the author write again to the copyright owners and request some concession. An approach like this is often successful for educational books, where the copyright owners can see that inclusion in a particular anthology serves an educational purpose or will help to disseminate their work to a wider audience. If no agreement can be reached, the author may have to delete or replace the material.

Details of repeat or additional fees or terms for reapplication specified by the copyright owner must be clearly understood by the author, editor and publisher. These details are recorded for future reprints and new editions. A system for highlighting such permissions or advising the production manager is essential.

For details on compiling and editing acknowledgements, see chapter 4.

Acknowledgements

Appropriate acknowledgement must be made to all copyright holders for any copyright material included in a publication. Often a precise wording will be requested.

Defamation and plagiarism

The publisher is responsible for ensuring that the publication meets all legal requirements, but the editor should also alert the publisher immediately to any possible legal problems. Apart from copyright, these can include defamation and plagiarism. The publisher may then seek legal advice before deciding whether the material should be altered or deleted.

The editor should be particularly careful to identify any possible defamatory material in either the text or the artwork. Anything that seems potentially defamatory must be clarified with the author, deleted or rewritten, or referred to the organisation's legal advisers. It is important to look at the context as well as the meaning, as sometimes what precedes or follows a statement or quotation will affect the way in which it is read. Similarly, the position of artwork, or the captions or comments that accompany it, may also affect the reader's interpretation. When seeking permission to reproduce material, the editor must give the copyright holder the context in which a quotation or piece of artwork will be used.

Plagiarism—where authors attempt, wittingly or unwittingly, to pass off another's work as their own—is another hazard. Plagiarism can be difficult to detect, but is surprisingly often recognised by a kind of editorial instinct. Signs to watch for are a section of text written in a different style or format, an illustration or table that is more elaborate or detailed than others, photocopied material

from an already printed work, or a nagging feeling that the editor
has read or seen this material somewhere before.

If in doubt, the editor should double-check that it is the author's
work. While using computers to copy and paste makes plagiarism
very easy, technology also makes it much easier to detect the
stealing of other writer's words. A simple search on Google can be
used to check suspect passages if there aren't too many; however,
where there is a great deal of material to check, then it might be
necessary to use one of the many software programs and online
services available for this purpose (type 'plagiarism checker' into a
search engine). Although these options can be quite effective, they
are unlikely to catch extensive unacknowledged paraphrasing or
lifting of ideas.

Safety issues

The editor must always be alert to any content that could involve
danger to the reader. This is particularly important in educational
texts, but safety problems can also arise in texts such as technical
manuals, health publications and recipe books. Problem areas to
look out for include:

- scientific experiments in school textbooks

- health or fitness programs or advice that might pose dangers
  to people with heart or muscular problems, asthma or severe
  allergic reactions

- recipes for children that involve the use of open flames, high
  heat or sharp knives

- physical procedures that could cause bodily strain; for
  example, lifting or carrying

- accounts of experiences such as sexual assault that may
  trigger a reader to relive their trauma.

A potential problem section might need rewriting or replacing
with a safer option, or a safety warning might need to be inserted
to alert potentially at-risk groups.

Inclusiveness and exclusiveness

Although public debate on inclusive language has tended to focus
on individual words in a text, questions of exclusion also need to be
borne in mind at all times when dealing with manuscripts. Often
sexist or racist language is a symptom of attitudes that exclude or

denigrate women or other groups, and much more fundamental matters may also need to be dealt with. There are a number of guides available to help with finding solutions for these symptoms, and this is an encouraging sign.

The chapter on inclusive language in the *Style Manual* provides helpful guidelines for dealing with individual instances of sexist language (the use of *they* as a singular pronoun is discussed later in this chapter). However, other kinds of problems can arise from discriminatory language, the most obvious being excluding or denigrating people based on their race, ethnicity, perceived physical or mental disabilities, sexual orientation, age or social status.

These are often matters of structural balance; it is no good having equal numbers of male and female politicians in the examples at the back of a book on politics if analysis reveals that all the female politicians are shown in unfavourable circumstances.

It is also important to avoid excluding population groups. For example, the sentence 'We Australians have still not faced the fact that we are not an Anglo-Celtic country any more' implicitly assumes that all Australians have Anglo-Celtic origins. Similarly, in a medical textbook the sentence 'Doctors often have difficulty in communicating with their female patients because they have not experienced what it is like to be a woman' assumes that all doctors are men.

The expression of overt prejudice on the basis of such factors as race, disability or ethnicity is unusual in publications these days (unless it is for artistic reasons), but sometimes a token reference is worse than none at all. An editor can play a very important role in deciding where the line is drawn between inclusiveness and tokenism. Because experienced editors are attuned to the nuances of language, they are particularly well placed to pick up these fine distinctions and to make creative suggestions for dealing with them.

In fact, if editors have enough common sense to avoid terminology like *personhole cover*, they will probably find that devising elegant ways of writing around a sexist or racist statement will not only help educate the writer about what is currently acceptable, but will also become a creative highlight in what might otherwise be a somewhat pedestrian editing project.

Indigenous peoples

When writing about indigenous people as a group it is important to use terms that will be acceptable to the people concerned. For example, in Australia the preferred generic term is *Aboriginal and Torres Strait Islander people/Australians*. The term *Indigenous Australians* is also sometimes used.

When referring to individuals, it is preferable wherever possible to refer to the specific group to which the person belongs; for example, *an Anangu man* or *a Pitjantjatjara painting*. The *Style Manual* has details of preferred names for indigenous regional and language groups in Australia.

It is important to use specific rather than general terms for indigenous peoples from any country: *a Seminole school* rather than *an Indian school; an Inuit woman* rather than *an Eskimo woman*.

When referring to the people of New Zealand, it is important to remember the dual heritage of both Māori custom and culture and that of the *pakeha* (white Europeans). The two official languages of New Zealand are English and Māori. The Māori language, like English, has more than one dialect, and Māori people may have several tribal affiliations and preferences according to their social grouping; however, the term *Māori* (used for both singular and plural, preferably with a macron over the 'a') is generally used when identifying all the indigenous people of Aotearoa (New Zealand).

macron
a diacritic printed as a line above a letter, usually to indicate a long or stressed vowel

Language accessibility

In addition to the issue of being inclusive or exclusive when writing about particular groups of people, the editor must pay attention to the level and complexity of language used in order to appropriately address the publication's intended audience. Is the publication aimed at people who have a cognitive disability or those for whom English is not their first language, or at younger readers? Is the level of language used appropriate for these groups?

The Australian federal, state and territory governments have mandated that materials on their websites meet accessibility guidelines, which means ensuring that all publications are written in plain language and allow those with cognitive impairments, physical disabilities or other problems with accessing information to more easily use and understand the information. Editors play an important role in meeting these requirements.

Language level is further discussed later in this chapter, and in the section on government publications in chapter 10.

Artwork

After looking at the structure of a manuscript, and weeding out any offensive words or statements, the editor should examine the illustrations. It can be frustrating to have conscientiously removed all sexist or racist (or both) text references only to find that the illustrator has drawn all business managers as men in suits, all women as housewives in aprons, and everyone but the office cleaner as very plainly Anglo-Celtic.

For more detail on illustration briefs, see chapter 9.

This is why there should be as much input from editors as possible in the briefing of line illustrators, cartoonists and photographers. The editor should also consult with the author at an early stage if the existing artwork or roughs do not appear to be inclusive. It is not only gender that needs to be considered—if it is the editor's job to choose photographic artwork, a conscious effort must be made to look for pictures that show an appropriate range of ethnic groups. Pictures of people with disabilities can also show them participating in daily life—at work, at school, playing sport, using computers, enjoying a concert—rather than being shown as somehow 'other'. The editor would do well to think of all the people who might read the book, and ensure that it reflects life in all its diversity.

For the special requirements of fiction editing, see chapter 10.

Although it is part of the editor's role to eliminate any elements of sexism or racism in non-fiction publications, especially educational non-fiction, the situation is different when editing works of fiction. In fiction, such elements may be deliberate and entirely in keeping with the intentions of the narrative.

Parochialisms

It is important not to limit a book's potential market by using parochial terms and examples. A book that is to sell in Australia and New Zealand should include references to both countries or examples common to both. A secondary economics textbook for Australian schools should not give examples using only New South Wales statistics. Conversely, a book originally published in the United States or Britain may need to be adapted for the Australian or New Zealand market if it includes many localised references and examples; for instance, a gardening book might be changed to refer to planting by calendar months instead of by seasons.

Even within a particular country or culture, it is important not to exclude particular audiences, or to assume knowledge that not everyone may have. For example, a general book about sport cannot assume that all readers will know about a tennis player who is referred to only by a nickname, so the editor should ensure that full details are included with the nickname the first time the player is mentioned in the text; the nickname can be used thereafter.

Some books, however, intentionally and appropriately use parochialisms. For example, in a biography of an internationally known Australian sportsperson, the use of Australian slang and other colloquialisms might give a flavour of the protagonist's personality and background. In such cases, the author and editor should consider how to explain these terms to readers who are unfamiliar with them.

As with inclusive language, the editor should try to read the manuscript from the points of view of all likely readers to detect, eliminate or explain parochialisms, as appropriate.

Specialist terms

Non-fiction works may use specialist terms that require explanation. The author may gather these together in a glossary that appears at the beginning or end of the book; use explanatory footnotes; or insert call-outs throughout the work, usually in the margin near the relevant text. In ebooks it is possible to hyperlink terms in the text directly to a separate glossary of terms.

margins
the space surrounding the type area at the top, bottom and sides of a page

In addition, manuscripts may include historical or other measurements that require explanation for the expected readership; for example, by translating between the metric and imperial measurement systems. The editor can adopt either of two methods, depending on the frequency of occurrence. If there are few instances, the conversion could be placed in brackets after the reference in the text. For example:

Benedict held 640 acres (260 hectares) of good grazing land.

Boil the soup for five minutes and then add half a pound (227 g) of flour.

Note that in some cases, such as in recipes, it may be vital to provide exact conversions, while in others it may be sufficient to round the converted amount. If there are more than a few instances, a note explaining the conversion rates used can be placed at the beginning or end of the glossary. If there is no glossary, it can be placed in the prelims, combined with the acknowledgements or preface, or placed on its own.

In works of fiction, it may be preferable to rewrite the text to incorporate conversions or explanations, or to use a footnote.

QUESTIONS OF STYLE

In this section we will look at two kinds of style:

- writing style (tone or voice)

- copy editing/house style.

What style is that?

Writing and copy editing styles should not be confused with electronic styles, which are used to identify structural elements virtually within a digital manuscript (see chapter 6).

Writing style

Writing style, which includes such things as choice of vocabulary, sentence length, use of punctuation, and formal or informal language and construction, is the way in which authors communicate with their audiences. Ideally, the style should be appropriate for the type of publication and its audience, and include issues of voice (active or passive construction), tone (formal or informal language, use of humour, point of view), language level and so on.

Establishing appropriate writing styles

When reviewing an author's writing style, the question is not 'What do I think of this style?', but 'Is this style appropriate for this publication?' For example, no matter how much the editor might dislike a folksy, jocular, colloquial writing style, it would be perfectly appropriate for a book of cricketing anecdotes. Such an approach, however, would be inappropriate for a government white paper or a textbook on company law.

How does the editor know whether an author's style or tone is appropriate for the audience? How does the editor judge whether the tone is too formal or informal? Although the publisher's brief may contain some information about the intended audience, many publishing organisations will also require authors to complete an author's questionnaire (see appendix 7 for an example from an educational publisher). Ideally, this will provide a profile of the audience, as well as details of the major competing publications and the reasons for the author's belief that their book will be competitive. This questionnaire, combined with a thorough reading of the file and any readers' reports, will give a sound idea of the anticipated market. Armed with this information, the editor is in a strong position to decide if the author's style is appropriate.

If the manuscript is too formal or informal in tone for its intended audience, major rewriting may be necessary. It is normally the author's responsibility to make sure that the tone is appropriate for the audience, and usually the manuscript will be returned to the author for rewriting in a more appropriate style. In this case the editor may need to provide a sample of edited text to show the author what is required. Major rewriting by an editor (or a ghost writer) is costly, and should be done only at the publisher's request and with the author's agreement.

Sense and meaning

Problems with understanding the author's meaning are more difficult to resolve. Editors should carefully probe each sentence and paragraph in the manuscript to ensure that (a) the sentence itself makes sense; (b) the sentence makes sense within the paragraph; and (c) the paragraph makes sense within that section of the work. It is quite common for authors to insert sentences that could be misinterpreted, or that are unambiguous in themselves but then contradict other text in the paragraph or section. This could happen, for example, if the author simply inadvertently excludes or includes the word *not*, thus making the sentence say the opposite of what is intended.

Another common occurrence is an author introducing new names, concepts or ideas without explanation, or placing the explanation so that it appears, too late, in a later section of the text.

A good editor will not resort to guesswork but will seek clarification from the author. This can usually be accomplished in Word by using the *Comment* facility. When querying the meaning of a passage, it is good practice to give the author an idea of what the problem appears to be and perhaps suggest some options that might solve it. For example, simply saying 'I'm not sure what this means' is not very helpful compared to 'This passage could be interpreted as meaning either X or Y. Perhaps if it was phrased as Z, this would clarify the issue?' or 'This section is difficult to understand because no definition of X is given, and X underpins the discussion. Please expand on and clarify what X means'.

Some authors who have difficulty in expressing themselves on the page will be able to give a clearer verbal explanation, and if there are only a few instances, a phone call may be sufficient to resolve them.

If there are more problems than can be dealt with by email or a phone call or a meeting with the author, the editor may need to return the manuscript to the author for rewriting. If the editor thinks this is necessary, the problem should be discussed with the publisher before approaching the author.

Language level

The level of language used is crucially important in educational publishing, but can also be important for general or trade books. Primary and secondary textbooks are usually written by teachers familiar with the educational level of the target audience. Tertiary textbooks and references, however, are often written by people who teach at a level higher than the one the book is aiming for, and the language level may therefore be set too high. A book that began life as an academic thesis often needs to be recast into an acceptable style for a more general readership.

Language level is judged by two criteria: length and structure of sentences, and difficulty of vocabulary. If the sentences are too complex, then rewriting will probably be necessary throughout the manuscript. If the problem rests mainly with the vocabulary, it may be possible to replace unsuitable words with simpler synonyms.

To both recognise and correct language-level problems the editor must be familiar with the needs of the intended audience. For educational publications it is helpful to obtain copies of competing books on the subject, or a range of popular texts for that age level. Education departments in some states provide lists of suitable vocabulary for different year levels.

As well as making sure that the vocabulary is of an appropriate level, it is also important to ensure that sentence structure is not too complex (or too simple) for the expected readership. One way to check this is to count the number of sentences per hundred words in a representative sample of manuscript (this may be done using the readability function available in recent versions of Word). The more sentences the editor finds in 100 words, the shorter the sentences would be expected to be, giving a reading level at the simpler end of the scale. The more words the editor finds in each sentence, the more complex the assumed reading level. However, this method should be used with caution, as short sentences, and even short words, can contain complex meanings. For example, 'To be or not to be: that is the question' would pass a readability test for seven-year-olds, but would they appreciate its full meaning?

Other factors to consider are the number of syllables per hundred words, and whether the text uses grammatical structures and concepts that are appropriate for the level required.

Before making any changes to the vocabulary, it is important for the editor to explain to the author what is intended and why. Many authors are proud of their choice of words and will resist attempts to simplify the vocabulary. The editor will need to explain to them how important achieving the appropriate language level is in marketing a book for any part of the educational market. If the editor expects resistance, it may be helpful to show the author relevant comments from readers' reports, or a vocabulary list for the target age group. It is important for editors to be firm about this, as teachers check books carefully for language level, and will not order a book if the level is too high (or too low).

Occasionally a book will be specifically aimed at the upper or lower end of a particular audience. For example, a Year 12 English course might be specifically designed for schools with a more academic orientation, and therefore a higher language level could be an advantage; or a tertiary text might be aimed at a group including a large number of students for whom English is a second language, in which case a simpler language level would be appropriate.

As with all other aspects of editing, a sound knowledge of the intended audience and an awareness of budgetary and time restrictions are invaluable in making editorial decisions about language level.

Copy editing and house style

Copy editing style, unlike writing style, involves more technical aspects of writing, including issues of consistency, grammar, spelling and word use.

Establishing appropriate copy editing styles

The question most frequently asked by trainee editors and editing students is 'Which is the right style?', in the belief that there is one correct decision to be made on all matters of word use, grammar and spelling. Sadly (or happily, for lovers of the flexibility of the language), there is no such standard for English usage.

For example, in writing this book we had to consider style issues such as how to lay out and punctuate lists, whether to capitalise words like *internet*, and whether to use *-ise* or *-ize* endings in words like *organise*. In each of these cases there are two or more choices available that are considered to be 'correct', depending on which style manual or other reference is being used.

For most of these decisions, we were guided in the first instance by the publisher's house style guide, the current edition of *Macquarie Dictionary* and the most recent edition of the *Style Manual*. Where these references were silent, we made our decisions by looking at the options and discussing which would be the most appropriate for this particular book. In making these choices, sometimes we would consult three or four other references—*The Australian Concise Oxford Dictionary*, *The Cambridge Guide to Australian English Usage*, and perhaps Strunk & White's *The Elements of Style*.

Such references are the editor's tools of trade. It is vital for practising or trainee editors to keep up with the changes that occur in English language usage and, in particular, in Australian style. Only by becoming familiar with the views (and that is all they are) of these commentators on style can editors develop their own judgement of what is and is not appropriate for a particular manuscript.

The editor may have been taught certain rules that seemed to be set in stone; for example, not splitting an infinitive or ending a sentence with a preposition, or writing *an historian* rather than *a historian*, or using *whilst* rather than *while*. But any background reading about infinitives and prepositions will quickly reveal that the matter is not so simple, and that the best language depends on elegance of expression rather than arbitrary rules, with usage shifting and changing over time.

Grammar and punctuation can be formal or informal. Editorial decisions made about, for example, a chatty, informal guide to successful party-giving will probably be quite different from those made about an academic book on linguistics, or a technical manual.

The *Style Manual* is an example of an invaluable guide to such matters as how to express weights and measures, how to express numbers, dates and abbreviations, and when to use italics (e.g. in book titles), and is the preferred authority on these matters for most Australian publishers and government departments. Editors and would-be editors will find it useful as a reference for many such matters. However, if the publishing organisation specifies styles differing from those recommended in the *Style Manual*, the editor should follow the house style.

Consistency

Ensuring consistency within manuscripts is one of the most important aspects of copy editing. This includes consistency not only of details of style but also of language, presentation of artwork, structure and, in some cases, layout.

Inconsistencies in the spelling of names, the layout of tables, the structure of chapters, or the presentation of figures, tables and other illustrative material will all cause unease, as readers' initial sampling of the publication will have set up expectations that are later frustrated. They may not know what is causing their unease, but they will be uncomfortable as they read; even if the narrative seems to flow smoothly, they may decide that the publication is 'hard to read'.

Part of the editor's task is to ensure that this does not happen, by examining the structure, language and layout to make sure they are logical and consistent, and by checking all details of spelling, capitalisation and so on. This is where the use of style sheets comes to the fore.

Style sheets are discussed in more detail later in this chapter.

Consistency of structure is particularly important in educational publications, where chapters often include different sections for theme, glossary, text, activities and references. Where possible, these sections should be standardised so that teachers and students will know what to expect in each chapter. The editor should ensure that the sections appear in the same order, and aim for the same number of sections, in each chapter. Academic and general reference books, and government and corporate reports may also follow a pattern that should be adhered to throughout the text.

The layout of special components of a manuscript should also be checked carefully for consistency. For example, if there is a list of references for each chapter, they should be checked against each other to ensure consistency of style and accuracy of citation and layout. In this type of segmented structure, it is useful to mark up the first chapter very carefully and then use it as a model for all subsequent chapters. Lists, tables and boxed items should also be standardised in this way.

If the editor's organisation has a recommended style for bibliographies, lists and tables, it is useful to keep model copies readily available and standardise these elements to that style. If there is no house style, the editor should decide on a style appropriate for the type of manuscript and discuss it with the author; or the author's style may be retained if it has been used consistently. The agreed style should then be recorded and referred to regularly when copy editing every bibliography, list or table.

With a complex manuscript, the editor may accrue a sizable pile of word lists, model layouts and house-style reminders, but the small effort required to assemble them will be amply repaid when the chaotic manuscript is transformed into a clean and consistent set of proofs.

Another aspect of consistency is ensuring that parallel structures are used wherever necessary. Parallel structures are those where words, phrases or clauses linked in a series, such as in a list, use the same pattern. In the following example, the elements in the first sentence are not parallel but those in the second sentence are:

> Petra's hobbies include collecting stamps, listening to music and *to go running*.

> Petra's hobbies include collecting stamps, listening to music and *going running*.

Headings should also preferably be in parallel; for example, it is better to avoid mixing headings that are short and descriptive with those that are posed as questions, unless there is good reason for doing so.

Grammar, spelling and word use

There are numerous style guides to spelling and word use, some of which are listed in the bibliography. Unfortunately, they often differ in their recommendations. We recommend *The Cambridge Guide to Australian English Usage* for its commonsense approach to Australian usage and style. Fowler's *Modern English Usage* is also excellent. The *Style Manual* has chapters on grammar and word use, and a very clear and up-to-date chapter on punctuation. However, there are a number of matters on which these authorities either differ widely or fail to make any definite recommendation.

One of the most plaintive cries to be heard from authors after their manuscript has been edited is 'You've changed all my *whiches* to *thats* and *thats* to *whiches*!' Most authors, and many editors, use these two words, when they are functioning as relative pronouns, randomly. Fiction writers may also choose to use *which* because it has a 'softer' sound than *that*. There is, however, a rule that is recommended by most style guides. If the editor wishes to follow it so that the use of these words has a logical and consistent pattern, here it is:

Use *that* for defining clauses, and *which* for non-defining clauses.

A defining clause limits or restricts the meaning of the word or words it applies to. For example:

Penny likes pearls that are expensive.

In this example the words *that are expensive* cannot be removed from the subject of the sentence without changing the meaning. They define which pearls are under discussion, so Penny, in this case, likes expensive pearls, not inexpensive ones.

A non-defining clause gives further information about the word or words it applies to, but does not limit or restrict the words. For example:

Penny likes pearls, which are expensive.

In this case the words *which are expensive* could be removed from the sentence without altering the basic meaning. They give additional information, so in this case Penny likes pearls (any pearls) and, as it happens, pearls are expensive. Non-defining clauses that begin with *which* should normally be set off from the main clause by commas. Once editors become familiar with this distinction, they will find that it improves both the consistency and the rhythm of sentence structure.

Another vexed question is the use of *they* as a singular pronoun. The generic *he* is no longer acceptable to a great many readers, writers and book buyers, and *they* appears to be emerging as the most acceptable alternative to avoid using *he* where *he* or *she* is meant. Many people believe this to be a grammatical sin, but in fact it has a long and distinguished literary history that is very well described in chapter 2 of Miller & Swift's *The Handbook of Nonsexist Writing* and in *The Shorter Oxford Dictionary*. Even though some authors, editors and publishers will fight the singular *they* to the death, usage and attitudes are changing. The *Macquarie Dictionary*, which once listed it as 'regarded as bad usage', since its fourth edition has regarded it as 'increasingly accepted in written English'. Nevertheless, in the face of resistance, the editor may need to change the wording to avoid the problem.

Most well-written manuscripts define their subjects precisely and do not present problems of this kind. A manuscript that contains many instances of the use of the generic *he* is often carelessly written and in need of firm editing. One solution is to recast the text in the plural, which often makes better sense. For example, in a prospectus for a college that has already been described as including both men and women, the sentence 'Each student has his own room' will sound odd. Recasting it to say 'All students have their own rooms' will make more sense. Rewriting badly written sentences into well-written ones makes even more sense.

We suggest that using *they* as a singular pronoun can be an acceptable solution if it reads well, but where it can be avoided, especially in more formal texts, it is sensible to do so. If there are only a few instances, using *he* or *she*, or *him* or *her* may be appropriate, but if much used this becomes very unwieldy. Avoid using *he/she* or *s/he*, as they do not reflect language as it is used and are visually ugly, impeding the flow of the text.

Editors need to be sensitive to changes in accepted style and to be able to incorporate them as part of their editing function. To do this, they need to keep up to date with what is happening in the language and check the latest usages in a current dictionary. Here are some examples of words or conventions that have changed in usage over time:

- *Colour* versus *color*. Words like *colour*, *honour* and *labour* are spelt without the 'u' in American style, and this style is becoming common in Australia in newspapers and magazines, but has not yet spread to any extent to general and government publishing. For this reason, we have used the *-our* spelling in this book, but if the company or department recommends the *-or* style, follow the house style. Again, editors may find that authors will resist these spellings. Note that the Australian Labor Party uses *-or*, but the British and New Zealand Labour Parties use *-our*.

- *Program* versus *programme*. For a time a distinction was made between these two spellings, with *program* being used in computer terminology and *programme* reserved for literary use. *Program* is now the preferred form for both uses in all Australian style guides and dictionaries. A journey into its history will reveal that *program* is the original form (from the Latin *programma*) and that *programme* is an affectation introduced from the French—as also is the *-our* form in such words as *honour* and *valour*.

- *Email* versus *e-mail*. This is an example of a growing trend towards dropping hyphens. Increasingly, previously hyphenated words are either being combined to form single words or treated as two or more separate words. While in many cases this causes no problems, and indeed simplifies things, there are also instances where confusion can occur or meanings can change when the hyphen is dropped or added; for example, *resign* versus *re-sign*, or *heavy metal equipment* versus *heavy-metal equipment*. The editor should always be on the lookout for overzealous hyphen-dropping or hyphenating habits and ensure that the addition or lack of a hyphen does not change the meaning or readability of the text. Again, a good current dictionary or the house style guide will assist in deciding whether to hyphenate.

- Feminine endings. The use of feminine endings in words such as *hostess*, *aviatrix* or *chairwoman* draws attention to the gender of the person rather than the role that is being described. This practice is increasingly being avoided in the move towards using nonsexist language. Instead, the stem word is used as the neutral form that applies to all those who perform the role, regardless of gender; for example, *host*, *aviator* and *chair/chairperson*.

There are also other styles that differ according to national conventions. For example, it is Australian style to use 's' in words like *organise* and *organisation*, but 'z' is used in American style, and either may be used in British style. If a book is to be distributed in several countries, careful editorial decisions need to be made about which style to follow.

Related to this is the spelling of the names of organisations. Dictionaries may convert all names to be consistent with national spelling conventions; thus, in the *Macquarie Dictionary*, the *World Trade Organization* becomes the *World Trade Organisation*, accompanied by a note about the difference in spelling. Editors need to consider carefully whether to follow this practice, as the organisations themselves may not take kindly to having their names spelt incorrectly (it would be akin to spelling a personal name incorrectly, say, *Margret* instead of *Margaret*). We encourage editors to follow whatever spelling the organisation uses, no matter what the dictionary might specify.

This confirms the importance of consulting widely regarding usage. Using dictionaries alone will not necessarily provide all the answers; for example, they do not always distinguish between spoken, written and colloquial language. The *Macquarie Dictionary*, for example, includes *Xmas* and *bar-b-q* in its word list. These spellings, although acceptable in advertising copywriting and widely used, are colloquial abbreviations, and would not be acceptable in book or government publishing.

The editor's best guide to good style is how they respond to the look and sound of a sentence or phrase. It can be useful to read an awkward sentence out loud or to break down complex sentences into their component parts in order to determine what is wrong and how to fix it. Large doses of common sense and reference to as wide a range of style guides and dictionaries as possible will also serve the editor well.

House style

No matter what style decisions an editor is used to or would prefer to make, these will often be trumped by house style. Publishing companies often develop a guide, known as house style, that covers many of the basic decisions an editor might otherwise have to make, including preferred spellings, punctuation and layout. House style must be adhered to for all of their publications. Most government departments follow the *Style Manual*, and many publishing organisations also use the manual as the basis for their house style, often recommending that authors and editors use it for matters of general style, with a specified dictionary, most commonly the *Macquarie Dictionary*, as a guide to spelling.

Although a house style guide can simplify editorial decision making, it can create extra editorial work if an author's style differs from house style yet is consistently and logically applied. In such a case, the editor should discuss with the publisher the desirability of maintaining the author's style, particularly if the book has budgetary or time constraints. However, books that are part of a series, or that target a particular educational market, should adhere to the required style.

The editor should always let the author know straight away if a manuscript is to be altered to conform with a house style. Many publishing companies give authors of commissioned books a copy of the house style, and if the editor has any contact with authors while manuscripts are in preparation it makes sense to encourage them to use the required style.

The editor must be sure to check how much discretion is possible before they speak to the author. If the author objects to a particular aspect of the style, and if the company gives editors a degree of flexibility in such matters, it may be worth agreeing to the author's style on that point. If, however, the house style is always rigidly adhered to, or if a particular style is necessary for a particular book, the editor should explain this pleasantly but firmly to the author.

The editor should always confirm in writing any telephone discussions with the author, and remember, if a style decision cannot be justified to the author it may not be justifiable.

Style sheet

Once it has been established which conventions to use in matters of detail, it is time to prepare a style sheet for the manuscript. A style sheet records all the style and spelling decisions made about a particular text. It usually comprises two parts: the first is a list of style decisions, such as using spaced em rules for dashes, italicising foreign words, or using metric measurements; the second is an alphabetical word list containing all spelling decisions, including names, capitalisation and hyphenation. Proper use of a style sheet ensures that editorial consistency is maintained throughout the text.

It is essential that both the author's name and the title of the publication are recorded in the style sheet.

If editors are working to a house style, they will not need to list items that are dealt with in the house style guide, such as the spelling of *program* or the style for spelling out numbers. Freelance editors, however, may be working to several different house styles for different manuscripts, so should always keep a copy of the relevant styles with each manuscript. In either case, editors need to include in the style sheet any items that are subject to variation, even if they are following the author's choice of style. For example, an inattentive author might consistently write *co-operative* in the first few chapters but then introduce *cooperative* in a later chapter.

The editor should keep a record of all words that can be written with or without hyphens, as one word or two, and if possible make a firm decision about them at their first appearance. It is helpful

For an example of a style sheet and word list, see appendix 8.

to use one dictionary as a basis for these decisions, both to give a rationale for explaining them to the author and to save time agonising over which of the author's three styles to favour.

Names of people and places and foreign words and phrases, unless very well known, should also be recorded in the word list. If the editor runs into a variation later in the book, they can find the earlier variants using the word processing program's search function. It is particularly common to have problems with names like *Clark/Clarke* or *De la Roche/Delaroche* that have more than one variant, or names with unusual spellings, such as that of Australian author *Katharine Susannah Prichard*.

It is also a good idea to check the names of organisations at their first appearance to avoid errors with names such as *Pearl Harbor* or the *World Trade Center* (both of which have the American spelling). The names of some organisations even include a mix of American and British spellings, such as the *International Labour Organization*.

With a complex reference book, or a translation that retains many foreign words, the editor may need to keep several word lists, with one for general vocabulary, spelling and punctuation, one for names, and one for foreign words and phrases. This may sound like a lot of extra work, but the decision regarding the correct usage needs to be made only once and it is vital for consistency, saving time later on as the editor progresses through the manuscript. In this way, the editor need only glance at the word list to know how to deal with a phrase, name or date.

In the case of a series, it is a good idea to establish a general word list for the series, plus a separate list for each manuscript within the series, with names, places, dates and words that occur only in that manuscript.

A word list can be recorded by hand on a prepared sheet comprising a series of blank boxes, each representing one or more letters of the alphabet (see appendix 8 for an example of this). This makes it easy to add words as the editing progresses and find the words for later reference, though sometimes some of the boxes can get quite crowded. However, if the editor is working onscreen, it is probably easier to simply create a separate Word document that lists the words. The advantage of doing this is that any number of words can be added, without worrying about having to cram them into a predefined box, and they can also be easily sorted alphabetically using Word's *Sort* function. To sort the words, select the relevant text and choose *Sort* under the *Table* menu. Choose the *Sort by: Paragraphs* option, *Type: Text* and in *Ascending* order, which is usually the default. Choose *OK* in the dialogue box and the selected words will be sorted alphabetically. Note that Word sorts text in word-by-word order, not letter-by-letter order.

For more discussion about word order, see chapter 13.

The style sheet is an essential tool not only for the editor, but also for the author and proofreader, as adherence to it avoids needlessly revisiting decisions or even reversing them later on. It can also be used when briefing the page designer.

6

Editing practice: onscreen editing techniques

In chapter 5 we identified the principles of editing for structure, content and style. In this chapter we will look at the four major features in Microsoft Word for editing text onscreen: applying global corrections, applying electronic styles, using the *Track Changes* feature to record edits, and checking spelling and grammar. We will also look at setting up Word's default settings for effective editing.

Chapter 7 will deal with the application of these onscreen editing techniques to the practice of copy editing.

On Microsoft Word

The industry standard word processing program is Microsoft Word and editors use different versions of this software, on either the Windows or Macintosh (Mac) platforms, which themselves come in varying forms.

Rather than providing step-by-step details for everything, we will concentrate in this chapter on the general features and tools that are available in Microsoft Word, and how to use them effectively in the process of editing. This is because, while most editing functions in Word perform similarly across various versions of the program, the exact methods of accessing and using these tools differ (some features are even missing from certain versions of Word) and it is beyond the scope of this book to cover them all.

(continued)

On Microsoft Word *(cont'd)*

Word comes with its own extensive and useful help system, which the editor can search to find out how to access a specific function. There are also plenty of manuals, guides and online tutorials available, as well as hands-on workshops offered by organisations such as the various societies of editors, to assist users to get the most out of the software.

Useful references on using Word for Windows and Mac are listed in appendix 11.

We strongly encourage editors to take the time to *first* become highly proficient with the particular features of their own version of Word. It is only then that they will be able to concentrate on effectively editing the *content* of the manuscript instead of on the mechanics of preparing the text for production.

WHY ONSCREEN?

Few publishers and editors still work in hard copy only; it is mainly those working in fiction who do so. This is not to say, however, that there is no purpose or value in working on hard copy. Long, complex manuscripts that require a lot of cross-checking between sections or major restructuring are often more easily dealt with in hard copy, because the pages can be spread out for broader overview, and quickly flicking from one part of the book to the another can be faster. Even for those working primarily onscreen, it may be easier to occasionally work from printed copies when manuscripts are complex. The editor is also able to move about more freely when reading a printout compared with being chained to a computer, not to mention the eyestrain caused by staring at a screen for long hours! And, of course, there is always the ever-present fear that an electronic file might be accidentally deleted or overwritten or 'lost in cyberspace'. Nevertheless, because it is now not commonly used in publishing, the mechanics of hard-copy editing are not covered in this book. We recommend that editors who are required to work in hard copy refer to this book's website at www.wiley.com/go/aeh3 for more information.

The widespread demise of hard-copy editing has come about because it has several drawbacks, or at least fewer advantages, compared with onscreen editing, especially in a world where speed and efficiency (read: budgetary constraints) dictate the methods used. Some of the benefits offered by onscreen editing include being able to:

- track editorial changes electronically and choose to see only a selection of the changes (by person or type)

- easily switch between a marked-up and corrected view

- insert complex queries to the author at the appropriate point in the text

- identify the semantic elements of the text (headings, quotes, lists, boxed text etc.) using electronic styles

- view the heading structure of the manuscript once electronic styles have been applied

- use electronic styles to prepare the text for typesetting and later output to an electronic publication

- easily clean up and remove manual or inappropriate formatting

- apply templates to text to ensure consistency with house style

- apply global corrections (such as to spacing, names and spelling)

- search for all instances of specific words or characters

- run checks for spelling, grammar and readability (but use with caution!)

- number pages, chapters, headings and text automatically

- insert and automatically number footnotes and endnotes

- generate an automatic table of contents and lists of figures and tables

- reduce double-handling of the manuscript, as corrections are inserted directly, instead of being marked on a hard copy first

- make backup copies easily and reduce the chance of work being lost (in the post or if loose pages fall out).

Some publishers and editors use a combination of these methods in order to take advantage of the strengths of each, but increasingly time pressures dictate that many publications are only edited onscreen.

SETTING UP WORD FOR ONSCREEN EDITING

Straight out of the box, Microsoft Word comes with default settings that may be helpful for general consumers but are not necessarily useful for editors. Publishing companies may supply editors with Word set up according to the house requirements; however, freelance editors and those in smaller organisations may need to tweak their settings to their own liking before they start.

General settings

The options for changing the general settings can be found and adjusted in the *Options* (Windows) or *Preferences* (Mac) dialogue boxes of Word. There are several common setting adjustments to consider.

- Turn off all *Autocorrect, AutoFormat as You Type* and *AutoText* options except for converting straight quotation marks to typographic ('smart' or 'curly') quotation marks.

typographic quotes (smart or curly quotes) quotation marks that are curved rather than straight

- The spell checker is useful, especially the *Check spelling as you type* option, but many editors prefer to turn off the grammar and readability checkers, as they are not very reliable and when the *Check grammar as you type* option is used, they can be rather distracting.

- Turn on non-printing characters, which reveals all the underlying paragraph, tab and space markers, optional hyphens and other hidden text. With these, the editor can detect problems such as tabs in the middle of a paragraph or multiple paragraph returns being inserted in order to start text on a new page.

- Ensure that the options for *Typing replaces selection* or *Typing replaces selected text* and *Drag-and-drop text editing* or *Allow text to be dragged and dropped* are turned on. In some versions of Word, these are not turned on by default.

- Turn off the option *When selecting, automatically select entire word*. It is better to be able to manually choose to select a whole word or part of it.

- *Enable click and type* should also be turned off, as this inserts undesired and uncontrolled formatting in the text.

It is also useful for the editor to set up their preferred margins and page size and save these in the Normal (standard) template. The default settings are based on inches and the US Letter page size, so the editor may want to alter these to base them on the metric and ISO systems (e.g. the A4 page).

Keyboard and toolbar shortcuts

As mentioned earlier, it is very important to become familiar with and proficient in Word and all its features relating to editing. Setting up shortcuts and toolbars can take some time initially but, once done, will save the editor hours of unnecessary mousing up and down to the menus and searching for commands hidden in submenus and dialogue boxes.

If possible, the editor should memorise or set up new keyboard shortcuts for the most common features used. Table 6.1 shows a few of the more common built-in keyboard shortcuts.

Table 6.1: common built-in Word shortcuts

Command	Windows shortcut	Mac shortcut
Cut	CONTROL (CTRL) + X	COMMAND (⌘) + X
Copy	CTRL + C	⌘ + C
Paste	CTRL + V	⌘ + V
Undo	CTRL + Z	⌘ + Z
Redo	CTRL + Y	⌘ + Y
Save	CTRL + S	⌘ + S
Find	CTRL + F	⌘ + F
Repeat Find	ALT + CTRL + Y	SHIFT + F4
Heading 1 (or 2 or 3)	ALT + CTRL + 1 (or 2 or 3)	⌘ + OPTION + 1 (or 2 or 3)
Toggle Track Changes on/off	CTRL + SHIFT + E	CMD + SHIFT + E
Insert a comment	CTRL + ALT+ M	⌘ + OPTION + A
Toggle case (lower to title to uppercase)	SHIFT + F3	SHIFT + F3
Copy formatting (including style)	CTRL + SHIFT + C	⌘ + SHIFT + C
Paste formatting (including style)	CTRL + SHIFT + V	⌘ + SHIFT + V
Clear paragraph style back to Normal	CTRL + Q	[Set up manually]
Clear character style of selected text	CTRL + space	CTRL + space
Em rule	ALT + CTRL + minus (number pad)	OPTION + SHIFT + hyphen
En rule	CTRL + minus (number pad)	OPTION + hyphen
Ellipsis	ALT + CTRL + full stop	OPTION + semicolon
Non-breaking space	CTRL + SHIFT + space	OPTION + space

em (typesetting)
the square of any type body, so named because the letter 'm' in early fonts was usually cast on a square body; a 10-point em is 10 points wide, a 12-point em is 12 points wide etc.

em rule or **em dash**
a rule or dash taking up one em width

en
half an em

en rule or **en dash**
a rule or dash half the width of an em rule

ellipsis
a mark of punctuation (three fixed-spaced dots), usually to indicate an omission

Astute readers will notice that many of the shortcuts for the Windows and Mac versions of Word are very similar and generally only require a substitution between CTRL (Windows) and ⌘ (Mac) and sometimes ALT (Windows) and OPTION (Mac). This certainly makes it easier to work across different versions, but obviously there are quite a few other differences too, so platform-jumping editors need to take care.

All keyboard shortcuts can be replaced and new ones can be added. Editors might find it useful to create new shortcuts for the following commands:

- the most commonly used paragraph and character styles, such as for heading levels beyond Heading 3, bulleted lists and italics

- frequently used special characters, such as the degree sign or multiplication sign.

Keyboard shortcuts can be created and changed through the *Customize Ribbon > Keyboard Shortcuts* (Windows) and *Customize Keyboard* (Mac) dialogue boxes. Custom shortcuts that have already been set up in a particular copy of Word can be found through the *Print* dialogue box, where the editor can choose to print just the *Key Assignments* instead of the document.

Many other functions that are used less often but are nevertheless important for editing can also be made more accessible by adding them to or creating new toolbars. For example, it is useful to keep the *Reviewing* options (for managing tracked changes) visible in the toolbar, and to add any macros created to a new toolbar.

macro
a single-command shortcut for performing a string of operations in a software application; it can be created and customised by the user

Choosing which ways to work with Word

There are often several ways to do the same thing in Word; for example, by keyboard shortcut (there might be a few different ones built-in for the same action), by using the ribbon (the toolbar that runs across the top of the document window in recent versions of Word), or by using the menu system. Editors may find that one way suits them better than another, so it is worth exploring all the possibilities.

Styles panel

Finally, it is essential for the editor to have the *Styles Task Pane* (Windows) or *Styles Toolbox* (Mac) always open on the screen. This panel lists all the styles available in the document as well as (depending on the version of Word) just listing those in use, and some other useful functions that will be discussed further.

GLOBAL CORRECTIONS

Once Word has been set up to the editor's satisfaction, the focus can move back to the manuscript in hand. One of the most valuable functions of onscreen editing is the ability to carry out corrections that apply consistently across the manuscript, using *Find and Replace*. There are many editorial issues that arise regularly in any manuscript that should always be corrected, such as the use of double spaces or the incorrect use of hyphens and en and em rules. In addition, the editor will note various other inconsistencies and issues specific to particular manuscripts that could easily be fixed with global corrections, such as the incorrect spelling of names and variations in hyphenation.

Performing a global correction

Simple text replacement

To perform a global correction, open the *Find and Replace* dialogue box in Word. Enter the string of characters to be found in the *Find what:* box and enter the replacement text in the *Replace with:* box. For example, if Winston Churchill's name has been regularly misspelt as 'Wintson Churchill', simply type 'Wintson' in the *Find what:* box and 'Winston' in the *Replace with:* box, and choose the *Replace All* option. When it has finished, Word will advise how many occurrences of the word have been replaced. If the *Track Changes* function has been turned on, the changes will also be shown in the text.

For more information about Track Changes, see 'Recording changes and inserting author queries' later in this chapter.

Double spaces can also be replaced with single spaces in this way. If Word has been set up to automatically correct typographic quotation marks, then straight quotation marks can easily be replaced with smart quotation marks, simply by typing the same quotation mark in each of the find and replace boxes.

Narrowing the search and being selective

Simple text replacement is straightforward. But what if the editor wants to refine the search or be more selective about what is found and replaced? For example, it might be that the author has used 'percent' instead of 'per cent' throughout the text. If a simple text replacement was performed, as in the previous example, Word would also replace all instances of 'percentage' to 'per centage', an undesirable result. Fortunately, Word provides a means of searching only for whole words rather than a string of characters.

Firstly, make sure that the bottom panel of the *Find and Replace* dialogue box is showing (figure 6.1). If it isn't, click on the *More* button (Windows) or the dropdown arrow button (Mac) as circled in figure 6.1. In the bottom panel the editor can refine the search by checking the *Find whole words only* option before running the find and replace. This bottom panel also provides other ways of refining a search, such as by matching the case, format, style or language of the text.

case (capitalisation) the use of capital and non-capital letters in a word

Figure 6.1: Word's Find and Replace dialogue box with the bottom panel showing

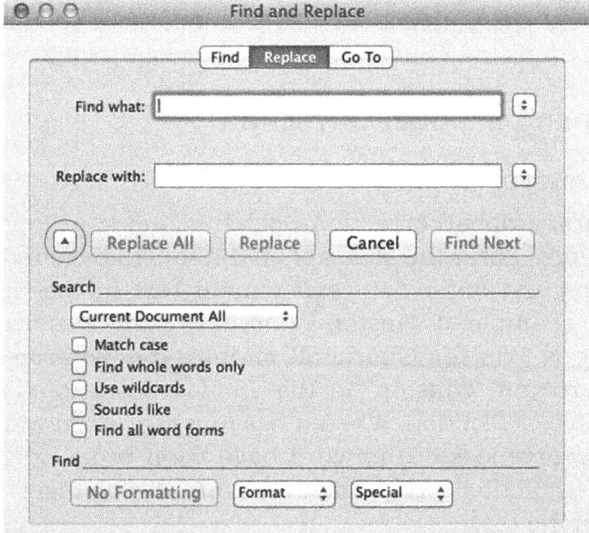

Sometimes even these options will not help, and the editor will have to resort to selective replacement. For example, if the author has used *-ize* spellings (e.g. organize) and the house style is to use *-ise* (e.g. organise), the editor cannot perform a simple text replacement of all instances of *ize*, because otherwise words such as *size* and *prize* will become *sise* and *prise*. It is also important not to inadvertently change the original spellings in quoted text.

In such cases, instead of *Replace All*, use the *Replace* option, where each instance is reviewed before replacing. So, for example, if the house style is to replace *-ize* with *-ise*, take the following steps:

1   Enter 'iz' (which will find both *organize* and *organization*) in the *Find what:* box.

2   Enter 'is' in the *Replace with:* box.

3   Select the *Find Next* button, which will find the first instance 'iz'.

4   If this instance of 'iz' is to be corrected, select the *Replace* option, which will replace the text and then automatically find the next instance.

5   If the instance is not to be replaced, use *Find Next* to go to the next instance.

In this way, the editor can quickly and semi-automatically make all the relevant changes, without fear of missing an instance or incorrectly replacing text. This will still save time from having to change the text manually as the edit proceeds.

Non-printing and special characters

What happens if the editor is required to find, remove or insert extraneous spaces, hard returns, tabs, manual line breaks, non-breaking spaces or hyphens? If non-printing characters have been turned on in *Options* or *Preferences* the editor will easily be able to see where such spacing and other special characters have been inserted and how. Table 6.2 shows some common non-printing characters and what they represent.

hard return or **paragraph break**
a manually inserted break in text that creates a new paragraph

Table 6.2: examples of non-printing characters and their symbols

Non-printing character	Symbol
Paragraph (hard return)	¶
Tab	→
Manual line break	↵
Non-breaking space	˘
Non-breaking hyphen	—˘—
Optional hyphen	⌐

To replace non-printing or special characters, the editor must use Word's special codes. These can be found in the *Find and Replace* dialogue box (in the bottom panel in the *Special* menu), but to save time it is useful to learn the ones that occur more frequently. For example, Word represents paragraph markers (hard returns) as ^p. To replace two paragraph markers with one paragraph marker, type the code ^p^p in the *Find what:* box and ^p in the *Replace with:* box, effectively replacing two paragraph markers in a row with one.

Other common codes for special characters are: ^t for tab, ^l for a manual line break, ^m for a manual page break, ^~ for a non-breaking hyphen and ^s for a non-breaking space.

Find and replace formatting and styles

For further information about paragraph and character styles, see 'Working with electronic styles' later.

It is also possible to find and replace text that has been formatted in a specific way; for example, to find a specific paragraph style that has text with italics manually applied and replace the formatting with a character style.

The *Format* dropdown list in the bottom panel of the *Find and Replace* dialogue box allows the editor to select the format and/or style of the text to be found. The formatting of the found text should always be replaced with a style, never with manual formatting. By leaving the *Find what:* and *Replace with:* boxes themselves empty, all text with the specified formatting/style will be replaced.

Using wildcards

rule or dash
a horizontal line used to link characters, words or numbers

While the standard *Find and Replace* functions are very powerful, they do not cater for instances in which the editor wishes to replace text only within a specific context. For example, it is common for authors to use a hyphen in a number span rather than an en rule (e.g. '2013-14' instead of '2013–14'). How would the editor go about fixing this without changing *all* the hyphens to en dashes?

The answer is to use wildcards. With this function, Word can search for text that matches a *pattern* rather than matching exactly. The wildcard function is turned on by ticking the *Use wildcards* option in the bottom panel of the *Find and Replace* dialogue box.

In the example given above, the editor would ask Word to find any number followed by a hyphen followed by any number, and replace them with the first original number followed by an en rule, followed by the second original number. The wildcard sequence would be: *Find what:* ([0-9])-([0-9]) and *Replace with:* \1–\2. The sequence can be further modified to find number spans with a spaced hyphen, an em rule, and other combinations.

Wildcard searches can also be used to find and replace unspecified multiple instances of characters, such as multiple spaces or paragraph returns. For example, replacing multiple paragraph returns could be done by running a search for two paragraph markers replaced with a single paragraph marker several times, using standard *Find and Replace* techniques. However, with wildcards, this could be done with just one wildcard sequence: *Find what:* (^13)@ and *Replace with:* ^p.

Coding wildcard searches is not for the faint of heart, and great care has to be taken to make sure that unexpected replacements don't occur. If they do, this is where the *Undo* command (see table 6.1) earns its keep! However, once mastered, wildcards have the potential to widen the range of global corrections that can be made, saving the editor a great deal of time.

Creating and using macros

Manually applying even just the standard global corrections listed in table 6.1 would result in having to make tedious changes one after the other. It is also all too easy to forget to apply one or other command or to apply them in the wrong order, which leads to inconsistencies and missed corrections.

Again, Word comes to the rescue, this time with its *Macro* function. This allows the user to string a whole sequence of commands together into one command that can be invoked with one click or a keyboard shortcut. Macros are most easily created through Word's *Record New Macro* dialogue box (under the *Tools* menu). Here the macro is given a meaningful name (with no spaces, e.g. 'BasicGlobalEdits') and a short description of what it is meant to do. The macro can also be assigned to a keyboard shortcut or toolbar item. Once *OK* is clicked, then any actions performed in Word are recorded until the process is stopped. The editor should then perform each of the global corrections required, in sequence, until all have been completed, and then stop the recording (under the *Tools* menu).

For more information on how to create macros for a particular version of Word, see the onscreen editing resources listed in appendix 11.

With careful planning, the savvy editor can develop a suite of macros that will perform in a few clicks what would otherwise be a laborious series of commands.

Macros can also be created and edited manually by amending the text file containing the commands (see figure 6.2, overleaf). However, this requires detailed knowledge of how macros work and is not recommended for novices.

Figure 6.2: example of macro instructions

```
Sub EditForPrint()

' EditForPrint Macro
' Macro recorded 22/12/03 by
'
    With AutoCorrect
        .CorrectInitialCaps = False
        .CorrectSentenceCaps = False
        .CorrectDays = False
        .CorrectCapsLock = True
        .ReplaceText = False
        .ReplaceTextFromSpellingChecker = True
        .CorrectKeyboardSetting = True
    End With
    With Options
        .AutoFormatAsYouTypeApplyHeadings = False
        .AutoFormatAsYouTypeApplyBorders = False
        .AutoFormatAsYouTypeApplyBulletedLists = False
        .AutoFormatAsYouTypeApplyNumberedLists = False
        .AutoFormatAsYouTypeApplyTables = False
        .AutoFormatAsYouTypeReplaceQuotes = True
        .AutoFormatAsYouTypeReplaceSymbols = False
        .AutoFormatAsYouTypeReplaceOrdinals = False
        .AutoFormatAsYouTypeReplaceFractions = False
        .AutoFormatAsYouTypeReplacePlainTextEmphasis = False
        .AutoFormatAsYouTypeReplaceHyperlinks = False
        .AutoFormatAsYouTypeFormatListItemBeginning = False
        .AutoFormatAsYouTypeDefineStyles = False
    End With
    Application.DisplayAutoCompleteTips = False
    With Options
        .AutoFormatApplyHeadings = False
        .AutoFormatApplyLists = False
        .AutoFormatApplyBulletedLists = False
        .AutoFormatApplyOtherParas = False
        .AutoFormatReplaceQuotes = True
        .AutoFormatReplaceSymbols = False
        .AutoFormatReplaceOrdinals = False
        .AutoFormatReplaceFractions = False
        .AutoFormatReplacePlainTextEmphasis = False
        .AutoFormatReplaceHyperlinks = False
        .AutoFormatPreserveStyles = False
        .AutoFormatPlainTextWordMail = True
    End With

    Selection.Find.ClearFormatting
    Selection.Find.Replacement.ClearFormatting
    With Selection.Find
        .Text = " "
        .Replacement.Text = " "
        .Forward = True
        .Wrap = wdFindContinue
        .Format = False
        .MatchCase = False
        .MatchWholeWord = False
        .MatchWildcards = False
        .MatchSoundsLike = False
        .MatchAllWordForms = False
    End With
    Selection.Find.Execute Replace:=wdReplaceAll
    Selection.Find.Execute Replace:=wdReplaceAll
    Selection.Find.Execute Replace:=wdReplaceAll
    Selection.Find.Execute Replace:=wdReplaceAll
    Selection.Find.Execute Replace:=wdReplaceAll
    With Selection.Find
        .Text = "^g"
        .Replacement.Text = "^&*****"
        .Forward = True
        .Wrap = wdFindContinue
        .Format = False
        .MatchCase = False
        .MatchWholeWord = False
        .MatchWildcards = False
        .MatchSoundsLike = False
        .MatchAllWordForms = False
    End With
    Selection.Find.Execute Replace:=wdReplaceAll
    With Selection.Find
        .Text = "^l"
        .Replacement.Text = "^p"
        .Forward = True
        .Wrap = wdFindContinue
        .Format = False
        .MatchCase = False
        .MatchWholeWord = False
        .MatchWildcards = False
        .MatchSoundsLike = False
        .MatchAllWordForms = False
    End With
```

It is important to remember that a macro will always perform *all* of the actions recorded within it. It isn't possible to perform just some of them. Therefore the editor should ensure that each command in a macro always goes together with the others and will not occasionally need to be ignored. For example, say the house style specifies the use of double quote marks but the standard macro includes commands to both replace multiple paragraph returns *and* convert double quote marks to single quote marks. In this case, the macro could not be used because the quotation marks would be replaced (incorrectly) along with the other changes.

Nevertheless, once a suite of macros has been developed, it is a powerful means for editors to perform dozens of commands very quickly and painlessly. Publishing organisations may supply their editors with Word templates that have the required macros built in.

WORKING WITH ELECTRONIC STYLES

What are electronic styles and why use them?

A major aspect of copy editing is to identify the various components of a manuscript. Such components can be as simple as just chapter titles, opening paragraphs and normal paragraphs (for a fiction work), or be extremely complex and include a heading hierarchy, figure and table captions, footnotes, quotes, references, equations, call-out text, boxed text and so on. By treating these elements distinctively and effectively in the page design, the reader is given clues and markers as to the author's intentions, and the text will be much easier to read and understand.

Most casual Word users (including many authors) apply manual (also called direct or local) formatting to customise the formatting of the text to their own liking and to visually distinguish parts such as headings from each other. For example, to make a top-level heading authors might select the text and change the typeface to Arial, 18 point, bold. Next time they come to a top-level heading, they will make the same formatting changes. By the time they get to the next chapter (or even earlier), they may have forgotten the exact formatting they used and the top-level heading might have transformed into Times New Roman at 16 point and italic. Any editor trying to untangle the heading structure in such a text would struggle to make sense of it all. The same thing could happen with block quotations, boxed text and other text that needs to be distinguished from regular body text.

point
a printer's unit
of measurement
(approximately
0.35 mm), used
principally when
dealing with typefaces

Further problems arise if the headings are to be numbered, especially when the numbering is in outline format (e.g. 1, 1.1, 1.1.1). It is all too easy for authors to forget where they are in the sequence and miss or duplicate numbers. Changing the order of sections amplifies the problem, as all sections need to be renumbered accordingly. It is obvious that a huge mess can result if authors rely only on manual formatting.

Electronic styling can bring order to the chaos, as it allows the parts of the text to be identified 'virtually'. For example, applying the styles *Heading 1*, *Heading 2* and so on, will correctly identify the relative status of a heading within the text; that is, whether it is a major heading, a subheading, a subsubheading, and so on. The styles can also be automatically numbered or outline numbered, allowing for limitless rearranging of numbered sections without worrying about having to manually fix the numbering.

Once the headings have been styled, editors can also create an automatic table of contents based on those styles, or view the headings in *Outline View* or in the *Document Map*, all of which isolate and illuminate the heading structure more clearly (refer to figure 5.1 on p. 67). It is much easier to spot inconsistencies in the heading structure using these methods.

Style names may also be used by typesetters to generate tables of contents, and lists of tables and figures in the final book, so it becomes even more important in those circumstances to use appropriate style names. Automated contents and lists are preferable because they can be created quickly, they reduce errors and they ensure that any changes to headings, captions and pagination are easily and accurately updated.

Using styles also ensures that all parts of the text that are conceptually the same (e.g. all headings at level 1, all list bullets, all quotes) can be formatted and re-formatted consistently. Formatting a *Heading 1* style as Arial Narrow, 18 point, roman with 12 points of space before, will ensure that all text that has that style applied will appear with that formatting. Should the editor decide later that actually all *Heading 1* text should be Times New Roman, 20 point, italic with 24 points of space before, only the *style* needs to re-formatted in that manner and all text styled as *Heading 1* will automatically update to the new format.

roman (type)
upright type (not italic)

Formatting and naming styles

The other great advantage of using electronic styling is that the virtually identified text components translate directly across to the layout phase, thus reducing typesetting errors. However, it is important for editors to realise that the formatting 'look' applied to styles in Word is not how they will appear in the final typeset document. In fact, it is quite possible for all the parts in a correctly styled Word document to look like plain, identically formatted text. Similarly, the text could be formatted as pink and bold or purple and italic, or any other combination, and still be correctly styled (if a little hard on the eyes)!

In a similar vein, technically it doesn't matter what the styles are called (e.g. they could be simply called *Style1*, *Style2* etc.), as long as they are applied consistently. This is because it is the consistent virtual *labelling* of the text that is important, not how the document looks or what the label names are. The typesetting program simply takes the style *names* in the Word document, matches them with the style names in the text design, and overrides the Word formatting to replace it with the required appearance in the typeset document.

So why bother formatting or naming the styles in Word at all? Because this makes it easier to visually distinguish one style from the other and for the editor to ensure that the correct styles have been applied to the various textual components of the manuscript. It is much more useful if a style for a quote makes the paragraph indented left and right with more space above and below than for ordinary text, and likewise if it is called *Quote* rather than *Style52*. Being able to visualise text components more clearly—roughly as they might appear in the final document—helps the editor analyse the structure and catch errors that might otherwise slip by if all the text used the same font and spacing. It also helps to communicate the intended formatting to the typesetter, especially for complex layouts. Nevertheless, it is important for editors to remember that the purpose of electronic styling is to identify parts of the text *conceptually*, not visually.

> indent (typesetting) a line or paragraph of type set so that it begins or ends inside the normal margin

Word's built-in styles

Word comes with many built-in electronic styles, with default names and formatting, such as *Normal*, *List Bullet*, *Heading 1*, *Heading 2* and so on. Many publishers prefer not to use these built-in styles and create their own custom sets of styles for their publications. This is because in the past the built-in styles created problems in the typesetting process; however, these issues have largely been solved, and it is safe to use all the built-in styles except for *Normal* (see below).

Paragraph versus character styles

Two types of electronic styles can be applied to text: paragraph styles and character styles.

Paragraph styles, as might be guessed, are used to identify the purpose of whole paragraphs of text, such as headings, body text, list bullets, block quotations or references. Once identified, each of these paragraph styles will be treated differently during the typesetting process, with different type sizes, weights and styles applied, along with varying spacing and justification, all of which help the reader to understand the relationships between the elements of the material.

Character styles, on the other hand, apply only to specified characters within a paragraph. Thus, *all* text in a Word document has a paragraph style applied (even if it's just the default *Normal* style), but only some text within those paragraphs might have character styles applied.

justified text
words and letters
spaced to a given
measure, producing
vertical alignment
at right, left or both
margins

paragraph spacing
the spacing between
paragraphs; not to be
confused with leading

Perhaps the most common character styles to be applied are those that indicate emphasis (often indicated by italic or bold formatting). They only override specified typeface attributes of the underlying paragraph style (such as the style or weight); they cannot change paragraph-level attributes, such as space before or after the paragraph, justification or indentation.

Character styles are also useful for identifying text that might need special treatment at the typesetting stage. For example, special characters (such as fractions, multiplication signs, symbols or non-roman scripts) often do not translate well from Word to typesetting programs due to the differences in typefaces used. Applying a character style to these instances and briefing the typesetter accordingly will ensure that those words are easily identified and set properly in the typesetting process.

Character styles (like paragraph styles) identify parts of text *conceptually*, but only within the context of the particular paragraph style in which they sit. Emphasising words within a paragraph identified as body text is not the same as emphasising words within other types of text, such as text in a table or call-out.

On a practical level, this means that the editor must distinguish between these different types of uses; for example, there might be a need to create separate character styles for italic body text, italic table text, italic reference text, and so on.

Why use different character styles?

font
a specific size, weight
and style of a typeface

Technically, the requirement to create different character styles for different contexts is due to the fonts used in typesetting programs. Typographically, italic, bold, condensed and various other combinations of styles found in a typeface are each expressed as separate fonts; Frutiger Light, for example, is a different font from Frutiger Light Italic.

Confusion arises because word processing programs such as Word do not manage fonts in the same way as typesetting programs and will just fake it when making text italic or bold or superscript; any text in Word can be made italic, for example, whether or not there is a proper italic font available. By contrast, in a typesetting program, the instruction to make some text italic must be associated with a specific font; it can't be faked. So body text that is Garamond Light must use a character style of Garamond

Light Italic for italic text, and table text that is Helvetica Neue Condensed must use a different character style specifying Helvetica Neue Condensed Italic to make it italic.

It is not necessary for the editor to actually use any of these specific fonts in Word, and indeed editors are unlikely to even know which will be used in the final layout. So long as the character styles are applied correctly in Word, the typesetting program will match the style names and use the correct typeface and font in the typeset publication.

Word templates

All Word documents are based on a template. For most users, this is the default 'Normal' template, which contains all of Word's built-in styles, margin settings, macros and so on. When a new document is created, Word opens a blank copy of the 'Normal' template, which can then be saved as a standard Word file.

While editors may find that they then need to create from scratch a whole suite of electronic styles for a particular manuscript, larger publishing organisations will often supply their editors with a set of customised Word templates and settings from which to work. These templates can include a built-in set of paragraph and character styles, macros, toolbars, keyboard shortcuts and other settings. Using such templates ensures that the style names used will match those used in the typesetting process, which will minimise errors when translating Word files.

Opening a custom template will create a blank copy of that template and the 'Normal' template will be overridden. Existing documents that were originally created with a 'Normal' or other template can have a custom template 'attached' (using the *Templates and Add-Ins* function under the *Tools* menu) that will override the original template's settings.

If the editor is required to use custom templates, the publishing organisation should provide detailed instructions for using them.

Sample settings

Publishers may ask a typesetter or designer to produce a sample setting of the text design (in hard copy or PDF) with the style names marked. This is usually created using sample text that has been supplied with styles applied. The sample text may have been styled by a copy editor or by another member of staff at the publishing organisation.

In any case, sample settings allow editors to make sure that they use the correct style names for the correct text types, and also help them to visualise what will happen to the styled text once it is typeset. It also means that editors can flag any special text components that might be missing from the design or that might require a different treatment from that originally envisaged.

Creating and applying styles

Applying existing styles

Applying styles to text is a straightforward matter. First, make sure that the *Styles Task Pane* (Windows) or *Styles Toolbox* (Mac), under the *View* menu, is open on the screen (see figure 6.3).

Figure 6.3: the Styles Task Pane (Windows; left), and Styles Toolbox (Mac; right) in Word

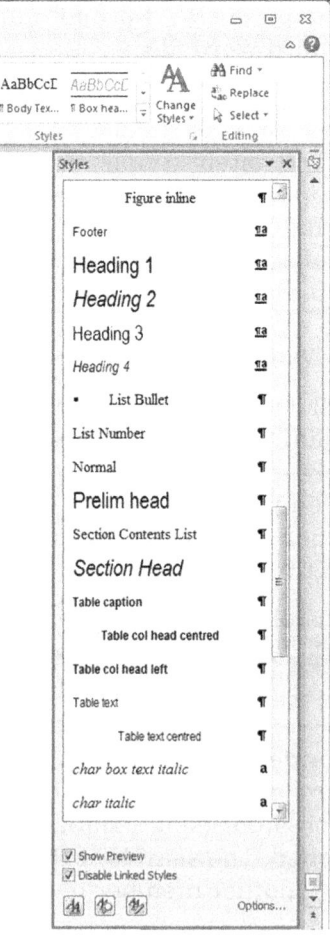
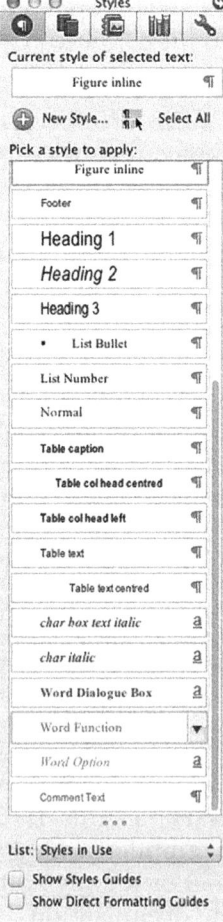

To apply paragraph styles, insert the cursor somewhere in a paragraph in the document, and click on the appropriate style. Do not do this by selecting parts of the text in the paragraph, as Word will incorrectly apply the paragraph style only to the selected text and not to the entire paragraph.

For character styles, select only the relevant text and choose the appropriate character style in the *Styles Task Pane* or *Toolbox*.

Note that paragraph styles are indicated in the *Styles Task Pane* or *Toolbox* by the '¶' symbol and character styles by the 'a' symbol on the right of the style name.

Creating and naming styles

If the editor has to create a *paragraph style* from scratch, it is easiest to do so as follows:

1   Make sure that the *Styles Task Pane* or *Toolbox* is open on the screen.

2   Select the text in a paragraph and apply all the formatting that is desired (such as font size and type, line spacing, space before and after, and indentation).

3   With the text still selected, click on the *New Style* command in the *Styles Task Pane* or *Toolbox*, which will open the *New Style* dialogue box.

4   Name the style with a meaningful label, such as *Figure caption*, *Box text*, and so on.

5   At this stage, it is possible to make additional changes to the formatting of the style, using the various options available in the dropdown menus.

6   Under the *Based On:* dropdown list it is advisable to choose what style the new one will use as its source. If say, a *Bullet List* style is based on the *Body Text* style, then changes made to shared characteristics in *Body Text* (such as font type and size) will be passed on to *Bullet List*. This makes it easy to change the overall look and feel of a document. However, if the style is to remain independent of the other styles, then it should be *Based On: (no style)*.

7   Click *OK* when finished.

To create a new *character style*, follow the same steps as above, except that in the *New Style* dialogue box, under *Style Type:*, choose *Character* from the dropdown menu. Also make sure that under *Style Based On:* the dropdown menu says *Default Paragraph Font*.

The *Normal* style

In Word, the default paragraph style is called *Normal*. Any time that formatting or styling is cleared from a paragraph, the style will return to *Normal*, and this style by default forms the basis of all other styles. In addition, the *Normal* style will vary from one computer to another because it always defaults to the style that is included in the user's 'Normal' template, not the style applied by another user. For these reasons, it is best to avoid using *Normal* as a style when preparing documents for typesetting, even if it is for standard body text.

Reusing and re-formatting styles

There are many existing Word styles (either built-in or created earlier) that can be reused or re-formatted to suit the requirements of a specific manuscript. In particular, it is useful to reuse Word's built-in heading styles, as this allows the editor to easily review the heading structure in *Outline View*.

If an existing style is to be used, but the editor wishes to make it appear with different formatting, it is easiest to use the following steps:

1 Make sure that the *Styles Task Pane* or *Toolbox* is open on the screen.

2 Select all the text in the relevant paragraph and apply the style required.

3 Change the formatting of the paragraph as desired (e.g. change the font size and type, line spacing, indentation).

4 With the text still selected, click on the '¶' or 'a̲' symbol to the right of the style name in the *Styles Task Pane* or *Toolbox*. A dropdown menu will appear.

5 Select *Update to Match Selection* from the dropdown menu. The style will then be changed to match the formatting of the selected text.

Checking the application of styles

Checking that a style has been applied correctly is generally a straightforward matter. If the formatting for each style is different, then each time a style is applied the text should change formatting to indicate that the style has been applied correctly.

However, editors often receive manuscripts from authors who are not familiar with electronic styles and therefore might have applied a mixture of styles and manual formatting, or applied styles incorrectly, based on their appearance and not on their conceptual place in the text.

One option for dealing with these situations, especially if the text is extremely messy, is to clear *all* the formatting from the text and start applying the appropriate styles from scratch.

If the styling is reasonably clean but needs checking for consistency, then it may be more efficient to use Word's facility to display the style name used for each paragraph and then clean up any stray styling or formatting that way. This facility is set in the *Options* (Windows) or *Preferences* (Mac) dialogue boxes by turning on the *Style Area* in the *Advanced* tab (Windows) or *View* pane (Mac). In the *Draft* and *Outline* views (but not the *Print Layout* view), there will now appear a panel on the left of the text that shows which styles have been applied to the text. Unfortunately, this option does not show character styles (see figure 6.4).

Figure 6.4: Draft View with the Style Area showing

Heading 1	# The action of bituminous coal
Body Text	Coal **chokes** the air spaces within the bed of coke, which shuts off the air supply needed to burn the gases produced from the fresh coal. There is a very rapid **evaporation** of moisture from the coal, which chills the mixture, thus reducing the heat in the furnace.
Body Text	Next, water-gas forms by chemical reaction, as the steam becomes **decomposed**, and its oxygen burns the carbon of the coal to carbonic oxide. The hydrogen is then **liberated**. The reaction takes place when steam is in contact with carbon that has been greatly heated, also leading to a chilling process, which absorbs heat from the furnaces. The two fuel gases generated would give back all the heat absorbed during their formation, but due to the chilling, there is not enough air in the furnace to burn.
Heading 2	## *Effect of air*
Body Text	Allowing more air to enter through the fire door has no effect, because the gases are now relatively cool and cannot be burned unless the air is heated again. After the moisture has been driven off, the hydrocarbons begin to be **distilled**, and a substantial portion escapes without being burned, due to the lack of hot air. In the meantime, huge volumes of smoke escape from the chimney, together with all the fuel gases—hydrogen, hydrocarbons, and carbonic oxide that have been unburned. At the same time soot is deposited on the hot surface, reducing its efficiency in transmitting heat to the water.

Recent Mac versions of Word also have a facility for viewing the styles in the *Print Layout* view (see figure 6.5). At the bottom of the *Styles Toolbox*, checking the *Show Styles Guides* will colour-code and number the text with the relevant style, which can be cross-checked with the corresponding colour and number in the *Styles Toolbox*. This function indicates character styling to a limited extent.

The other option at the bottom of the Mac *Styles Toolbox*, *Show Direct Formatting Guides*, is also useful as it highlights with light shading any text that has had manual formatting applied.

Figure 6.5: Print Layout view showing the Styles Guides and Direct Formatting Guides, with corresponding numbering in the Styles panel

· *Picture books* ¶

Picture books are the first introduction most children have to the joys of reading. They are usually read aloud to young children, at least initially, so vocabulary level is not as limited as in school readers, where the children themselves are reading the books. One of the great values of picture books is their ability to extend children's knowledge and enjoyment of words. Editors who can recognise the difference between an ordinary word that is too difficult for a picture book, such as *initiate* for *start*, and a special word that will be long remembered, such as *soporific* in Beatrix Potter's *The Tale of Peter Rabbit*, probably have the makings of a good children's book editor. ¶

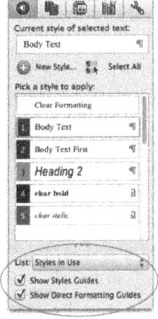

An important part of the editor's role is **liaison between the author, illustrator (or photographer) and designer**, especially if the illustrations are commissioned after the text is received. Often the editor will help the designer choose the right illustrator for the book, then work closely with both author and illustrator to ensure that text and pictures match perfectly. ¶

Because there is so little text in a picture book, every word must be **exactly right**. Sentence structure should be simple, beginning with the main clause, and there should be no unnecessary words or phrases. Read each line aloud to find out how it sounds. Look for imaginative ideas, rhythm, flow and repetition, which form the basis of many much-loved picture books. ¶

RECORDING CHANGES AND INSERTING AUTHOR QUERIES

The *Track Changes* feature (also called *Reviewing*) in Word is one its most powerful editing features. When *Track Changes* is turned on, all editorial and styling changes are recorded in the document, which can then easily be sent to the author via email or a file transfer service, such as Dropbox. In this way, both the editor and author can see exactly where changes have been made and can then accept or reject them, individually or en masse. Once an edit is accepted, no rekeying is required (as would be needed with hard-copy editing), as this has already been done in the document, thus both saving time and reducing keying errors. Likewise, if an edit is rejected, it is easy to go back to exactly the way it was originally, without having to rekey anything.

In addition, with Word's *Comments* facility the editor can insert author queries directly into the document, linked to the specific text, so that it is easy to see exactly what the comment is referring to and without having to retype it on a separate page or refer to page and line numbers. Gone too are the days of losing queries that were attached to a printout with a paperclip or sticky note!

Nevertheless, a major disadvantage of using *Track Changes* is that, even with recent improvements in the functioning of this feature, a heavily edited manuscript can become quite difficult to read and it can be hard to tell what has been changed and where. Another problem arises if major structural changes must be made. Again, though tracking these sorts of changes has improved with recent versions of Word, it is still problematic and may cause confusion.

Fortunately, there are ways to work around these limitations.

Turning on and viewing Track Changes

As with many functions in Word there are several methods of turning *Track Changes* on and off. But probably the easiest (and most efficient) way is to use the built-in keyboard shortcut for the action (CTRL [or ⌘] + SHIFT + E) or create a more memorable shortcut for it. The reason it is worth using a shortcut is that editors will generally find that they have to do this frequently while editing, because if *all* edits were faithfully recorded, the manuscript might become almost unreadable!

For information on how to create shortcuts, see the earlier section on 'Keyboard and toolbar shortcuts'.

It is also important to show either the *Review* ribbon tab at the top of the page window (available in more recent versions of Word) or the *Review* toolbar. These provide the editor with all the options for tracking changes, including toggling the function on and off, changing what is viewed, commenting, and accepting and rejecting the changes.

There are two main modes for viewing tracked changes in Word. The first, and original, method is in *Draft View* (see figure 6.6, overleaf). In this mode, all markup appears directly in the text, with insertions appearing as new coloured text and deletions appearing as strikethrough text. Comments are inserted and amended using a separate panel, though once inserted they can be read by hovering the cursor over the comment marker.

Figure 6.6: a passage with Track Changes, viewed in Draft View

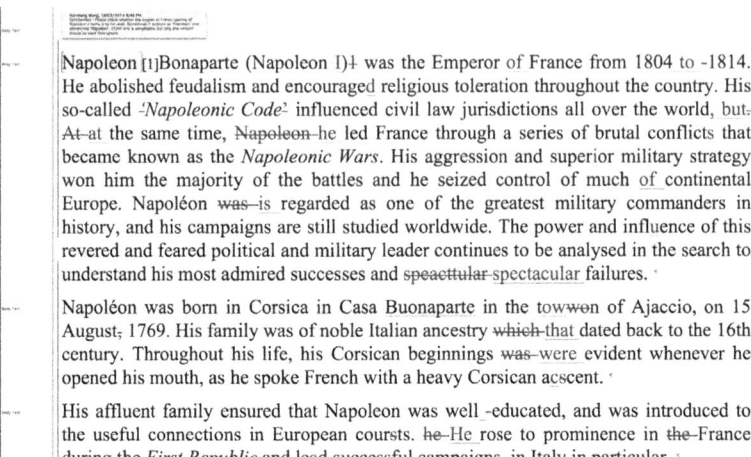

Napoleon [1]Bonaparte (Napoleon I)⊦ was the Emperor of France from 1804 to -1814. He abolished feudalism and encouraged religious toleration throughout the country. His so-called ‑'Napoleonic Code'‑ influenced civil law jurisdictions all over the world, but. At‑at the same time, Napoleon‑he led France through a series of brutal conflicts that became known as the *Napoleonic Wars*. His aggression and superior military strategy won him the majority of the battles and he seized control of much of continental Europe. Napoléon was‑is regarded as one of the greatest military commanders in history, and his campaigns are still studied worldwide. The power and influence of this revered and feared political and military leader continues to be analysed in the search to understand his most admired successes and speacttular‑spectacular failures. ·

Napoléon was born in Corsica in Casa Buonaparte in the towwon of Ajaccio, on 15 August, 1769. His family was of noble Italian ancestry which‑that dated back to the 16th century. Throughout his life, his Corsican beginnings was‑were evident whenever he opened his mouth, as he spoke French with a heavy Corsican acscent. ·

His affluent family ensured that Napoleon was well ‑educated, and was introduced to the useful connections in European coursts. he‑He rose to prominence in the‑France during the *First Republic* and lead successful campaigns ‑in Italy in particular. ·

A much more practical and less cluttered mode of viewing the markup is in *Print Layout* view, where insertions also appear directly in the text, but deletions, formatting changes and comments are viewed in the right margin in 'balloons' (see figure 6.7). This makes it much easier to see what the final version will look like, although even with this improvement it can still cause problems. For example, it is quite easy to miss punctuation and other very small changes because the fine lines and small triangles used to show which edits the balloons in the margins relate to can sometimes get in the way. In addition, if there are a great number of edits, the balloons will collapse into summaries in which only the first line is visible, making it very difficult to see exactly what has been done. In such cases, the editor has three options:

• hover the cursor over the location of an individual edit to bring up a box showing the change

• click on the summary balloon to open a separate panel with the corrections listed in full (but no longer within the text)

• switch over to *Draft View*, which will allow the individual edits to be seen in situ.

Every one of these options has its merits, and the editor can choose the one that best suits the occasion.

Another viewing method is to change the dropdown menu in the *Review* ribbon or toolbar from *Final Showing Markup* to *Final*, which can be done in both Draft View and Page Layout View. This will instantly hide from view all comments and markups so that the editor can see what the final document will look like. Note that if *Track Changes* is turned on, any edits made in this view will still be recorded, even if the markup is hidden. It can be a bit dangerous to edit using this method, because if *Track Changes* is turned off by accident, it is easy to miss this, and edits will not be recorded.

Figure 6.7: the same passage with Track Changes, viewed in Page Layout View

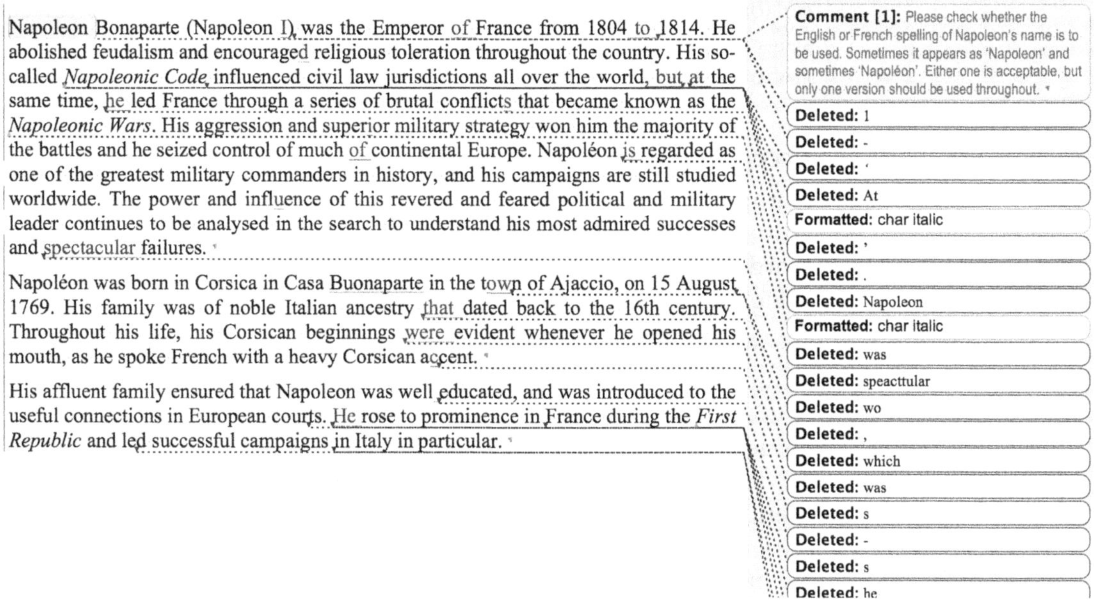

Napoleon Bonaparte (Napoleon I) was the Emperor of France from 1804 to 1814. He abolished feudalism and encouraged religious toleration throughout the country. His so-called *Napoleonic Code* influenced civil law jurisdictions all over the world, but at the same time, he led France through a series of brutal conflicts that became known as the *Napoleonic Wars*. His aggression and superior military strategy won him the majority of the battles and he seized control of much of continental Europe. Napoléon is regarded as one of the greatest military commanders in history, and his campaigns are still studied worldwide. The power and influence of this revered and feared political and military leader continues to be analysed in the search to understand his most admired successes and spectacular failures.

Napoléon was born in Corsica in Casa Buonaparte in the town of Ajaccio, on 15 August 1769. His family was of noble Italian ancestry that dated back to the 16th century. Throughout his life, his Corsican beginnings were evident whenever he opened his mouth, as he spoke French with a heavy Corsican accent.

His affluent family ensured that Napoleon was well educated, and was introduced to the useful connections in European courts. He rose to prominence in France during the *First Republic* and led successful campaigns in Italy in particular.

Comment [1]: Please check whether the English or French spelling of Napoleon's name is to be used. Sometimes it appears as 'Napoleon' and sometimes 'Napoléon'. Either one is acceptable, but only one version should be used throughout.

Deleted: 1

Deleted: -

Deleted: '

Deleted: At

Formatted: char italic

Deleted: '

Deleted: .

Deleted: Napoleon

Formatted: char italic

Deleted: was

Deleted: speacttular

Deleted: wo

Deleted: ,

Deleted: which

Deleted: was

Deleted: s

Deleted: -

Deleted: s

Deleted: he

Managing tracked changes

As mentioned earlier, a heavily edited manuscript can be quite difficult to read with all the markups in view. This can be further compounded when the author receives the edited manuscript and revises it accordingly, also using *Track Changes*. If there are multiple authors, each of them may also add their own corrections and comments. These are then returned to the editor and the circle continues. After a few rounds of this, it is not too hard to imagine what a mess might result! So, what is the best way to manage all those tracked changes?

Selective viewing of markup

A very useful function in Word is the ability to select what markup to view, either according to type of markup or by the reviewer (user) who made the markup.

On the *Review* ribbon or toolbar click on the *Show Markup* dropdown menu. The options allow the editor to show or hide

Comments, Insertions and Deletions, and *Formatting.* This is especially useful for hiding formatting balloons, which generally contribute unnecessarily to the clutter. As usual, creating a shortcut for these simplifies life greatly.

Further down the *Show Markup* dropdown list is another option called *Reviewers.* This brings up a submenu that lists all the reviewers who have contributed to the document. There is also an option to show or hide *All Reviewers.* With this list, the editor can selectively show or hide the markup made by one or more or all reviewers.

Accepting or rejecting changes

Authors may agree or disagree with an editor's changes; likewise editors may agree or disagree with the author's revisions. Word's reviewing features include several mechanisms by which reviewers can accept or reject suggested edits.

To ensure that all edits are reviewed individually, the editor or author can find each marked-up change by clicking on the *Previous* or *Next* icons in the *Review* ribbon or toolbar. At the first change found, the user can click on the *Accept* or *Reject* icons in the *Review* ribbon or toolbar to reveal another dropdown menu. This menu allows the user to accept or reject a change and, if required, automatically find the next one. It is also easy to accept or reject an individual change by right-clicking on the changed text and choosing *Accept Change* or *Reject Change* from the contextual menu. Again, it is more efficient to create keyboard shortcuts for these frequently used functions.

Once an edit has been accepted, the markup disappears and the text appears normal again. The change is no longer recorded and the previous version of the text is no longer visible.

There is also an option available to *Accept/Reject All Changes in Document* or *Accept/Reject All Changes Shown.* The latter is used after the author or editor has selected to view only some of the changes, as described earlier. In that way, it is possible to accept, for example, all the formatting changes, or to accept all changes made by a particular reviewer. These options both offer much faster ways of managing changes but, of course, care must be taken when using them.

Managing tracked changes between author and editor is discussed in more detail in chapter 7.

It should be noted that it would be rare to use the 'reject all' versions of these commands, assuming that most authors would agree with most of the edits that editors make.

Tracking moved text

Sometimes an editor will have to move text that appears in an illogical place to a more appropriate spot. Before Word 2007, cutting and pasting text from one place to another using *Track Changes* resulted in the moved text being indistinguishable from edited text. If further edits were made to the new text it was not possible to easily see what had been changed. However, since Word 2007, the *Track Moves* function treats moved text differently from normal corrections, with the original text being marked with a double strikethrough in a different colour from regular edits and the moved text being marked with double underlining in yet another colour. In the new location, the moved text can be further edited and corrections will show up as normal corrections. This ensures that any text that has simply been moved is easily distinguishable from text that has been edited.

Note that moved text is not correctly marked if the text being moved already has some tracked changes in it. Therefore it is important, if possible, to move text before it is copy edited.

File management and version control

Another vital element in keeping tracked changes under control is implementing an efficient file management system. Under such a system, at each stage of the editing process (first edit, author response to first edit, second edit and so on), the editor or author always starts working on a copy of the most recent version of the document so that there are progressively backed-up versions of the manuscript.

As changes are agreed with and accepted in *Track Changes*, the markups associated with those changes are removed, leaving a relatively clean document from which to start the next stage of editing. The archived documents still record the original changes in case it is necessary to go back to an earlier version to review a decision or query.

Potential disaster lies ahead if two or more authors or editors work on copies of the same manuscript at the same time. Even if *Track Changes* is used by everyone, trying to reconcile all the different changes between two or more documents is very time-consuming, and it is very easy to miss some changes or find several conflicting edits that then have to be resolved separately.

version control managing versions of an electronic file so that there is no confusion about which is the latest version; older copies are archived and only the current version is worked on for the next stage

File management practices are dealt with in more detail in chapter 7.

121

Comments and author queries

In the course of the editing process, it is often necessary to insert a query to the author, or an explanation as to why a certain edit has been made. For example, the author may have used the name of a historical figure inconsistently and it may not be clear which of the versions is the preferred one; or the editor may need to explain that it is the house style to include percentages as rounded whole numbers or to use double instead of single quotation marks. Whatever the case, it is easiest to do this using the *Comment* function in Word.

Simply insert the cursor at the desired point in the text, or select the relevant text, and choose *New Comment* from the *Insert* menu or from the *Review* ribbon or toolbar. Again, the most efficient method is to use the built-in keyboard shortcuts (CTRL + ALT + M in Windows, and ⌘ + OPTION + A in Mac). This brings up a balloon in the margin of the *Page Layout* view into which the editor can type a query or comment.

Compare documents

It is not uncommon for authors to be unfamiliar with, or downright hostile to, using the *Track Changes* feature in Word. This is not surprising given that a manuscript with many edits can look quite a mess when all the markup is shown. So an editor may receive back from the author a revised manuscript with no markup at all, or with only the original editing markup showing.

Again, Word has a feature, *Compare Documents* (or similar—the name varies quite a bit between versions), that can help with this. Although not entirely bug-free, this function compares two documents and produces a new version that contains all the differences marked-up in a similar way to a document with *Track Changes*. The main issues to be aware of are choosing the correct document to be the base document against which the other is to be compared (so that the markup shows the new version, not the old), and ensuring that both documents contain no markup (it is alright to leave in comments), as existing tracked changes will cause problems during the comparison process.

In the scenario discussed earlier, the editor should first ensure that all changes in both documents are accepted. These should be saved as new files, so that there is a backup in case anything goes wrong. Then the editor's earlier document is tagged as the 'original' and the author's document as the 'revised'. On creation of the new, marked-up document, the editor should check that the markup reflects the changes correctly, and then save the document as a new version. The comments from both documents will be included, thus ensuring that queries and responses remain.

Another method is to use the similar *Merge* command, which involves opening the original document (with all changes accepted) and then merging the revised document into it. Again, the differences show up as marked-up changes.

CREATING CROSS-REFERENCES

Cross-references are used to refer the reader to other parts of the book that have related content. Traditionally, cross-referencing with page numbers was avoided because they could not be completed until the final page proofs were ready, and any last-minute changes could be costly or error-prone. For this reason, it was more common to refer to chapter or heading titles, though even these could change and therefore require changes to all cross-references. However, Word and modern typesetting programs can quite easily set up cross-referencing to specific page numbers and heading titles that update as the pagination or titles change, so this task is no longer as onerous as it used to be.

cross-reference
a pointer in a text or index to related material elsewhere in a publication, usually indicated using *see* or *see also*

The author or editor may choose to set up cross-references in Word using the *Cross-reference* function (under the *Insert* menu). In the dialogue box that appears, the dropdown menu *Reference type:* identifies the type of text that will be referred to, such as a heading, bookmark, note or caption. The *Insert reference to:* menu indicates what will appear in the cross-reference, such as a page number or heading text. The box below these two menus then allows the editor to choose which heading, bookmark and so on, to refer to. Choosing *Insert* will then insert the page number or heading text wherever the cursor has been placed. These fields will then translate over to a typesetting program such as InDesign as live, instantly updating cross-references.

Before going to this effort, though, it is worth checking with the typesetter that their typesetting program will indeed allow these cross-references to transfer correctly, and that the typesetter has the expertise to ensure that they will work as intended.

CHECKING SPELLING AND GRAMMAR

Another Word function that can be useful is the *Spelling and Grammar* checker. Each element of this function can be turned on or off independently of each other, and can help to highlight spelling and grammar errors either 'as you type' or in a complete sweep through the entire document.

All of these depend on the language (under the *Tools* menu) that is set for the document; for example, there are four versions of English that could be chosen: Australian, US, UK and Canadian. Obviously, 'English (AUS)' would be chosen for manuscripts that are intended for an Australian market. If the language is set in the *Normal* style, then all styles based on *Normal* will take on that language too. The language set dictates which dictionary and grammar rules will be used when running the spelling and grammar checkers, so that *organise* will be recognised as being correctly spelled when 'English (AUS)' is chosen, but not when 'English (US)' is selected.

Perhaps the most effective of the options available is to have Word spellcheck 'as you type'. In this mode, Word will place a wavy line under all those words that have been misspelt, according to the specified language dictionary. Using this option, as the editor progresses through the manuscript, any anomalies will be highlighted and can be fixed individually or with judicious use of the *Find and Replace* function. This is arguably more efficient and effective than running a spellchecker through the entire document, since many specialist words and proper nouns and names will unnecessarily be brought up as errors during a spellcheck. This means the editor will then have to decide whether to ignore once or all the time, or change once or all the time, while also having to take into account context and other issues. However, every editor will have their preferred way of working, and using a combination of these techniques will also be effective.

It must be noted of course that neither of these methods will find correctly spelt words used incorrectly, such as *their* versus *there* or *they're*.

Using Word to check grammar is a little less useful, as the feature is more difficult to implement properly due to the complexity of the language. There is a readability checker that tests the level of language used and can provide a variety of raw statistics about the words and sentences used. While this is a crude way of measuring readability, it can be useful as a quick overall check that might indicate that there are problems with the manuscript, especially if preparing material specifically for reading onscreen.

Tips for managing files

Don't forget to save files regularly to avoid the danger of losing hours of work should there be an unexpected technology failure, such as the program or computer crashing. Learn the shortcut CTRL + S (Windows) or ⌘ + S (Mac), and invoke it often.

Back up all working files at least daily, preferably to both an external hard disk and the cloud (that is, a server that is located elsewhere), to prevent loss of work due to a hard-drive failure, computer virus, fire, theft or other disaster.

backing up
(file management)
regularly making
and securely storing
copies of electronic
documents to avoid
losing work

Editing practice: copy editing techniques

Once the editor is familiar with onscreen editing techniques for cleaning up a manuscript, using *Track Changes* and setting up electronic styles, the actual task of copy editing the text can commence.

The vast majority of authors submit their manuscripts and associated files (such as images) as electronic documents via email or a file-sharing service such as Dropbox. An in-house or freelance editor edits and electronically styles the manuscript onscreen, normally using Microsoft Word, and then returns the edited file to the author to address queries and approve the suggested edits. There is usually a bit of toing-and-froing as editorial issues and queries are sorted out. Once the manuscript is considered to be final, the file is sent for typesetting using a program such as Adobe InDesign. The editor or proofreader and the author then proofread the typeset document, either in hard copy or digitally in a PDF (using the Adobe Reader program), and corrections are taken in by the typesetter. There may be several iterations of the typeset document, and proofreading may be repeated several times. When the document is near completion, an index may be prepared. In the final stages, the editor and typesetter work together to add the index and all last-minute material before the typesetter outputs the final version for sending to the printer or ebook conversion service.

For a diagram of a typical production workflow, see figure 2.1.

There are many variations to such a process, but most follow similar steps. This scenario will form the basis for the following section on how editors go about the actual copy editing process. Subsequent chapters will examine the remaining steps in the production process.

THE MANUSCRIPT

It is essential for editors to learn how to prepare for and manage the electronic files submitted by the author. The better the author and editor prepare for and manage all facets of the manuscript, the smoother the editing and production processes will be, reducing the likelihood of problems emerging further down the track.

Briefing the author

It is to the editor's advantage to brief authors carefully about how to present their manuscript. While the author's primary focus will, of course, be on the writing, they should also be provided with guidance by the editor about editorial style as early as possible, especially if there is already an established house style and word list available.

editorial style
editorial decisions
made about the
grammar, punctuation,
usage and spelling
of text

Authors should let the publisher know from the start if they intend to use non-standard software programs, so that any potential file format issues can be addressed as early in the process as possible. For example, if the author's word processing program can only produce plain text files (which would not allow the manuscript to be electronically styled), the editor should instruct the author on how to mark up the headings and other text manually. Fortunately, such circumstances are rare these days.

Authors can help ensure their manuscript is set up and laid out correctly if they assist by paying some attention to the setup of the file and the use of electronic styles and formatting. Authors who are familiar with the use of electronic styles should be asked, at minimum, to apply Word's built-in electronic styles to the headings. Many publishing organisations can supply authors with Word templates with the required styles and formatting built in, which helps ensure that styles are applied according to the organisation's requirements.

For a more detailed discussion about electronic styles and templates, see chapter 6.

A little knowledge can be a dangerous thing, though, and overzealous authors may end up applying styles and formatting inappropriately and excessively. Unless authors are working with an established template that they know how to use fully, they should be encouraged to keep both styling and formatting to a minimum—just enough to illuminate the structure—and to provide any special instructions as additional comments or highlighted notes in the text. The more complex and detailed styling is then left to the editor to finalise.

Any author who is not familiar with electronic styles could be provided with basic training or else be requested to at least use consistent formatting (especially for headings) so that the structure of the text is apparent.

The author should also be briefed as to whether separate files should be provided for each chapter, prelims and endmatter, and on the file naming system to be used for each. Normally the author would provide the text files in Word document format, although generic RTF (rich text format) files are also acceptable, as these can be opened easily in Word, with formatting and electronic styling intact. If the author is unable to supply files in either of these formats, the project manager needs to check the compatibility of the author's files with the publishing organisation's own equipment as early as possible in the process.

RTF (rich text format) a widely accessible text file format that allows text to be styled and formatted

It used to be that authors were asked to supply tables separately, especially if they were complex. However, this is a hangover from older typesetting methods and is unnecessary if current desktop publishing programs such as InDesign are being used. It can be counterproductive if the tables are supplied separately, as they need to be tediously copied and pasted into the appropriate spot in the text, with the possibility of errors being introduced in the process. It is also easier to edit both text and table if they are adjacent in the document so they can be cross-checked for accuracy.

The author will need to be informed of the preferred formats for the manuscript and artwork, and told how to submit them (usually by email). Artwork can be supplied in a number of formats. Some publishers prefer the artwork to be supplied separately (preferably electronically), with approximate locations marked in the text using square brackets (e.g. [Insert Figure 3.2 near here]) or other distinctive marking, while others are happy for artwork to be inserted directly into the text at the required point. Depending on the format and type of artwork and whether it will have to be redrawn for reproduction, it may need to be both inserted in the text and supplied separately. All artwork files supplied electronically should be clearly identified; for example, with the book title or author, and figure number and title.

For a detailed discussion about the format and supply of artwork, see chapter 9.

The author should also supply either a hard copy or PDF of their text against which the electronic file can be compared. A Word document that is transferred to a different computer could potentially lose information in the process, especially if unusual fonts or special characters or images are used, but also if authors provide the wrong version of a file. If such issues arise, a hard copy or PDF allows the editor to check what has gone wrong.

Basic requests from editors to authors

Do

- adopt the house style consistently and as much as possible

- supply a word list of the spelling and usage of terms in the manuscript

- apply electronic styling to semantically identify parts of the text, such as headings, quotes, boxed text, poetry and emphasised characters

- insert manual instructions about the treatment of text if it has not been electronically styled

- use automatic bullet lists

- use Word's *Table* facility to create tables

- identify boxed text, preferably by applying electronic styling, or by adding instructions before and after the text, or by inserting the text into a table cell

- use automated footnotes or endnotes

- include a header or footer that contains the name of the publication, the chapter and the page number

- use standard Word typefaces, such as Times New Roman or Arial, to ensure compatibility

- supply artwork according to the publisher's requirements, including clear labelling of the files

- use unique and useful file names, including chapter number or name for text files, and figure numbers for figures, and always add the date to make it clear which is the latest version

- keep backups of files, and save files frequently while working

- supply a printout or PDF of the manuscript against which to compare the Word version.

Don't

- apply manual formatting to the text — use electronic styles
- use more than the minimum amount of styling required
- insert manual hyphenation in non-hyphenated words, line breaks or bullets
- create tables using tabs, spaces and/or columns — use Word's *Table* facility
- add extra paragraph returns, tabs or spaces — one of each at a time is enough
- underline text or apply special formatting such as outlining or drop shadows
- use Word's *Text Box* feature for boxed text
- use all caps (all capital letters).

all caps
all letters in a word, phrase or sentence are capitalised

Receiving the manuscript

Ideally, the author will submit the manuscript in its entirety; however, in the case of very long books or those with multiple authors or a tight deadline, it is sometimes necessary for the text to be supplied in batches. If the editor is not dealing directly with the author, the project manager or publisher should ensure that the editor is aware of this.

Once the entire manuscript has been submitted, the project manager will check the total number of words in the manuscript (including all chapters) to ensure that it tallies with that specified in the original contract. Since preliminary costings for the book are made based on this word count, it is important to ensure that there has been no major variation that might affect the budget. The extent and size of other elements, such as tables and artwork, must also be included in the final estimate (also known as a cast-off).

cast-off
an estimate of the number of printed pages a manuscript will make when set in a given typeface and measure, following a predetermined page design

Managing files

On receipt of the author's files, it is important to immediately institute good file management practices to ensure that all versions of the manuscript are kept secure and orderly. It is, unfortunately, extremely easy to accidentally delete electronic files or overwrite them with a different version, especially if a number of people are working on the same publication. It is therefore important to create a new copy of the text as it progresses through each stage of the editing and production process so that editorial decisions can be tracked and, if necessary, earlier versions of the text can be reinstated.

Care needs to be taken to ensure that the original files are stored separately, and the editor must work only on a copy. Each version of the file must also be managed carefully and, if all is going well, only the most recent copy should proceed to the next stage.

A common system of naming and storing files must be used to ensure that different versions of the manuscript are clearly identified. Some examples of good practice include the following:

- Establish a system of folders and subfolders for storing the text and graphic files appropriately, such as by stages of production (e.g. original, editing, typesetting), with subfolders for parts of the book (e.g. prelims, each chapter, endmatter) and, depending on the complexity of the publication, possibly further subfolders. It is also useful to create folders for storing administrative material, such as the production schedule, readers' reports, the budget and so on.

- The original files should be changed to read-only status so that they cannot be overwritten (although they can still be deleted!).

- Label text files with a useful and meaningful name, such as the chapter number and title, and the date and initials of the person who last worked on the file. Label artwork with the chapter and figure number and the date.

- Format chapter and figure numbers in file names with a leading zero to ensure they file electronically in numerical order (e.g. 'chap07' instead of 'chap7').

- Format the date as: YYYYMMDD (year, month, date); for example, 28 October 2014 would be formatted as '20141028'. This ensures that the files will be organised chronologically and the latest version will be easily identifiable.

Each time an editor, author or other person works on a file, they should save it as a new version and rename it accordingly so that it is obvious who worked on the file and the date on which they saved it. Often publishing organisations will have an established system for ensuring version control; but, if not, editors should implement their own system. All those involved in the project should be given instructions about how the file management system is to operate, to ensure consistency.

All author's files should be scanned for viruses (especially macro viruses), particularly if the author is using the Windows platform. If a virus is detected, the files should be disinfected using anti-virus software. If this is not possible, the project manager and author should be notified immediately and the files returned for repair.

All email and other correspondence should also be filed carefully as a record of discussions and decisions made. Emails should be stored to a separate mailbox or folder that has been created for the project, and, if there is any hard-copy correspondence, this should also be filed into a dedicated hard-copy folder.

A strong backup system is necessary to ensure that in the case of equipment failure, theft, fire or other disaster, the work that has already been done will not be lost.

For more discussion about security measures, see chapter 3.

THE FIRST READING

Before reading through the manuscript for the first time, it is essential for the editor to read all correspondence between the publisher and the author, any readers' reports, the publisher's brief (see appendix 1), the author's questionnaire (see appendix 7) and the author's contract, if available. This information will help with the most crucial aspect of the first reading—ensuring that the manuscript is what the publisher commissioned or agreed to. If it becomes apparent that it is not, the publisher should be informed immediately.

The editor should check the manuscript to make sure that it matches the printed or PDF version. It is not unheard of for the author to inadvertently supply an earlier version of a manuscript, so it is best to catch this before beginning work. All pages should be numbered for ease of referral, especially if the pages are to be printed out at any stage.

Both a lack of and excessive styling or formatting can be problems that make editing more difficult; the former because no formatting can make the heading structure invisible, and the latter because excessive formatting can make the text hard to read and may require a great deal of undoing. It may be necessary in these cases to go back to the author to resolve these issues, but, in any case, assessing the condition of the styling and formatting early on will give the editor an idea about what level of work will be required when preparing the manuscript for publication.

If feasible, the initial reading of the manuscript should occur in one uninterrupted session. Some editors prefer to do this first reading in hard copy, as this removes them from the technical aspects of editing so that they can focus on the overall structure and content, which should be the editor's main focus at this point. Reading a hard copy also makes it much easier to detect major problems relating to structure, repetition, omissions and variations in style, as the pages can be spread out and the editor can compare one section with another without having to scroll or squeeze everything onto one computer screen. Although it is best to read straight through without pausing to make copy editing marks, it is a good idea to highlight any obvious problems, missing text and anomalies, such as spelling variations, along the way, so they can be revisited later.

For information about managing artwork, see chapter 9.

Keep a running checklist of any artwork, tables and other non-text material mentioned in the text, and make sure they have been supplied with the manuscript. The publishing organisation may supply an artwork checklist, or the editor may be required to develop the list in a separate Excel spreadsheet or Word document.

The author may also have inserted special characters (such as Greek characters, equations or symbols) that are lost or transform into different characters when the file is opened using a different platform or version of Word. In such cases the editor should check these against the printout or PDF to correctly identify the missing or transformed text. All major issues should be reported to the project manager or author immediately to ensure they do not cause problems later in the production process.

RESTRUCTURING TEXT

With the first reading done, the editor may have discovered a number of places where some restructuring must take place. It is not uncommon for authors to become so engrossed in the detail of the content that they lose track of the structure and order the text in an illogical manner or neglect to address an issue that is a necessary part of the argument or story.

Depending on the nature of the publication, the editor may either suggest the change in a comment or actually move the text using *Track Changes*, adding a comment explaining the move so that the author can review it and agree (or disagree) with the change. Sometimes actually moving the text first helps the author to see better how the change would improve the manuscript.

The editor may find that some text is missing. For example, an author may list five issues to address in detail but then only provide further information for four (or list four and address five!). Such instances should be dealt with by inserting a comment requesting that the missing content be supplied.

If the structural changes are significant, then it would be best to discuss the suggested restructuring directly with the author (or with the project manager, as appropriate) before any further work is done. If there is to be substantial rewriting, the author will usually need to undertake this work.

COPY EDITING TECHNIQUES AND CONVENTIONS

Global corrections

During the first reading, the editor will have noted some of the more obvious inconsistencies in the manuscript, such as the spelling of names or use of punctuation. Some of these will need to be edited individually, while others can easily be corrected using global corrections.

The number and types of global corrections that could potentially be made are many, and will vary with each manuscript. Nevertheless, there are some standard corrections that can safely be applied to almost any Word document (see table 7.1, overleaf). Many of these relate to applying spacing, indentations and other layout features, which is the task of the typesetter, not the author or editor. Thus, all extra spacing between words and paragraphs must be removed during the editing process, leaving only single spaces, hard returns and tabs. Manual line, page, column and section breaks should be avoided and preferably removed altogether. (If it is imperative that a break should appear at a certain point — for example, before a figure or at a break in the narrative — then this is better indicated with a specific instruction to the typesetter.) Manual line breaks (or soft returns) that are being used instead of hard returns should be replaced with hard returns.

For details about how to use Find and Replace to make global corrections, see chapter 6.

soft return or **line break**
a break in text that creates a new line, but not a new paragraph; can be inserted manually or calculated automatically by typesetting software

Table 7.1: common global corrections that may be applied to
Word documents

Find what	Symbols/ characters*	Replace with	Symbols/ characters*
a manual line break in the middle of a sentence or paragraph	^l	one space	[one space]
a manual line break being used as a hard return	^l	a hard return	^p
a manual column, page or section break	^n ^p ^b	a hard return	^p
two spaces†	[two spaces] OR use wildcards: ([two spaces])@	one space	[one space]
a hard return followed or preceded by a space	^p[space] [space]^p	a hard return only	^p
a non-breaking space or hyphen	^s ^~	a normal space or hyphen	[one space] -
an optional hyphen	^-	nothing	[blank]
a space before a full stop, comma, colon or semicolon etc.	[space]. [space], etc.	only the punctuation mark	. , etc.
a space after an opening bracket	([space]	opening bracket only	(
a space before a closing bracket	[space])	closing bracket only	)

Find what	Symbols/characters*	Replace with	Symbols/characters*
straight quotation mark (single and double)	' "	typographic (smart) quotation mark (with Autocorrect on)	' "
a space before or after a tab	[space]^t ^t[space]	a tab only	^t
two tabs †	^t^t OR use wildcards: (^t)@	one tab	^t
a tab before or after a paragraph marker	^t^p ^p^t	a paragraph marker only	^p
two paragraph markers †	^p^p OR use wildcards: (^13)@	one paragraph marker	^p
a space before or after a hyphen	[space]- -[space]	an unspaced hyphen	-
a hyphen in a number span	use wildcards: ([0-9])-([0-9])- ([0-9])-([0-9])	an unspaced en rule between numbers (using wildcards)	\1–\2
a spaced en rule between numbers	use wildcards: ([0-9])-([0-9]) – ([0-9])-([0-9])	an unspaced en rule between numbers (using wildcards)	\1–\2

*Descriptions in square brackets (except when using wildcards) are used to indicate characters that are otherwise difficult to show in the table, such as spaces.
†For these searches, there are two methods possible: (a) using standard Find and Replace, repeat the first command shown until Word says that no replacements were made, and (b) using wildcards, use one instance of the second command shown to find multiple instances. See chapter 6 for further details.

Other global corrections might be applied differently, depending on the house style being used (see table 7.2 for some examples).

Table 7.2: global corrections that depend on purpose and house style

Find what	Replace with (according to purpose and house style)
a spaced or unspaced em rule	an unspaced em rule or a spaced en rule
a spaced or unspaced en rule	an unspaced or spaced en rule
an unspaced or spaced ellipsis	a spaced or unspaced ellipsis
double (to single) quotation marks	single quotation marks (except for quotes within quotes)
single (to double) quotation marks	double quotation marks (use *Find Next* and manual *Replace*)

Warning

It is important to note that while global corrections are great time-savers that help to achieve a high level of consistency, blindly applying them can lead to disaster. All such corrections must be thought through carefully and the results checked.

For this reason, it is best to perform all global corrections at the beginning of the edit, so that if anything unexpected has occurred, they will be found during the detailed copy editing process.

Should everything be recorded in Track Changes?

It is best not to record standard or minor global corrections (such as removing double spaces) with *Track Changes*, as they do not affect the content of the text and marking up all of them would make the amended text unnecessarily difficult to read. It is also usually not necessary or particularly desirable for authors to view styling changes, so it is also best not to use *Track Changes* to record those either.

Styling and editing text elements

After applying the initial global corrections, the editor will find it useful to go through the entire manuscript and apply the major electronic styles to the text (with *Track Changes* turned off), particularly elements such as the headings, body text, lists, block quotes, boxed and call-out text and table text, if present. This will impose a consistency in the text formatting that will help the editor to visually identify the different elements of the text and assist with the copy editing process. The editor can then turn on *Track Changes* and focus on copy editing the text itself, although of course the styles will need to be further refined and applied as required as the editing progresses.

block quote
a separate paragraph containing a long quotation, set differently from the main text, such as indented and in a smaller font

Even if using a publisher's pre-styled Word template, it is quite possible that the editor will need to create new styles to accommodate a particular manuscript. And of course in the absence of such a template the editor will be required to create the entire set of styles from scratch.

It is useful to create a separate style for typesetting instructions so that they can easily be found and removed before final publication. To make them stand out, it is preferable if the instructions appear in bold and in a bright colour.

Headings

Book and part titles

The title and subtitle of the publication and any section and chapter titles are all treated differently from text headings and should be given styles of their own (e.g. *Book Title*, *Book Subtitle*, *Section Title* and *Chapter Title*), to keep their treatment separate from the rest of the text. Note that ideally the book title and subtitle should have separate styles, as they are usually treated differently. Subtitles for section and chapter headings may also need to be styled differently (e.g. *Chapter Subtitle*), depending on the text design.

Provide any special instructions to the typesetter regarding the layout of the title page and part title in square brackets (e.g. [Part title on recto; leave verso blank]). If sections and chapters have their own opening pages, this should also be indicated (e.g. [Chapter opening begins] and [Chapter opening ends]).

It may also be necessary to create separate styles for the headings used in the prelims and endmatter, as these may be formatted or treated differently. For example, chapter titles in the main text may appear in a different format than the titles for the acknowledgements or appendixes, so for the latter it may be necessary to use a style such as *Prelims Title*. Such decisions should be made in consultation with the designer or typesetter.

Text headings

Text headings must be placed in a hierarchy in order to make it clear to the reader the relative importance and logical sequence of each section and its subsections. In hard-copy editing the editor would mark up the text parts using accepted conventions, such as writing A, B, C next to each heading to identify the heading hierarchy. In onscreen editing, editors use electronic styles to indicate the purpose of each text element. Thus, the first-level heading below the chapter title level is usually styled as *Heading 1* or *Heading A*, the second-level heading as *Heading 2* or *Heading B*, and so on. Ideally, text headings should not have more than four levels, as too many headings make the text difficult for the reader to follow and may indicate that there are structural problems within the manuscript.

Some parts of the prelims and endmatter of a book (e.g. an executive summary or an appendix) may also contain text headings, and these would usually be given distinctive style names too, such as *Heading 1 Prelims* or *Heading 1 Appendix*.

If there are any italic or bold words in the headings, these should be styled using character styles. As the fonts used in headings are often different from those used in body text, these character styles should have distinct names (e.g. *Heading Char Italic* or *Heading Char Bold*).

In complex texts such as scientific papers or reports the author may have introduced a numbering system for headings, with major headings numbered 1, 2, 3, subheadings 1.1, 1.2, 1.3, and the next level 1.2.1, 1.2.2, 1.2.3. If these heading numbers are referred to in the text (e.g. see section 1.3.2) then they need to be retained. The question then arises as to whether to number the headings automatically or manually. The advantage of automatic numbering is that if sections are moved or headings deleted or added the numbering will update throughout, without manual intervention, reducing errors and saving a great deal of time. Cross-references to these headings can also be automated, so that if a heading number changes, the reference to it does as well. This numbering also translates quite well to typesetting programs. However, if the heading styles have not been set up or used properly, automatic numbering in Word can sometimes work in mysterious ways, and undesirable outcomes can easily result. For example, the numbering can skip levels, or the cross-references can suddenly start generating errors. Manual numbering, on the other hand, can ensure that the intended numbering doesn't change and that the numbers are not inadvertently omitted when the manuscript is converted to the typeset document.

As mentioned in chapter 6, once the heading styles have been applied, it is useful to use *Outline View* in Word to check that the hierarchy is logical, consistent and correctly identified. This can also be used to check that the headings are parallel (use a similar structure), and to identify the shortest and longest headings to assist with the text design.

All headings should conform to the house style in terms of capitalisation, which will usually be either sentence case or title case. They should never be in all caps. If the headings are in all caps, it will be left to the typesetter to decide on capitalisation, which is not desirable. If small caps are to be used in the headings (increasingly rare), the editor should still apply the house style for capitalisation in Word; the typesetter will then apply the small caps formatting to the heading.

sentence (minimal) case
capitalising only the first word and any proper nouns in a heading, title or phrase

title (maximal) case
capitalising every significant word (excluding prepositions, articles and conjunctions unless they are the first word) in a heading, title or phrase

Capitalisation

There are a number of styles used for capitalising the titles in headings and bibliographic citations, ranging from minimal to maximal capitalisation, but they can be broadly grouped into two main types:

- *Sentence case or minimal capitalisation.* Capitalise only the first word and proper names (e.g. *The structure of the Australian economy: an American perspective*). Some editorial styles capitalise the first word of the subtitle as it is considered to begin a new part.

- *Title case or maximal capitalisation.* Capitalise all significant words, excluding prepositions, articles and conjunctions except when they start the title (e.g. *The Structure of the Australian Economy: an American Perspective*). Some styles also capitalise minor words if they are 'long' (e.g. four or more letters), or capitalise the second part of hyphenated words.

There are many minor variations to these approaches, so follow the house style if there is one, or choose one accepted style reference (such as the *Style Manual* or *The Chicago Manual of Style*) and be consistent.

Body text

The paragraphs in the main text form the bulk of most manuscripts and generally are set in the same typeface and size throughout. The main difference in treatment is how the beginning of a new paragraph is indicated. In most books, the first paragraph following a heading, an indented quote or a section break would normally be set full out to the margin. The first line of all other paragraphs is indented (traditionally by one em), and there is no extra space between the paragraphs. This convention was introduced to save space and therefore reduce page extent and printing costs, but it is also well suited to dialogue in fiction texts, as it reduces the space between the lines and therefore aids in fluid reading.

full out
type that is set so that all lines in a paragraph are flush to the left and/or right margin; the first line is not indented

Full-out paragraphs may be styled differently depending on what element they follow (e.g. *Body Text First* or *Body Text After Quote*), what the requirements of the text design are, and to allow for different treatments. The remaining (indented) paragraphs are usually styled as *Body Text*.

Where the commercial imperative to save space is less of an issue (such as in electronic texts or government publications), all paragraphs may be set full out, with extra space between each paragraph, so they can all be styled the same. Some texts use both devices (indenting and extra space) to denote new paragraphs, but this is overkill. Ebooks, despite not usually having page extent issues, often follow the print convention of using indented paragraphs, perhaps to retain an element of familiarity for readers.

Text breaks

dinkus
a typographic device (such as an asterisk, fleuron or other element) used to mark a break between text passages

If there needs to be a break in the text that is not marked by a heading, insert an instruction to the typesetter to this effect (e.g. [Insert text break here]). Such breaks may appear as simply more space between paragraphs. Sometimes, particularly in works of fiction, a typographical device (a dinkus)—such as asterisks, a fleuron or other ornamental element—is inserted to mark the break. If this might be appropriate, it must also be included as an instruction to the typesetter.

fleuron
stylised form of flowers or leaves that serves as a typographic device, used, for instance, to mark a break in text

Textual emphasis

Text may be emphasised using italics or bold, but these should be applied sparingly, otherwise the effect of the emphasis will be lost. Italics are normally used to denote titles of books and periodicals, names of plays and works of art, foreign words, scientific names of fauna and flora, words that are being used in a special sense and statistical abbreviations. Follow the house style to determine where to use italics. Bold text is used rarely in the body of the text, but is often used in headings, tables and captions.

To mark italics and bold text for the typesetter, character styles should be applied (e.g. *Body Char Italic*). A different character style needs to be created for each different context in which it is to be used, such as in headings, quotes, tables, lists and references (e.g. *Quote Char Italic* or *Reference Char Italic*).

In technical works, such as computer manuals, it is common to provide a different typographical treatment to instructions, software programming code and other special terms. For example, programming code is often formatted using a fixed-width serif font, such as Courier. Again, such special treatment should be indicated using a character style (e.g. *Program Code*).

Underlining used to be necessary to convey emphasis in typewritten text, but is almost never used in printed books as it obscures the descenders of letters such as 'g' and 'p' and can be mistaken for an internet hyperlink.

Special characters

Care needs to be taken when dealing with special characters, such as Greek letters, symbols, diacritics and fractions. The world of typefaces is a complex one and some typefaces contain larger character sets than others and are therefore more useful when there are special typographic requirements. Designers should be briefed fully on the nature of the text and any special characters that may be required so that they can choose typefaces that will suit the needs of the publication. For example, a publication on Māori culture would need to use a typeface that has the macron 'a' diacritic (ā), which many font families do not include. Likewise, scientific texts often require Greek characters, which may not be available in some typefaces. Do not assume that because the characters appear correctly in Word, they will transfer across to the typeset document.

All such special characters therefore need to be marked up using character styles and with instructions to the designer or typesetter to ensure that they are set correctly in the final publication.

fixed-width or **monospaced typeface**
a typeface in which every character takes up the same horizontal space

serif
short cross-line or stroke at the end of the main vertical or horizontal stroke of a printed letter

descender
the part of a letter that descends below the x-height or baseline of the text (such as in 'p' or 'y')

hyperlink
a virtual link or reference between elements within an electronic document or from elements within a document to an external file

Cross-references

Cross-references between parts of the publication must be checked carefully to ensure that they are correct, especially if section, chapter or caption numbers or page numbers are used. Preferably any use of numbers and heading titles should be inserted using Word's automated numbering and cross-referencing functions to ensure that if any parts are moved or deleted or added, or if headings are changed, the wording and numbering will update accordingly.

The editor should check with the typesetter that Word cross-referencing will translate correctly to the typesetting program. If not, occurrences of cross-references may need to be marked up manually in the text with the heading or caption title or number to be linked either included in the text or given as an instruction to the typesetter (e.g. see section 4.2 on page XX). It may be useful to highlight the placeholder for the page numbers with a brightly coloured and bold character style so that the typesetter can easily find them. All manual cross-references will need to be double-checked after copy editing has been completed, to ensure that they are all still correct and pointing to the appropriate places in the manuscript.

> **placeholder text** dummy text (e.g. XX) that is inserted in the early stages of editing and production to indicate where text needs to be updated

Footnotes and endnotes

Notes are mostly used in academic, scientific and technical works to provide reference sources and brief explanations of terms that are incidental and would otherwise unnecessarily interrupt the flow of the text.

For a detailed discussion of referencing systems, see chapter 8.

From the outset, a decision must be made as to whether such notes are to be included as footnotes, which appear at the bottom of the page where the footnote marker has been inserted, or as endnotes, which appear together at the end of the book or at the end of each chapter. The decision may be influenced by the type of referencing system used, the number of notes in the text, and readability considerations. Footnotes have the advantage of being easily accessible; the reader doesn't need to keep flicking to the back of the chapter or book to find the additional information. On the other hand, lengthy footnotes can take up large amounts of space on a page and even flow over two or more pages, hindering the smooth flow of the narrative. Footnotes also may not work in ebooks, particularly in the EPUB format, which have no set 'pages'; notes in ebooks are therefore usually treated as hyperlinks and take the reader to another part of the book, acting more like endnotes.

Where there are only a few notes, they are better presented as footnotes and may be indicated in the text with a footnote symbol such as an asterisk. The sequence of symbols to follow is: asterisk (*), dagger (†), double dagger (‡), section mark (§), parallel mark (‖) and hash mark (#), which restarts on each page. Alternatively, the last symbol can be a paragraph mark or blind P (¶). If more than six notes appear on the same page, the *Style Manual* recommends the symbols be doubled (e.g. ** and ††).

If the notes are extensive, they are better indicated in the text with superscript Arabic numerals that run sequentially through either the chapter or the entire book. In Word, note markers, whether symbols or numbers, can be generated and updated automatically by using the *Footnote* function under the *Insert* menu. Note that although the function is called *Footnote*, it can also be used to generate endnotes. When footnotes or endnotes are inserted in Word, they are automatically given the paragraph style names of *Footnote Text* or *Endnote Text* and the note markers have the character styles *Footnote Reference* and *Endnote Reference* applied.

Footnote text is usually separated from the main text by a line space, often with a short rule above the note. Endnotes appear in a separate list either at the end of each chapter or at the end of the book (often divided by chapters). Both footnotes and endnotes are set down (reduced) by about two points in type size and set as hanging indents, where the symbol or number 'hangs' out to the left, with the text of the note indented. If the sequence of numbers reaches double or triple figures, these should be aligned on the right (although this practice is becoming less common and it is impossible to achieve in most electronic publications). If right-alignment of note numbers is essential, the typesetter should be given a global instruction to do so.

set down
set type in a smaller size

hanging indent
type that is set so that all lines in a paragraph are more indented than the first line; the first line may be full out or indented

The editor should be aware that deleting footnotes or endnotes when in *Track Changes* mode means that the numbering of subsequent notes will not be updated correctly until the change has been accepted. To avoid confusion, it is a good idea to delete the note and then select the *Track Changes* balloon on the right showing the deleted note marker, right-click on the balloon and select *Accept Change*. All subsequent note numbers will then be renumbered accordingly. Note also that when a note is deleted, the text of the note is not included in the balloon and so is therefore not recorded as a change.

Quotations

Short quotations are normally enclosed in quotation marks and run into the text. The use of single or double quotation marks depends on the house style, but they should always be typographical, or curly or smart quotes (', "), never straight or dumb quotes (', ").

Longer quotations (the definition varies but may be, for example, any quote over 30 words) are usually set off without quotation marks in a new indented paragraph. By convention, such block quotations usually have extra space before and after the paragraph and are indented from the left and sometimes from the right as well. The text may be set in a different font type, size, face or colour. Block quotes are indicated by giving the paragraphs a different style name (e.g. *Quote*).

Any omissions within a quote should be marked with an ellipsis, which may or may not be preceded and followed by a space, depending on the house style. Ellipses should never be replaced with three full stops; not only can full stops be separated by a line turnover, but they are spaced differently and are typographically incorrect substitutions.

turnovers
the second and subsequent lines of a paragraph, bibliography or index entry

Lists

There are two main types of lists: numbered and bulleted. Numbered lists are those in which each item is part of a hierarchy or must follow a particular sequence, such as parts of a legal document or the instructions for changing a car tyre. Items may also be numbered if they are referred to in the text (e.g. see discussion topic 3). Bulleted lists are those where the items are not part of a hierarchy or sequence, such as a list of services provided by an organisation, although the items may appear in an order that links them in a logical manner or relates to the order of related elements (such as headings) in another part of the text.

Short lists can usually be run on within the text. For example:

> She had in her bag her usual mess of must-haves: keys, wallet, tissues and handcuffs.

However, even short lists may be set out for clarity and ease of reading where this is appropriate, such as in primary-level textbooks or in technical manuals.

The traditional method for setting out lists where the items are all fragments of the same sentence has the list following a colon, with each item numbered or bulleted and closed with a semicolon, except the last item, which closes with a full stop or other end punctuation. Sometimes the second last item ends with a semicolon and 'and'. This system is still commonly used in scientific, technical and academic publications. For example:

> The approach that will be taken is to:
> - establish the existing parking situation in the study area;
> - establish the parking demand likely to be generated by the new development; and
> - make recommendations regarding road and parking improvements.

Increasingly, lists of fragments are being set out with no end punctuation except for the last item (see the *Style Manual*). This is the style we have followed in this book. For example:

> The approach that will be taken is to:
> - establish the existing parking situation in the study area
> - establish the parking demand likely to be generated by the new development
> - make recommendations regarding road and parking improvements.

A less formal style has no end punctuation in the sentence fragments following the bullets, including the final fragment, which is popular for general and educational books and for onscreen publications as it is visually less distracting and reduces errors in punctuation.

If items in a list form full sentences, they should begin with a capital letter and end with a full point or other appropriate punctuation mark. For example:

> The following rights have been established:
> - You have the right to access the information relating to your child's progress.
> - You have the right to see any records relating to your child.
> - You have the right to stand for election to local school–parent organisations.

These differing systems of punctuation should not be combined within one list; however, it is acceptable to have different list types in the same work, depending on the context. In textbooks with separate exercises or activities sections, for example, it may be appropriate to use an open, informal style within the text, and a more formal style in the separate sections. Whichever list types are adopted (or dictated by the house style), it is important to ensure that all comparable lists use the same system of punctuation.

Tables

Tables are used to present information that can be related in rows and columns. Check all tables as a separate procedure to ensure consistent numbering and copy editing of the text. The copy editing should follow the same style as for the main text, even when the material comes from another source (unless the copyright owner has expressly forbidden this).

Check that the wording of the caption accurately describes the content of the table, and that all necessary information is included. All captions for tables that contain similar data should be consistent with each other in style and content. The captions should include the table number for cross-referencing purposes. If there are numerous tables, it may be advisable to number them by chapter; for example, as Table 1.1, Table 1.2, Table 2.1. In Word, this numbering can be automated so that the numbering updates when tables are moved, deleted or added. Once the caption numbering is automated, then any cross-referencing to those table numbers can also be automated.

The accompanying text should refer to or comment on the significance of the most salient information in the table, rather than simply repeat it. Consider whether the information is better given as text (or whether text should perhaps be presented as a table).

Tables should have their own set of style names to accommodate their different components and ensure consistency. These include styles for column headings, row (side) headings, text in cells (using different alignments, such as left, centred or right, or aligned by decimal point), bold and italic formatting, and table notes. Table cells that contain numbers are usually aligned by the decimal point and these should be styled as such.

When notes occur in tables, the superscript indicators are usually lowercase letters (a, b, c) rather than numbers, because table cells often primarily contain numbers. The note sequence should be self-contained for each table and not be included in the numbering of footnotes or endnotes in the rest of the document. In works containing statistical tables, asterisks and other symbols should not be used to indicate notes, as these often have a separate and specific meaning in statistics.

All numbers in tables should be checked for errors in addition, rounding or other mathematical inconsistencies. If a column or row should add to 100 per cent but the figures only add to, say, 99.9 per cent, it is likely to be due to rounding and this should be included in the table notes. Errors should be queried with the author.

Sometimes the tables are set up in the Word document as tabbed text, or worse, using columns. These must be converted to Word tables before they can be typeset.

Marginal notes

Marginal notes may be used to add further information, such as definitions of terms or linkages to another part of the book. As their name suggests, they appear in the margins and therefore are usually not very long. Marginal notes may present design problems, and the advisability of using such notes and how to set them up for typesetting should be discussed at an early stage in the publication process.

In Word, marginal notes may be inserted as separate paragraphs at the appropriate point within the running text. They should be styled appropriately (e.g. *Marginal Note*) and, if necessary, the words to which the notes refer may be highlighted or styled so that the typesetter can find them.

Text boxes

Text boxes are commonly used in textbooks and reports to highlight or focus on a topic, exercise, list, summary or other, often self-contained, material. They may vary considerably in length, from one or two sentences to whole pages of information. They should not be inserted using Word's *Text Box* function because such text

149

boxes are treated more like graphic objects and may not transfer correctly to typesetting programs. Text inserted in a text box is also not included in the word count, which may be undesirable.

It is preferable to include them in the appropriate place in the text, but style them separately. Boxed text should have its own set of styles to accommodate headings, text, bullet lists, notes and so on, because it is often set in a different typeface and font style. Although the styles themselves will tell the typesetter where the boxed text starts and ends, it can nevertheless be useful to insert simple instructions (e.g. [box starts] and [box ends]) to make this clear. It may also be necessary to give specific instructions, for example, if there are illustrations or other artwork to accompany the boxed text.

Other special material

Poetry

Poetry extracts can be treated typographically in the same way as text quotations, or separated from the text and set in text type. Very short extracts can be run into the text within quotation marks, with a solidus with a fixed thin space on either side separating the lines of poetry ('the moon / in June').

solidus
an oblique stroke dividing alternatives or ratios; not to be confused with the forward slash on a typical computer keyboard

If set off from the text, it is important to ensure that the lines are given their own electronic style to match their appropriate typographic treatment (e.g. *Poem Fullout* or *Poem Indent*).

thin space
a space that is one-fifth or one-sixth of an em wide

For complex layouts it may be necessary to create a different style for each type of line format (see figure 7.1). However, if the particular layout occurs only once or twice in the book, it may be easier to eschew styles altogether. Instead, replicate the formatting in Word (using margin indents and space before or after rather than tabs, spaces or returns) and provide instructions and a printout to the typesetter. If possible, discuss the layout with the typesetter to ensure that the instructions are clear and translated correctly.

The title and source of the poem should be given their own styles.

Figure 7.1: a complex poetry layout, styled and formatted

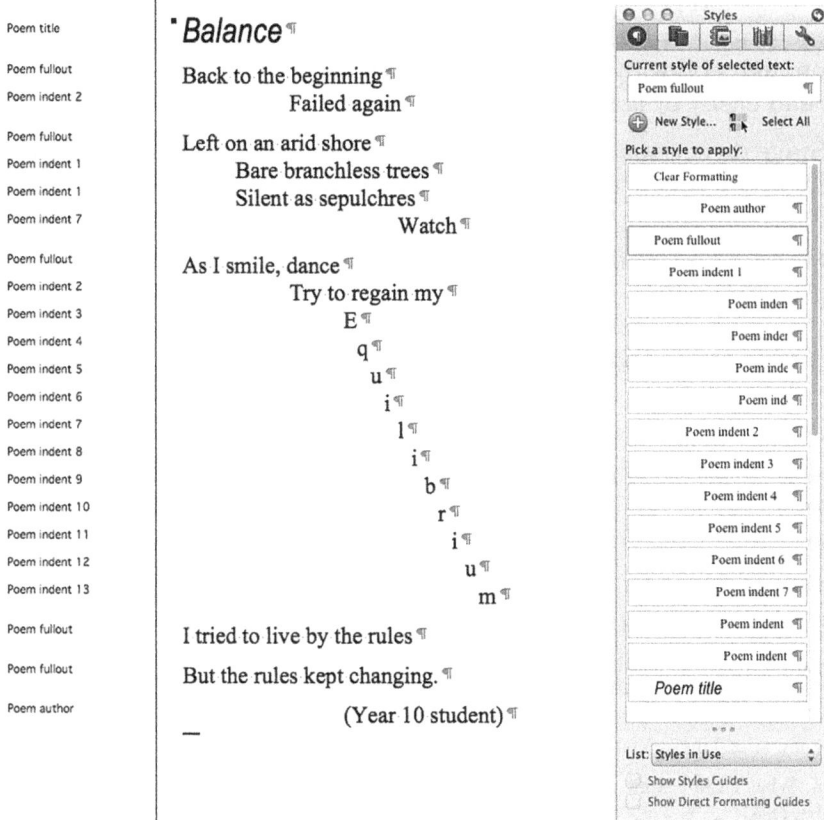

Play scripts

Certain conventions are normally followed when editing play scripts.

A list of characters should appear before the first page of the full text of a play. Acts are numbered in roman capitals, scenes in roman lowercase (e.g. Act I, Scene ii), and are usually placed on a separate line in the same typeface as the text.

The names of speakers should be set in small capitals. Each new speaker's name should begin full out to the margin, followed by a one- or two-em space, a full stop or a colon. The speech can either follow on the same line or begin on a new line, depending on the space available and the design.

The text may be tabulated or treated as hanging indents so that the speakers' names and their speech form two columns. If the material is to be used for performance, it should be set large enough and with sufficient leading (space between the lines) to be read easily by actors on stage.

leading or **line spacing**
the spacing between lines of type; not to be confused with paragraph spacing

Stage directions should be enclosed in square brackets and styled to be set in italics with no end punctuation (see figure 7.2).

Figure 7.2: a styled play script

ACT 1, Scene ii

[*Dave is lying on the couch with his feet up, reading a newspaper, when the doorbell rings*]

DAVE: Maree!

[*Maree comes out of the bedroom and lets Pete and Sharon in, while Dave continues to read his newspaper*]

MAREE: Coffee?

PETE: Be great.

[*Pete and Sharon remain standing while Maree goes into the kitchen area*]

PETE: Well, are you going to take it?

DAVE: What do you think?

PETE: You know what I think. You'd be letting the team down.

DAVE: Mmm. What I can't work out is why they offered it to me. Chip's the Number One.

Film scripts

Published film scripts differ from play scripts in a number of ways, although if there is a need to save space the dialogue may be set out similarly.

uppercase
capital letters, as distinct from lowercase letters

Scene indicators are set in uppercase, full out to the margin, and include the scene number (although it is becoming increasingly common to omit this), whether the scene is interior or exterior (INT/EXT), a brief location summary and the time of day (DAY/NIGHT/SUNSET).

Descriptive material is set in italics, full out to both margins, but is not enclosed in brackets. Character names within the description should be in capitals for the first mention in each scene, and thereafter in lowercase with initial capital only.

Names above dialogue are given in capitals, either centred or set out as for a play. Dialogue description—(*voiceover*), (*angry*) and so on—appears in brackets, in italics, all lowercase, either centred beneath the name or in brackets at the beginning of the speech.

Speech is indented at least four ems from both left and right margins under the speaker's name (see figure 7.3), unless set as for stage plays.

For discussion about broader editing approaches used with specific areas of editing, such as fiction and children's works, see chapter 10.

Figure 7.3: a styled film script

1   124   INT   LIVING ROOM   DAY

2   *The room is in chaos. Furniture has been slashed and overturned. There is broken glass everywhere and the television screen has been smashed.*

2   *INGRID enters.*

4   INGRID
5   Oh, my god!

2   *She moves dazedly towards a chair and tried to right it, but cuts herself on a sliver of glass.*

4   INGRID
3 6   (*calling*)
5   Sven!

2   *SVEN rushes in and stops in his tracks. Ingrid runs into his arms.*

4   SVEN
5   What is this, sweetie? Ingrid,
     what the hell is going on?

2   *It is only then that they see the foot protruding from behind the overturned settee.*

Final check

Whenever possible, read the entire manuscript one final time after the copy editing is finished. At the very least, check the heading hierarchy, all numbered and alphabetical sequences (including footnotes or endnotes), artwork and tables, and other text elements for consistency and completeness.

Check that all artwork has either had a draft version inserted or the position keyed in, and that all tables have been inserted in the correct position.

key in indicating the approximate position of artwork by inserting a note, comment or draft image in the manuscript

LIAISING WITH THE AUTHOR

Once the copy editing is complete, the editor sends the edited document, with its tracked changes and comments, to the author, either directly or via the project manager, usually by email. The editor should include a covering letter explaining in broad terms the level of editing and highlighting any issues that apply across the manuscript (such as an inconsistent use of voice). However, it is preferable to ensure that these are also included as comments in the Word document so that all issues are recorded in one place. The letter must be positive and polite, as with all correspondence with the author and others involved in the publication.

The author then reviews the tracked changes made by the editor. It is often preferable if the author leaves untouched all edits with which they agree and deals only with changes with which they disagree and with any author queries (using *Track Changes*). It is also best if they can use the *Comment* function to explain why they disagree with a change or to respond to queries. This will ensure that there is a record of all decisions made.

When the revised document from the author is received, the file is saved with a new name, using the naming conventions established for the project. In Word, the editor chooses to show only their own markup from the author's document (using the *Show Markup* option described in chapter 6). This will hide any changes made by the author. The editor then applies the *Accept All Changes Shown* option, which, as would be expected, accepts only those changes that are visible (in this case, the editor's original edits). The author's revisions are then made viewable again, leaving the editor with a relatively clean document to work on for the next stage. These steps, which can be repeated, save both the author and the editor from the tedious task of individually accepting each change at each stage of the editing process.

When the editor is preparing the final document for typesetting and is satisfied with the manuscript, the *Accept All Changes in Document* option will clear out all remaining tracked changes so that the file is cleaned up for typesetting.

DESIGN SPECIFICATIONS

When copy editing is completed the typesetter should be provided with details about the manuscript, such as:

- the title, author, series and other bibliographic details
- the format of the book

- estimated extent
- the parts of the book, including prelims and endmatter
- the artwork and permissions brief
- a list of tables
- a list of material that is still to come.

For more information about dealing with illustrations and other artwork, see chapter 9.

Even if the typesetter and editor are able to discuss the manuscript face-to-face, it is still essential that all the necessary information is put in writing, as a record and to avoid misunderstanding. For the same reason, the editor should always keep a copy of any written communications with the author, designer and illustrator.

Many publishing organisations also require that a list of all the styles in the manuscript be compiled, indicating the context in which they have been used, along with a description of how each style is to be typeset. There may also be instructions relating to how parts of the text should appear globally or in specific sections, including any special symbols that might require the use of particular typefaces. For example, it may be that all boxed text must be set in a different typeface from the main text, or there may be special instructions for setting student exercises in a textbook. This can be a two-way process, as the text designer may already have supplied a sample setting that shows how most of the components of the manuscript will be set.

Sample settings are often prepared by the designer before the text design is confirmed. The editor gives the designer a styled selection from the manuscript including sections of straight text and a full range of other book elements, such as part and chapter headings, subheadings, epigraphs, set-off quotes, lists, tables, figures, captions, appendixes, notes, glossary, bibliography and index. The designer uses these excerpts to create a sample setting that will accommodate all the required elements, including the longest headings and captions in the manuscript.

The sample setting is checked by the editor and publisher, and sometimes by the author. Some modifications may be necessary: type styles, sizes or leading may need to be changed, or spacing or other readability or design features may need to be adjusted. Once accepted, the chosen design can be implemented, corrections made and proofs prepared. A sample setting is also used to check whether it is possible to match the setting in a pre-existing or out-of-print book that is to be reprinted with corrections or revisions.

Editing practice: other elements

8

Although the text is the major part of any publication, the other elements—the prelims, endmatter, headers, footers and cover—are also important components. The editor must ensure that these are all compiled, complete and edited in preparation for publication.

For a description of the parts of a book, see chapter 4.

PRELIMS

Title page

At the outset, the editor should confirm how the author's name is to be expressed; for example, should it be *Jan Smith*, *J.W. Smith* or *Janice W. Smith*? Note that an author's honorific is not usually included on the title page, unless it is considered to be particularly relevant to the marketing of the book. For example, a book on managing Type 1 diabetes might sell better if the medical doctor who is the author is called *Dr*.

In multi-author publications it is important to establish which author's name should appear first; it cannot be assumed that the names will appear in alphabetical order of surname. For example, the name of the coordinating (contact or key) author may appear first, with the rest in alphabetical or other order; the authors may have agreed between themselves on an order of seniority, and this should be strictly adhered to in prelims and cover copy, and in all publicity material.

Imprint page

The editor should check the imprint information to ensure that all required elements are present and that there are no spelling or grammatical errors.

Some information, such as the name of the indexer or the printer, often cannot be added until late in the production process, so it is essential that these items are marked to be checked later so that the publication is not printed with the line 'Printed by [TBC]'!

Publication details

The publication details on the imprint page include:

- the name, address, website and branch addresses (including overseas offices) of the publisher

- the date of first publication, and the dates of all subsequent editions and reprints; often reprints will be indicated by the progressive deletion of the right-hand number from an initial printing carrying the line '10 9 8 7 6 5 4 3 2 1'

- the copyright notice with the symbol ©, followed by the name of the copyright holder(s), and the year of first publication of the current edition, along with the publishing history of all previous editions (giving the years and the names of publishers, if different from the current edition)

- the publisher's notice about conditions regarding any reproduction

- the CiP data, including the book's unique ISBN(s) and ISSN(s) (if applicable)

- the name (and location) of the printer

- optional information, such as the names of the editor, designer, typesetter, photographer, illustrator, cartoonist or cartographer, or a description of the typeface.

ISSN (International Standard Serial Number)
an international numbering system that identifies each serial publication (newspaper, journal, magazine, newsletter etc.) by a unique number

Cataloguing-in-publication data

The cataloguing-in-publication program of the National Library of Australia provides a system by which publications are catalogued before they are published. The cataloguing information is immediately made available online to librarians and the publishing industry to encourage advance orders and the speedy availability of publications in libraries and reference centres. The program also provides information on Australian publications internationally through online catalogue records.

It may be the editor's job to apply for CiP data. Freelance editors should find out whether this is part of their brief or whether someone in-house will do it. To apply for CiP data:

- obtain ISBN(s) or ISSN as appropriate (see the next section)

- complete an online CiP application (available on the National Library's website), including publisher details, publication details, author information, description of the content and publication format or edition

- attach a copy of the title page, the table of contents and publisher's blurb to the application, to help with correct cataloguing.

The application will usually be processed by the CiP unit of the National Library within 10 days. The CiP entry is printed on the imprint page under the heading *National Library of Australia Cataloguing-in-Publication data*. The entry should be set, line for line, exactly as sent. The only permissible editorial change is to convert spaced hyphens to dashes, according to the publisher's style, and the text may be ranged left or centred to suit the publication's design.

When the publication is printed, an advance copy must be sent to the National Library to fulfil the publisher's legal deposit obligations. A revised catalogue entry will then be published in the Australian National Bibliographic Database.

ISBNs and ISSNs

The CiP data will include the publication's International Standard Book Number (ISBN) or International Standard Serial Number (ISSN); if a book or report is part of a series, it may require both. These numbers identify a particular edition or format of a publication or a serial in a worldwide cataloguing system. ISBNs consist of 10 or (since 2007) 13 digits and ISSNs have eight.

ISBNs are purchased from the Australian ISBN Agency, administered by Thorpe-Bowker, while ISSNs are issued free by the National Library. Major publishing organisations usually purchase blocks of ISBNs (associated with that particular publisher), which they then assign to specific titles as they are published. ISSNs may only be issued after the first issue of the series has been published.

Each separately available edition and format of a publication (e.g. hardback, paperback, audiobook, ebook) must be given a different

range
to align elements either vertically (e.g. for line endings or a caption with an illustration) or horizontally (e.g. for table elements)

Legal Deposit Scheme
a requirement under the *Copyright Act 1968* for publishers to deposit a copy of any print work published in Australia with the National Library of Australia and the relevant state library

ISBN. A multi-volume work that is available both as a complete set and as individual volumes should have one ISBN for the set and different ISBNs for each volume in the set.

The ISBN for a new manuscript is usually listed in the publication file. If not, the editor should check with the project manager if the publisher already has a block of ISBNs from which to take the number. Otherwise, the editor may need to contact Thorpe-Bowker to purchase a new number.

barcode
a printed code for the ISBN and EAN, consisting of vertical lines of various thicknesses, to be read by an optical scanner

Printed and audio publications that are sold through retail outlets should also have barcodes that conform to the European Article Number (EAN) standard. These can be purchased at the same time as the ISBN.

EAN (European Article Number)
an international product numbering convention consisting of a 13-digit barcode

Foreword

A foreword should not be edited or altered in any way without the writer's permission, except to correct typographical or grammatical errors. If it is too long for the allotted space, the editor should obtain the writer's permission before reducing it.

Contents

The wording on the contents page must match exactly the wording of the headings in the text. Contents pages can be generated automatically in Word, using the *Insert Index and Tables* function and selected heading style names. Ideally, these should not be used in the final typeset document, but should be included in the edited manuscript so that the typesetter knows what level of headings to include in the contents of the final publication. The published table of contents should be generated by the typesetting program (based on the heading style names) so that page numbers and headings match exactly and are automatically updated if changes are made. However, the generation of such a list in either Word or typesetting programs can be tricky, especially if there are several parts to the document, so it is essential that the editor rechecks the contents page after editing, and again after proofreading, to ensure that the numbers correspond to the relevant part and chapter titles and headings.

List of artwork and tables

The wording used to identify artwork or tables in these lists should correspond exactly to the captions in the text. Again, these can and should be generated in Word and typesetting programs using the caption styles, but, as always, the editor should check that the captions and page numbers correspond with the text at final proof stage.

ENDMATTER

Lists of abbreviations and acronyms

Abbreviations and acronyms are usually presented in two columns, with the shortened form on the left and the expanded form on the right. Ideally they should be inserted into a two-column table in Word and sorted alphabetically (using Word's *Table Sort* function). This is preferable to simply using a tabbed list, as it provides the typesetter with more options for layout and ensures that full forms are not accidentally separated from their shortened forms.

The editor should carefully cross-check the abbreviations and acronyms to ensure that they are all included in the list and in the text, and that the full forms are accurate.

Glossary or chronology

Keywords and their definitions are also usually set in tabular format, in two columns, with the keyword on the left. In a long and detailed glossary the definitions may follow straight on from the term to save space, with turnover lines indented one or two ems. If turnovers are set flush to the margin, adequate space should be inserted between entries to improve readability.

Glossaries are arranged alphabetically, which is easily achieved using Word's *Table Sort* function. If the list is extensive, it may be useful to group the entries in separate tables under each letter of the alphabet.

It is important to ensure that only appropriate words relating to the text are included in the glossary. It is crucial to recheck this if large parts of the text have been deleted or amended since the glossary was created. Take care that the spelling of names, political groups, and foreign words and phrases is the same in the glossary as in the main text.

Foreign words that are not in common English usage are normally set in italics in the text. If many of the keywords in the glossary are not English, the glossary should be set in roman type, with only other foreign terms in italic. If a lowercase style is to be used for keywords, any proper nouns should retain their initial capitals.

If cross-references within the glossary are necessary, use *see* and *see also*, both italicised. *See* cross-references can be set off from the definition with a space, a comma or a colon. If the definition ends with a full stop, capitalise the *See also* cross-reference; otherwise use lowercase after a colon. Check after editing is completed that no cross-referenced terms have been deleted or changed.

Chronology entries must be in date order and be checked very carefully for accuracy. Entries must also match the dates and information used in the main text.

Other lists

If lists of contact names and addresses are included, check the accuracy of the information where possible, and try to ensure that telephone and fax numbers, and email and website addresses are up to date.

If the list is divided into sections under subheadings, check the alphabetical order within each section. The editor will also need to check:

- consistency in spelling and abbreviations (e.g. avoid using both *St* and *Street*, *Rd* and *Road*)

- consistent and appropriate use of names of states (e.g. *NSW* and *WA* in a telephone directory; *New South Wales* and *Western Australia* in an electoral directory)

- that postcodes and telephone area codes are listed.

Delete punctuation at the ends of lines, and style the text and any headings appropriately. Lists in the endmatter should have their own suite of styles (e.g. *Resources Heading 1* or *Resources List Bullet 1*) because as a whole they may be treated in a different way typographically (e.g. set in a different typeface or font size).

In a resources list of suppliers, include a brief description of the organisation along with their website address. It may be preferable not to include details such as prices or even contact details, because this type of information can change.

Appendixes

Appendixes are usually numbered using Arabic numerals (e.g. Appendix 1, Appendix 2) or letters (e.g. Appendix A, Appendix B). It is a good idea to use the opposite system to that used in the main text; thus, if chapter numbers use Arabic numerals, the appendixes should use letters, and vice versa. This practice makes it easier for readers to distinguish between the two sections. Roman numerals may also be used, but these are harder to read and can become unwieldy if there are many appendixes.

Appendixes may be set in a different typeface or size or in a different layout, again to allow readers to more easily identify the separate sections. Any tables, figures or notes in the appendixes should be numbered distinctively; for example, if tables in the text are numbered from Table 1.1, tables in appendix A could be numbered from Table A.1. Endnotes specific to an appendix should be self-contained within that appendix.

If the appendix material has been written by the author, copy edit the appendix to conform with the rest of the text. If it comes from another source, treat it as a quotation, and include a precise source and acknowledgement; if the editor finds an occasional misspelling, the insertion of '[sic]' after the word is permissible. Ask the author to supply footnotes for clarification if necessary. Ensure that permission to use the material is obtained. Proofread the material, and make permissible house style corrections such as dashes and spacing, but otherwise keep to the original.

References and bibliographies

If possible, discuss the bibliographic system to be used with the author at an early stage in the preparation of the manuscript, and provide guidelines on house style. The author–date system is commonly used in academic and government publications, while the footnote or endnote system of citation is widely used in legal and historical works.

Academics often use an automated referencing system such as EndNote, which can output the bibliographic data in a large number of different styles. However, even software programs cannot prevent misspellings and inaccuracies from being introduced during the data entry process, so whatever method is used by the author, editing references and bibliographies often takes up a large amount of time.

It is a good idea to edit the bibliography or references before beginning work on the text. This will familiarise the editor with the authors and titles, and will reduce the amount of work required in cross-checking if inconsistencies are discovered in the bibliography.

When editing onscreen, the most efficient way to cross-check entries between either the notes or the author–date references in the text is to print out the edited references and cross each one off as they are mentioned in the main text. This serves three purposes:

- to check that citation details in both the text and references match and are free from errors and inaccuracies

- to make sure that all the items in the references are mentioned at least once in the text and that no citations mentioned in the text are missing from the references

- to alert the editor when a multi-author work has been cited more than once (which often entails different rules for listing authors; see later in this section).

Cross-checking can also be achieved entirely onscreen by either splitting the Word window or opening the references in a new window; however, the constant need to switch between windows or panes is cumbersome, even if the editor has the luxury of having a large monitor.

If there are any discrepancies or any missing information, these should be queried with the author. If the matter is minor, such as a missing page number or year, it may be easier for the editor to check this through an internet search. Obviously if the reference is missing entirely or there is doubt as to which reference is being cited, then only the author can answer those questions.

Follow the house style, or a style agreed with the author, for all references, which may vary depending on whether the publication is intended for an academic, general or educational market. There are a number of systems of referencing, including those described in the *Style Manual*, *The Chicago Manual of Style*, the *Australian Guide to Legal Citation* and the *American Psychological Association [APA] Publication Manual*, to name just a few. Each has its own system of setting out the information in a citation, including:

- *punctuation*, with some using mainly commas, others full points

- *alphabetisation*, with some alphabetising word by word, others letter by letter

- *capitalisation*, with some using title case and others sentence case

- *use of quotation marks*, with some using quotation marks for article titles, others not

- *inclusion of elements*, with some including more information than others

- *order of elements*, with, for example, the date following the authors' names or appearing at the end of the citation

- *abbreviations*, with some using standard journal title abbreviations and others spelling them out

- *numbering of volume, number and pages*, with each using different combinations of brackets, colons and commas.

There are also different systems of referring to the source within the main text. In the notes system, following the initial full entry any succeeding references to the same source can refer to the author by surname only, together with a short title (essential if two or more publications are by the same author), or to the author only, followed by 'op. cit.' or 'ibid.'. These abbreviations are often confusing to an inexperienced editor or author, and, because many readers are also baffled by them, it is becoming common practice to use a short title instead. However, in academic and technical publications they are still frequently used, so it is important to know what they mean and how they work. Likewise, when using the author–date system, in the second and subsequent mentions of multi-author works, the author names may be shortened using 'et al.', which is frequently incorrectly punctuated. Note that these abbreviations are not capitalised or italicised.

Referencing abbreviations

- The abbreviation 'op. cit.' is used in the second and subsequent references to a particular publication or article using the notes system, and follows the surname only of the author of the work. It means 'in the work cited' (that is, the title of the publication).

- The abbreviation 'ibid.' means 'in the same place'. It is used to indicate the publication or article given in the note or entry immediately preceding the present one. Include a page reference only if it differs from the page reference already given.

- The abbreviation 'et al.' (meaning 'and others') may be used after the first full reference to a multi-author work in the main text when using the author–date system. It follows the name of the first author, and usually indicates more than one other co-author (although this practice varies).

If source details are to be presented in an abbreviated form in the notes, ensure that the bibliography or list of sources provides the full information.

If the bibliography is annotated, allow a line space between entries. The annotation may be run on after the title entry or set on the following line, indented to match the turnover lines.

Where a title ends with a question or exclamation mark, do not add a full point. Remember that punctuation marks that are part of an italicised title (such as a colon between title and subtitle, or a question mark at the end of a title) must also be italic.

Tables 8.1 and 8.2 illustrate how citations can differ depending on the style manual adopted and whether they are notes or author–date systems.

Table 8.1: examples of citation systems for notes

Style rules	Example citation in the notes (first mention)	Example citation in the bibliography
Style Manual	S Heller & V Vienne, *100 ideas that changed graphic design*, Laurence King Publishers, London, 2012.	Heller, S & Vienne, V 2012, *100 ideas that changed graphic design*, Laurence King Publishers, London.
The Chicago Manual of Style	Steven Heller and Véronique Vienne, *100 Ideas That Changed Graphic Design* (London: Laurence King Publishers, 2012).	Heller, Steven, and Véronique Vienne. *100 Ideas That Changed Graphic Design*. London: Laurence King Publishers, 2012.
Australian Guide to Legal Citation	Steven Heller and Véronique Vienne, *100 Ideas That Changed Graphic Design* (Laurence King Publishers, 2012).	Heller, Steven and Vienne, Véronique, *100 Ideas That Changed Graphic Design* (Laurence King Publishers, 2012).
APA Publication Manual	Note system not used	Note system not used

Table 8.2: examples of author–date citation systems

Style rules	Example citation in the text	Example citation in the references
Style Manual	(Heller & Vienne 2012) or Heller and Vienne (2012)	Heller, S & Vienne, V 2012, *100 ideas that changed graphic design*, Laurence King Publishers, London.
The Chicago Manual of Style	(Heller and Vienne 2012) or Heller and Vienne (2012)	Heller, Steven, and Véronique Vienne. 2012. *100 Ideas That Changed Graphic Design*. London: Laurence King Publishers.
Australian Guide to Legal Citation	Author–date system not used	Author–date system not used
APA Publication Manual	(Heller & Vienne, 2012) or Heller and Vienne (2012)	Heller, S., & Vienne, V. (2012). *100 ideas that changed graphic design*. London: Laurence King Publishers.

Editing bibliographies and references—a checklist

- Check organisation of the citations under relevant headings.

- Check alphabetical order of the references according to the house style.

- Check consistency in the use of authors' given names or initials.

- Check consistency of abbreviations for words such as *edition*, *volume*, *number* and *page(s)*.

- Check the order of elements as per the house style.

- Check consistency of all punctuation, capitalisation, italicisation and quotation marks (if any).

- Is there any missing information?

- Are there any inconsistencies between the bibliography and the notes or in-text citations?

Acknowledgements

For further
discussion about
copyright and
permissions, see
chapter 5.

All copyright material (original text or poetry, extracts from letters, diaries, newspapers, websites, artwork of all types) must be acknowledged, and permission sought and received before the material can be reproduced. Many publishers add a disclaimer in an attempt to protect themselves against any dispute about permission or copyright ownership. However, such a disclaimer has no standing in law, so it is best to be very wary of using material for which there is no written permission from the copyright owner.

If the copyright owner stipulates a particular form of acknowledgement, this must be followed exactly, particularly if the material falls under US copyright law. If no precise wording is given, be brief and consistent.

Acknowledgements may be arranged alphabetically by source, with the page reference at the end of each acknowledgement, usually in brackets, and with a space between each item; or the page number may appear first, followed by a colon, with the items in order of appearance in the text. This second method makes the source of the material more readily accessible for anyone trying to trace it, especially if the page reference is given in bold.

If not listed by page number, poetry should be listed alphabetically by author surname, with the first or given name or initials following the surname. Give the title of the poem (in quotation marks), followed by the other source details: publisher, place, date, edition and page number (if known).

Where several copyright items share the same source, these may be grouped (e.g. pp. 17, 28, 121, National Library of Australia; pp. 19, 35, *Financial Review*).

If space is a problem, all acknowledgements can be listed alphabetically by author source and run on; however, this makes locating a source more difficult, and also poses problems when inserting new acknowledgements in later editions.

When there is more than one piece of artwork per page, they should be identified according to their position on the page (e.g. p. 64 (top), p. 72 (centre), p. 146 (lower left)).

Figure 8.1 illustrates two styles of presenting acknowledgements.

Figure 8.1: formats for presenting acknowledgements

Acknowledgements

The author and publisher wish to thank the following authors and publishers for permission to reprint copyright material:

> **p. 62**: 'A Very Special Day' from *Memories of Mother Earth*, © Martha Seger 2004, reprinted by permission of Barnaby & Sons; **p. 84**: *Who Knows When the Sun Will Return?*, © James Brumby 2012, Mitchell Books; **p. 103**: *We'll be Back*, © Felicity Watson 2009, Sunday Publications.

Acknowledgements

Sources of illustrations are as follows:

Sunday Times: Figs 3.2, 4.7, 7.1

Smithsonian Institution, Washington DC: Figs 3.1, 5.4, 6.2

RUNNING HEADS AND FOLIOS

If the publication is to have running heads, the wording should be confirmed at the copy editing stage so that the running heads can be included in the design. Running heads are used mainly in reference books and textbooks. However, they may be included in general books and even some fiction books, where they would be helpful to the reader.

Running heads appear at the head of the page, or sometimes at the foot (when they are called, rather charmingly, running feet), separated from the text and often combined with the folio (page number), which is set at the outer edge. In computer programs these are more commonly called headers and footers.

The typesetter can create master headers and footers to ensure consistency, as well as generating them automatically to make sure that they match the chapter and part titles exactly, even if they are changed later on. Titles can be read from the titles that appear in the main text, providing styles have been applied correctly. Even dictionary headers can be automated by telling the program

head
the margin from the top of the page to the top of the type area (text block)

foot or **feet**
the margin from the bottom of the type area (text block) to the bottom of the page

to insert the first and last entries on the page as the headwords. Again, this requires accurate and consistent application of styles.

It remains for the editor to specify what should appear in the running heads and feet, and where. In deciding whether there should be running heads and what form they should take, think about how the reader will use the publication. Traditionally, the following conventions are used:

- If the main text is organised in parts, the part title will appear on the verso running heads, and the chapter title on the rectos.

- A simple textbook with no part divisions will have the book title on the verso running heads and the chapter title on the rectos.

- A complex reference book might have the chapter title on the verso running heads, and the section of the chapter on the rectos.

- Many fiction books do not have running heads; if they do, a common style is to place the book title on the recto and the author's name on the verso. If there are chapter titles, the chapter title usually appears on the recto and the book title on the verso.

- Running heads for prelims and endmatter do not include the book title, but repeat each prelim and endmatter heading on both verso and recto (e.g. Notes, Bibliography, Index).

- In endnote running heads (particularly in heavily annotated academic texts), for ease of use include the chapter or page numbers; for example, 'Notes (Chapter 1)'; 'Notes (Chapters 2–3)', where endnotes for the next chapter begin mid-page; or 'Notes (pp. 14–17)', where a small number of endnotes for several text pages occur on one page.

The editor should indicate in the page design brief when a chapter or section must start on either a verso or a recto.

Folios also tend to be placed according to certain conventions:

- Prelims are usually paginated separately, using lowercase roman numerals.

- The main text pages are usually numbered with Arabic numerals.

- In most books, the folios form part of the running heads, but sometimes they are placed at the centre or outer edge at the foot of each page.

- Where chapters have a foot folio only, the folio should be centred or aligned on the outer edge.

- Many fiction books without running heads include a decorative element in the folio design.

- In dictionaries, the folio may be centred in the running head between the headwords.

Folios should not appear on any of the following pages (although they are included in the pagination):

- blank pages

- the half-title and half-title verso

- the title and title verso (imprint page)

- the dedication page

- a page carrying an epigraph or an illustration

- the first page of the contents and other lists in the prelims

- part titles (and blank versos, if part of the design).

Running heads and folios are usually omitted on pages with full-page turned tables or artwork, and on those including artwork that extends (bleeds) into the margin where the header or number would usually appear. However, the sequence should be arranged so that no more than two consecutive text pages appear without a running head or folio.

To avoid confusion, running heads should be set in a style that differentiates them from the text headings, and are usually set down a point size from the main text. They may be set in italics or small capitals, but this can cause complications if the running heads include words that should be italicised, especially if the heading appears directly under the running heads. The design may include decorative elements to separate chapter titles and folios.

Long titles should be reduced to a manageable length. It is useful to provide the designer with the longest running head to ensure that this will suit the design. Make sure the author sees and approves any abbreviated headings.

COVER COPY

Editors are often required to organise the copy for the front cover, the spine and the back cover of the book.

Ebooks, of course, do not have spines, back covers or dust jackets; however, the front cover should match the text of the print version

bleed
the part of an artwork or other element that runs out past the edge of a printed page; when the page is trimmed, there is no space between the edge of the page and the artwork

spine
the binding edge of a book's cover or jacket; the outside of the spine is visible when the book is stored on a shelf

thumbnail

a smaller version of
an image, such as a
cover, that is used in
publishing catalogues
and on reading devices
to more easily identify
a book

(if there is one) and the designer should consider if the cover design works both in print and as a thumbnail (in a reduced size) in ebook readers. Blurbs are also used on websites and e-stores to help market the ebook.

Front cover

The front cover copy carries:

- the title and subtitle

- the author name(s), in the order in which they appear on the title page

- the edition number if this is not the first edition

- the publisher's name and logo.

It may be necessary to omit the subtitle if there is insufficient space. It is vital that the names and titles on the front cover match those on the title page, and that the names are spelt correctly and in the desired form and order.

flash

a design element
added to a book cover
to draw the reader's
attention to a special
aspect of the content,
such as a new edition
or map inserts

The front cover may include promotional material, such as a flash indicating a new edition, a pertinent quote or an accompanying website.

Spine

The spine will include:

- author surname(s), and often the first name as well

- the title (usually without subtitle)

- the publisher's logo or company name.

Some book spines place the author name first, while others start with the title. Some paperbacks include the ISBN on the spine. The copy may run either from the top down or across, depending on spine width and design.

Check that the order and spelling of the author name(s) are the same on the front cover, spine and title page.

Back cover

The back cover of a book may carry:

- the blurb (see later in this chapter)

- a barcode that incorporates the ISBN, the EAN and often a price code, which must match the information on the spine and in the CiP data

- an author photograph

- a subject classification

- quotes or extracts from the book

- the publisher's name and website address.

Some organisations also include catalogue numbers or in-house reference numbers on the back cover, or categories for shelving in bookshops or newsagents.

Dust jacket

Most hardback books have dust jackets that differ from paperback covers in a number of respects. The front cover and spine copy generally match those for paperbacks, but the blurb is usually placed on the inside front flap, while the author biography and photograph are placed on the back cover or on the inside back flap. A long blurb may carry over from front to back flap, with the biography and photograph placed below this or on the back cover. The back cover usually contains the barcode (including the ISBN), the publisher's name or logo, and a website address. Again, check that the information on the cover (title, author, ISBN etc.) matches the CiP entry.

When a book is published with a dust jacket, the front and back hard covers are normally left blank, but the spine copy is usually repeated on the case spine. This is known as die copy, and should be presented to the printer as separate cover copy.

There is a growing trend for hardcover publications to dispense with the dust jacket and print the copy directly onto the case; the cover copy will then follow the conventions for paperback publications. Alternatively, there may be both a dust jacket and a printed case.

Case copy

If a publication is to be presented as a boxed set or in a presentation case, separate case copy must also be prepared. This may be identical to the dust jacket or printed cover, or the publisher may choose to feature additional information, such as a listing of the publications contained in the set. Again, the title, author and other details must be carefully checked against the cover and CiP, as well as the dust jacket, if there is one.

dust jacket
the wrapper around a hardback book, giving publication information, and designed to protect the case and attract attention

case (binding)
the assembled front, back and spine covering material into which the book block is bound

die copy
copy, such as author and title, printed on the spine and case of hardback books

Blurbs

The blurb usually appears on the back cover of a paperback or the front flap of the jacket of a hardback. It may be written by the publisher who commissioned the manuscript or by the author, but frequently it is the editor's responsibility. Notes from the publisher and the draft blurb included with the author's questionnaire may offer some guidance, but otherwise the editor must rely on their knowledge of the manuscript's content, the profile of the author(s), and the market.

The blurb is an important part of the sales strategy for any publication. It is one of the first things that people look at when they pick up a book, and needs to be compelling enough to entice them to buy it. The blurb is also frequently used as the basis of the publisher's catalogue entry and other marketing material.

Depending on the kind of publication and the market, the blurb needs to catch the reader's attention; explain why this book is better than all others of its kind; advertise new, controversial or particularly useful attributes; and describe the qualifications and experience of the author(s).

The blurb for a novel will aim to catch the reader's imagination, whereas the blurb for a secondary educational text will focus on its relevance for a particular syllabus and promote it as the most up-to-date textbook on the market. Adjectives commonly found in fiction blurbs include *extraordinary*, *passionate*, *powerful*, *haunting*, *spine-chilling*, *turbulent* and *compelling*. The paperback edition of a previously published hardback will often carry selected excerpts from published reviews. Language commonly used in the blurbs of educational and reference texts includes *new*, *expanded*, *thoroughly revised*, *extensively illustrated*, *with accompanying website materials*, and a paragraph will often be devoted to the experience and qualifications of the author(s).

To decide on the style of the blurb, the editor should write down all the marketing strategies included in the background information received with the manuscript and list the main strengths of the book that relate to these marketing strategies. Add any other outstanding features (e.g. original maps, lively cartoons, multinational recipes or adherence to a recently revised standard), and then draft and redraft, aiming for language that is lively and accessible.

Many inexperienced editors worry about writing blurbs. Like all skills, good blurb-writing technique can be acquired with practice.

One of the best exercises an editor can use for improving their blurb writing is to write a rough blurb for every publication they read, non-fiction or fiction, then compare it with the existing blurb. The editor will soon begin to see what makes a good or poor blurb, and how different styles suit different markets, age groups and tastes. Figure 8.2 shows examples of blurbs that might be written for different markets.

The publisher, the marketing department and the author will check and often suggest changes to the blurb before it is approved and signed off.

Figure 8.2: blurbs for different markets

Myths and Landscape in Australian Film (academic text, 364 pp)

This book examines the way in which cultural myths in Australian feature films reflect changing political and social attitudes of their times. The myths up to and including the 1970s were male, Anglo–Celtic, colonialist myths. The next two decades witnessed a slow but dramatic return of all those whose presence had been excluded or repressed—indigenous Australians, women, multicultural Australians. By following this progression through Australian films up to the present, the book is able to map the journey from a monocultural, masculine myth of 'Australianness' to the plurality of depictions of 'Australians' now made possible by the deconstruction of those earlier myths.

An important feature of this book is that it examines the different paths taken by different fields of film—drama, documentary, comedy, even children's film—drawing on examples of the films themselves, and also on critical reviews, both contemporary and retrospective, to place each path in the context of what was happening at the time these films were released.

Each section is generously supported by stills and quotes from a wide range of Australian films, making it a valuable text for students of media studies and Australian history. Professor Mary Rowan has drawn on a lifetime's study of both local and world film to produce a work of great significance about Australian national mythology.

(continued)

Figure 8.2: blurbs for different markets *(cont'd)*

The Lady in the Tomb (detective thriller, 500 pp)

On a snowy Christmas Eve, the Cathedral in the Marsh is unusually well attended. A rumour is circulating that the tomb in the Lady Chapel has cracked open, revealing the body of a young woman, newly dead.

Many locals believe that the original occupant, Lady Mary Bernard, herself gruesomely murdered in the 15th century, has claimed her own victim. But Detective Euan Partridge has seen the state of the body. To make sure he never sees anything like it again he enlists the help of forensic historian Henrietta Talbot.

Author Tessa Molloy is at her spine-tingling best as Detective Partridge once again finds himself in a world where nothing is quite as it seems.

Mary, Mary (picture book for ages 3 to 6, 24 pp)

Mary wants to go outside but she can't find her shoe.

Where can it be?

Not under the bed.

Not in the toy box.

Join Mary in her search as she looks high and low in some surprising places.

Can she find her shoe?

9

Editing practice: artwork

Chapters 7 and 8 discussed copy editing techniques used to deal with the text in a book. This chapter looks at the editing and management of artwork.

Artwork brings a text to life and helps to explain or illustrate concepts that might otherwise be difficult to describe in words alone. All artwork that is intended to add to the reader's comprehension, including diagrams, maps, graphs and technical drawings (that is, other than purely decorative images), should be described and referred to in the text and any important features should be pointed out.

If the author is thorough and well briefed, the editor will not have a great deal to do in organising any artwork required for a publication. The author will provide the artwork in suitable formats, numbered in sequence, with all label copy consistently prepared, and inserted (keyed in) to the appropriate places in the manuscript. The editor need only check the artwork for content and suitability, and ensure that it has been appropriately referred to in the text, and that the numerical sequence is correct before compiling an artwork and permissions brief. If the brief has not been followed, however, the editor will need to do more work to organise and key in the artwork.

format (artwork) the method of encoding a digital image to suit particular purposes (e.g. JPEG for raster images or AI for vector images)

All original artwork should be supplied electronically if possible. A range of formats could be supplied (see later in this chapter), depending on the nature of the images. If the artwork has been supplied in hard copy only, the publisher may arrange to have it scanned so that everyone can work from electronic copies. All supplied artwork must be checked for suitability by the designer, publisher and editor.

Each image file should be named with a sequential figure number that matches the text, including chapter number if required, plus a brief description of the figure (e.g. Figure 5.4 Maslow hierarchy). As usual, the original files must all be stored in a secure archive and copies made for working on.

If the artwork is to be handled in hard copy, two photocopies must be made of all the paperwork: one set for the editor's reference and the other to stay with the original artwork for the publisher and designer. Attach abbreviated labels securely to the back of each illustration (do not use paperclips) and include the chapter and figure numbers. Double-check that all artwork has been keyed into the text. The originals should be stored untouched until passed to the designer, with photocopies marked up to indicate any suggested cropping, edits to labels or other changes to the content.

Publications such as art, children's, cooking, educational, medical and geography books usually contain colour illustrations, but as colour printing can be expensive it is not used extensively in most general books. One way to introduce colour at a lower cost is to print using two colours, usually black and one spot colour, such as in this book. Ebooks can include colour images at no additional cost; however, it must be remembered that many older ebook reading devices cannot display colour.

After reading the manuscript the editor may feel that some artwork proposed by the author is unnecessary, inadequate or inappropriate, or that additional images are required. Any changes to the artwork and permissions brief should be discussed with the publisher and the author, as they may affect the costing of the book.

If it is necessary to commission illustrations that are not the author's responsibility, decisions about which illustrator to use are made by the publisher, designer and editor, sometimes in consultation with the author, depending on the nature of the book and the artwork required. If the author does not know how to organise the artwork efficiently, the editor may need to assist or be asked to obtain appropriate images, either from sources provided by the author or publisher, or through picture research.

PICTURE RESEARCH

Picture research is normally the responsibility of the author, although the publisher may decide to employ a professional picture researcher where this is warranted. Sometimes the editor will be asked to find appropriate roughs for line illustrations, such

For more details about handling printed photographs, see the 'Photographs and scans' section later in this chapter.

cropping
trimming or masking off unwanted portions of an artwork

spot colour (printing)
a coloured ink that is pre-mixed so that it can be printed in a single run rather than using CMYK or other colour combinations that require four or more runs

as parts of the body or clothing styles of a particular period, or photographs or paintings of a particular bird or flower. Picture research is easily done through the increasing number of websites that offer rights-managed and royalty-free photographs and illustrations (and sometimes even video, audio and animations). These sources allow the editor to search for photographs by subject, colour or black and white, picture orientation, the presence of people, animals or other features, and many other attributes. The sites also allow the user to download a free 'comp', which is a low-resolution, watermarked version of the photo that is used for drafting layouts. Longstanding sources of professional photography — such as Corbis Images, Getty Images, Newspix and AP Images — are particularly useful for journalistic photographs and very high quality images. However, these can be very expensive and images are often rights-managed, so many publishers use semi-professional royalty-free sources like iStockphoto, fotolia or Fotosearch, or find public domain or low-cost images using search engines such as Google Images. Large publishing organisations often buy subscriptions to royalty-free stock libraries so that the whole library is accessible for a reasonable cost.

Apart from commercial sources, many major public photographic collections, such as those of the Australian War Memorial and the National Library of Australia, have been or are in the process of being digitised and made available online. This makes photographic research relatively straightforward, requiring only an internet connection and some relevant keywords. However, many photographs are still only available in physical form, so finding those still requires contacting the relevant organisation by email or by visiting in person.

The author, permissions assistant or editor each will review the photographic brief, and group material likely to be obtainable from the same source. Military images, for example, may be obtained from the Australian War Memorial (for Australian or New Zealand subjects) or the Imperial War Museum in London (for British and European). Major metropolitan newspapers keep extensive files of photographs of public figures and important events, and will often be the best source of photographs of politicians or sporting stars, or globally significant events such as space launches, earthquakes and the Olympic Games. National and state libraries can often supply photographs of historical figures as well as famous contemporary figures (scientists, writers, musicians and artists), and most national and state galleries take high-quality photographs of the paintings in their collections. Museums and government research organisations are good sources for scientific illustrations.

rights-managed image artwork that is licensed for one-off, limited use, e.g. for a specified duration or location, with any further uses requiring the payment of additional royalty fees

royalty-free image artwork that is licensed with a one-off fee that allows reuse over an unlimited period without the need for the user to pay further royalties

For a detailed list of image sources, see appendix 11.

For more unusual photographs, the editor may need to research books on the subject, referring to their source acknowledgements to find out where they obtained their photographs. The key is to be resourceful. For example, for photographs of trains or agricultural machinery, try the publicity section of the relevant government department; for workers in a particular industry, ask the relevant trade union body.

If the editor is required to assemble the artwork, sources should be contacted early in the editing process, listing the material required in as much detail as possible. If a copy of an Australian painting is needed, give the name of the artist, the title of the painting and its date if known; if a photograph of a politician or other prominent figure is required, indicate whether it should be contemporary or relating to a particular event; if the photograph is to illustrate something described in the text, send a copy of the relevant text. It can be useful to search online for an image that is either a copy of what is sought or something that is similar, which can be sent along with the request in order to improve the chances of finding the correct and appropriate artwork.

Picture research can be creative and challenging, but it is often time-consuming and expensive. The publisher will normally expect the author to carry out the basic research, although a permissions assistant may then send out the request letters, based on a detailed list compiled by the author or, more commonly, by the editor. It is important to stress to the author early in the development of the artwork list that if photographs that have appeared in other publications are to be used, the author must provide both the title and publication details of the original book, along with any acknowledgements giving the source of the photograph. If the photograph is from a source other than a book, complete details of the owner of the copyright should be supplied, so that permission and a copy of the original photograph can be sought.

A wide variety of artwork materials could be required for the publication, and each will need to be dealt with differently, depending on the type of publication, the type of artwork and the format in which it has been supplied.

IMAGE FORMATS

Editors may not be expected to deal with the more technical aspects of artwork management, such as checking image quality, ensuring that the file format used is appropriate and that the paper quality is suitable, or accurately sizing each illustration, but it is important to have some understanding of the technical aspects of artwork reproduction in order to be able to flag likely problems, such as if a low-resolution format suitable only for ebooks is being used for high-resolution printing.

There are two broad types of graphic files that are used in publishing: vector and raster images.

Vector images are based on mathematical formulas that form a picture by creating lines that join specified points, rather like a 'join-the-dots' puzzle. Because they are based on formulas, the file sizes tend to be relatively small and they are almost infinitely resizable (limited only by the capabilities of the devices used to reproduce them). They do not lose quality, no matter how large or small they are. It is also relatively easy to change any colours used, either to different colours or to greyscale. In fact, all digital typefaces are vector-based, which is why they can easily be scaled up or down, and made bold, italic and so on.

greyscale
gradations of tints between black and white; sometimes simply called black and white

Vector images are best suited to illustrations that have defined areas of flat colours or black, including:

* logos

* technical illustrations or diagrams, such as flow charts, graphs, maps or cutaway models

* crosswords and other puzzles.

A common file format for vector images used in publishing is AI (Adobe Illustrator). EPS (encapsulated postscript) and PDF are also commonly used, but technically these can also contain raster images. Unfortunately, none of these formats can be used directly in EPUBs or on websites.

PPI (pixels per inch)
the density of pixels in an image; the higher the density the higher the resolution (quality) at which the image may be printed

Raster images, on the other hand, are based on pixels—tiny digital squares of different colours or greyscale tints that combine to display images. Usually, the more pixels per inch (PPI) in the image, the higher the resolution and quality at which the image may be reproduced. Low-resolution images are usually unsuitable for print reproduction as they will appear pixellated or blurred (see figure 9.1, overleaf), but may be suitable for ebooks or websites, which generally require a lower PPI.

pixellation
the unwanted visibility of individual pixels, rather than smooth gradations, in a raster image when it is reproduced at a larger size than the resolution allows

Figure 9.1: vector images (left) look good at any size; low-resolution raster images (right) can become pixellated if enlarged too much

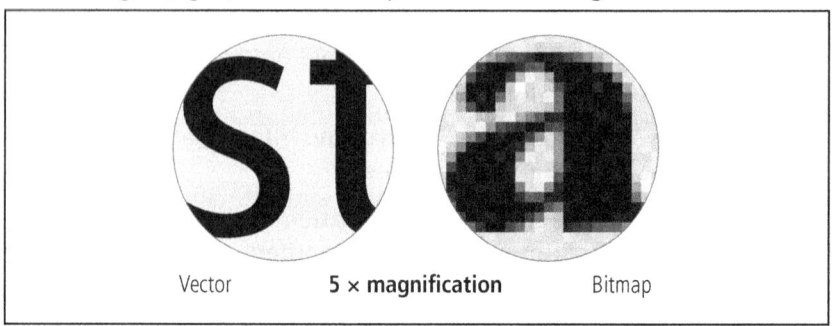

Vector   **5 × magnification**   Bitmap

Although file sizes may need to be quite large, the raster format is ideal for displaying gradations of complex colours or greyscale, such as in reproductions of:

- paintings

- photographs

- freehand drawings such as handwriting, cartoons or sketches.

It is also the only type of graphic file that will support duotone printing, where (usually) greyscale artwork is overlaid with one other contrasting colour. Duotones are widely used for adding interest and contrast to photographs; for example, to create a sepia effect, or when full-colour printing is considered too expensive but two-colour printing is affordable.

Common file formats for raster images used in print publishing are: TIFF (tagged image file format), JPEG (Joint Photographic Expert Group) and BMP (bitmap). PNG (portable network graphics) and GIF (graphics interchange format) files are highly compressed formats that are commonly used for ebooks and websites, particularly as substitutes for vector images.

sepia
a warm tone added (usually digitally) to a black-and-white photograph and printed using the duotone method

Some types of artwork, such as cartoons and maps, may be supplied in either vector or raster format, depending on the nature of the illustration. A cartoon, for example, may be drawn freehand and supplied as a scanned raster image or may be drawn in a vector program in the first place. Most modern maps are computer-generated as vector images, but older hand-drawn maps would usually need to be scanned as high-resolution raster images.

For more information about ebook production, see chapter 15.

Because of the need to ensure high-quality production in print publications, the editor should keep a sharp eye out for images supplied by the author that are low resolution rasters or in an inappropriate format. If, for example, the author supplies a raster image that is a colour photo of a painting meant to occupy a whole page in a printed book, but the file size is small—say, 1 MB (megabyte)—then it is highly likely that the image will not be suitable for reproduction, and this will need to be flagged with the publisher and designer. A common rule of thumb is that images to be printed should be about 300 PPI at the reproduction size. Images destined for ebooks, on the other hand, need only be between 72 and 96 PPI, depending on the reading device. An author may also supply images in PNG or GIF formats for a print publication, but these are inherently low quality, even if they are supplied at high resolution, because they are compressed formats and are therefore unsuitable for reproduction. In these situations, the publisher and designer need to be alerted to the problem.

> **MB (megabyte)**
> one million bytes of electronic data

Note that the reverse situation, where the image supplied is of high resolution and quality but is only to be used in an ebook, should not cause problems. This is because raster images do not lose quality when they are scaled down, only when they are scaled up.

Low-resolution watermarked raster images are often used by typesetters to place draft images (comps) into a typeset document. Once they are approved, the typesetter will replace them with high-resolution versions. Editors and proofreaders need to check the final pages proofs carefully to ensure that all comps have been replaced with high-resolution images.

> For further information about proofreading, see chapters 11 and 12.

LINE ILLUSTRATIONS

Line illustrations are distinct from photographs because they rely heavily on lines to denote edges and shapes, rather than on shading or colour. They include technical and scientific illustrations, maps, logos and freehand drawings.

Technical illustrations

Complex technical illustrations (e.g. circuitry diagrams, architectural drawings and cutaway models) are often generated in specialist programs, such as statistical software or CAD (computer-aided design) tools, and therefore can usually be output as vector files. These can then be easily resized and modified (such as by changing the colours or text) if required.

Authors may create simpler diagrams (e.g. flow charts, graphs and molecular structures) using one of the Microsoft Office programs. For example, they may use the *SmartArt* function in Word, Excel or PowerPoint to create a flow chart, or they may use Excel to create a graph or pie chart. The advantage of this is that the labels in all of these can be checked by the editor within the Office program to ensure they are free from spelling errors and other inaccuracies. It is then usually possible to export the diagrams as vector files for further design work (e.g. to make them match the size, colour and style used in the book). However, artwork produced in this way can be so unattractive or poorly laid-out that designers often prefer to recreate the diagram completely. This can permit spelling and other errors to creep back into the artwork, so the editor must carefully check redrawn illustrations.

If only a hand-drawn rough is supplied, the designer, illustrator or typesetter will need to start from scratch. The instructions for the roughs must be detailed and all lines and labels clear to minimise errors. If there are a lot of labels, the editor may need to type them out (and edit them) for the illustrator.

If technical artwork from another source, such as a published book or article, is to be reproduced, then permission and, if possible, the original artwork needs to be obtained. Illustrators may also be asked to create artwork based on an existing illustration, in which case the new artwork must be clearly differentiated from the original.

The illustrations should be checked carefully for appropriateness and inaccuracies. Questions the editor should ask include:

- Does the illustration aid understanding?

- Does it clearly show what is intended?

- Are all the required elements included?

- Are there any elements that are unnecessary?

- Do the labels in the diagram match the terminology and style used in the text?

- Does the illustration match the description in the text?

- Is the illustration drawn accurately? Do lines meet precisely? Is the perspective correct?

- Do the colours, shapes and shading used help to clarify relationships?

- Are elements of the diagram appropriately distinguished from each other?

- Is the illustration a reproduction? Have permission and the original artwork been obtained?

Maps

Maps may be generated by a software program, scanned from an original (with permission), redrawn from existing maps to include only the required information, or drawn from the author's roughs.

Maps may be drawn initially by the author as rough freehand illustrations, then passed to an illustrator or cartographer. Simple maps (of black lines and type on a white background) are usually created as vector graphics. If a map contains continuous tones, it may be treated in the same way as a photograph.

If permission is being sought to use an existing map that exists only in hard copy, a high-resolution raster scan may be supplied on request (usually for a fee). If parts of different maps are being combined or scanned, or if part of an existing map is being redrawn, it is important to apply for permission for any original concepts included on the map. If, for example, only the outline of Australia along with the major cities and ports is being used, this would not require permission, as this information is in the public domain. However, if a map of Ludwig Leichhardt's 1848 expedition is to be reproduced from an original map devised by the author of a history of Australian exploration, the editor must note that permission is required.

For more information about permission requirements, see chapter 5.

Maps should be as clear and simple as possible. If another map is being used as a source, eliminate any information not relevant to the current author's purpose. If a map is to be drawn from a rough, examine it carefully to ensure that it does not include unnecessary detail. Should it cover the whole of New Zealand's North Island or just Tongariro National Park, with perhaps a small inset to show the park's position on the map? A map should give all the information required for the particular context, and no more.

Check that all the information the reader will need in order to use the map effectively is included on the rough: a comparative distance scale, a compass point (usually showing at least 'N' for north), latitude and longitude lines, or other geographical information. This is particularly important in, say, a secondary-level geography book in which exercises follow the map, or if the map has letters and numbers in a grid, as in a street directory. Check the author's roughs with relevant atlases and reference books to verify that contours are accurate and that borders and names of places are up to date, before passing the rough to the illustrator.

Except in the case of a reproducible copy of an original map, new labels must be created to fit the style of the book. The conventions traditionally followed for labelling maps are:

- countries and other major political divisions—roman caps

- towns—roman bold, caps and lowercase

- oceans, mountains and other major geographical bodies—italic caps

- rivers, lakes and other minor geographical bodies—italic caps and lowercase

- villages—roman caps and lowercase.

Unless the book contains only a few illustrations, number the maps separately from other artwork, according to chapter (e.g. Map 6.1, Map 6.2).

Freehand drawings

Freehand drawings include illustrations, cartoons, sketches and other drawings. As the name suggests, such illustrations are traditionally created by hand and then scanned for reproduction in a book. However, many illustrators have now moved to creating such illustrations using software programs that convert their freehand drawings directly into vector-based art, thus allowing the images to be easily edited and resized to suit the requirements of the publication.

Sometimes the author will supply rough drawings or specifications for the artwork to be drawn by an illustrator. The editor must check any roughs and specifications against the manuscript to ensure that the planned artwork is necessary and appropriate, and within the publication's budget, before an illustrator is commissioned. If line drawings are requested by the publisher, the editor may be asked to prepare an illustration brief.

Ensure that the illustration brief includes information about the market—particularly the age group being addressed—and a reminder, if appropriate, to avoid stereotypes and to include representation of a wide range of possible readers. The editor may need to specify any particular points referred to in the text that must be reflected in the illustration. For example, if the text describes the different stages of development, including size, of an embryo, the illustration should show these differences.

Particularly when working from hand-drawn roughs, the illustrator may not immediately recognise the points that need to be emphasised. For a complicated or technical image, provide the illustrator with a copy of the manuscript to enable a better understanding of the publication's direction and content.

PHOTOGRAPHS AND SCANS

The author may supply photographs that they have created themselves (such as medical imaging photos or photos of a historic landmark). These days, photographs are usually taken with a digital camera and so are already digitised, ready for reproduction.

The author may also supply digital scans of printed photographs, art or other images. However, for reproduction in printed books, digital photos must be high-resolution raster images, as free from flaws as possible, well-lit, well-composed and in focus. In reality, unless the author is a skilled photographer, uses scientific imaging devices or is knowledgeable about scanning, self-taken photographs may not meet these criteria. The editor may need to ascertain whether the photographs supplied are meant to be merely indicative of what is required (in which case the photograph will need to be replaced using a good stock-photo archive or a professional photographer), or whether the exact photo must be used, for example, because it is an image of a one-off event (in which case the editor will need to flag the quality issues with the designer and publisher to see if the problems can be rectified or if the photo should be used at all, as well as ensuring that permission for its use has been obtained).

The author may also supply printed photographs or film transparencies or negatives to be scanned by the designer. The best sources for scanning are film transparencies or negatives, because prints are not as high quality as the original. If only a printed photograph is available, then glossy prints on good quality unglazed photographic paper are preferable.

Reproducing photographs directly from another book is rarely satisfactory, although authors frequently believe it is acceptable. It may be possible to obtain the original print for a fee when seeking permission from the artist or photographer and the owner (e.g. the museum or gallery, private collection or corporation holding the work). However, if the original photograph is not available, scanning it directly from the printed book may be the only option. Keep in mind that photographs printed in books lose detail, and unwanted (moiré) patterns are often evident. If permission cannot be obtained, do not use the photograph.

moiré
unwanted patterns that appear in images in printed books due to the overlaying of printed dots during the printing process

Photographic prints should be scanned as soon as possible to avoid excessive handling, and because it is easier to manage digital assets. The resulting scanned files must be clearly labelled and, if appropriate, any identifying information, dates, photographer name and other details should be recorded in the metadata of the file (using a program such as Photoshop). This ensures that all the data associated with the photograph is embedded in the file and cannot be misplaced.

The prints themselves must be stored carefully in a labelled box of suitable size, in padded envelopes or in folders between stiff cardboard. Identifying information should be written on a label, then attached to the back of each print using archival tape to avoid damage. Never write on the back of a photograph: pressure marks may show through when the photograph is reproduced. For the same reason, do not use paperclips or bulldog clips on prints. Prints should be returned to the author or owner as soon as practicable after scanning to avoid loss or damage.

With digital photographic processing, it is very easy to edit photographs to suit the requirements of a publication, such as cropping out parts of the image, erasing or adding people or objects, changing colours and even distorting shapes. Some types of editing might be acceptable (such as cropping the image to focus on the most relevant part), while other types might be considered unacceptable (such as manipulating a photograph of a person so they look younger or older, or adding in people who were not in the original). The line between acceptable and unacceptable editing can be blurred, and the editor should look out for potential overstepping at all times. For example, is it acceptable to remove a bystander from the edge of the photo in order to be able to focus on a particular person? What if the bystander is a person whose presence might contradict or change the nuance of the narrative?

If suitable photographs cannot be obtained, sometimes they may need to be commissioned. Compile a detailed brief for the designer, photographer or photo stylist listing what photographs are required. Occasionally, especially if a staff photographer is used, the editor (and sometimes the author, especially for recipe books) may be required to attend the photographic sessions to offer helpful or creative suggestions, or help in setting up or providing props. All commissioned photographs, including cover photographs, should be approved by the publisher, editor and author to ensure that they fulfil the brief and are appropriate to the text.

CAPTIONS

Artwork that adds to the content and understanding of the book, such as photographs and diagrams, should include a caption describing the image. Decorative images do not have captions.

Captions should be as brief as possible, while including all necessary information. If they do not form full sentences, they should not include end punctuation. All captions should be consistent; if some contain one or more full sentences, all of them should be rewritten to conform, with appropriate end punctuation. Sometimes authors include substantial information in a caption that should be transferred to the text. If long explanatory captions are required, they should supplement the text, not repeat it.

Captions should be electronically styled and ideally be included at the appropriate point in the text, along with an instruction to the typesetter (e.g. [Insert figure 3.4 near here]). It is also useful to insert a low-resolution digital copy of the required illustration, as this helps the typesetter to identify the correct figure to use rather than having to rely only on a file numbering system, which sometimes changes during editing (see figure 9.2).

Figure 9.2: figure inserted in a Word document showing caption, source and typesetting instruction

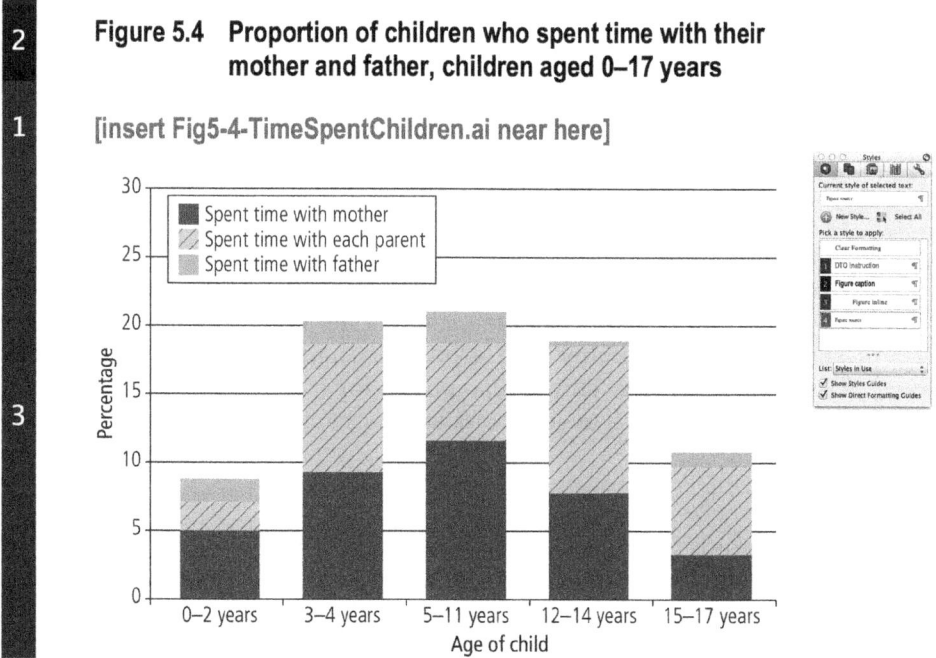

Figure 5.4 Proportion of children who spent time with their mother and father, children aged 0–17 years

[insert Fig5-4-TimeSpentChildren.ai near here]

Source: Australian Census 2006

For more
information
about ebooks,
see chapter 15.

Note that some house styles require captions to be placed above the figure, while others dictate below. In ebooks it is better to place the caption above the figure, especially if there are hyperlinks to the figure captions from other parts of the book; if the caption is below and a reader is directed there by hyperlink, the caption will appear at the top of the page and the reader will have to scroll up in order to see the figure itself.

Source lines acknowledging the use of copyright material may be required to appear with the illustration to meet the copyright owner's requirements or, in the case of graphs, to show the reader where the data came from. These should be included with the caption in the appropriate place in the text (see figure 9.2) and electronically styled as a source line. If it is not stipulated that sources should appear with the illustration, they may be placed in the list of illustrations in the prelims, or listed in the source acknowledgements.

Usually captions are numbered. If there are numerous figures (or tables), the author or editor can use Word's caption numbering and naming function (*Insert Caption*) to ensure that the numbering is sequential. This is particularly useful if the text is restructured and figures have to be moved around, as Word will then automatically renumber them. Captions can be numbered sequentially throughout the book (e.g. Figure 1, Figure 2), sequentially within each chapter (e.g. Figure 4.1, Figure 4.2) or sequentially according to illustration type (e.g. Figure 1.1, Graph 1.1, Map 1.1). The word *Figure* may be spelt out or shortened to *Fig*. Even if captions are not numbered, the illustrations themselves are usually numbered for easier management.

An easy way to check the correct sequential numbering and consistency of captions is to use the *Table of Figures* function found in the *Index and Tables* dialogue box under the *Insert* menu in Word. This allows the editor to compile a table of figures based on the figure captions' electronic style. Once created, the editor can easily spot if any figures have been numbered incorrectly or if any are missing. This is also useful for checking in one place that all captions have used a consistent structure and format.

LABELS

Any labels for new or redrawn artwork must be edited and typeset in a consistent style. This includes checking that the labels are appropriate and none are missing, the terminology matches that in the text, capitalisation and punctuation are used consistently, and spelling and grammar are correct.

If the author has prepared diagrams using the Office suite of programs, the editor may be able to edit these directly in Word. Mostly, though, the illustrations are likely to be images that are only editable using specialist programs or that are indicative roughs.

For illustrations that have just a few labels and need only a little editing, the amendments can be given as simple instructions in the illustration brief, or marked up on a hard-copy or digital version of the image (see figure 9.3). Where there are substantial amendments to be made, it may be more appropriate to retype all the labels and indicate on a digital or hard-copy version of the image where they are to be placed or replaced. Some figures are further complicated by the fact that different labels must be treated in different ways. In a complex map, for example, the editor might need to electronically style the labels according to their different uses (e.g. city names, geographic features, country names). The illustrator will then decide how best to format them.

For more information about adding comments using Adobe Acrobat, see chapter 11.

Figure 9.3: editing labels using Adobe Acrobat's commenting features

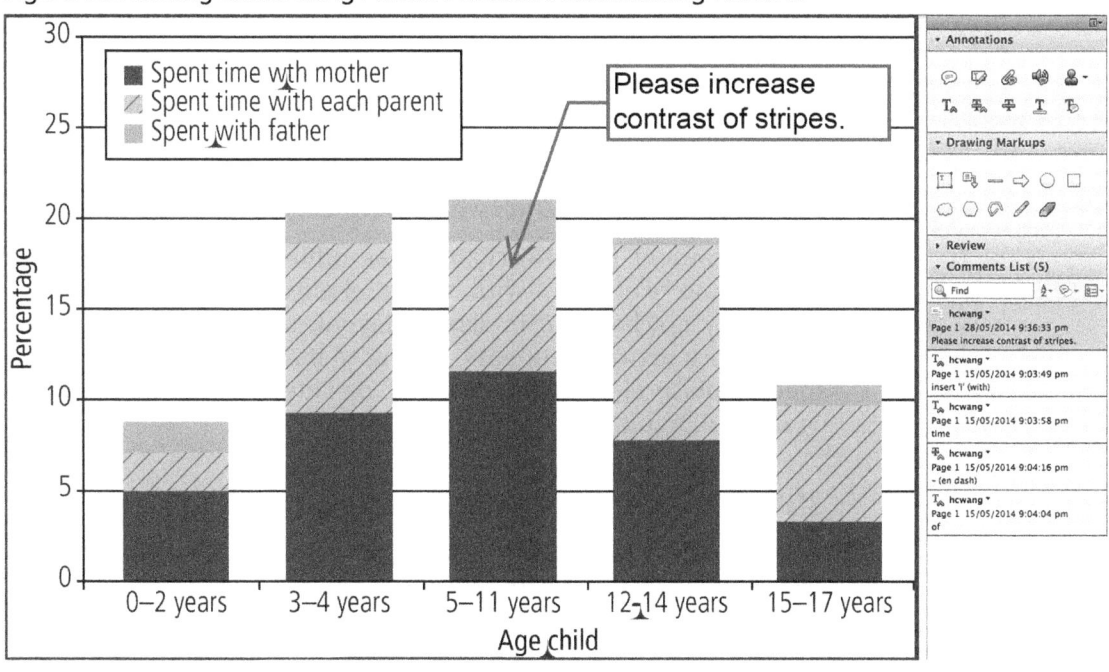

PLACEMENT OF ARTWORK

By convention, artwork should appear immediately after the first paragraph in which it is mentioned. However, the constraints of a printed book mean that it is not always possible to insert artwork exactly where required in the typeset layout, so the typesetter will insert it as close to the position marked as possible, but always after the first text mention.

If an illustration must be placed in a particular position, add a note to indicate this. If the artwork does not fit, it may be necessary at the proofreading stage to insert, delete, transpose or even rewrite some text to adjust the fall of the pages appropriately. If figures need to be placed side by side or in a particular position in relation to the text (e.g. in a children's book, an art book or an instruction manual), provide instructions or a rough layout or storyboard for the designer. This can easily be done in a word processing program.

storyboard
a rough layout of the text and artwork elements in a publication, provided to a designer

Wherever possible refer to all artwork in the text by number (e.g. see figure 12.8) rather than referring to it by position (e.g. 'see below' or 'see left') because it is not possible to guarantee that such positions will be retained during the layout process.

It is vital to ensure that all artwork is keyed in, numbered and placed correctly, particularly if other illustrations have been inserted or deleted. Leaving out an important illustration can mean having to repage the whole chapter, or even the entire book.

For more information about ebooks, see chapter 15.

The placement of artwork involves different considerations in EPUBs and websites. With these electronic publications, the page may not be fixed in size or layout, so there is less control over where artwork appears. Trying to make figures appear in a specific place on a page or sit side-by-side with specific text can be more difficult.

BRIEFING THE DESIGNER AND ILLUSTRATOR

All artwork should be listed in an artwork and permissions brief (see appendix 3), giving details of:

- the author and title of the book

- the chapter number

- the figure number

- a description of the artwork

- the source or possible source of the artwork

- type of artwork (photo or line drawing)

- the file name of the artwork

- whether it has been supplied by the author or is still to be obtained or drawn

- the file format used or required

- whether it is to be in colour or black and white

- whether permission must be sought or fees paid

- any other issues, such as notes about the appropriateness or quality of the artwork.

This information is usually prepared in a spreadsheet program such as Microsoft Excel or a database program such as Microsoft Access or FileMaker. This allows the information to be sorted according to different categories, as required. For example, the artwork could be sorted in standard numerical order, or by type of artwork, or by whether permission has already been sought and obtained. In this way, it is easy to identify all the artwork that needs to be handed off to an illustrator or be scanned, or all the items that need to be chased up for permissions.

For more information on how to obtain permission to reproduce artwork, see chapter 5.

If new illustrations are to be created, the editor may need to write an illustration brief for the illustrator, listing what is needed in each piece of artwork (see appendix 4). If the author has provided roughs for the illustrator, ensure that they are accurate and appropriate. Any labels must be checked for spelling and grammar, and the artwork must match the description given.

COVER ARTWORK

The editor works closely with the designer, and sometimes the author, on the choice of artwork for the cover of a publication. An illustrator, cartoonist or photographer may need to be commissioned, or a picture library may be used. The proposed design then has to be approved by the marketing department, and the publisher or managing editor.

Covers are normally printed in four colours but some have additional spot colours or include embossing, foils, forme cuts (such as rounded corners) or other decorative features.

Covers of government and corporate publications may include logos. Organisations can spend considerable money and time creating their logos and often have very strict guidelines as to how they may be used. The Commonwealth Government, for example, provides specifications for the size, layout, colour and positioning of the Australian Government logo, along with the circumstances under which it can and cannot be used. Editors should ensure that logos are reproduced according to the organisation's requirements, especially in regard to position, orientation and colour.

10

Specific areas of editing

The amount and type of editing required is partly dependent on the type of publication. Although the general principles of editing are the same for all publications, there are areas where particular knowledge or skills may be required. This chapter gives an introduction to some specific areas of editing.

FICTION

Editing fiction requires special skill and sensitivity. In non-fiction publishing it is usually quite clear what should be done about unusual grammar or punctuation, misspelt words, sexist or racist material, disorganised structure or ambiguous writing. In fiction the editor must not only discover whether these things are intentional or unintentional, but also be able to help the author to decide whether they are acceptable or not in the context of that particular book.

Even more than in non-fiction publishing, this is the author's book. The editor's role is to make sure that it is the best possible version of that book, not to rewrite it into another kind of book altogether. A fiction editor has to make judgements about the world an author has created or presented, rather than the world as the editor would like to see it. The question is 'Does it work?', not 'Do I like this?'.

Ideally, the editor should like the book and understand the author's aims in creating it, and then look for any matters of structure, language, punctuation, voice and style that do not work towards those aims. All editors need to be tactful, but a fiction editor needs to be exceptionally so. Even clear-cut matters such as missing plot strands, characters who appear then disappear never to be seen again, or dead spots where the narrative gets stuck, need to be treated gently; the author may believe they serve a literary purpose that is not apparent to the editor. In this case, all the editor can do is point out the problem and leave it for the author to think about.

How much editing is needed?

It is always difficult to know how much editing is needed on a work of fiction. This may depend very much on the author, and on the author's relationship with the publisher. Some authors are aware that their grammar and spelling are not good, and are grateful for the work of an experienced copy editor. Others use grammatical, spelling or punctuation variations as literary devices, and will be furious if so much as a comma is altered.

If there are many unintentional typographical or grammatical mistakes, this will usually be apparent. But what of intentionally naive or ungrammatical structures? Or a spelling or grammatical fault that appears to be making a literary point? The best thing to do is to ask the author (tactfully, of course) to confirm that its use is intentional. If, for example, French words are misspelt in a piece of dialogue, but spelt correctly in the rest of the text, the editor might ask, 'Am I right in assuming that these words are incorrectly spelt to indicate Michael's ignorance of French, or should we correct them?' If the errors are intentional, this gives the author the opportunity to think again about the reader's possible reaction to them. If they are not intentional, this is a polite way of pointing them out.

Special problems

Although many copy editing concerns, such as headings, tables and endmatter, do not normally arise in fiction, issues such as consistency, copyright ownership and potential libel or defamation should be kept in mind. For example, an author who has based characters on a real family may use their fictional names most of the time, then lapse and use a real person's name on one or two occasions. Keeping a word list of names of characters and their age and appearance, places, streets, houses and so on is extremely valuable, as authors frequently change such details as they draft and redraft, and it is very easy for an earlier usage to slip through. For books with a number of related characters, drawing up a family tree can also be very helpful in keeping track of who is who, and preventing such inconsistencies as a character being referred to as Tran's niece on page 32 and then as his cousin on page 105.

The editor must be alert for any quoted material requiring permission for reproduction, such as poetry or song lyrics. It is also becoming increasingly important to ensure that the publisher is made aware of any potential for litigation over libel or defamation. If it seems likely that a character could be recognised as a person in real life, this must be discussed with the author, and brought to the publisher's attention. Most fictional characters, of course, are based at least partially on real people the author has known or heard about, and this rarely presents legal problems, but there have been cases where authors and publishers have been sued. If there appears to be a risk of litigation, a decision on how to proceed will have to be made by the publisher and the company's legal advisers.

Most problems with fiction manuscripts are less serious than this. They tend to be identified by questions such as the following:

- How can I tell the author that the bar incident that is supposed to introduce comic relief is just plain corny?

- Are three suicides in one novel too much?

- How did they get from Zanzibar to Rome? Did I miss something?

- Does the author know any mercenaries, or is this all guesswork?

- Would Genevieve really say that?

- Would Mr Dellasandrio really do that?

- Why is everyone suddenly writing about mass murderers?

Fiction editors are a very special breed. They need impeccable judgement, consummate tact, a perfect memory for trivia, the ability to hold several themes and subplots in their minds at once, and the stamina to endure the phone call at two in the morning from the irate author who has just discovered the altered semicolon on page 104.

The reward comes when that same author announces that the book could not possibly have reached its present state of perfection without the help of 'my wonderful editor'.

CHILDREN'S BOOKS

Children's book editing, although similar to fiction editing in some respects, is governed by a number of constraints. Even fiction and picture books may be destined for educational or book club distribution, and so must meet official or unofficial standards set by these distributors. Book club distributors may not accept certain swear words. Educational buyers may apply standards for language level, or for gender or racial balance. Books to be sold in countries outside Australia may encounter language and content restrictions. For example, some American publishers will not accept nudity in their publications — even when the subjects are children under the age of three! Publishers faced with these market pressures must try to strike a balance between integrity and pragmatism. In such situations the editor should follow the publisher's advice about how much 'censorship' to apply to a particular book.

Other market pressures come from the readers. Adult fiction readers may accept ambiguous writing or flat patches within a story. Children will not. Books written for children up to the age of 14 must have a good, simple story that keeps moving, and is clear, believable, topical and lively in style. Novels for older teenagers can be more complex, but must still hold the reader's attention throughout.

Picture books

For most children, picture books are their introduction to the joys of reading. They are usually read aloud to young children, at least initially, so vocabulary level is not as limited as in school readers, where the children themselves are reading the books. One of the great values of picture books is their ability to extend children's knowledge and enjoyment of words. Editors who can recognise the difference between an ordinary word that is too difficult for a picture book, such as *initiate* for *start*, and a special word that will be long remembered, such as *soporific* in Beatrix Potter's *The Tale of Peter Rabbit*, probably have the makings of a good children's book editor.

An important part of the editor's role is liaison between the author, illustrator (or photographer) and designer, especially if the illustrations are commissioned after the text is received. Often the editor will help the author, publisher or designer choose the right illustrator for the book, then work closely with both author and illustrator to ensure that text and pictures match perfectly.

Because there is so little text in a picture book, every word must be exactly right. Sentence structure should be simple, beginning with the main clause, and there should be no unnecessary words or phrases. Read each line aloud to find out how it sounds. Look for imaginative ideas, rhythm, flow and repetition, which form the basis of many much-loved picture books.

Picture books for very young readers are usually 16 pages in length; for slightly older readers they may be 24 or 32 pages (always in multiples of four for printed books).

Picture book manuscripts can be presented in various ways. If the author is also the illustrator the book will usually be received as a mock-up, with roughs of the illustrations and sample text laid out as double-page spreads. The editor will need to examine the text to ensure that it is clear and lively, and that it flows well from spread to spread. In consultation with the publisher, an assessment is made as to whether the illustrations are appropriate and the cost of production will be within the budget. If there is anything that should be changed, it is often the editor's role to negotiate this with the author. The editor will also need to discuss with the designer the technical aspects of production, and compile prelims, cover copy and publicity material.

mock-up
a model of a finished page or book to show how the elements will be combined

Many unillustrated manuscripts are submitted with the text already broken down into double-page spreads, and an illustration brief for each page, or even rough sketches of the author's ideas. The editor must ensure that this breakdown flows well and fits the book's planned extent, as well as review the style and content. Then, together with the designer and publisher, a list of possible illustrators is compiled. Samples of the work of these illustrators will often be discussed with the author, and an appropriate illustrator chosen. The illustrator will be asked to provide sample rough sketches for the book.

If a manuscript is submitted as text only, then the editor (preferably in consultation with the author) must decide on the page divisions and the book's extent before compiling an illustration brief (see appendix 4).

When the roughs have been completed, the publisher, editor and designer will check for suitability, cost of finished artwork, accuracy, safety and, if necessary, gender and ethnic balance. For example, if children are shown visiting a factory, is the machinery correctly drawn and up to date? Are the workers wearing safety helmets and boots? Are both women and men depicted, and different ethnic groups represented? The editor or author may need to provide roughs for the illustrator: botanical drawings for a book about flowers, appropriate costume designs for a historical story and so on. Illustrations for picture books are usually in full colour.

Picture storybooks

Picture books generally have very little text, the emphasis being on the illustrations. In picture storybooks the illustrations, although important, are secondary, and may not occur on every page or may take up less space than the text.

Except in the case of work by author–illustrators, manuscripts usually arrive with text only, with perhaps brief suggestions for illustrations. Take into account the target age group in working out the extent, the number, position and style of illustrations, and whether they will be in black and white or colour, or a mix of both, perhaps on alternate spreads.

Picture storybooks are produced for children as young as four and as old as 12, but in general the same editing principles apply—simple, lively story, uncomplicated sentence structure, and no unnecessary words or concepts. Vocabulary should be monitored carefully for readers over six, who may be reading the book themselves.

Teenage novels

Although teenage novels can include more difficult concepts than books for younger readers, they still need to be simple and direct in style. They should be written in the active rather than the passive voice, should focus on the actions and thoughts of the protagonist or protagonists, and should avoid diversions into side issues.

There is a distinction between editing teenage novels and young adult novels, as the latter can be subject to both teenage novel and adult fiction criteria.

Informal language is usually more accessible, but colloquialisms that will date quickly should be avoided. If the book is to be sold overseas, care must also be taken to ensure that the language is appropriate for those markets. If there is a moral message in the story, it should be implicit in the plot development, not heavily spelt out in the text. Conversation should be lively, and the language used should be appropriate for the characters; for example, colloquial and brusque for contemporary playground conversation, old-fashioned and colourful for a historical adventure story. All facts, dates and descriptions of places should be checked carefully. It is important not to include concepts or information that are likely to be beyond the target age group's understanding.

School readers

Although part of the educational publishing market, school readers require many of the same editorial skills as children's fiction. However, they also impose a number of constraints. They may need to be written to fit specific word lists, and sometimes to fit specific themes. They are often produced on a smaller budget than general picture books, and may be illustrated in one or two colours only, or even in black and white. This poses special challenges in making them lively and attractive; they must be as appealing as possible—especially the cover—and must also meet all the market requirements.

Cover or jacket copy

Covers or jackets of children's books are vitally important, and a great deal of care goes into choosing the best possible cover for each book. The editor will be responsible for compiling front cover copy and writing a blurb that will encourage a casual browser to buy the book.

Blurbs must take into account who is going to be buying this book—parents, teenagers, teachers or relatives. This will influence the language level and pitch of the blurb. Many authors supply their own blurbs. These are often excellent, as the authors know their own books so intimately, but the editor must check them for any inaccuracies or misrepresentation.

Picture book covers usually include one of the illustrations from the text, perhaps as a wraparound from front to back, with the main part of the illustration on the front cover. For other books a cover illustration will be specially commissioned, not necessarily from the same artist who did the text illustrations.

A detailed cover rough, including text mock-up, artwork and colour samples, will be circulated to the publisher, designer, editor, managing director and marketing manager, as well as to the author. Cover roughs for children's books are often amended many times before everyone is satisfied with the design.

The protagonist should feature on the cover, particularly in junior and teenage novels, and it is very important that this character's image is dynamic and appealing. It is the editor's job to ensure that the picture matches details in the text—age, hair colour, clothing, unusual characteristics—and that any action shown is depicted in the story. It is also important that the style of the cover gives a clear understanding of what kind of story it is: adventure, fantasy, comedy or science fiction, for instance.

What makes a good children's book editor?

Perhaps the most important characteristic of a good children's book editor is a love of children's books. Extensive reading will help to develop a feeling for appropriate language levels. Look through picture books, picture storybooks and teenage novels in bookshops, libraries and online bookstores. Get a copy of books that were recent finalists in the Children's Book Awards. Reread old childhood favourites. This reading is not only enjoyable, it is the best way to develop a feeling for what makes a good children's book.

RECIPE BOOKS

Before starting to edit a recipe book, consider these questions:

- Is it to be formal or informal in tone and presentation?

- Will it be full of useful information, hints and ideas, as well as the recipes?

- Will it be illustrated with anecdotes, photographs, cartoons or sketches?

- Is it intended for adults or children, experienced cooks or novices?

- Will it be sold overseas, and if so should it include imperial as well as metric measurements?

- How are the various elements—headings, ingredients, method, cooking times, illustrations—to be arranged?

- Is there a house style that must be followed?

It is essential to have a sample setting at an early stage in the preparation of a book of this kind. Look critically at the layout and the information to be included:

- Are all the elements required (recipe name, ingredients list, method etc.) included in the layout?

- Is the design well laid out, with plenty of white space and good use of design elements?

- Is the typeface and size easy to read from a distance (from eye height at standing position to bench height)?

- Will each recipe fit on one page or spread? If the page needs to be turned to complete the recipe, is this made obvious?

Food photography is a specialised art, and most cookery books include full-page colour illustrations that aim to make the food look even more mouth-watering. The editor may be required to commission and brief a food stylist and a photographer, help obtain the necessary props, and be present at the photo shoot.

Step-by-step diagrams or photographs may be necessary to illustrate any tricky preparation stages, such as jointing a chicken, dicing a mango, or rolling and shaping croissants. Sketches and cartoons may also add to the visual appeal of recipe books.

Editors should follow the instructions given in chapter 9 on dealing with illustrations, copy edit or create any captions, and ensure that all permissions and acknowledgements are in order.

Recipe books sometimes include descriptive sections on foods of certain regions, or on techniques of food preparation and cooking. Edit these for consistency.

The index is generally ordered alphabetically, though sometimes it is ordered alphabetically under subheadings, such as Appetisers, Soups, Meat and Fish and so on, that follow the order of the meal or region or the main ingredient.

Recipe books—a checklist

General issues

- Are the recipe names appropriate, parallel and consistent?
- If the recipe names are in a foreign language, are English-language equivalents given?
- If the recipes have short introductions, are they consistently included and similar in length and style?
- Is there an indication at the beginning of the recipe of preparation and cooking times, and of how many people can be served from the amounts given in the recipe?
- Does each photograph appear on the same spread as the matching recipe or are captions and cross-referencing required?
- Will there be a separate section for basic cooking methods (such as how to blind-bake pastry or prepare eggplants)?
- Will there be a section that lists measurements, conversions, abbreviations etc.?

Ingredients

- Are ingredients listed in the correct order (either in order of use or amount)? Cross-check with the instructions. Are they subdivided into, say, pastry and filling?
- Is there a separate list of equipment needed, given in order of use?

(continued)

Recipe books—a checklist *(cont'd)*

- Are the amounts given in both metric and imperial measurements?

- Are the amounts correct? Check for mistyping; for example, should 1000 g butter be 100 g?

- Is the wording consistent both within and between recipes? (One recipe may specify '3 stalks celery, chopped finely', and the next '2 stalks finely chopped celery'.)

- Are the descriptions accurate and detailed enough? (For example, is a cup of chopped parsley finely or coarsely chopped?)

- Are standard abbreviations used: g (gram), Tbsp (tablespoon), tsp (teaspoon), L (litre), mL (millilitre) and so on. A list given as:

  240 g of plain flour

  180 grms salted butter

  mineral water (60 mL)

  should be corrected to:

  240 g plain flour

  180 g salted butter

  60 mL mineral water

Instructions and method

- Edit all the instructions in the normal way, checking spelling, punctuation, grammar, paragraphing, and especially fluency and accuracy of expression. For example, 'Drape the pastry over tin, and then roll over' would be better (and less ambiguously) expressed as 'Drape the pastry over the tin, and then roll the edges with the rolling pin'.

- It may be useful to number the steps to follow in preparing a recipe, where appropriate; for example, in a beginner's recipe book.

- Double-check that all the ingredients mentioned in the instructions are listed under the ingredients, and vice versa.

- Think through all the steps, and check with the author that all the recipes have been tested. Has anything vital been omitted? For example, did the instructions for making a filling specify 'Cream the butter' but neglect to mention that the sugar had to be added and beaten in too?

- Are mixing and preparation times given consistently?

- Are cooking times and temperatures (in both Celsius and Fahrenheit if necessary) specified?

- Are cooking times and temperatures given for conventional, fan-forced and microwave ovens, where relevant?

- What shelf position should be used in a conventional oven?

- How and when does the cook test that the food is ready?

- Are there any serving suggestions? What accompaniments are recommended? Any such additional information must be supplied consistently.

- Are there cross-references to other recipes—perhaps to a sauce, to vegetables or to side dishes? Check that they are included in the book.

- Are any safety precautions mentioned, especially in cookery books for children?

DICTIONARIES AND REFERENCE BOOKS

Each dictionary or reference book presents a different problem in organisation and layout. The first thing the editor must determine is whether the book will be organised by subject category, by chronology, in alphabetical order, or by some other system, such as chapters subdivided according to the types of information to be presented.

An encyclopaedia is usually arranged alphabetically by subject, possibly with subheadings, and includes a detailed index. An encyclopaedia presents a body of information for each entry; the material can run to several paragraphs or pages, often with explanatory illustrations or photographs.

A thesaurus may be divided into two sections: a list of words and synonyms indexed to paragraph numbers, and a numbered section of keywords divided according to parts of speech and differences in meanings. Or it may be presented alphabetically.

Reference books, and even some dictionaries, may also include tables, maps, graphs, diagrams and other illustrations. A biographical dictionary gives details of people's names, birth and death dates, birthplaces, occupation and main achievements. Entries may end with referenced sources, in which details and dates are often abbreviated according to a predetermined style. A dictionary of quotations gives precise details of the sources of the quotations; it is arranged alphabetically, and has a detailed index.

General dictionaries contain information on the pronunciation and origin of words, with brief explanations of the meaning of each word. The explanations must not contain the word or phrase being defined (e.g. *departure point* may not be defined as *point of departure*). If the word has several meanings or can be used as different parts of speech, the entry is subdivided, each section starting with the relevant italicised abbreviation such as *adj.*, *n.* or *v.*, and meanings numbered, with the most frequent meaning given first. If the word has several distinctive meanings that need lengthy explanation, the word is repeated as a separate entry, but with a following superscript number. Compound words are also included, and may be numbered in groups. The dictionary may use the international phonetic alphabet to indicate pronunciation.

It is useful to study the presentation of different types of dictionaries or reference books before discussing the proposed layout of the project with the designer.

Whatever the style of the book, follow general copy editing and copyright rules for the text, and for including any quoted or illustrative material. Check that every entry includes the same elements (e.g. headword, variant spellings, pronunciation symbols, grammatical category), in consistent order, and using consistent punctuation and electronic styling.

Detailed checking and cross-checking of spelling, forms of names and titles, dates and numbers, presentation of sequences of information and especially of alphabetical order are essential in reference books. Do not take anything on trust!

The preliminary pages in reference books may include a foreword, a preface or introduction, acknowledgements, glossary, a key to pronunciation, an explanation of terms or of how to use the book, and a list of contributors.

Layout of entries

Attention must be given to all aspects of the layout of dictionaries and reference books. It is imperative that a sample setting is prepared at a very early stage so that all copy can be electronically styled and typeset according to the design requirements.

Some points to consider:

- The copy may be typeset in one, two or more columns, perhaps separated by a vertical rule.

- The main words may be set in bold caps, or in bold upper and lowercase, in small capitals or in italics; they may all begin with a capital letter, or a capital letter may be used only for proper nouns.

- The entries may be set full out, with a line space separating each entry, or they may be set closed up, with all turnover lines indented.

Ensure that all entries follow a pattern; for example, surname followed by first name or initials, birth and death dates, birthplace, occupation; or a place name followed by the population total, distance and direction from a capital city, type of rural area; or a river name followed by its length and location.

If any entries appear overlong, check with the author. Reduce the content to an agreed length, or break it, as appropriate, into several smaller entries, with cross-references if necessary.

Cross-references

Cross-references can be indicated in various ways; for example, by using asterisks before or after the term or name cross-referenced, by using bold or italic type or small capitals, or by using *see* or *see also* at the end of the explanations. Strings of cross-references should be separated by roman semicolons.

If both an abbreviation and a full name are given, refer from the abbreviation to the full name; for example, 'ABC, *see* Australian Broadcasting Corporation'; 'CSIRO, *see* Commonwealth Scientific & Industrial Research Organisation'. Remember also to include the abbreviation after the full name; for example, 'Australian Broadcasting Corporation (ABC)'.

Refer from a pseudonym to the real name, if known; for example, '"Collins, Tom" *see* Furphy, Joseph'. Also include the pseudonym in parentheses after the real name; for example, 'Furphy, Joseph ("Tom Collins")'.

Birth and death dates

When preparing biographical reference books, if the person listed is still alive, leave one em space after the en rule following the birth date (1917–   ). If the date of birth is unknown, add a question mark in front of the possible birth date (?1978–); if the date of birth is known approximately, add 'c.' in roman type before the birth date (c. 1912–); and if the birth date is estimated, add a question mark after the estimated birth date (1912?–).

Copy editing

Modern dictionaries are often generated entirely from a database, which helps to ensure consistency in the order of elements, styling and formatting throughout. Nevertheless, even for these types of listings, all entries must be edited carefully to check for data entry and outputting errors.

Other editorial considerations include the following:

- Are distances and measurements to be given with the unit of measurement in full or abbreviated; for example, kilometres or km, centimetres or cm, litres or L?

- Will numbers from 10 000 upwards or 1000 upwards use a comma or a thin space to separate three-digit groups?

- How will phonetic pronunciation or emphasis be indicated? Is this really necessary?

- Are footnotes to be included, or should the information be written into the text?

- What form of dates will be used? Is length a problem, and should dates and other terms be abbreviated?

- Are there to be subheadings within the running text? For example, an entry on the Boyd family could list individual members alphabetically within the entry, perhaps with their names in bold.

Page layout

Start a new page for each new alphabetical section, headed by the letter of the alphabet. Headwords are used in place of running heads in reference books. A common practice is to use the first and the last entry or surname on each page, or the first headword on the verso as the verso head and the last headword on the recto as the recto head. Abbreviate any long titles to fit. As discussed in chapter 8, headwords can be generated automatically during typesetting. Folios will be positioned at the head or foot of each page, as decided in the sample setting.

Remember that tight setting is usually required for such books, and there will be a greater need for hyphenation to avoid wide word or letter spacing. Check for widows and orphans on the page proofs, although these are harder to eliminate than in books with continuous text.

A continuation line may be needed where an entry runs from a recto to a verso, but is not required between columns of one page, or across a double-page spread.

MATHEMATICS AND SCIENCE BOOKS

The main requirements for presenting mathematics and science (including medicine) in books are for clarity of expression, accuracy of calculations, and precision of editing, typesetting and proofreading. Because the typesetting, particularly of mathematics, is more difficult than for books with continuous text, the production process is slower and more expensive than for general books. Careful attention must be paid to choices of typefaces, font styles and layout of displayed material.

The editor of a mathematics or science textbook should have at least a basic knowledge of general maths or science, while the editor of a specialist maths or science book should be qualified in the relevant discipline. Editors without these qualifications should consult mathematical and scientific resources or a colleague with a specialised background when they find their knowledge of a particular subject is deficient. If necessary they should refer the manuscript to an expert reader or referee with appropriate qualifications in the area or commission a freelance editor with relevant qualifications or experience.

Mathematics books

Type conventions

In mathematics the following formatting conventions are followed:

- letters as symbols—light italic (A, B, x, y)
- vectors and tensors—bold or bold italics (**A**, $\boldsymbol{X}$ or **x**)
- abbreviations of mathematical functions—lowercase roman, without a full point (cos, sin, tan, log)
- numerals—roman (1, 2, 3)
- Greek alphabet—standard type (Σ).

widow
the last line or word of a paragraph that sits on its own at the top of a page

orphan
a single word or part of a word that sits on its own in the last line of a paragraph, or the first line of a paragraph that sits on its own at the bottom of a page

All typefaces, including any special characters that the designer or typesetter may need to obtain, must be matched in size and horizontal alignment.

Layout of mathematical equations

Equations are usually created by the author in Word, using the inbuilt *Equation Editor*. However, typesetting these equations is less straightforward because the industry-standard typesetting programs, InDesign and QuarkXPress, do not handle them well. Professional maths typesetters therefore prefer to use specialist programs such as LaTeX and Mathematica for this purpose.

Equations must be separated from running text with extra space above and below the equations and any explanatory expressions. Any equals, plus, minus, multiplication and division signs should align horizontally with the main fraction bar of any equation. The first equals sign in each line of a multi-line equation should align vertically with the others. For example:

$$dN_{\text{coll}} = \left(\frac{\partial f}{\partial t}\right)_{\text{coll}} \Delta t d^3 \mathbf{r} d^3 \mathbf{p}$$

$$= \Delta f d^3 \mathbf{r} d^3 \mathbf{p}$$

superscript
a character in a smaller font size that prints above the x-height or at the top of a line; used, for example, in footnote references and equations

The standard order of enclosure of brackets, working from the inside out, is { [(< { [( )] } >)] }. It may be necessary to check with the author on the use of differently shaped brackets in mathematical expressions, as they sometimes denote a difference in meaning.

subscript
a character in a smaller font size that prints below the x-height; used, for example, in equations

Fractions within displayed equations are often set in two-line form, but within running text they must be converted to run on, with a solidus separating the components. To avoid ambiguity in expressions such as $\frac{2}{x+7}$, use brackets as follows: $2/(x+7)$.

All copy, including equations, should read as a sentence, even when the symbols replace the words. For example, $A + T = N$ reads as *A* plus *T* is equal to *N*.

baseline
an imaginary common line in type on which all capital letters, x-heights, Arabic numerals and ascenders rest

Spaces must be left on either side of joined expressions or mathematical signs, and italicised, superscript and subscript numbers and letters must be styled appropriately.

Decimal points should be located on the baseline, not centred on the x-height (the height of the letter x). The decimal point is almost always preceded by a figure; for numbers below one, add a zero (e.g. 0.789); exceptions are for probability values ($p < .05$) in hypothesis testing, and for the calibre of firearms (.22 rifle).

Where ratios are expressed in words or figures, there should be equal or no space on either side of the colon (e.g. 3 : 4 or 3:4).

Expressions of magnification should be given as '× 100', not '100 ×'.

Distinguish between the letter x and the multiplication sign (×); between hyphens, en and em rules, and minus signs; and between the degree sign (°) and the masculine ordinal indicator (º).

Equations, if referred to in the text, should be numbered in brackets in a consistent way on either the left or the right. If equations are long, break the sequence before a sign, and align the turnover to the text above.

Names of units are given in lowercase (e.g. metre, gram), but some abbreviations are capitalised, such as V for volt, L for litre. Whether the names are abbreviated or not, there must be a space between the number and the name (e.g. 7 millimetres or 7 mm, 20 grams or 20 g, but not gm or gms); note that there is no following punctuation with such abbreviations, and no final 's' to indicate more than one unit.

The spacing of the degree measurement can vary, depending on house style. Where a degree sign is accompanied by the letter indicating the temperature scale, some styles (e.g. the *Style Manual*) require a fixed space between the number and the degree name (e.g. 32 °C, 56 °K), while other styles specify no space (e.g. 74°C). However, if the degree symbol is used on its own, all style guides agree that there is no space between the number and the symbol (e.g. 100°).

fixed space
a space between two characters that does not break when it falls at the end of a line

Chemistry

Symbols used for elements are given in roman; for example, Pb (lead), Au (gold). Note the capitalisation. Formulas in running text must be kept together, and not broken at the end of a line. Note the use of superscripts and subscripts, bonds (e.g. C=C), arrows, and negative and positive signs; for example:

$$H_2SO_4 + H_2O \rightarrow HSO_4^- + H_3O^+$$

Prefixes, if italic, are followed by a hyphen (e.g. *N*-methyl); if roman, they are closed up (e.g. polypropylene). Complicated compounds in common usage are often abbreviated to initials (in capitals, without punctuation); for example, DNA (deoxyribonucleic acid).

Note also that the American spelling of a word often differs from the British spelling—*oestrogen* (British), *estrogen* (American). Before making any changes, check whether substantial sales might be expected in the US, and discuss with the publisher whether American spelling should be used. If an edited collection of articles from international authors, including Americans, is to be published in Australia, then British spellings should be used.

Botany, biology and zoology

The biological sciences have stylistic requirements regarding initial capital letters, and roman or italics for taxonomic groups such as phylum, division, class, order, family, genus and species.

Note that species (singular) is abbreviated to sp.; species (plural) to spp. The genus is given in italics with an initial capital, the species in italics (first word with an initial capital, subsequent words in lowercase), followed by the common name in brackets; for example, *Populus nigra italica* (Lombardy poplar). Derivatives and common names are always given in lowercase roman (except for proper nouns); for example, eucalypt, Paterson's curse.

Geology

Use initial capitals for geological ages; for example, the Jurassic period. Many house styles prefer to use small capitals for the abbreviations of the eras BC (before Christ) and AD (anno Domini), or BCE (before the Common Era), CE (Common Era) and BP (before present). Usually these abbreviations appear after the year, separated by a space, though in some styles AD appears before the year.

Astronomy

Use an initial capital for the names of planets, stars and constellations (e.g. Venus, the Pleiades, the Southern Cross). Names such as *earth*, *sun* and *moon* are given in lowercase, unless they are referred to in combination with other planets; for example, 'A spacecraft was sent from Earth to Mars'.

Medicine

Editors of medical publications will normally need some medical background, such as a qualification in medicine or nursing, or experience in medical research. A familiarity with a wide range of medical terminology is essential, although very specialised texts will usually also be sent out to expert readers or referees with specific knowledge of the field.

When editing general books or magazines dealing with health issues, use a reliable medical dictionary for reference. Editors new to medical editing may also refer to several books and online resources related to medical publishing.

For suggested resources, see appendix 11.

Note that the Vancouver system of citation is normally followed in medical publications (the *Style Manual* has a detailed section on the use of this system). The *Publication Manual of the American Psychological Association* is usually followed in the fields of psychology and psychiatry.

Medical books may be extensively illustrated with medical imaging, illustrations and diagrams. The editor must ensure they are accurately drawn and clear, and that all labels are included and located correctly.

LEGAL PUBLICATIONS

Most editing of legal publications is done by qualified legal practitioners, but in some cases specialised texts may be sent out to experts in the particular field of law for detailed checking, and to a general editor for copy editing. The *Australian Guide to Legal Citation* is a valuable resource in this area, though it should be noted that the style suggested differs in many respects from that specified by the *Style Manual*.

The titles of Acts, Ordinances, Regulations and other legislative material should be cited exactly, without any alteration to capitalisation or punctuation. The titles are usually italicised. If required, the jurisdiction is placed in parentheses, in roman type, after the date. Examples using the *Australian Guide to Legal Citation* include:

Trade Marks Act 1994 (Cth)
Frustrated Contracts Act 1959 (Vic)
Associations Incorporation Regulations 1998

Acts and Ordinances are divided into sections, abbreviated as *s* (singular), *ss* (plural), without a full stop. Legislation is further divided into regulations, abbreviated as *reg* (singular) and *regs* (plural).

Parliamentary bills take the same form as Acts but are in roman type. For example:

Corporations Amendment Bill (No 1) 2005 (Cth)

GOVERNMENT AND CORPORATE PUBLICATIONS

Government departments and large corporations usually have communications areas that employ project managers, designers, editors and writers to produce reports, newsletters, brochures, websites and media releases. These sections may have a number of subsections; for example, one for publications, one for the website, and one for public relations—each with its own staff and hierarchy of responsibility. Large organisations also frequently use freelance or contract editors, writers and designers. In smaller government agencies and companies, all of these functions may be supervised by a publication or communications manager, perhaps assisted by a production manager, publications assistant or editor.

Government publications

Many government publications—technical reports, annual reports, discussion papers, management plans, policy documents—whether in print or on departmental websites, have an established format, often as part of a numbered series, and the editor must ensure that the manuscript fits the required format and adheres to the series style. The *Style Manual* was created to detail the preferred format for Commonwealth Government publications. Since the format is usually fixed, structure should present few problems, and the editor need carry out only basic copy editing on the manuscript for consistency, style, accuracy and clarity of expression.

For resources about using accessible language, see appendix 11.

The Australian Government is increasingly adopting the principles of plain language in its publications, which aims to ensure that all communications are well structured, clear, concise and readable. Related to this is the mandatory requirement for all material released on Commonwealth Government websites to be made accessible. Some of this involves addressing technical specifications, but editors play a vital role in ensuring that the language used in the materials and the presentation of tables and figures are crafted to address the needs of people with a physical disability, those whose first language is not English and those with a cognitive impairment, among others.

The editor may also have responsibility for compiling the prelims, obtaining the ISBN and CiP data, and editing or compiling the acknowledgements list for publications. Many government publications do not use barcodes, as they are usually not sold in bookstores.

The title page will include the title, series and number of the report, the name of the department issuing the report, possibly the section in which it was compiled (although not always the name of the authors) and the place of publication. Look at previous documents from the series to determine the format and placement of the various elements.

A foreword, if included, is signed by the head of department or the relevant government minister, or a letter of transmittal from the head of the reporting body to the relevant minister or other authority may be required. These should not be changed or edited except for correcting misspellings or grammatical faults. The publication manager or editor must ensure that a copy of the writer's signature is incorporated into the foreword, along with the date of submission. Acknowledgements may include the name of the author of the document and all those who helped in compiling it, including technical advisers, field officers, the typesetter and the editor.

Government publications often go through a long series of clearances after the first draft has been copy edited, and there may be several sets of (often conflicting) changes that have to be incorporated into the final document. Consultation with the author and sometimes the head of department may be necessary in deciding whose comments must be complied with and whose can be taken as suggestions only.

With some government publications the editor may be held responsible for ensuring that the document endorses or at least does not contradict government or departmental policy, and for ensuring that no legal problems can arise from statements in the document.

Commonwealth Government departments are expected to make all their publications freely available to the public by default (unless there is a legal reason not to), generally through a Creative Commons licence. This has led to a substantial reduction in printed publications and a corresponding increase in the availability of the materials on government websites, whether as Word documents, web pages, PDFs or EPUBs.

Creative Commons a copyright licensing system that encourages the free but responsible sharing of information, generally via the internet

Corporate publications

Annual reports

Because company annual reports are both official documents and an important component of the company's communication to shareholders, they should be presented in clear and accessible language, and be informative and accurate. If the company is aware of these objectives, the briefs for writers and editors will reflect them. However, some members of management who produce source materials for the reports may be resistant to having any changes made.

It is important for editors to find out before they begin exactly what the aims for this particular work are, and how much scope they have to make style and even copy editing changes. Since the format of such documents is fixed, there should be no need for structural editing, but bias, unnecessary jargon and meaningless expressions and clichés should be removed where possible.

Technical publications

Company publications might include project reports, policy and discussion papers, tender documentation and operation manuals. The detailed content in these documents is usually the responsibility of the writer, although the content may also be checked by suitably qualified company personnel or outside referees. The editor will be responsible for general copy editing of language, style and accuracy.

It is particularly important to check numbering systems, figures and tables for continuity and accuracy. If there is time, all totals in tables should be checked. If not, check a sample, and, if problems are found, return all tables to the responsible department for detailed checking.

Newsletters and journals

Many large companies have in-house newsletters or journals, often the responsibility of a publication manager or officer who combines the functions of commissioning editor, copy editor and editorial writer. Sometimes the publication manager will also act as a project manager, organising design, typesetting, printing and all other aspects of production. Some companies will carry out all these functions in-house. Alternatively, companies may contract out the entire production process.

Media and advertising

Most company advertising is contracted out to advertising agencies. However, smaller jobs such as the production of information kits and brochures may be carried out in-house and require copy editing and proofreading, and checking illustrations by either in-house or freelance editors. Large projects, such as a new health campaign requiring a coordinated set of leaflets and accompanying media packages, may be contracted out to a project manager or agency.

Company policy

It is important when working on corporate publications to ensure that all logos, slogans and colour schemes align with company policy, and that all publications in the company's name have been approved and signed off by the responsible department.

ACADEMIC PUBLICATIONS

Academic publications include journals, collections of conference papers, teaching materials, scholarly books and theses. As with many other sectors of publishing, academic works are increasingly being published online, with some being published only through this medium, especially open access journals.

open access publication
a system that provides unrestricted access to books and articles online, often under a Creative Commons licence

Academic journals

Academic journals are frequently attached to a university department, but may have their own office and staff, typically the academic editor and an assistant. The academic editor, assisted by an academic board, will select and reject submitted papers, often after sending them out to suitable referees, and organise copy editing, proofreading, and placement and checking of advertising. Larger journals may have their own copy editing staff, but more commonly freelance or contract editors will be used.

Prospective contributors are provided with a copy of the journal's 'Advice to authors', often available online, and sometimes given access to a copy of the most recent edition of the journal. Design and formats for citation of references, figure captions and so on must be followed scrupulously, and the academic or copy editor will return papers that do not meet these requirements to be corrected by the author.

Then either the academic editor or the copy editor will assemble the prelims, including the imprint page, contents, and a list of contributors for each edition of the journal, and any endmatter, which may include short reviews, advertisements for other publications, or order forms for previous editions of the journal or associated publications. If, as is often the case, the journal is also published online, all these elements may still be required, but they may appear in a different position relative to the articles in the issue (e.g. they may all appear on a single 'home page' for that issue).

Conference papers

Editing conference papers is in many ways similar to editing academic journals, although often the academic editing will be carried out by a small group of academics or editors from different universities, with the administrative centre temporarily located at one of these institutions. Sometimes the editors will collect the papers before or during the conference. The restrictions on format may not be as strict as for an academic journal; the editor will usually send a copy of the required conventions to the contributors when a paper is accepted for the conference.

After the conference, selected papers are assembled into a formal printed or electronic publication, and edited and proofread for conformity to the chosen style. The editor prepares the cover copy and prelims, and in consultation with the conference organisers or editorial board decides on the sequence of the papers and organises the index, if one is included.

offprint
a printed copy of a single article or part from a book or journal

In collections of conference papers it is customary to commence each new paper on a recto so that offprints of individual papers can be produced easily.

Teaching and learning materials

Many universities and other tertiary institutions have learning resources departments that specialise in desktop publishing, planning and production management, copyright, and design and technical development. They also undertake editing and production of websites, coordinating such areas as multimedia development, graphic design, audio, video and photography. They produce course materials (e.g. printed and electronic study guides, unit information guides, assessment booklets), corporate documentation (e.g. annual reports, policy documents, agendas and reports), promotional materials and other support materials such as university handbooks.

The editors in such departments are responsible for translating the education designs for curriculum material into resources used by lecturers and students, and for establishing guidelines for copyright compliance and web accessibility for people with disabilities. The editorial team, usually headed by a managing editor, includes both full-time and part-time editors, with freelance editors called upon at peak times. Editors edit and manage the production of websites and print-based study materials in standard templates. They work closely with:

- academic authors

- educational and instructional designers and developers

- web developers and designers

- educational technologists

- photographers

- audio and video producers

- multimedia developers and producers

- digital media technologists (including typesetters)

- graphic and visual designers

- copyright officers.

Many tertiary institutions also have their own printing and binding departments, and their own website development teams, which helps to reduce the time frame for production of educational materials.

Scholarly books

Some universities have their own scholarly press, such as the University of Queensland Press, University of Otago Press and Oxford University Press, often combining academic with general publishing. Books presented for publication may include adaptations of PhD theses. In these cases it is the task of the publisher and editor to decide whether the book is likely to attract a large market of academic readers (an unusual situation), or whether the topic is potentially of interest to a general readership, in which case it may require a great deal of change and editorial guidance.

Many academic authors are well aware of the needs of a general audience and will have written or adapted their work to make it accessible to a wide readership. In other cases, the editor may be involved in the transition of a thesis through restructuring and editing into a lively and engaging book likely to be read by a wider audience. This often involves removing many of the trappings of thesis-imposed styles of writing and structure.

In the past it was common for editors to work closely with academic authors to help to make these changes. Academic publishing is rarely cost-effective, however, and authors may now be sent off with a list of instructions and a 'Guide to authors'. They will sometimes, at their own expense, employ a freelance editor to assist them in rewriting the manuscript.

Authors are increasingly required to obtain funding from an academic body or research organisation to contribute to the cost of production.

Theses

Many students writing their masters or doctorate theses seek the services of editors to help them prepare their work for submission. It is important for editors to be very clear about the nature and extent of the work required. The editor is not responsible for providing structural and content advice for theses as that is the task of the student and supervisor. Rather, the editor's role should be restricted to copyediting and proofreading, and no more. Editors working in this area should consult the Institute of Professional Editors' 'Guidelines for editing research theses', available on the IPEd website (www.iped-editors.org). Universities may also have their own requirements.

PART C

The production
process

The editor's role does not stop once substantive and copy editing is completed and the edited manuscript moves through the production phase. An editor may be required to manage the project through to publication, to proofread or index the publication or to be involved in the quality control of ebook formats. Part C describes proofreading procedures and techniques, dealing with indexes and printing issues. The final chapter provides an overview of the editor's role in ebook production.

11

Proofreading processes and techniques

The editor spends many hours preparing a manuscript for publication, but this careful work needs to be followed up during the production stages to ensure that the published book is free of errors, well laid out, and as complete and accurate as possible. This is where the quality control work of the proofreader comes in.

This chapter looks at the processes and techniques of proofreading. The practice of proofreading is covered in the next chapter.

Proofreading ebooks

Proofreaders of ebooks apply the same principles as proofreaders of typeset books when checking for typos and other textual errors. However, proofreading ebooks usually occurs at a different stage of the production process and involves checking for issues specific to that format, which are discussed in more detail in chapter 15.

THE PROOFREADING PROCESS

Once the text has been electronically styled and copy edited and all or most of any illustrative material has been prepared, the relevant files and appropriate instructions are sent to the typesetter. In turn, the typesetter lays out the material according to the text design, and adds all the other elements of the book that are generated by the typesetting program (such as running heads and feet, contents pages and cross-references).

The typesetter will then generate either hard-copy printouts or PDF files for the proofreading stage. The master copy of the publication will always be the most current version of the file prepared by the typesetter. PDF versions are more or less fixed and function in a similar manner to hard-copy printouts—as a means for proofreaders to instruct the typesetter as to what changes need to be made to the master typeset copy—except that they are marked up onscreen.

Once the proofs have been generated (the first pages), an in-house or managing editor usually manages the proofreading process. The editor may outsource the proofreading to a freelance editor or proofreader or give the task to in-house staff or undertake the work themselves. Even though the two roles (management and proofreading) are quite distinct, sometimes the same person may perform both. In this chapter when we talk about the editor or the proofreader, we are referring to the roles rather than the individuals who perform them.

The translation of a Word document and image files into a typeset publication is fraught with potential errors and conversion issues. Even if the manuscript has been carefully styled and prepared, there are numerous opportunities during production for images to be placed incorrectly or omitted, for text and files to be accidentally deleted, misplaced or duplicated, and for other unexpected layout issues to arise. And, of course, there will always be errors that were missed during editing.

It is therefore the proofreader's responsibility to check all the elements of the book, including reading the text word for word (usually once, at the first pages stage), while the author also proofreads the publication. The complexity of the proofreader's task will vary depending on the complexity of the book.

The proofs are ideally read against the edited manuscript, if supplied, either by the original copy editor or by a proofreader (often as a freelance commission or contract). The proofreader may be asked to collate the author corrections by incorporating them into the master copy of the proofs. Alternatively, this may be done by the in-house or managing editor, who will also:

- resolve any queries raised by the proofreader or the author

- ensure that all corrections are clear and consistent (that is, copy edited in the same style as the manuscript)

- ensure that any changes conform with what was agreed at the copy editing stage.

As with the editing process, proofreading is an iterative process. The first page proofs are proofread and the corrections are taken in by the typesetter, who then produces the second pages. The proofreader skims the second pages to ensure that all changes have been taken in correctly and to catch any further errors that may have been missed. The typesetter again takes in these changes and produces the third pages and so on. The number of times new pages are produced will vary depending on the budget available, the schedule and the complexity of the publication. Proofreaders are rarely requested to proof more than two rounds of pages; any checking of further sets of pages is usually carried out in-house.

WHAT MAKES A GOOD PROOFREADER?

A good proofreader possesses the following attributes:

- an intelligent approach

- an eye for detail and an ability to spot errors

- a capacity for thoroughness

- an excellent memory

- a thorough grasp of the English language

- a passion for grammatical/factual/typographical accuracy (but with enough pragmatism to accept the need to compromise where necessary)

- patience and persistence

- an ability to work under pressure to meet deadlines, without sacrificing accuracy.

WHAT ARE A PROOFREADER'S RESPONSIBILITIES?

The proofreader has two broad tasks:

- rechecking the text to ensure that no factual or other errors have been missed, including:

  — checking that the house style (or any other agreed style) has been used consistently

  — checking and correcting previously undetected errors in spelling, grammar and punctuation

— indicating (without changing) any obvious errors of fact that appear to have been overlooked

— marking, querying or checking any inconsistencies, such as discrepancies in the spelling of names, styles of figures, spans of numbers or periods of time, dashes, inconsistent capitalisation and punctuation

- checking that the pages have been correctly typeset, including:

— marking for correction all typesetting errors, and faults in layout and type specifications

— marking any material repeated, transposed or deleted accidentally

— checking against the manuscript, and artwork and permissions brief, that all illustrations, figures, tables and maps are properly placed, or that sufficient allowance is made for their insertion

— checking that the sequence of all materials is correct and complete

— checking that hyphenation at the end of lines (word breaks) is correct

— marking and listing any material still to be supplied

— checking that page numbers and cross-references in the text and prelims have been correctly inserted

— checking the consistency of headings with those in the contents.

word break
splitting (hyphenating)
a word at the end of
a line

A proofreader must develop a healthy scepticism; on close examination, apparently clean and well-presented proofs may reveal inaccuracies in typesetting and layout. Nothing can be taken for granted—everything must be checked. Normally people read for sense, taking in words and phrases by their general shape, influenced by what they expect to read, without pausing to spell out each one. But proofreaders must be alert to the problem of seeing what they expect to see, rather than what is actually there or omitted.

Proofreaders are not required or meant to be copy editors, and making sweeping changes at the proofreading stage is not acceptable. The proofreader's task is to do a final quality control check on the content of the publication to ensure consistency and accuracy. It is *not* to make editorial decisions such as changing the voice, altering quotations, changing tenses or marking other extensive changes. If a proofreader has concerns about a particular issue, they must consult the in-house or managing editor, or the author, as decisions may already have been made for reasons the proofreader does not know. If a proofreader tries to make substantial changes without consultation, such corrections may prove to be unnecessary, expensive and time wasting, especially if the proofs later have to be recorrected to the original version.

That said, the processes and responsibilities described here are indicative of what traditional proofreading encompasses. In reality, proofreaders are often called upon to work with a wide variety of publications, in a broader capacity than just straight proofreading, and must be prepared to be flexible. They may be required to be more proactive, take on additional tasks or even rewrite material, often at the last minute. For every job, the editor or client should ensure that the proofreader is fully briefed and sure of the limits and extent of the tasks they are to perform.

GETTING READY TO PROOFREAD

Proofreading is commonly performed using either hard-copy printouts or PDF files. Whichever format is used, the proofreader must have the same eye for detail and apply the same principles for checking the material.

The proofreader should always ask the managing editor before starting the job whether there is an in-house style guide, or style sheet and word list that can be used to check for inconsistencies. If there isn't one, proofreaders should create one themselves.

If checking hard-copy proofs, the proofreader should assemble the following before starting:

- fine-pointed pens to mark corrections

- pencil and eraser (for queries, if required)

- highlighter pens

- correction fluid or tape

- repositionable sticky notes

- paperclips and bulldog clips

- spare paper

- ruler or card

- essential reference books.

Hard-copy proofs may be provided on A3 sheets, so being able to spread them out on a large desk is very useful. Clear the desk of all extraneous material. Work on the material for only one publication at a time. If possible, work in a quiet, well-lit room, where there will be no interruptions.

If checking PDF files onscreen, the proofreader will need to use Adobe Reader (version 9.0+), Adobe Acrobat (version 7.0+) or similar software to make corrections electronically. Both Reader and Acrobat are available on Windows and Mac platforms, and Adobe Reader is available free of charge. This software allows the proofreader to electronically mark up text and insert queries, in a similar manner to working with hard-copy proofs.

One of the limitations of Adobe Reader is that it does not allow the proofreader to overlay the layout with a grid and rulers, which is useful for checking page drops, measurements, alignment and spacing. If obtaining exact measurements is a critical aspect of the proofreading work, then consider using either another PDF reader—such as Adobe Acrobat (available for Windows and Mac, but must be paid for), Foxit Reader or PDF X-Change Viewer (both available for Windows and free)—or a free virtual screen-ruler such as A Ruler for Windows (Windows) or Free Ruler (Mac). Otherwise, there is always the low-tech option of using an actual ruler to measure and check alignments on the screen.

As with editing onscreen, proofreading onscreen can be hard on the eyes and be a challenge physically. Onscreen proofreaders must make sure that their workstations are set up ergonomically and that they take frequent breaks. Having a large, high-resolution monitor to work on is also useful, as it helps make text more readable.

HARD-COPY OR ONSCREEN PROOFREADING?

As with the differences between hard-copy and onscreen editing, there are both advantages and disadvantages to using either hard copies or PDFs for proofreading.

Hard-copy page proofs allow the proofreader to spread out the pages and cross-check references across the publication quite easily. They also allow simple corrections, such as adding punctuation, to be made very quickly. When proofing page spreads, it is also easier to view the pages as the printed book will appear when opened to facing pages, which can be crucial for some publications, such as textbooks or art books. On the other hand, it is possible to lose pages of hard-copy proofs and it can be difficult to mark up long or numerous corrections when text margins are narrow. If large amounts of text need to be inserted, the typesetter may need to retype the material themselves, which can potentially introduce new errors.

Proofreading onscreen using PDFs can help with some of these issues. Corrections can be inserted clearly, no matter how narrow the margins, and longer pieces of text can easily be copied and pasted from the PDF to the typeset document. Consistency can also be more easily checked in PDFs by using the search function to locate all instances of a particular sequence of letters or words. PDFs can also be sent back and forth almost instantly rather than waiting for couriers. It can, however, be difficult to select individual words and characters (especially punctuation) accurately, and, as always, meticulous file management and backup is crucial.

Many publishers use printed page proofs, while others use onscreen PDF proofing, so both formats will be discussed in this chapter.

MANAGEMENT OF PROOFS

Sets of hard-copy page proofs will be supplied to the proofreader either as single pages on A4 sheets or (particularly with highly illustrated books) on A3 sheets as double-page spreads. PDF proofs may be supplied in separate files, one for each chapter, or combined into one large file, depending on the length and complexity of the publication.

It is vitally important to keep to scheduled dates for delivery and return of proofs. Even a few days' delay can snowball into much longer delays that upset the delivery of the publication and critical marketing plans. Proofreaders should ask to be advised if the typesetting is running behind schedule.

Editors who are managing hard-copy proofreading must check that they have received the required number of complete sets of first page proofs, and that all the pages are included in each set, in sequence and numbered.

- Label one set as 'Master proof, first pages' (companies may have special stamps for this), and add the date of receipt. The master proof collates both the proofreader's and author's corrections.

- Another set of proofs, to be marked 'Proofreader's proof', may be needed for a freelance proofreader, if the editor is not proofreading. If the proofreader will be required to incorporate the author's corrections into their own set of proofs, then this copy would be the master copy.

- Label and date the next set 'Author's proof', to be sent to the author, along with the Word version of the final edited manuscript.

- If the typesetter is not the designer, send another set, labelled 'Designer's proof' and dated, to the designer.

- Keep a set on file, marked 'Unread, uncorrected proof, first pages' and dated, for reference.

- Other sets may be requested for co-authors of a multi-author publication (also labelled 'Author's proof', together with the name of the particular author); for a legal check; or for marketing and publicity purposes. All these sets should be clearly labelled 'Unread, uncorrected proofs, first pages' and dated.

Editors who are managing PDF proofing should check that the PDF contains all the required pages. The original should be filed for reference and copies sent to the proofreader, author, designer and others, as required. Each copy of the file should be named appropriately; for example, 'ProofreaderProof', with the date appended in the format YYMMDD.

At this point the editor will have a rough page extent. Advise the production department immediately if the extent now differs significantly from the original estimate based on the manuscript.

In hard-copy proofs, each part or chapter or article or section should start on a new page. As the proofreader finishes checking each chapter, those pages should be clipped together (or the openings can be tagged) for ease of cross-checking. If PDF proofs are supplied in a single file, ideally the typesetter should be instructed to generate a file that includes bookmarks based on the styled headings, so that navigation from one section to another is easier.

When all the hard-copy proofs have been checked, label the pages clearly (e.g. 'First proofs, proofreader's set, checked against edited MS', or if the author's and proofreader's corrections are being collated, 'First proofs, master set, corrections from author and proofreader collated'), and sign and date the set. For PDF proofs, save the proofread versions as new files, also with a meaningful title, such as '2nd pages-ProofreaderAuthorCollated', and append the date in the format YYMMDD.

PROOFREADING TECHNIQUES

Errors and inaccuracies distract the reader and detract from the value of the author's and editor's work. Good writing and copy editing can be let down by poor proofreading. Proofreaders must read slowly and carefully, examining every word, every letter and space, all punctuation, as well as the design instructions, all the while keeping alert for any inconsistencies or possible errors. If their attention wanders or starts flagging, they should take a short break. This is intensive work, and no one can concentrate fully for long stretches.

The first time the pages are proofread may be the only time the typeset version of the publication is read in full (except by an indexer at the final proof stage, when it is too late to make any major corrections). It is therefore essential that all proofreading is careful and precise, all queries are answered, and any design problems are resolved.

Major changes to the text or other elements already in proof may be expensive. As adherence to the schedule is vital, the proofreader should exercise discretion at all stages, and ensure that only absolutely necessary corrections are made.

There are two broad approaches to proofreading:

- Read the proofs through first for sense, pencilling any queries in the margin of the hard copy or inserting notes on the PDF. Then reread in detail, if possible, cross-checking against the manuscript to ensure that all the material has been typeset correctly. Check for textual errors, such as inconsistency of spelling and punctuation, missing or repeated words at the end and beginning of lines, and the sequences of figure and note numbering.

- Alternatively, adopt the reverse order, first cross-checking in detail between the manuscript and the proofs, then rereading the proofs for overall sense and flow, and to settle any queries marked.

What to look for

Take nothing on trust. Even if the original Word document has been electronically styled and edited to a high standard, read the proofs as though the manuscript has been entirely retyped. Even if earlier typeset versions were laid out correctly, cast an eye over all the pages, not just those where corrections have been requested. The current version of the proofs may not agree with earlier versions for a variety of reasons:

- The typesetter may have had to retype some sections due to technical difficulties, sometimes without this being indicated on the manuscript or proofs.

- The typesetter may not be adept at using styles or templates, both of which aid in consistency.

- The wrong version of the manuscript may have been typeset.

- The wrong line of text may have been corrected or additional errors introduced in the retyping of marked corrections.

- Changes made in one paragraph that make the text flow differently may inadvertently change the layout further on, and this may have been missed by the typesetter.

- There may have been hidden gremlins in the files, or the files may have been infected by a virus.

Check that the proofs correspond exactly to the manuscript. An alert typesetter should notice major differences, and notify the editor, but the proofreader cannot depend on this. As the proofs are being checked, look for any extra unedited text or for missing or duplicated text.

Remember, editors who proofread their own copy editing must be alert to any blind spots in the editing! For this reason it is always helpful to have another pair of eyes checking the proofs.

Watch especially for the following:

- When an error is found in a line, it is easy to skip over nearby words containing other errors. To avoid this problem, as soon as the initial correction is marked, reread the whole line before continuing.

- The typesetter may have run a spellcheck and chosen an incorrect but similar-sounding word (*feted/fated*; *principal/ principle*; *to/too/two*), so read carefully for the sense of each word.

- Possessives and apostrophes may have been mistyped during corrections (*it's* for *its*; *yours'*; *does'nt*; *cake's* for *cakes*).

If the proofreader is only given the page proofs and there is no edited manuscript with which to compare them, this is called blind proofreading. In this case, the proofreader must be especially careful when querying inconsistencies and errors as it will be unclear as to who created the error or inconsistency, and why.

How to look for errors

When proofing against the edited manuscript, the manuscript and page proofs should be placed side by side for easier checking. In hard-copy proofing, a right-handed proofreader would place the proofs on the right and the manuscript on the left (and vice versa for a left-handed proofreader). Onscreen, the placement is a matter of preference.

When checking hard-copy proofs, an initial aid in reading carefully is to place a strip of card, or a ruler, across the proof, and move it down one line at a time, while using a finger or another card or ruler to mark the place in the manuscript. As confidence and experience comes, just use the tip of a pen or pencil to mark the place in the manuscript, paragraph by paragraph.

When proofing onscreen, it may help initially to focus by selecting some or all of the text in each paragraph as the proofing proceeds.

How to query issues

When proofreading for an in-house or managing editor, make queries clear and concise. If there are any inconsistent spellings not included on the editor's word list, list or flag the instances, and explain what the problem appears to be. If there is no style sheet and word list and the proofreader needs to create one, highlight words for the list as they occur, until the preferred or more frequent form can be determined. In hard-copy proofs, circle the relevant words in pencil and note the page numbers for reference. In PDF proofs, words can be flagged using the *Highlight Text* tool in Adobe Reader or Acrobat.

Check with the in-house or managing editor if there are any doubts about the editorial style to be followed (a style may have been agreed between author and editor during copy editing, but not imposed consistently throughout the manuscript). Where the proofreader cannot easily resolve inconsistencies, they should all be marked for the responsible editor's attention.

Electronic styling and proofreading

If possible, and in consultation with the editor and typesetter, it can be very helpful if the proofreader is provided with a complete list of electronic styles used in the typeset document. That way, if the style of a piece of text needs to be changed, the proofreader may simply request that a new style be applied rather than having to manually mark up the layout changes. For example, if a few paragraphs of body text should have been styled as a bulleted list, this change can be requested in a simple instruction (e.g. [Change to *List Bullet* style]) rather than the proofreader having to laboriously mark up indents and spacing, and insert bullet markers.

MARKING UP HARD-COPY PROOFS

Symbols used in proofreading

The symbols generally recommended in style manuals for use in proofreading are shown in appendix 9.

How to mark the proofs

Some publishers may use the following colour coding for marking corrections on typeset proofs, for charging purposes:

- red—all typesetting errors

- blue (do not use black)—author's, editor's and proofreader's corrections and changes (additions and deletions, changes for consistency, for accuracy or for updating information).

If this is the system being used, add a note to the proofs to inform the typesetter of this requirement.

When blind proofreading, it is not possible to ascertain who caused the errors, so only one colour is used to mark corrections.

Queries may be marked in pencil or pen, but must be circled to show that they are not to be set. Label clearly whether the query is directed to the author, the original copy editor, the designer, or the typesetter. Keep a running sheet of queries for reference at the end of the proofreading.

Instructions for the typesetter should be written in pen (printing in upper- and lowercase is preferred) in the margin and circled. It is easier for the typesetter to find the queries if the relevant pages are marked with sticky tags. In addition or alternatively, a list of the queries can be prepared in a separate Word document, cross-referenced to the relevant pages of the proofs. A list of global corrections should also be prepared. If they are not extensive, it may be sufficient to write these on the first page of the proofs; otherwise, prepare a separate document for the typesetter.

Errors in writing corrections on the proofs can be concealed with correction fluid or tape. If using correction fluid, tag the spot, and continue checking while the fluid dries. This marks precisely where the rewritten correction is to be inserted, without having to reread to find it. Worse, without a tag it is quite easy to forget about it altogether!

Where to mark the corrections

Proofreading changes and corrections differ both in style and in position from those used for hard-copy editing. The lines of text in a hard-copy manuscript are usually double-spaced, so a copy editor can write changes directly within the text and between the lines. On single-spaced typeset proofs, there is often not enough space for this, so the *position* of the corrections must be clearly marked within the text, and the corrections themselves written in the left and right margins.

A typesetter keying in proof corrections will look down the margins for corrections, so if there is nothing marked in the margin, small changes (e.g. to single letters or punctuation) written directly above or within a line can easily be missed. All text marks must therefore have a corresponding correction marked in the margin, and vice versa.

Write the correction or addition clearly in ink in the nearest margin, level with the error. If possible, write any correction to the left of the centre of the proof in the left margin, and any correction to the right of the centre of the proof in the right margin. Sometimes proofs are supplied without an adequate left or right margin or the text is set in two or more columns with only a small gutter in between; in these cases all corrections should be written in the available margin in sequence from left to right. If there is more than one correction, add them in sequence from left to right. Separate and end all corrections with a vertical or oblique line.

If the correction affects more than one line, start it opposite the point at which the correction is to begin, and indicate that the lines of the correction run on.

If the correction is long, running to two or more lines, take care that it is not confused with any other correction immediately below it; add run-on marks or insert a dividing line between the correction and the one below, or circle the entire correction and indicate clearly where it is to go. To avoid any confusion when a slash is part of the correction, circle the word 'solidus' or 'slash', and add an arrow to indicate its position in the correction.

Write or print clearly in upper- and lowercase; if there could be any doubt about which letters are capitals, add the triple underscore, or the double underscore for small capitals.

If a caret mark is inserted between words, make clear to the typesetter whether the correction is a separate word (mark the spaces) or joined to the word preceding or following it (add close-up marks). Remember to circle all typesetting instructions.

As the typesetter makes each change, they should tick the relevant markup to indicate that the correction has been made.

See figure 11.1 for an example of corrections marked up on a hard-copy proof.

Figure 11.1: corrected hard-copy proof

was the perfect day for viewing this extraordinary sight!

We lunched at the Beatrix Pavillion, which features an enormous room full of the most amazing orchids. These flowers are truly amazing, with their intense colours, unmistakable filaments and stems, and seemingly growing out of thin air.

Even though there were 50 tourist buses parked outside the park and its layout absorbed the crowds well enough for a sense of space within which to enjoy the marvellous gardens and pavilions.

○/
ay/
wonderful/

ay/

stet
③/

⊏

After spending three hours wandering around, we saddled up and again rode with the wind at our backs through more fields of tulips and parklands and canals. Experiencing the landscape from a bike allows one to see the watery wonderland that is The Netherlands.   ɔed/ us/

Our final stop for the day was the Cruquius Museum, an old water pumping station built in 1849. The museum housed one of the original four steam engines purpose-built to pump water from the Haarlem Lake, thereby reclaiming rich farming land (poders, which is drained land enclosed by embankments, separate from the other lakes and canals). Dutch history is built around keeping the sea back, as much of the country is below sea level. When it comes to water management and the machinery to achieve it, the Dutch are your people. However, the giant steam engine (said to be the largest steam engine ever) was manufactured in Cornwall (using tin mining technology) and transported by ship to the pumping station, where they were fitted in sections directly from the ship.   t/ are/ pieces of/   ay/

Now a World Heritage sight, the museum keeps the pump in basic working order (minus the steam) for demonstration purposes. The pump was capable of moving 60,000 litres of water per minute and, along with the other pumps, took some three years to completely empty the lake. Quite an achievement!   site/

We also were interested to view a model of the Dutch coastline and landscape, which showed when and where land reclamation happened across time. It makes complete sense that The Netherlands is the very model of a knowledge nation, as their very existence relies on the ability to innovate, solve problems and use various technologies to build their economy.   ay/

After that, the short ride into Haarlem took us along ubiquitous canals and into the old city, where we viewed one of the most

Marking deletions and insertions

Indicate clearly how much is to be deleted: mark a small vertical stroke through the beginning and end of what is to be deleted, and draw a line through the letters and any punctuation to connect the strokes, taking care to indicate whether preceding or following punctuation is to be retained or deleted, especially if the deletion occurs mid-sentence. For example:

> As he entered the dimly lit room, he saw her standing by the window, ~~framed in silhouette by the deep red velvet~~ ~~curtains,~~ her outline almost ghostly in the gloom.

Otherwise the typesetter will waste time trying to decide whether the comma is to be left in or deleted and may make the wrong choice. Carelessly marked deletions are confusing to the typesetter, and risk further error and correction.

If only one letter, character or punctuation mark is wrong, cross it through using the caret or delete sign, and write the correction in the margin. Do not write the delete sign as well as the insertion sign and the corrected letter in the margin; cross through the error and in the margin add the substitution only, followed by a vertical or oblique line to mark the end of the correction. If the deletion is in the middle of a word and there could be confusion as to whether the correction creates one word or two, add close-up marks for one word, or a space mark for two.

If more than one group of letters is to be corrected or if the form of the word is unusual, write the whole word, circled, in the margin for the typesetter's reference, in addition to marking the correction in the text and margin.

If there are many errors in one or more following lines of a short passage, cross out the whole section and write the corrected version in the margin. It will be faster and easier, with less room for error, for the typesetter to retype the revised text than to try to match up numerous small corrections in a short passage.

Long corrections or insertions should be copy edited to conform in style to the edited manuscript, typed into a separate Word document and proofread. Identify each new passage with a page proof number (e.g. 'p. 195A' for an insertion on page 195) and mark the position of the correction on the proof (e.g. Take in new copy 195A supplied in separate Word document). If more than one typed correction or addition is to be inserted on a page, identify each one as, say, 195A, 195B and so on. It is useful to securely attach a printout of the revised passage to the proof page for reference.

Reinstating text as set

If a correction is marked but for some reason all or part of the original is to be retained, add a row of dots or short dashes below the words or letters to be retained, and write 'stet', circled, in the margin.

stet ('let it stand') used to mark where a written correction in page proofs is to be ignored

Moving text or other elements

If lines of text or other material are to be moved from one place in the proofs to another, circle the material to be moved and label it with a letter (e.g. A) and write in a circle the instructions for moving (e.g. Move to p. 45). On the destination page, mark the proof appropriately (e.g. Take in copy A from p. 41 here).

Alignment

One of the most misunderstood hard-copy proof correction marks is that indicating a change in vertical alignment (⌐⌐). Think of the lines of text as being attached on one side to the vertical line as to a piece of string, mentally pull both ends of the 'string' taut, and the lines of text will be pulled to the left or to the right accordingly.

Global corrections

Depending on the type of correction, the typesetter can be asked to run a global find and replace on, say, a particular spelling or symbol or text dashes. Take care, though, to specify very clearly how this is to be done, especially if quoted material is involved or if the text to be replaced could appear in more than one context.

For example, if, say, in a university handbook, because of inadequate instructions the word *unit* is carelessly changed globally to *subject*, the following oddities may appear: 'subjectarianism', 'Subjected States of America', 'subjecty of time and place'. Remember to give a more specific instruction: 'Replace "unit" with "subject" when they occur as whole words'; repeat the search for plural or other versions of the words to be replaced. It should be possible for the typesetter to highlight all such global changes (as part of the find and replace process) so that they can each be checked by the proofreader.

Tagging queries

While reading, the proofreader should tag any pencilled queries so that they can be found again easily once proofreading is completed. Colour coding the tags may also be useful (e.g. yellow for editorial queries, blue for author queries, orange for the designer, green for the typesetter). However, great care needs to be taken to ensure that the tags stay in place.

MARKING UP PDF PROOFS

As with different versions of Microsoft Word, the functions available in Adobe Reader and Acrobat (or indeed any other program that is capable of annotating PDFs) will vary across different versions and computer platforms. It is beyond the scope of this book to describe all the features of the available software programs in detail, so for simplicity the examples given relate to Adobe Reader 11. To ensure the best functionality, proofreaders should at minimum download and install the latest version of Adobe Reader (free of charge) that is available for their computer operating system.

Proofing tools

PDFs can be annotated by using Reader's *Comment* tools, which are available by selecting the *Comment* button in the toolbar at top right. By default this reveals three submenus: *Annotations*, *Drawing Markups* and *Comments List*. To discover what each tool in the first two submenus does, hover the cursor over each icon. The most useful tools for proofreading are:

- *Add Sticky Note*, for creating a freestanding note

- *Insert Text at Cursor*, for inserting new text

- *Add Note to Replace Text*, for replacing existing text

- *Strikethrough*, for striking through text to denote deletion

- *Add Note to Text*, for highlighting text and adding a query or note

- *Attach File*, for attaching a file such as a Word document or illustration file.

There are also a number of drawing tools that can be used to hand-draw markup such as run-ons or to create a text box.

Setting up

Adobe Reader or Acrobat comes with certain default settings that should be changed for improved proofreading.

It is important to be able to view page spreads when proofing, especially when checking that page drops match or when checking layouts that are meant to be viewed across the spread. To turn on this option, go to the *View* menu and choose *Page Display* and *Two-Page Scrolling*. Importantly, the option *Show Cover Page in Two Page View* must also be selected to ensure that the first page starts on the recto and all following pages appear correctly as spreads. If the monitor is big enough, it may be workable to have this set up permanently by going into the program's *Preferences*, selecting the *Page Display* option on the left and choosing *Page Layout: Two-Up Continuous* from the dropdown menu.

It may also be useful to change the settings for *Commenting* functions. In the *Preferences* dialogue box, choose *Commenting* on the left. If not already selected, it can be useful to set the PDF to *Print notes and pop-ups* that have been added or to *Automatically open comment pop-ups for comments other than notes* (but the *Hide comment pop-ups when Comments List is open* option might then be better turned off).

Another default setting is that each time a commenting tool is used, the cursor will change back to the *Select* tool so that the comment can be moved, resized or otherwise amended. However, if desired, this behaviour can be changed by right-clicking on the tool and choosing *Keep Tool Selected*.

It is useful while proofreading to open the *Properties Bar* and keep it open, as this allows the properties of the selected annotations to be edited. For example, the colour of the markup symbols and text in the *Comments List* can be changed to indicate which corrections are typesetting corrections and which author corrections. To view the *Properties Bar* right-click in the toolbar and select the option from the dropdown list, or use the built-in keyboard shortcut CTRL + E (Windows) or ⌘ + E (Mac).

Applying markup

It is essential that those who are proofing onscreen learn how to use Adobe Reader or Acrobat correctly to mark up corrections; otherwise the typesetter may find it difficult to identify where to make changes. To apply markup and comments, select the appropriate tool and the cursor will become a text cursor. Some of the most common actions include the following:

- Select the *Insert Text at Cursor* tool and click the cursor at the appropriate point in the text. A note box will appear automatically, into which the new text can be typed.

- Use the appropriate tool to select text to be deleted or replaced and the text will be struck through. The *Add Note to Replace Text* tool will also automatically open a note box for the replacement text.

- Select the *Add Sticky Note* tool to add a generic note. Click at the appropriate spot on the PDF and this will open up a note box. Note that sticky notes are not attached to any particular text or object and should never be used to mark up specific text changes.

Markup such as indents, run-ons and alignment instructions require symbols that in hard-copy proofing are drawn and therefore can be difficult to replicate exactly in PDFs. Instead they may be indicated either by using the *Add Note to Text* tool to highlight the relevant text and adding an instruction in the accompanying note box, or drawn directly onto the PDF using the drawing tools and adding an appropriate note. Some publishers provide proofreaders with special stamps that emulate hand-drawn markup symbols, and these can be imported and inserted using the *Add Stamp* tool.

As with hard-copy proofing, the proofreader must be very careful when selecting text to be deleted or replaced to ensure that spaces and punctuation are included or excluded where necessary.

If it is necessary to provide additional material, such as several new paragraphs, the correct version of an illustration, or new text that requires special symbols or layouts, it is possible to attach these in separate files, such as in Word or Illustrator, so that the typesetter need only click on the attachment symbol to retrieve the material. Note that attaching a file in this way actually embeds the attached document into the PDF, so the proofreader need only send the one PDF file, and all the attached files will travel with it. However, keep in mind that this might result in the PDF file becoming very large and thus being unable to be delivered by email, so don't overdo it if email is the only means available for transferring files.

All of the annotations are collated into the *Comments List* on the right-hand side of the PDF. Clicking on a markup in the PDF will highlight the relevant annotation in the *Comments List* and, likewise, clicking on an annotation in the *Comments List* will move the cursor to the relevant markup in the PDF.

Figure 11.2 shows some of the tools used for PDF proofreading and the markup in the text linked to the annotations in the *Comments List*. Figure 11.3 (overleaf) shows how the page proof in Figure 11.1 could be marked up using Adobe Reader's *Comment* tools.

Figure 11.2: PDF proofreading tools

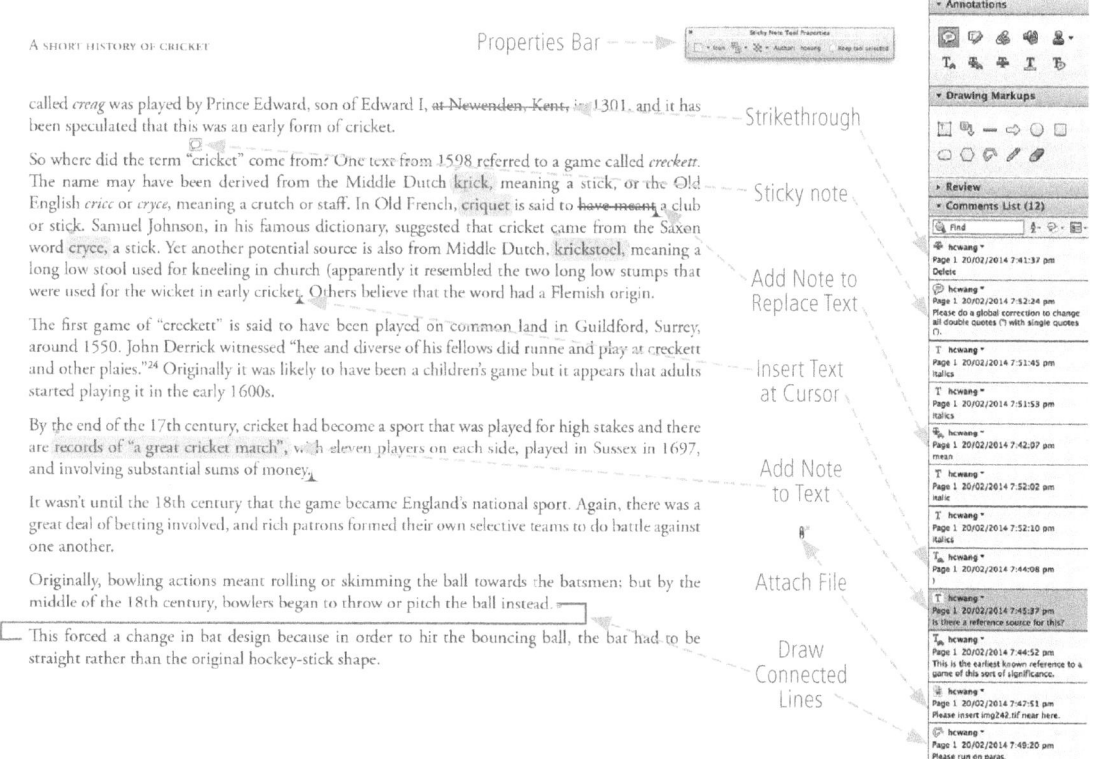

Figure 11.3: corrected PDF page proof

was the perfect day for viewing this extraordinary sight.

We lunched at the Beatrix Pavillion, which features an enormous room full of the most ~~amazing~~ orchids. These flowers are truly amazing, with their intense colours, unmistakable filaments and stems, and seemingly growing out of thin air.

Even though there were 50 tourist buses parked outside, the park and its layout absorbed the crowds well enough for a sense of space within which to enjoy the marvelous gardens and pavilions.

After spending three hours wandering around, we saddled up and again rode with the wind at our backs through more fields of tulips and parklands and canals. Experiencing the landscape from a bike ~~allows one~~ to see the watery wonderland that is The Netherlands.

Our final stop for the day was the Cruquius Museum, an old water pumping station built in 1849. The museum housed one of the original four steam engines purpose-built to pump water from the Haarlem Lake, thereby reclaiming rich farming land (~~poders~~, which ~~is~~ drained land enclosed by embankments, separate from the other lakes and canals). Dutch history is built around keeping the sea back, as much of the country is below sea level. When it comes to water management and the machinery to achieve it, the Dutch are your people. However, the giant steam engine (said to be the largest steam engine ever) was manufactured in Cornwall (using tin ~~minning~~ technology) and transported by ship to the pumping station, where they were fitted in sections directly from the ship.

Now a World Heritage ~~sight~~, the museum keeps the pump in basic working order (minus the steam) for demonstration purposes. The pump was capable of moving 60,000 litres of water per minute and, along with the other pumps, took some three years to completely empty the lake. Quite an achievement!

We also were interested to view a model of the Dutch coastline and landscape, which showed when and where land reclamation happened across time. It makes complete sense that The Netherlands is the very model of a knowledge nation, as their ~~very~~ existence relies on the ability to innovate, solve problems and use various technologies to build their economy.

After that, the short ride into Haarlem took us along ubiquitous canals and into the old city, where we viewed one of the most

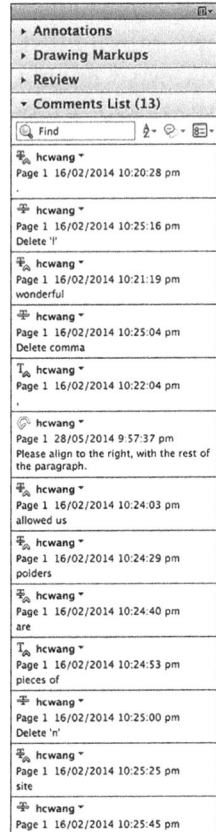

It is clear here that PDF markup has far fewer symbols and tools for use than hard-copy proofing. Much of this is compensated for by the use of the notes boxes and the fact that the copy is electronic. If in doubt about the efficacy or clarity of any given markup in onscreen proofreading, the proofreader should provide extra instructions in the notes box to make sure there is no confusion.

Each comment box also includes a small check box at top right. This can be used by the typesetter to indicate that the correction has been made in the typeset document.

AUTHOR CORRECTIONS

While the master set of first page proofs is being proofread, the author will also proofread a set of proofs, preferably against a copy of the edited manuscript. The author should be given the opportunity to check all changes made to the manuscript, no matter how minor. It is, after all, the author's work and reputation that will be reviewed critically, not the efforts of the (usually uncredited) editor. If changes have had to be made to the content or wording of the manuscript after the author has reviewed the edited manuscript, for instance to fit design requirements, these should be explained in the covering correspondence when the proofs are sent out, along with any other relevant information.

The covering letter should include other necessary instructions; for example, to discourage any rewriting or extensive changes the author should be cautioned that excessive corrections may be charged to the author. It should state the required date for return of the proofs (usually within two to three weeks unless the text is long or complicated) and emphasise that any delays could affect the publication date and marketing plans.

When the author's proofs are returned, the author's corrections are collated by the editor into the master set of proofs (if this has not already been done by the proofreader).

The author's corrections must be copy edited in the same manner as on the edited manuscript before incorporating them into the master proof.

What does the author take for granted? The author will assume that everything is in order. It is up to the editor to check for commonly missed errors, especially in the prelims, numerical sequences and note indicators, as well as all punctuation (in particular, opening and closing quotation marks and parentheses), word breaks, spacing, drops, positioning of illustrations and tables, and overall consistency in text and layout. Editors and proofreaders invariably detect more errors than the author, although it is always salutary after proofreading to see what has been found by another pair of eyes when it appears that the proofreader has checked the proof thoroughly.

The editor (or proofreader) will need to make informed decisions on which of the author's suggestions or changes should be incorporated; where necessary, any disputed changes or additions should be discussed with the author. Be watchful for cases where the author has reinstated earlier material or backtracked on already agreed decisions. In making these decisions, consider time and expense, as well as relevance. As each of the author changes is incorporated (or not), mark off each one on the author's set with a tick or a cross, annotated if necessary to explain the decision in case of any future dispute. If required, colour-code the corrections as typesetting errors or as author changes.

Once the author's (and proofreader's) corrections have been collated, resolve any outstanding queries with the author.

On hard-copy proofs, sign and date both the master set and the author's set, indicating on both that the author's corrections have been collated to the master set. On PDF proofs add a text box or sticky note to this effect.

12

Proofreading practice

Chapter 11 examined the processes and techniques of proof-reading. This chapter looks at their application when working with first and second page proofs.

PROOFREADING THE FIRST PAGE PROOFS

Read the proofs at several levels simultaneously:

- for accuracy in transferring the manuscript and design specifications to the proofs

- for sense and internal consistency

- for any possible (overlooked) legal problems

- for errors of fact.

It is very useful for proofreaders to keep a running sheet of matters still to be checked as they proceed through the proofs. Otherwise it is easy to forget to follow these up, especially if the work must be checked before the next round of proofs arrives.

Typesetter queries

Generally any queries from the typesetter are addressed by the in-house or managing editor, who should answer them as concisely and politely as possible. The editor should also thank the typesetter if they have noticed an inconsistency in the editing or made a perceptive or useful suggestion. When agreeing with a suggestion on hard copy, tick it, or write something like 'Yes' or 'Please do this', circled. In a PDF, add these comments in a text box or by using the *Add Note to Text* tool.

Layout issues

Grids, margins and page drops

backing up (printing)
when every line of
text on the recto of
a printed page aligns
with the line of text
behind it on the verso

Traditionally, a good page design is built on a grid so that the lines of text on each recto and verso leaf align (or back up) with each other. Thus, if a leaf from a printed book is held up to the light, the lines of text on both sides can be seen to align with each other.

text block or area
the lines of text that
are bound by the
margins on a page

Increasingly, grids are not used and instead the emphasis may be on ensuring that the text block on each page occupies the same space, top to bottom, with the lines within the block not necessarily aligning with each other.

Still other text designs let the lines fall unadjusted, causing the text blocks to be uneven in height, as in this book.

The proofreader needs to ascertain which system of page design is being used and then check that it has been applied consistently. In either case the running heads, feet and folios should always back up to each other and the margins around the top and sides of the text block should always be the same.

If this is part of the proofreader's brief, on hard-copy proofs use a ruler to measure the drop (distance) on part title or chapter opening pages from the top of the page to the headings, and from the headings to other elements on the page (such as text or illustrations), and to the foot of the page. Mark any variations for correction.

For more
information about
proofreading
software, see
chapter 11.

When proofing PDF files onscreen, one way to measure drops is to turn on a set of virtual gridlines that overlay the PDF, but PDF readers other than Adobe Reader must be used to achieve this. Drops can also be measured using a ruler against the monitor screen, or a virtual ruler.

On regular text pages, check the consistency of the drop from the top of the pages (other than part titles or the first page of each chapter) to the running head; from the running head to the first line of the text; from the last line of a full page of text to the foot folio (if in the design); and from the folio to the foot of the page. If there is no foot folio, check the drop from the last line of text of a full page to the foot of the page.

Widows and orphans

Typesetters can avoid widows and orphans automatically by making such settings part of the style of the paragraph. Text styles can be set up so that at least two lines at the start and end of every paragraph are always kept together, and headings and subheadings can be set up to always stay together with the next line of text, thus avoiding the awkward occurrence of having a lone subheading or a subheading and one line languishing at the bottom of a page.

When working with a design that is based on the text block, there is then usually not much else to do, as the vertical spacing of the text block is adjusted automatically to ensure that there are no gaps at the bottom, even when an extra line is taken over to the next page to avoid a widow or orphan. This can lead to ugly spacing between paragraphs or lines though, and, if this is part of the brief, it may still be necessary for the proofreader to shorten or lengthen paragraphs to improve the layout.

When working on a book that is based on a grid, avoiding widows and orphans can often result in the text block being one or even two lines short, which is especially noticeable where uneven text blocks sit side by side on facing pages. Such occurrences can be adjusted, as follows:

• Make both facing pages one line short or long (even over several double-page spreads before and after, but avoid creating further problems).

• Add a line by forcing over a word somewhere in a paragraph ending with a full or long line to the next line, or by recasting a sentence.

• Delete a line by running back a short last line of a paragraph through subtle changes in the paragraph, such as by rewriting or manipulating word breaks to fit.

Where a page ends with a subheading, or a subheading with only one line below it, it may be acceptable to transpose the subheading to the new page, and leave the original page one or two lines short (even if paired with a full-depth page). It is also acceptable to leave a page a line short because of the required space after a set-down long quotation, or after an illustration, figure or table.

The other solution adopted by some publishers is simply to allow widows and orphans to occur, for the sake of maintaining the integrity of both the text block and the grid.

Section breaks

Where internal section breaks occur, check that the design specifications have been followed. The breaks may be indicated by a line space with the following paragraph set full out, or a decorative symbol or dinkus (e.g. an asterisk or group of asterisks) centred in the space between the two sections, again with the following paragraph set full out.

Paragraph indentation and alignment

Check that:

- all spaces above and below headings and set-down long quotations, text figures, illustrations and short tables, and line, word and letter spacing in text, poetry, equations, calculations, long quotations, tables and forms are consistent

- gutters between columns are sufficiently wide to prevent columns appearing crowded; text that flows around an illustration or figure should also be adequately separated from the illustration

- the indentation of all paragraphs, long set-down quotes and verse, and turnover lines (in references) is consistent with the design instructions

- first lines below a heading or subheading start flush with the left margin and have been electronically styled separately as such

- all indented turnover lines in tables, bibliographies and indexes are aligned, and that all vertical and horizontal alignments match those in the manuscript

- the paragraph indentation and turnover allowance is met (an em space is standard, although practice can vary widely; in indexes the turnover lines are usually indented two ems to avoid confusion with set-off subentries that are placed with a one-em indent)

- all source lines are consistently aligned: on the left or on the right.

unjustified type set with even word spacing so that successive lines are of irregular length, usually aligned on the left

Justified text is text that is aligned along both the left and right margins, although the last line of justified paragraphs should be unjustified. Check that, if the style is for justified text, all text has been formatted accordingly. If text has been styled correctly, typesetting programs will automatically apply justification. However, there may be instances when a stray tab or other extra white space may have been missed during editing, and if this occurs at the end of a line, the text may appear to be unjustified. It may also be that only some text elements are to be justified, such as the body text, quotes and lists, while other text is not justified, such as headings, captions and callout text. The proofreader should check that all of these accord with the specifications.

With an unjustified setting the line ends should be checked for being too 'ragged', especially where automatic hyphenation has not been used. In such cases, a long word may have been taken over unbroken to the next line, causing a large gap at the text edge. If necessary, use minimal hyphenation, or take short words over or back to balance the appearance of the right-hand margin, but be careful not to overdo this (see figure 12.1).

Figure 12.1: markup of corrections to unjustified text in a PDF proof (top), and in a hard-copy proof (bottom)

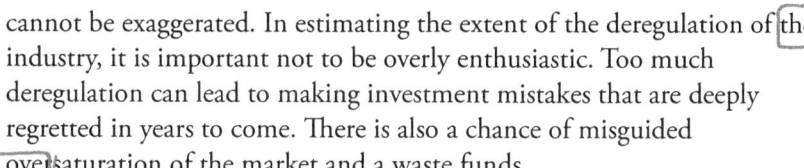

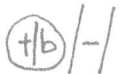

Word, letter and punctuation spacing

In unjustified type the word space throughout should be equal to a standard letter space. Justified text, on the other hand, can suffer from word spacing problems. Because text is justified by introducing tiny increments of letter or word spacing, this can create what look like rivers of white space running down the middle of the paragraphs, which can be distracting to the reader and interrupt comprehension.

Check that the word spacing is not too tight, too wide or uneven. Adjust the text to avoid any rivers, and to avoid tightly set lines followed by loosely spaced lines. Although modern typesetting programs are becoming very good at automatically correcting wide word spaces, these problems may still need to be addressed manually. Word spacing problems are quite easy to identify by sitting back from the text and squinting a little so that the individual words fade out and the white spaces in between become more obvious.

To correct spacing problems, take over or take back a word from the line above or below the line in question, or mark appropriate word breaks in a long word at the beginning of the line below or the end of the line above. (See the next subsection for more about hyphenation and word breaks.) An alternative is to recast the sentence to balance the appearance of adjacent lines. Check with the author and in-house editor if necessary before making changes to the text.

Note that if the page layout is not yet finalised it may be necessary to wait until final page stage before making these adjustments.

kern
adjusting the spacing between two characters so that they are visually more readable

With a bit of practice, extra letter spacing is quite easy to spot. In typefaces in which letters are evenly spaced, detectable space is often obvious after certain characters (e.g. capital letters *V*, *W*, *Y* when followed by lowercase *a*, *o* or *e*; lowercase *y* with following punctuation; italic capital *A* with following roman punctuation). Ask for these spaces to be kerned and corrected globally.

End-of-line word breaks

Breaking (hyphenating) words at the ends of lines is generally avoided in books, except when required to fix poor word spacing. It may, however, be set as the default if the text is set in narrow columns, where long words might otherwise make the word spacing awkward.

There are many different conventions used for determining where to break words. A few dictionaries, such as those published by Merriam-Webster, include word division suggestions in their headwords; however, most people now rely on word processing and typesetting programs to do the division. Arguably the proofreader has less to do in this area as a result; however, each word division must be checked for any awkward breaks, and the proofreader must still suggest where new word breaks should occur.

The main idea is to divide words in such a way that the reader is not led to 'mentally mispronounce' the first part of the word (e.g. ope-ration, coin-cidence, real-ign, rear-range, bed-evil). Some general principles include:

- Do not break words of one syllable, short words (usually six letters or fewer) or proper names.

- Take at least three letters over to the next line.

- Where possible, begin the second element with a consonant, although the word structure might dictate otherwise (e.g. draw-ing versus dra-wing).

- Breaks work well between the components of a compound word or a word with a prefix or suffix (e.g. data-base, pre-meditate).

Similarly, when examining numbers that occur at the ends of lines:

- Never break numbers. The only break permissible in some house styles is after a connecting en rule in a span of numbers (e.g. 100 000–/270 000), but this should be avoided wherever possible.

- Do not separate numbers from their following measurement or other element (e.g. 18 km and 21 April must always appear together on one line).

Adjust the text to avoid word breaks at the end of a recto page, before a full-page table or illustration, or before an inserted section or wrap of illustrations.

Ideally there should be no more than two end-of-line word breaks in sequence, though some house styles permit a maximum of three. Typesetting programs can be set up to avoid such occurrences.

Three types of hyphens are used in typesetting:

- *Hard hyphens* are those that are always required and have been inserted manually. These should have been applied at the editing stage, according to the house style and relevant dictionary suggestions.

- *Soft, discretionary* or *optional hyphens* indicate where words *could* be broken if necessary at the ends of lines, but are otherwise invisible. They are either inserted manually using a special soft hyphen marker or calculated automatically by the typesetting program according to inbuilt algorithms and dictionaries.

- *Non-breaking hyphens* are those that are always required but that should never actually be broken at the end of a line. While not as common, these may be used to prevent short hyphenated words from breaking and causing potential misreading (e.g. acronyms such as BCS-F).

Typesetters normally set the paragraph style to be unhyphenated, and should use only soft hyphens (manual or automatic) for improving word spacing. Using soft hyphens means that if further changes result in the hyphenated word flowing away from the end of the line, the break closes up automatically, thus avoiding unexpected hyphens appearing mid-line.

It cannot be assumed that the typesetter will choose the correct type of hyphen to use, so to minimise errors the proofreader should indicate the type of hyphen required at each word break requested.

When dealing with word breaks, the proofreader has a number of tasks:

- *Creating hyphenated word breaks* may be required, either to improve word spacing or to insert a hard hyphen that was missed during editing or deleted accidentally during typesetting. Indicate whether a soft, hard or non-breaking hyphen is required.

- *Changing hyphenation* might be necessary because the breaks are misleading or wrong. The (soft) hyphen should be transposed to a better position.

- *Removing hyphenation* may be needed where hyphens have been inserted incorrectly in the first place, or to adjust word spacing. Clearly indicate whether the two elements then become one word (mark to be closed up) or two (mark for a space to be inserted).

Typefaces and fonts

Check that the type specifications have been followed correctly, including typeface, type size, leading, changes in fonts, and weight of rules. Use the sample design as a guide, if there is one. The design specifications should provide details for the position, spacing and text type and size for any special elements, such as epigraphs.

Typeface and font style

The proofreader should carefully examine all changes in typefaces and fonts (such as serif to sans serif and back to serif; roman to italic to roman; medium to bold to light; see figure 12.2). Errors in the use of typefaces and fonts tend to occur most often when character styles have been applied incorrectly during the editing phase. For example, if the body text and the table text are set using different typefaces or fonts, then the same character style for the two types of text cannot be used to make the text appear italic. There would need to be separate character styles, such as *Body Text Italic* and a *Table Text Italic*. Because it is possible in Word to apply the same character style to both types of text so that they both look correct, it is easy to misapply such styles in Word, and discover the mistake only after migrating the text to the typesetting program. An astute typesetter might spot this problem, but the proofreader cannot rely on this and must check the text carefully.

sans serif
a typeface without serifs

For more information about applying electronic styling see chapter 6.

254

Figure 12.2: markup of changes in typefaces and fonts in a PDF proof
(top), and in a hard-copy proof (bottom)

References

Australian Bureau of Statistics 2011, **Disability**, *ageing and carers, Australia: user guide, 2009*,
cat. no. 4431.0.55.001, Australian Bureau of Statistics, Canberra.

American Diabetes Association 2013, 'Economic costs of diabetes in the US in 2012', *Diabetes
Care*, no. 36, pp. 1033–46.

Australian Institute of Health and Welfare 2008, *Diabetes, Australian facts 2008*, Diabetes series
no. 8, cat. no. CVD 40, Australian Institute of Health and Welfare, Canberra.

Boyle JP, Thompson TJ, Gregg EW, Barker LE & Williamson DF 2010, Projection of the year
2050 burden of diabetes in the US adult population: dynamic modeling of incidence,
mortality, and prediabetes prevalence, Population Health Metrics, no. 8, p. 29–32.

Buse JB, Ginsberg HN, Bakris GI, Clark NG, Costa F, Eckel R, et al. 2007, 'Primary
prevention of cardiovascular diseases in people with diabetes mellitus', *Diabetes Care*, no.
30, pp. 162–72.

Craig M, Twigg S, Donaghue K, Cheung N, Cameron F, Conn J et al. 2011, *National evidence-
based clinical care guidelines for type 1 diabetes in children, adolescents and adults*,
Department of Health and Ageing, Canberra.

References

Australian Bureau of Statistics 2011, **Disability**, *ageing and carers, Australia: user guide, 2009*,
cat. no. 4431.0.55.001, Australian Bureau of Statistics, Canberra.   *ital. not bold*

American Diabetes Association 2013, 'Economic costs of diabetes in the US in 2012', *Diabetes
Care*, no. 36 pp. 1033–46.   *rom*

Australian Institute of Health and Welfare 2008, *Diabetes, Australian facts 2008*, Diabetes series
no. 8, cat. no. CVD 40, Australian Institute of Health and Welfare, Canberra.

Boyle JP, Thompson TJ, Gregg EW, Barker LE & Williamson DF 2010, Projection of the year
2050 burden of diabetes in the US adult population: dynamic modeling of incidence,
mortality, and prediabetes prevalence, Population Health Metrics, no. 8, p. 29–32.   *ital/p/*

Buse JB, Ginsberg HN, Bakris GI, Clark NG, Costa F, Eckel R, et al. 2007, 'Primary
prevention of cardiovascular diseases in people with diabetes mellitus', *Diabetes Care*, no.
30, pp. 162–72.

Craig M, Twigg S, Donaghue K, Cheung N, Cameron F, Conn J et al. 2011, *National evidence-
based clinical care guidelines for type 1 diabetes in children, adolescents and adults*,
Department of Health and Ageing, Canberra.   *w/f*

Throughout, the proofreader should check that punctuation and
spacing have not had incorrect formatting (such as italic or bold)
applied. For titles of books, journals or newspapers in the text,
bibliography and notes, check that any punctuation and spacing
not included as part of the title is given in the correct font; any

punctuation and spaces that precede or follow a book title, for example, should be roman, not italic. Incorrect italic or bold spaces can be particularly difficult to detect, but it is most likely for these to occur around words or punctuation that have been formatted as such.

Expanded or condensed type

Expanded or condensed typefaces must be used only as specified by the designer, usually in headings or display material, and not to fill a line or to squeeze letters or words into a tightly spaced line. Text or headings that are too widely expanded or condensed are more difficult to read and comprehend, and often look ugly. It is a particular issue if the text looks obviously different from similar surrounding material.

Drop initial capitals

drop initial capital (drop cap) an initial capital at the beginning of a chapter or part set to drop down one or more lines in a larger point size than that of the main text, sometimes with additional decoration

Check all decorative drop initial capitals. They may have been set with the rest of the text, but if they are to be added later as artwork, mark the position in a hard-copy proof and add a circled note in the margin, repeating the letter to be added, or add a note in a PDF proof.

Check the spacing between the drop capital and the main text. When drop capitals such as *V*, *W* and *Y* are followed by certain lowercase letters, such as *a*, *o*, *c* or *e*, the typesetter can reduce any apparent 'extra' space by kerning the letters (closing up the normal letter spacing).

Running heads and folios

Are the running heads correctly placed—title or part title on the verso, chapter title on the recto?

Check that part and chapter titles have not been altered or abbreviated in any way without authorisation.

If the running heads are too long, the proofreader may need to suggest logical ways to shorten them (e.g. abbreviating the chapter title to fit the allotted length of the running heads set in the design specifications). Confirm any changes with the author and in-house editor.

Check that the type style of the headings is not repeated in the running heads, even in a different size, as this can be visually confusing. If the proofreader finds this has somehow been overlooked, it should be flagged for the designer.

Check that lowercase roman folios, if used, have been inserted for all prelims apart from the half-title and verso, title, imprint and first page of the contents, and any blank pages (these pages will still be included as blind folios in the sequence). As the prelims are usually numbered in a separate system (in roman numbers) from the main text (in Arabic numbers), any change in their number will not affect the page numbering of the rest of the publication.

blind folio
a folio counted in the numbering of the pages but not printed (e.g. on the title page and any blank pages)

Make sure the first page (usually page 1) of the main text starts on a recto, and that the numbers continue sequentially through to the last page of the endmatter. Check that the page numbering is correct, with odd-numbered folios on the recto, and even numbers on the verso.

If the house style allows it, folios (but not running heads) may appear on part title pages, although not on their blank versos.

The last full or part text page of every chapter should have a folio, unless it has been specified by the designer that all chapters must start on a recto, resulting in occasional blank versos at the end of some chapters. If so, double-check that where blank pages do not have running heads or folios, all blind folios are included in the continuous numbering.

The designer will have given instructions on the position of the folios: whether set as part of the running head, or centred or ranged left or right at the foot. Fiction books may have folios at the top or the foot of the page, either centred, or ranged left (on versos) or right (on rectos). Check that all the drops match, and that the text is aligned across the double spreads.

Text flow-on

A correction that will create or remove a line may affect the layout of subsequent pages. If the flow-on effect continues to the end of a chapter, it may even create or lose a whole page, causing a design and production headache. If it is within the proofreader's brief to check and correct flow-on, these are often marked in pencil, as only the typesetter is able to ascertain whether the suggested change will fix the problem.

Suggested strategies for avoiding this include the following:

• Reword a correction if appropriate, or indicate other possible alterations that might allow an essential correction to fit. If necessary, add the request, 'Please keep to the same number of lines'. The typesetter may be able to make subtle adjustments to line, word or letter spacing to achieve this.

- To save a line, look for the paragraph on that page with the shortest last line; then consider whether some text can be cut or reworded to reduce that paragraph by the required amount. If the addition is relatively short, look at the preceding and following lines to see whether a whole word or syllable can be taken over or back. This will depend on the number of characters of the inserted word, and how widely the words in these lines are spaced. It may be possible to delete an unimportant word containing the same number of characters to make room. If it isn't clear whether there will be sufficient space, on hard-copy proofs circle other possible words for deletion, and write 'Delete if necessary', circled, in the margin; or in PDF proofs, select the words using the *Add Note to Text* tool, and insert the instruction in the note box. To make it clear to the typesetter why this change is being suggested, add the note 'To save a line', as they may be able to make their own adjustments to ensure that this happens.

- To make a line, look for the paragraph on that page with the longest last line; then reword slightly somewhere in that paragraph to create an additional line. Turning over a word or words from a tightly spaced line may also force an extra line in the paragraph. Again, to make it clear why this change is being suggested, add the note 'To create a line'. Sometimes such adjustments are easier to do on the preceding page, so that it is possible to take over a complete line to the current page.

When moving lines of text from page to page, check that if there is a footnote attached to the text being moved there will be space on the new page to accommodate the footnote itself and that this doesn't lead to even more adjustments having to be made on subsequent pages.

Check also that subheadings near the foot of a page are followed by at least two lines of text, and that a short last line in the text, or a bibliography or index entry has not been taken over. Reword if necessary.

For any critical change to the text that may affect meaning, consult the author or editor. If page layout is not yet finalised, again it may be better to wait until the final page proofs to make any necessary adjustments.

Quotations and poetry

Long quotations extending beyond about thirty words (depending on the house style and text design) are usually set in a separate paragraph (block quote) using a variety of typesetting conventions to distinguish them from the body text; for example, the text could be set down (set in smaller type) or with reduced leading, indented from the left or also from the right, or even set in a different typeface (perhaps sans serif to contrast with the serif face used for the main text), with a set space above and below the block of quoted text.

For long quotes, check the following:

- They are consistently presented (e.g. in unjustified or justified type), in the correct typeface and size, and with the specified amount of space above and below the quoted extract.

- The position of any source lines (e.g. page references) is consistent.

- No opening or closing quotation marks are included, except where a secondary internal quote begins or ends the extract.

If the text has been incorrectly set as a block quote, the quotation should be run back into the text, using the run on (r/o) instruction, and placed within quotation marks. Remember to check for any internal secondary extracts in the quotation, which should then be placed within double quotation marks within single quotation marks (or vice versa depending on the house style).

If the quotation has been incorrectly run into the body text, the quote should be marked out as a separate block quote. If necessary, use the new paragraph (np) proofing mark to create the new block, and mark the required space above and below the quotation. However, it may be sufficient to simply request that the relevant block quote style be applied to the new paragraph. Don't forget to delete the opening and closing quotation marks. If the newly set-down quotation contains an internally quoted secondary extract, the quotation marks should be reversed (from double to single or single to double, depending on the house style).

Poetry, even if only two or three lines, will usually be displayed in a similar way to a set-down quotation. Check that the markup of this element in the manuscript has been followed, especially for any particular features such as progressive indentation or centring of lines.

Extent

Book pages are printed in sections that are multiples of four, because at minimum each sheet is printed as a two-page spread on each side. Most offset printers produce sections of 16, 24 or 32 pages (or sometimes even 8 or 48 pages). It is therefore ideal to prepare a publication in which the total page extent is in exact

offset printing
a process for printing high-quality, high-volume jobs by pressing large sheets over an inked rubber blanket; for colour printing, the printed sheet is repeatedly run through the printing press for each colour required

multiples of the printing sections to be produced or, at worst, a multiple plus one half of a section.

The proofreader may be required to check the current extent of the proofs and, taking into account any material that is still to come (such as the index), estimate the final extent.

For more information about page extents, see chapter 14.

If there will be blank pages, the proofreader should check with the in-house or project editor how these are to be dealt with.

Text and content issues

Typos

Proofreaders must keep alert for literals or typos (typographical errors) and must be careful not to accept what they *think* is there, but read exactly what has been typeset.

If more than one typesetter has worked on the same publication, each may have introduced a perceptible pattern of keyboarding errors. Look for repeated transpositions of a sequence of letters (*statoin* for *station*, *ot* for *to*), recurring misspelt words, or spacing issues, such as missing or extra spaces around punctuation. If proofing onscreen on a PDF, it is possible to perform a spellcheck or use the *Find* facility to search for these types of mistakes.

Missing copy

OSC (out, see copy)
a markup made in the margin of page proofs to indicate when there is a large amount of missing copy to be inserted that is supplied separately; for example, in a Word document

If a substantial amount of copy has been accidentally omitted from the proofs, mark this in the margin of a hard-copy proof as, for example, 'OSC: copy A in the accompanying Word file', and attach a printout of the missing text, preferably with tape or other secure fastening. When the proofs are returned, the text should also be provided in a suitably named Word document so that the typesetter can copy and paste the text into the document. If working on a PDF proof, insert a note at the appropriate point in the text and attach the missing text as a Word file using the *Attach File* tool.

overset or **overrun**
text that does not fit into a text area in a typeset document; it exists in the file but does not appear on the page because the text area is too small, or the text too long or the font size too big

Often the text is not actually missing, but has been overset (the text doesn't appear on the page even though it is contained in the file) or an object has been placed over the text without a wrap-around instruction, so the text is obscured. In these cases, it is a simple matter for the typesetter to reinstate the text without having to retype or copy text from another file.

Headings and subheadings

Check that the wording and numbering of headings is accurate, and consistent (e.g. not Part 1, Part 2, then Part III). These headings should be uniform, with consecutive numbering, and be set in the same type style, size and position.

Once proofreading is complete, cross-check these headings with those in the contents, and resolve any discrepancies either against the original edited manuscript or with the author or editor. Ideally, the contents listed will be generated automatically by the typesetter, using the actual heading titles as a reference, reducing the likelihood of errors occurring.

All subheadings should be read with the text for literal accuracy. Run through them all again as a separate step once proofreading is finished, and cross-check them with the contents list to ensure they are included there and that they match the wording exactly.

Wrong words

Be alert to the occasional error of incorrect words spelt correctly (e.g. there/their/they're; pair/pare/pear; four/for/fore). It may be that a computer spellchecker has been used and a wrong choice made in response to a query. Read for sense, and correct all such errors.

Repeated first and last words

Check carefully any text in which successive lines in the manuscript begin or end with the same word. Corrections may have been made accidentally on the wrong line, or a line omitted. Be alert to the possibility that the same word may have been mistakenly repeated in the manuscript at the end of one line and the start of the next line and overlooked in the original copy editing.

In some house styles a three-line sequence ending or beginning with the same word is unacceptable and adjustments may be necessary to correct this.

Capitalisation

Check that capitalisation is consistent throughout. The house style used and style sheet should be consulted closely, as capitalisation requirements can vary.

Issues that often need particular attention from the proofreader include the capitalisation of:

- abbreviated designations and titles after spelling out the name in full (e.g. *the Department of Human Services*, followed by *the department*)

- scientific nomenclature

- formerly capitalised names that have become household
  words (e.g. nylon, dutch courage)

- mid-capitals (e.g. iMac, AustLII)

- cross-references between sections of a book (e.g. chapter,
  section)

- titles in bibliographies and references.

If small caps are used anywhere, carefully check that words in
title case are correctly converted; for example, Horatio Nelson
should appear in caps and small caps as HORATIO NELSON, not
HORATIO NELSON).

Spelling, hyphenation, acronyms and abbreviations

Check (preferably against the house style guide, and style sheet
and word list) that spelling and hyphenation are consistent (e.g.
-ise or -ize, program or programme, co-ordinate or coordinate), as
are names of people, places and events, but observe the original
spelling, hyphenation and capitalisation in quoted material,
references, and company and brand names.

Recheck that, at first use, all acronyms and abbreviations are
explained in the text or in a footnote, or indicated in a glossary.
Check that acronyms and abbreviations are set according to
house style, with or without punctuation and spaces. Some house
styles dictate that the full form is only used once, while others are
less restrictive.

Also check any unusual and unfamiliar spellings or words that
could be misspelt.

Punctuation and other marks

Check all punctuation very carefully. When writing additions or
corrections on hard-copy proofs, it is important to circle all full
points, commas, question and exclamation marks, ellipses, colons
and semicolons so that they are not missed or mistaken as simply
stray marks.

Single closing quotation marks and apostrophes in particular must
be distinguished from a comma, with the former being written
above a superscript mark, and the latter circled. Always write
quotation marks, apostrophes and commas in the typographic

(smart or curly) forms. When prime (′) and double prime marks (″) are required (usually to indicate feet and minutes, and inches and seconds, respectively), these should be specially described as such to ensure that the correct characters are used. Sometimes straight single and double quotation marks are used instead of primes, but this is typographically incorrect and easily misunderstood, and so must be marked for amendment.

Make sure that all opening and closing quotation marks are present, and that they are correctly paired, in the right direction, as specified in the house style (either single quotation marks, with double quotation marks within single quotation marks, or vice versa). Where dialogue by the same person spans two or more paragraphs, each paragraph should start with an opening quotation mark but there should be no closing quotation marks in between the paragraphs in that dialogue sequence; only at the end of the final paragraph.

Check that the spacing of all punctuation follows the house style. There should be no space after an opening parenthesis or bracket or before a closing one, or after an opening quotation mark or before the closing one. There should be no space before and only one space after other punctuation (e.g. comma, full point, colon, semicolon, question mark, exclamation mark).

Ellipses may or may not be preceded and followed by a space, depending on house style, but whatever the style the spacing should be applied consistently. Be alert for the incorrect use of a series of three full stops instead of ellipses, identifiable due to their different spacing.

Again, according to the *Style Manual* or house style preference, non-breaking thin (or hair) spaces are frequently used in place of a comma in figures over either 999 or 9999 (except in quoted material, and often in tables), and between initials preceding or following a surname. Non-breaking thin spaces are also sometimes necessary to separate letters or punctuation, for example, when both single and double quotation marks fall together: as for ' "… (not '"…) and …' " (not …'"). Non-breaking spaces of any width ensure that the preceding and following elements cannot be separated over two lines.

Any corrections to brackets should be clearly written. If there is likely to be any confusion in hard-copy proofing, write an accompanying instruction in the margin. Check that both opening and closing brackets are given, and are correctly paired: round with round (…), square with square […], brace with brace {…}.

Text dashes (rules)

Check that the style of text dashes is used consistently: a closed or spaced em or en rule. When a spaced em or en rule is used, it is accompanied on either side by a fixed space (often a thin space). If the fixed space is not specified, the variable word spacing in justified setting may lead to very wide or cramped spaces either side of the dash, which are unsightly and distracting to the reader.

Do not leave a dash at the beginning of any line. Look for some way to take it back, or to bring over all or part of the last word from the line above. Solutions include changing the punctuation to commas or parentheses instead of dashes, or recasting the sentence (with the author's approval). Distinguish clearly between the text dash and hyphens in any corrections marked.

Dates

Check that dates are presented consistently (e.g. 10 December 1928), except for dates in quoted material, which should remain in their original form.

In spans of dates check that the following distinction has been made:

- a closed en rule in spans of days or years (e.g. 5–7 July, 1899–2004)

- a spaced en rule between compound terms (e.g. 9 January – 22 June).

Lists

The proofreader must check that each item in a list is set at the appropriate level. It is quite easy for one or more items to be assigned to the wrong level, or simply to appear as body text. Similarly, body text surrounding lists can sometimes be erroneously styled as being part of the list. This is where the text must be read carefully for sense to ensure that the list items are correct.

Unnumbered lists

Unnumbered lists are usually set as hanging indents itemised with a circular or square bullet, punctuation or symbols such as arrows or specially designed decorative elements. Sometimes open bullets (white in the middle) are used to allow for the insertion of a tick or cross.

Each level within a list should adopt a different bullet marker; for example, the first level might use circular bullets, the second level a square bullet, and the third an en dash. The proofreader must ensure that the symbols are used correctly and consistently for each level.

Numbered lists

Numbered lists are also set as hanging indents, itemised with Arabic numbers, letters of the alphabet or roman numerals.

As for unnumbered lists, each level within the list should use a different system of numbering; for example, the first level might use Arabic numbers, the second lowercase letters and the third roman numerals. Check that the correct numbering is used at each level.

The numbering should be sequential within the list. Depending on the nature of the publication, numbering may either be self-contained within each list (i.e. each list starts at number one) or continue the sequence from one list to another. Particularly in the latter case, the proofreader must check that the numbering does indeed continue sequentially from list to list, without omitting or repeating a number. In typesetting programs, automatic list numbering ensures that numbers are unlikely to be missing or repeated. However, they necessarily default to numbering items sequentially from list to list, so typesetters must manually restart the numbering for each list if self-contained numbering is being used. It is therefore more likely that proofreaders will encounter numbering that continues across from a previous list when it shouldn't, rather than the reverse. Alternatively, to avoid this problem, editors and typesetters may simply opt for manual list numbering, which of course brings its own problems.

If the sequence of roman numbers runs to double or triple numbers, check that the numbers are aligned on the right. For example:

    i
   ii
  iii
   iv
    v
   vi
 [etc.]

Notes

Check that all the text indicators for footnotes and endnotes are included, and correctly sized and placed. Make sure that the notes themselves are in the correct type size and style. Where the note numbers run to two or more digits, check that all the numbers align on the right.

If the notes are numbered, check whether the numbering runs sequentially from one chapter to the next or restarts for each chapter (especially where chapters have been written by different authors). Check that numbers are consecutive, and that no numbers in the sequence are repeated or missing. Highlighting the numbers in the text as proofreading proceeds makes the final check easier. Cross-check the note numbers against the text indicator numbers. Do they agree?

The ability of current typesetting programs to handle footnotes and endnotes is mixed at best, so although some functions are automated, others are not and this area is one where proofreaders have to pay special attention to ensure that numbering is sequential.

Footnotes

Footnotes will be placed, or at least start, on the same page as the footnote indicator, separated from the text by a preset space or a short rule below the last line of the relevant page.

If there is insufficient space to include the whole footnote at the foot of the page, it will run across to the foot of the following page. Ensure that it is clear the note is a continuation—the best way to indicate this is to add a longer rule (sometimes running the full page width) aligned left above the footnote continuation. Check that the same amount of space has been left above this rule as for the first part of the footnote.

If the footnote design is for a short rule on the left for both the start and the continuation of the footnote, add '(cont'd)' above the first line of the continuation on the next page. This will avoid confusing the reader if the continuation starts with a new sentence.

Endnotes

Endnotes may be grouped at the end of each chapter or at the end of the main text, after any appendixes and before the bibliography or other endmatter.

Check that all endnotes in the endmatter have been correctly matched to the respective chapters. Are they to appear in one long sequential run or are they meant to be separated by chapter? If separated by chapter using chapter titles, the headings must match the chapter titles exactly.

Numbers

Check all numbers against those in the manuscript. Do not take them on trust. Spot-check the simpler calculations.

Typographical style

Numbers can be set in four main typographical styles. They can be of proportional or fixed (tabular) widths combined with being old-style or lining. Old-style figures have descenders, so that the tails of numbers 3, 4, 5, 7 and 9 sit below the base line (e.g. 123456789), while lining figures do not descend below the base line. Proportional figures vary in width depending on the number, while tabular figures each occupy the same horizontal space. Tabular lining works best in tables, as the digits line up vertically and horizontally, while within the body text, proportional old-style is very attractive and is arguably more readable.

Proofreaders should be aware of these differences and be able to identify the typographical styles for numbers. This will assist in verifying that the correct styles have been used consistently for numbers in varying contexts.

Spelling out numbers

The house style will have specified the preferred style for spelling out numbers: some stipulate spelling out numbers up to 20 or 100, others only up to 10. Check all numbers for consistent style.

Check that amounts or measurements are not spelt out when followed by units of measurement, even if under 10 (e.g. 6 kg). Numbers and measurements are usually spelt out in a more general context (e.g. The children rode their bikes for twelve kilometres to reach the local school).

Number spans

Make sure spans of numbers are elided according to house style. Most usually the second number is reduced to be as short as possible without losing clarity, such as 3–5, 10–19 (note the difference for the teens), 20–9, 100–66. Other styles require that the second number appears in full (e.g. 201–230, not 201–30).

Number measurements and spacing

Spacing should be checked when numbers are followed by a unit of measurement or other symbol. In general, there should be a non-breaking space between a number and its associated measurement name (e.g. 21 kg, 40 mm), but no spacing between the number and the primes or the percentage sign (e.g. 50′, 47%).

The spacing of the degree measurement can vary, depending on house style. Where a degree sign is accompanied by the letter indicating the temperature scale, some styles (e.g. the *Style Manual*) require a fixed space between the number and the degree name (e.g. 32 °C, 56 °K), while other styles specify no space (e.g. 74°C). However, if the degree symbol is used on its own, all style guides agree that there is no space between the number and the symbol (e.g. 100°).

In research and technical publications it is important that any units of measurement accord with the International System of Units (SI). Some measurement names commonly used in general publications do not conform with SI specifications (e.g. kph should be km/h, 5 kg not 5 kgs), so proofreaders must look out for these where applicable.

Check that when measurements are compared, the same unit is used (e.g. 'the room measured 2.5 m by 3.6 m', not 'the room measured 2500 mm by 3.6 m').

In equations, mathematical symbols should always be surrounded by non-breaking spaces (e.g. $5 + 3 = 8$).

For positive and negative numbers, ensure that there is no space between the plus or minus sign (–) and the digit (e.g. +20, –5).

Percentages

Check that percentages are uniformly given:

- in the text—for example, *10 per cent* (*percent* may be the style if the book is intended for an American market)

- in tables and notes—often using the per cent symbol (e.g. 35%)

- in lists—where percentages may be expressed with the per cent symbol to save space.

Decimal places

For more technical publications, establish the number of decimal places to be used and the context for the usage. For example, percentages in the body text may be presented as rounded integers, while those in tables may be presented to one or more decimal points.

When numbers are presented to one or more decimal points, all of them should have the same number of decimal digits, even if the meaningful digits do not extend that far (e.g. at one decimal point, 5.0 not 5; at two decimal points, 86.40 not 86.4).

Tables

Check tables even more carefully than the text (remember that typos may be more obvious in words than in columns of figures). Do a quick scan of the columns to see whether values progressively increase or decrease across and down the page; this may help to detect errors.

Check the spacing and alignment of the headings (horizontal: ranged right or left, or centred; vertical: top, middle or bottom). What is the heading type style? What is the table text type style? Check that all formatting is applied according to the type design.

Make sure all the abbreviations are consistent (e.g. per cent or %; a.m./p.m. or am/pm; $million or $m; thousands or '000). There are many conventions regarding the presentation of statistical symbols and abbreviations, and these need to be checked for accuracy and consistency.

Check that the data in all table cells are aligned horizontally and vertically. Check across the page, line by line, and also down each column, each as separate operations. Do a spot check of the numbers to make sure they add up to the totals stated.

Points to check:

- *Captions*. These should appear above the table. Check that they are numbered sequentially and are consistent with the other table captions.

- *Alignment*. Decimal points should be aligned and are usually preceded by a unit (e.g. 0.1). Alternatively, numbers may be ranged right. Check that alignment is consistent.

- *Empty cells*. Data that are not available, not recorded or not applicable are usually represented differently (e.g. an en rule for data not available, and blank for not applicable). Check that they are represented consistently and are explained in the table notes.

- *Indicators*. Asterisks and other symbols or superscript letters such as *a*, *b*, *c* must be explained in the table notes, and all notes must have matching indicators in the table.

- *Notes*. The notes section below the table may begin with 'Notes:' (or 'Note:' if there is only one note) and is often set as a hanging indent. The notes for each indicator may each begin on a new line or run on from each other, ending with a full point, depending on the house style.

- *Sources*. The sources appear after any notes and must be given in a consistent form. House style may dictate whether there is a full point at the end.

The proofreader may need to mark the position of table corrections on hard-copy proofs with a fine line drawn out to the margin, or perhaps mark the corrections beside the errors in individual columns if there is sufficient space. Marking the position of the error and the corresponding correction with a coloured highlighter is useful in very tight settings.

If at all possible, tables should not be broken over a page unless they are very large. If a large table runs to more than one page and horizontal rules are part of the design, check that the bottom horizontal rule of the table on the first page has been omitted, and a byline such as 'continued' or 'cont'd' is added below the table and aligned on the right. On the following page make sure there is another byline at the top (e.g. Table 1.4 (cont'd)), and that all column headings are repeated. If appropriate for the design, make sure there is a horizontal line below the table after the last line, above any notes and sources, to indicate the end of the table.

Make sure the position of each table is correct. Ideally they should appear immediately after the paragraph in which they are first mentioned, but this is often not possible due to layout limitations, so the proofreader needs to check that the table appears as closely as possible to the ideal position. Tables should not appear before they are mentioned in the text.

landscape
the format of a page or illustration that is wider than it is deep

portrait
the format of a page or illustration that is deeper than it is wide

Tables that need to be rotated to fit a landscape shape must always be positioned so that the foot is on the right-hand side of the portrait page. Thus, the reader will turn the publication clockwise to read the table.

Ligatures

Ligatures are used to combine two characters in a typographically more pleasing manner. Technically, the two characters are combined into one. In modern typography, the letters that are most commonly set as ligatures include 'fi' (to 'fi'), 'fl' (to 'fl') and 'ff' (to 'ff'). If these are to be used, the proofreader must check that they have been applied consistently throughout.

Cross-references

A properly prepared and typeset publication should have had any cross-references (e.g. 'see p. 32' or 'see figure 4.1') inserted so that they update automatically, where possible. Even so, the proofreader should carefully check them to ensure that they all have been applied accurately.

As proofreading proceeds, or in a separate run at the end of the proofreading, check all references to other chapters, sections within chapters, illustrations, tables, equation numbers, footnote or endnote numbers, and appendixes, and flag any that are incorrect or missing. It is a good idea to highlight all these cross-references, even if they appear to be correct, so that when checking the next round of proofs references to elements that have moved can be found more easily. In hard-copy proofs, use a yellow highlighter, as this does not reproduce as a dark shadow when the proofs are photocopied. In PDF proofs, use the *Highlight Text* tool.

Where typeset documents do not include automated cross-referencing, highlight all cross-references and add notes about material still to come. The author will add any remaining cross-referenced page numbers at final proof stage.

Websites and other electronic references

Website addresses and other electronic references frequently change during the writing, editing and production process. While the author is responsible for making sure these are up to date, the proofreader or editor may also be asked to check these at the final stage to ensure they are as current as possible before publishing.

Specialist proofreading

Proofreaders may be required to proofread a publication with specialised vocabulary and symbols that are unfamiliar. The proofreader may then need to learn some basic concepts, important names and terminology, and commonly used characters. For example, art books may require knowledge of the names of techniques, art movements and relevant historical periods, while dictionaries may involve being familiar with the international phonetic alphabet and the correct setting of the symbols.

If unfamiliar material presents a problem, check the style sheet and word list, ask the in-house or managing editor, or consult reference books, dictionaries or technical texts on a similar subject to become acquainted with specialised symbols, terminology and vocabulary.

Scientific and technical publications often include characters that require special composition, such as superscripts and subscripts, mathematical symbols, equations and chemical formulas. It is important for proofreaders to be versed in the typographical differences between frequently confused symbols, such as an en rule (–) and a minus sign (−), a textual 'x' and a multiplication sign (×), or an ordinal indicator (º) and a degree symbol (°).

Always check equations against the original manuscript for spacing, positioning, superscripts, subscripts, italics and so on. Check spacing above and below equations, and whether they are to be centred or indented a standard amount. Are the equations numbered consecutively through the book or by chapter? Are any numbers missing or repeated?

Foreign words

Foreign words are usually set in italics. However, words and phrases that have been absorbed into the English language—for example, de facto, non sequitur, café (now frequently without the acute accent), tofu, jihad—are no longer italicised. If the style sheet, word list or dictionary does not assist, the proofreader should query the italicisation of any foreign words. Check a dictionary of the relevant language if the spelling seems incorrect, and flag any queries for the author.

It may be important for a proofreader to become familiar with accents, special characters, punctuation and other aspects of the relevant language. Otherwise it will be difficult to ascertain if an incorrect character or symbol has been used. In hard-copy proofing, write any accented characters very clearly; if necessary, spell out (and circle) the name of the accent (e.g. the French acute, grave and circumflex accents, the Spanish tilde and the German umlaut). Check whether corrections made to accented words are accurate (it is easy to confuse an acute accent for a grave, e.g. á for an à), and that they have not been inadvertently omitted. It may be clearer to rewrite the entire word or phrase to ensure accurate corrections.

Each language has its own idiosyncrasies. For example, in German all nouns are capitalised; in French inverted commas are represented by chevrons (<< ... >>); in Spanish questions begin with an inverted question mark and end with the normal one; and in most European languages the decimal point is shown as a comma (0,37).

The *New Oxford Style Manual* has a very useful and detailed section on rules for setting text in foreign languages.

Endmatter

Check recto or verso placement of all components in the endmatter against the text design, or for consistency if the specifications are not available.

Appendixes

Check that the appendixes are set consistently according to the text design. They may be set in a different typeface, size or font style from the main text or may be set with a different layout of margins, columns and other design features.

In technical publications, appendixes often contain a large amount of data in tables and these must be checked carefully to ensure they are laid out consistently with tables in the main text.

Glossary

As the proofreading proceeds, check against the glossary entries any terms or expressions in the text omitted from the glossary that should also be explained. Highlight and tag any glossary entries that are no longer mentioned in the text.

Check the glossary entries for consistency of presentation, spelling and capitalisation, and for any additional cross-referencing that would be helpful within the glossary.

Bibliography and references

While proofreading, double-check the alphabetical and date order of citations in the bibliography, the alignment of turnover lines, the use of the two- or three-em rule for repetition of an author's surname (if used), and for any widows or orphans.

Cross-check these entries with citations in the notes or in the text, depending on the referencing system used. Highlight or tag any discrepancies between the entries and citations, or missing details, and list them for the author to check. Make sure the same order of elements is used throughout, and that the referencing styles used, including all capitalisation, punctuation and italicisation, agree.

Other endmatter

Items such as lists of addresses, advertisements, forms and so on, may not be available for proofreading until final pages, when the final extent is confirmed. Proofread any that have already been set.

In lists of addresses check the headings, consistency within all addresses and telephone and other contact details, spacing, alphabetical order within sections and so on.

Forms require careful proofreading. Check that sufficient space has been allowed for the insertion of handwritten responses.

Artwork

Placement and layout

Check all artwork and captions for correct placement on the pages. The proofreader may be supplied with the artwork and permissions brief and be required to check all artwork against this listing to ensure nothing has been missed. Mark any artwork that is still to come and check that the space allowed is sufficient and correctly placed.

Check for any requested cropping, reduction or enlargement, or any other design requirements such as drop shadows or text wrapping around the shape of the image. Double-check that they are all the right way round and up, especially for photographs and art, where any problems might not be obvious at first glance. Make a visual check of all keylines (the borders around illustrations, maps, boxes etc.) for uniform thickness and colour or tint, and mark any discrepancies.

Be alert to any situation in which a picture box obscures nearby text, or a part of a diagram (such as the corner of a letter label on a geometry diagram) is partly obscured because the picture box overlaps the text.

Check that whole-page landscape (turned) illustrations are all positioned with the foot on the right-hand side of the portrait page, irrespective of whether on a verso or a recto. In other words, the reader should turn the book clockwise to view a turned illustration.

Illustration sections included as inserts or wraparound sections do not usually have running heads or folios, although the illustrations or plates may have their own numbering system. At this stage, the page references given in the list of illustrations in the prelims should be given as, for example, 'opposite p. XX', or 'between pp. XX and XX'. Unlike other items in the list of illustrations, these page numbers may have to be inserted manually and will be finalised after final proofs have been checked, and the extent and number of sections in the publication confirmed.

wraparound
a small group of pages (usually printed separately due to their different content or format) wrapped around a section, or part of a section, in the makeup of a book

If any logos appear in the publication, check that they are reproduced according to the organisation's requirements, including size, placement, colour and surrounding space.

If artwork does not fit on the same page as the associated text reference, it may need to be moved to the following page. In such cases, it may be the house style to add a cross-reference to any mention of it in the text (e.g. 'in figure 5.2 (on page 67)') so that the reader can find the artwork more easily. If this has been done by the typesetter, the proofreader should check it is correct, or insert the cross-reference if necessary.

If the positioning of artwork becomes a problem (especially if there are many images relative to the amount of text), the proofreader should alert the in-house or project editor. The editor may have to make a decision to make major adjustments to the layout, such as repositioning, resizing or even removing the artwork. Photographs in particular can be repositioned to bleed off the edge of the page, thus saving some space within the text block. If the changes become very complex and the editor is unsure whether the adjustments will have the desired effect, they should consult the typesetter or designer and let them know what the problem is, along with some suggested solutions. It may be that the typesetter will be able make finer adjustments and juggle the elements in a way that will resolve the issue.

Captions and labels

Check all captions are correctly paired with the illustrations, and flag any that are missing or incomplete. Ensure that they are consistently placed in the position dictated by the house style; that is, either above or below the figures.

Proofread all the captions carefully for consistent type size and style (including italics or bold), numbering, capitalisation and abbreviations (e.g. Figure 1.1 or figure 1.1; Fig. 1.1 or fig. 1.1), spacing, end punctuation, source lines (including acknowledgements if required to be placed with the illustrations) and catalogue numbers.

All labels, scales and legends must be checked to make sure that none are missing and for spelling, punctuation, capitalisation, type style and size, and so on. Check that pointers are correctly placed and actually point to the correct item in the illustration, without obstructing any other vital information.

First proofs—a checklist

Page layout

- Are all part titles on a recto with a blank verso, or, to save space, above the chapter title?

- Are there part or chapter contents pages? Are page numbers to be included?

- Are chapters to start only on a recto, or on either a recto or a verso?

- Have the typefaces, chapter and page drops, and all the headings been checked?

- Have the running heads and folios been checked?

- Are all long set-down quotes spaced correctly in the text, without opening or closing quotation marks?

- Have the prelims, notes, bibliography and other endmatter been checked for accurate layout?

Text

- Have all the following prelims been finalised as far as possible: half-title and verso, title page (recheck the title and the spelling of the author name(s)), imprint (including the CiP data—remember to double-check the ISBN), dedication, foreword, contents, list of illustrations, list of tables or graphs, list of contributors, preface, introduction, acknowledgements and so on?

- If any material is still to come, is it necessary to leave one or more blank pages for this, based on its known or estimated extent?

- Are all copyright permissions in hand? Has a list of acknowledgements been prepared?

- Are there any cross-references to be completed on the final page proofs? Have these been marked clearly?

- Is any material to be added or checked at the last possible opportunity (say, in a book on a current political situation)? If so, has the position and extent been specified?

- Have instructions been given about avoiding widows and orphans, and word breaks at the foot of rectos?

- Have all global corrections been listed?

Artwork

- Have all design instructions been followed?

- Is there any outstanding artwork? Do any illustrations have to be corrected or redrawn? Have these been listed for the designer or noted on a master checklist of illustrations?

- Have all design instructions for tints (to a specified percentage, e.g. 5%, 10%), colours or other treatment (boxes, rules, continuation lines etc.) been observed?

- Have any numbered items been reordered, deleted or added? Is the numbering now correct?

- Are all tables, illustrations, captions and labels, diagrams and maps correctly placed, or their position keyed in?

- Are there any remaining low-resolution images (comps) that must be replaced by high-resolution versions?

- Are the illustrations to be printed as wraparounds or inserted sections, or on text pages? Do any have to be resized—cropped, reduced or enlarged?

- Are all illustrations correctly matched with the corresponding captions, source lines, photo credits etc., including all legends and internal labels?

Extent

- Has the estimated extent of the book been checked? Remember to include all the prelims and illustrations, and to make an allowance for the index.

- On the last page of the proofs, has additional material, such as the index, been marked as being still to come?

- Will the index start on a recto or a verso?

(continued)

First proofs—a checklist *(cont'd)*

- Has the probable number of sections (of 16 or 32 pages etc.) been estimated, and has this been checked with the production department? Has a decision been made on the necessary changes that need to be made to fit the publication to this extent?

Final check

- Have all queries been resolved?

- If working with hard-copy proofs, has the master set been signed and dated? Has a security copy been made?

- Have instructions been prepared for the typesetter on any critical design or typesetting points that need attention, such as typefaces, fonts and sizes, running heads, headings, text spacing, layout and position of tables, chapter drops, illustrations, footnotes and endnotes, as well as listing any global corrections?

- For hard-copy proofs, have sufficient sets of revised proofs been ordered?

CHECKING CORRECTED (REVISED) PROOFS

Proofreaders may only be required to check a second round of proofs, with subsequent rounds being completed by the editor, but this will depend on the publishing organisation's practices.

For hard-copy proofs, the editor should check that the correct number of sets of ordered proofs have been received, together with the previous set of marked proofs. Depending on the nature of the project, timelines and budget, these might comprise:

- a master set for the proofreader or editor—label this according to the round of proofs (e.g. 2nd proofs, master set), and add the date

- a set for the author to check any major changes on the first proofs—label this according to the round of proofs (e.g. 2nd proofs, author's set), and add the date

- a set for filing—label this according to the round of proofs (e.g. 2nd proofs, uncorrected file copy), and add the date

- an extra set that can be photocopied as needed (e.g. for marketing and publicity, or for any organisation considering endorsing the book, such as Diabetes Australia for a book of recipes for people with diabetes).

Date and label all sets, and confirm that all the sets are complete, with running heads and folios in position, and that all the pages are in the right sequence.

With PDF proofs, make the required number of copies of the original files from the typesetter, labelling them appropriately before sending them to the proofreader, author and others.

Note that the author may not review subsequent proofs, depending on the publication, the number of rounds of proofing, and the number and types of changes required.

How to check revised proofs

Proofreaders usually do not read revised proofs in full, though it might be easier to do so, depending on the level of corrections. Check only that all the corrections marked on the first proofs have been accurately completed, with no new errors introduced.

It is preferable to place the marked set of proofs side by side with the corrected set so that headings and text line up across both for easier checking. Any misalignment of layout at both page and paragraph level will alert the proofreader to the need to check carefully for unwanted text flow-on or other errors.

If checking PDF proofs onscreen, a large monitor is the proofreader's friend, as this makes it manageable to compare different versions of proofs side by side on the screen.

What to check

Check, paragraph by paragraph, first proofs against revised proofs, that nothing is repeated or missing or inaccurately corrected.

Look carefully at all instances where any lines of text may have been marked to be respaced or reworded:

- to make or save a line within or at the foot or top of a page

- to avoid an orphan or a widow on the following page

- to fit tables, illustrations, footnotes or headings neatly into the page format

- to ensure that the baselines of facing pages (double-page spreads) are evenly aligned.

Meticulous checking at this stage is essential. Read the whole corrected line, as well as the lines above and below, especially if they begin with the same word; if necessary, read to the end of the paragraph. This is essential if the correction affects subsequent line endings.

Make sure that all corrections necessary at this point correspond as closely as possible to the previous number of characters and lines. Make sure that any corrections do not create further problems, such as flow-on of text, unwanted widows and orphans, split tables or artwork and tables appearing too far away from the associated text.

Check word breaks and words previously manually hyphenated but now in the middle of a line, and check whether the hyphen is still required; mark errors for correction.

As with first page proofs, it may be necessary to alter the layout by running text over or back, or adding or deleting some words to alter paragraph length, and creating long or short pages as necessary, but this should only be done as a last resort and only if the proofreader has been instructed to do so.

Check very carefully all corrections to mathematical and chemical equations and calculations, display material, forms, rules for writing answers, boxes and so on, especially for conformity to all type specifications and layout.

Recheck all the page numbers in the contents and in lists of illustrations, figures, tables, maps etc. Finalise any outstanding cross-references (e.g. see p. XX). The author can do this at the same time as preparing (or checking) the index, but the proofreader or editor should also double-check the page numbers in case for any reason some pages have had to be adjusted (with a flow-on or flow-back effect). Check all cross-references in the text to other chapters or pages, and to plates, figures, tables and chapters.

Do a final check of the page imposition for equal length of pages as a separate checking stage once all other corrections are completed. Also check all running heads and folios as another separate operation.

Artwork

Artwork is frequently added to proofs in stages, because the illustrator may still be working on some images, or the editor is waiting on high-resolution versions of photographs, or permissions are pending. It is therefore common for the proofreader or editor to be checking artwork even after a few rounds of proofs have been completed.

Check that the correctly imposed illustrations have been placed as closely as possible after the associated text references and whether a cross-reference by page number is necessary. Recheck captions, notes and sources to ensure that they still match the artwork.

Check that the labels in all diagrams and maps are now correct, and all scales, legends and keys have been included and checked.

It may also be decided at quite a late stage that artwork has to be deleted or changed (for example, if permission cannot be obtained), which may necessitate making major changes to the layout.

Second and subsequent proofs—a checklist

Final checks to run

As it is hard to keep more than a few elements in mind without overlooking some of them at some point, scan for one or two, or at most three, editorial points at a time. Check that:

- all text dashes are correct
- all word breaks are acceptable
- all widows and orphans are dealt with
- all cross-references are highlighted
- all running heads are correct
- spacing and layout conform to design specifications.

Questions to ask about layout

- Are all running heads and folios in place?
- Does each part title begin on a recto? Is there a folio? Is the part title followed by a blank page without a folio?
- Do all chapters begin on alternate rectos or versos, or only on rectos?
- Does each part or chapter opening page begin on the required recto or verso? Do these pages have folios?
- Do the first and last text pages of each chapter have a folio? Are folios deleted on preceding blank pages?
- Have blind folios been included in the page numbering?
- Are all long set-down quotes spaced correctly in the text?

(continued)

Second and subsequent proofs—a checklist *(cont'd)*

- Are there any remaining widows and orphans or word breaks at the foot of a recto?

- Have the typefaces, the headings and the chapter drops been rechecked?

Questions to ask about artwork

- Has the numbering of all the artwork been checked?

- Is the artwork correctly matched with the captions and labels?

- Is there any outstanding artwork? List this for the designer.

- Have all copyright permissions been received, and the required acknowledgements been added and checked?

Questions to ask about content

- Are there any cross-references still to be completed? Have these been marked clearly?

- Are there any outstanding queries for the author?

- Have all the prelims been finalised: half-title and verso; title page (recheck the title and the spelling of the author name(s)); imprint; dedication; foreword; contents; lists; preface; introduction; acknowledgements?

- Has all late copy (such as a preface or foreword) been checked, and have any late alterations to the notes, bibliography and other endmatter been copy edited?

For details on
editing an index,
see chapter 13.

- Is there any other material still to come (e.g. bibliography, index, foreword)? What is its extent, and is it to start on a new page, recto or verso?

For discussion on
the final stages
of proofing
and preparing
a publication
for print, see
chapter 14.

- Has the last page been marked in the hard-copy proof?

Management issues

- Have final instructions for the typesetter been listed?

- Has a copy of the hard-copy or PDF proof been stored securely?

Editing indexes

Depending on the nature of the publication the author or a professional indexer (sometimes the editor) may need to compile an index for the book. Even if an editor's duties do not include indexing, it is nevertheless useful to understand what indexing is and how it is done in order to better be able to assess the quality of an index and edit it once it has been submitted. This chapter provides a broad introduction to indexing and the editor's role in editing an index.

WHAT ARE INDEXES?

Indexes are mainly used in non-fiction publications. They are not commonly used in, for example, fiction books, certain categories of general books, books for young children, books with comprehensive tables of contents or dictionaries. Indexes consist of lists of words and phrases, arranged as entries (or headwords) and subentries that locate for the reader where in the publication significant topics, concepts, people and other matters are mentioned. Some books may have two or more indexes; for example, a restaurant guide might have one index for types of cuisines and another for locations. Anthologies usually have several indexes: one to titles and first lines, another to authors, and sometimes a general index to topics as well.

Indexes also usually include cross-references, which refer the reader to related or alternative terms in another part of the index. A *see* entry directs the reader from a non-preferred term to the preferred term and therefore does not include any page

entry or **headword**
the main term in an index or dictionary used for a concept, topic, name or other item, followed by the page number(s) where it appears in the book, and sometimes by subentries

subentry
an indexing term for a sub-topic of the main entry

preferred term
a word or phrase that is chosen to describe a particular topic, concept, person or other item

non-preferred term
a synonym or alternative spelling of a preferred term; readers are directed from non-preferred to preferred terms using *see*

references (e.g. felines *see* cats). A *see also* entry indicates to the reader that there is an additional, related entry in the index (e.g. lions 45, 89; *see also* leopards), and there are page references under each entry.

An index should not be treated as an afterthought as it provides readers with valuable additional information about the contents and helps them to get the most out of the book, especially if it is on a complex topic. Whatever the content, indexes should have neither too much nor too little detail. Deciding on the balance for this and ensuring a consistency of depth throughout is a skill that a good indexer develops with experience. The depth and length of an index is also affected by the number of pages, budget and time available.

Some argue that indexes are no longer necessary in digitised documents because they can be searched using keywords. However, keywords do not easily capture complex issues and topics (sometimes expressed over a number of pages), nor do they allow the grouping of similar concepts under preferred terms or cross-referencing to related entries. For example, a passage of text may discuss the political, social and economic circumstances that led to the onset of World War II, without ever actually mentioning the words *World War II*, *political*, *social* or *economic*, thus making the topic difficult to locate simply by using keywords. Only an intellectual analysis of the text would identify the meaning of such a discussion, and this is where indexing comes in.

PREPARING AN INDEX

The author may be contracted to prepare the index, or a professional indexer may be employed, paid for either by the publisher or the author. The publisher or the editor will negotiate with the author as to who commissions an indexer, and the contract may specify a procedure or payment for doing so.

> Wherever possible, the indexer should be chosen from among those registered with the Australian and New Zealand Society of Indexers. Contact details for registered indexers in all states of Australia are available on the Society's website (www.anzsi.org).

In some cases, particularly for academic works, the author or indexer may be asked to prepare an index early in the process, such as when the original manuscript is submitted or after the manuscript has been edited. More commonly the index is prepared at the page proof stage, once the pagination is final. Much like editing, indexing is still and will probably always be a heavily manual process, as it requires careful thinking about the concepts being indexed and the appropriate terms that can be used to group and link these concepts. However, the process can be assisted greatly by using either specialist indexing software or embedded indexing techniques.

When creating an index, some indexers prefer to read through the entire publication at least once to get an overall sense of the content and structure and decide on the key concepts and terminology to be used in the index. At this stage they will note potentially synonymous terms that could be combined, different spellings and any unusual issues. They will then read through the text again in more detail, adding entries and subentries linked to the page numbers (or locators) on which they appear. Other indexers, however, spend only a short time getting a feel for the text before they commence the indexing process.

locator
a page number or other device used in an index to pinpoint where a topic, concept, person or other issue is to be found in a book

The traditional method of indexing starts with the near-to-final page proofs, with indexers creating a separate index that is then incorporated into the typeset file. Another method is called embedded indexing, which, as the name suggests, embeds the indexing terms into the electronic file as metadata. This type of indexing can occur at almost any time during the writing, editing and typesetting process.

Separate indexes

To create a separate index, some indexers simply use Word to record the entries as (styled) text; however, this can be cumbersome and is not recommended for indexes to lengthy, complex works. Most professional indexers use specialist indexing programs such as CINDEX (Windows and Mac), Macrex (Windows) or Sky Index (Windows). These programs do not do the intellectual work of indexing, but assist with the often tedious mechanical tasks of managing the entries. The indexer inputs the entries and their page numbers into the program to create a special type of database that can, among other things:

circular cross-reference
a cross-reference, usually in an index, where two non-preferred terms refer only to each other (e.g. cats *see* felines; felines *see* cats), thus leading the reader nowhere

- cross-reference index terms to each other and check for errors (such as circular cross-references or references to non-existent entries)

- sort terms by alphabet, page number, date entry and other elements, using various methods (such as letter by letter, or according to specific foreign language rules)

- format (style) the entries appropriately and consistently (such as italicising *see* and *see also*)

- group terms by initial starting letter or other rule

- output terms as indented or run-in entries, using the required punctuation

- output entries in a range of formats, such as styled word-processing or typesetting files.

Such programs are very powerful and give the indexer a great deal of control over how the index appears in the final document (see figure 13.1). Providing the output format is set up correctly, according to the brief, this should mean that, when editing the index, the editor can focus on the entries and page numbers themselves rather than worry too much about the alphabetical order, formatting, punctuation or other mechanical issues.

Figure 13.1: example of index entries in CINDEX, showing an entry dialogue box (left), and formatted output (right)

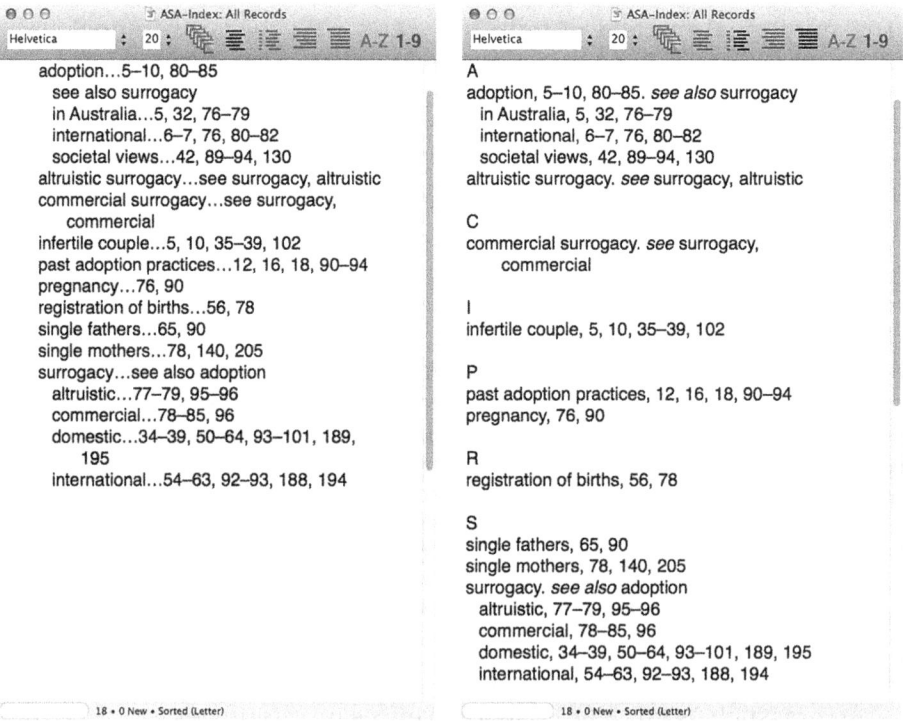

Reproduced by permission of Indexing Research, Rochester, NY, USA

Embedded indexing

Embedded indexing is indexing that occurs during the writing, editing or typesetting process. While the same intellectual analysis needs to be used to create the entries for the index, the main advantage of this method is that the indexing entries are inextricably linked to their location in the text. This means that the index is 'live' and travels with the text so that repagination can be updated with relatively little effort, saving considerable production time. An added bonus is that, in theory anyway, if there is a new edition, provided the author works from the correct version of the previous files, the index can simply be updated rather than re-created from scratch.

Embedded indexes can be created either in Word using the *Insert Indexes and Tables* function (see figure 13.2, overleaf) or directly in a typesetting program such as InDesign or QuarkXPress. The relevant text is selected or the cursor is inserted into an appropriate spot, and an entry and subentry (if required) or cross-reference is created using the program's indexing tools. If text is subsequently deleted or moved, the associated index entry is also deleted or moved, or if the text changes in a way that alters its meaning, the index entry can be changed to match. Index entries created in Word translate quite well into programs such as InDesign, allowing the index to be recreated and the pagination updated throughout to match that of the typeset document. InDesign CC and later versions can also output the index to EPUB format so that index entries are hyperlinked to the text.

For more information about indexing EPUBs, see chapter 15.

While this technique has potential, the indexing capabilities of Word and InDesign are not as sophisticated as those of specialist indexing programs, and so they are more suited to simpler indexes. Nevertheless, some publishers prefer to use this method to save time during production.

Figure 13.2: example of embedded index terms and generated index in Word, with coding shown (top), and hidden (bottom)

·A little knitting history{ XE "knitting history:history" }·

The word 'knitting' is derived from the Old English *cnyttan*{ XE "*cnyttan*" \t "*See* knitting" }, to knot. The Danish used to practise *nålebinding*{ XE "*nålebinding*" \t "*See* knitting" } ('binding with a needle' or 'needle-binding'), which was a technique for creating fabric that predated both knitting and crochet{ XE "crochet" }. It is believed, though, that the earliest known sample of true knitting originated in Egypt{ XE "Egypt" }—cotton socks made from knitted coloured strands have been dated to 1000 AD. ·

The first trade guild{ XE "trade guild" } devoted to knitting began in Paris in 1527. Perhaps surprisingly, the knitting members were men only. ·

Later on, the knitting machine{ XE "knitting machine" } was invented, and knitting by hand became a handicraft that was used by people in rural areas who had access to their own fibres, such as wool and cotton. Eventually knitting became a leisure activity for the wealthy. ·

During the 1940s, knitting became particularly popular in England{ XE "knitting:England" } but less so in the rest of Europe{ XE "knitting:Europe" }. This is perhaps because knitting was originally perceived of as a German{ XE "knitting:Germany" } craft, so during World War II, continental knitting fell out of style due to its relationship with Germany. ·

·Index·

blogging, 1 ·	knitting history ·
cnyttan. *See* knitting ·	history, 1 ·
crochet, 1 ·	knitting machine, 1 ·
Egypt, 1 ·	nålebinding. *See* knitting ·
knitting ·	podcasts, 1 ·
England, 1 ·	trade guild, 1 ·
Europe, 1 ·	
Germany, 1 ·	

A little knitting history

The word 'knitting' is derived from the Old English *cnyttan*, to knot. The Danish used to practise *nålebinding* ('binding with a needle' or 'needle-binding'), which was a technique for creating fabric that predated both knitting and crochet. It is believed, though, that the earliest known sample of true knitting originated in Egypt—cotton socks made from knitted coloured strands have been dated to 1000 AD.

The first trade guild devoted to knitting began in Paris in 1527. Perhaps surprisingly, the knitting members were men only.

Later on, the knitting machine was invented, and knitting by hand became a handicraft that was used by people in rural areas who had access to their own fibres, such as wool and cotton. Eventually knitting became a leisure activity for the wealthy.

During the 1940s, knitting became particularly popular in England but less so in the rest of Europe. This is perhaps because knitting was originally perceived of as a German craft, so during World War II, continental knitting fell out of style due to its relationship with Germany.

Index

blogging, 1	knitting history
cnyttan. *See* knitting	history, 1
crochet, 1	knitting machine, 1
Egypt, 1	nålebinding. *See* knitting
knitting	podcasts, 1
England, 1	trade guild, 1
Europe, 1	
Germany, 1	

MANAGING THE INDEXING PROCESS

Check the availability of the author or the commissioned indexer, and give advance notice of the anticipated date of delivery of the proofs. Provide an indication of the time allowed. An index that might take an author several weeks may only take a trained indexer several days. Even with a trained indexer, though, it is important to be realistic in scheduling and allow adequate time to produce a good index.

As always, the quality of an index is dependent not only on the skill of the indexer, but also on the initial brief, which should detail the publisher's requirements, such as:

- any specialist subject matter that needs to be taken into account

- how many and what type of indexes are required

- the level of detail and length of the index

- whether photographs and other images require separate treatment

- the budget available

- how the entries are to appear, including:

  — the method of ordering (using letter-by-letter or word-by-word or some other system)

  — whether the subentries are to be run-on or indented

  — the punctuation used between entries, page numbers and other elements

  — the treatment of numbers

  — paragraph and character styling to be used (such as for each entry level and the words *see* and *see also*) and so on.

Publishing organisations that regularly index their publications may have specific guidelines for indexing in their house style, which should be provided to the indexer during the briefing.

What should be done if the index has been badly prepared? There are two alternatives: tidy it up as much as possible or, after consultation, commission a new one (at additional expense for the author or publisher).

Once the index has been edited and proofread, any outstanding queries (especially those raised by the indexer) should be finalised with the author, emphasising the importance of swift responses at this stage. There will still be pressure to keep strictly to the schedule; as if the scheduled printing date is missed the printer may be unable to reschedule the job for some time, and essential publication dates or publicity may be affected.

Indexing from page proofs

Indexing is usually scheduled to occur after a specified number of rounds of page proofs have been corrected. However, regardless of the schedule, the pages should only be sent for indexing once the author and editor are sure that no further amendments are likely to occur that will cause changes to the pagination. In other words, there might be further minor corrections of missed typos, table data, cross-references and so on, but text should not be expected to reflow to another page nor elements such as tables, figures or images to move to another page. Changes made to pagination after indexing can incur additional costs and increase the chances of errors creeping in.

The editor should send the final page proofs (hard copy or PDF) to the author or indexer for the preparation of a separate index, along with a clear brief. An author creating the index should be advised firmly, but politely, to refrain from making any changes to the text that will affect the pagination. The date for returning the proofs and index should also be clear.

Preparation of the index may lead to the discovery of overlooked errors, especially in the spelling of names. The indexer should note any major errors for the editor to consider. The editor must use discretion as to how many corrections can be accepted at this point, given the available time and resources for completion of the publication; if in doubt, the managing editor, the publisher or the production manager should be consulted about what is possible.

When the proofs and index are returned from the author or indexer, any final minor corrections from the author must be checked by the editor and incorporated into the master copy of the proof. Be sure that no previously agreed decisions have been overlooked or overturned by the author at this point.

If the index has been created using a specialist indexing program, and there are errors in formatting, these are likely to appear consistently and be easy to spot, as they have probably been generated by the software. For example, the punctuation between entries and page numbers may not match the house style, or page ranges may not be expressed correctly, or elements such as *see also* may not have been styled correctly. These types of errors are much more easily fixed by the indexer, as they will merely involve a quick tweak or two of the indexing program's output instructions. Likewise any re-sorting of entries is something that is much more easily done with the indexing software, which can be set to use various types of settings, depending on requirements. As usual, time and budget will always be considerations when deciding whether to send the file back to the indexer.

If it transpires that space is a problem, it may be that entries can be edited down or combined or deleted altogether. If the index has been manually compiled, then those entries can be edited in Word or during proofreading, depending on the stage at which they are identified. However, if the index has been generated using indexing software, it may be preferable to send these edits back to the indexer for updating in the original indexing program, if time and budget allow. This ensures that any related cross-references that are affected are also updated, and other error checking can occur.

Indexing during writing, editing or typesetting

If the author is required to create an embedded index in the original manuscript, the editor will be able to check the index entries directly against the text during the editing process. Care must be taken to ensure that index entries are deleted or moved along with deletions or moves of the associated text, and that any editorial changes that might affect the meaning or context of the text are also reflected in the index entries.

Fewer problems are likely to be encountered if the indexing occurs later in the process, such as after editing or after the first set of pages have been typeset, when fewer editorial changes are likely to occur.

Again, outputting errors (such as punctuation) should be evident quite quickly and are usually easily fixed in the typesetting program. Complex entries or those involving page ranges may cause problems that might require manual workarounds. Consult the indexer or typesetter if necessary to ensure that, if the index is recompiled, any manual changes are re-inserted.

SOME INDEXING CONVENTIONS

Order of entries

Indexes are organised alphabetically using either the word-by-word or letter-by-letter methods. The word-by-word method orders each word of the entry separately. The letter-by-letter method ignores spaces (see table 13.1).

Table 13.1: comparison of word-by-word and letter-by-letter order

Word-by-word order	Letter-by-letter order
word order	wording
wording	word order
work groups	workers' compensation
workers' compensation	work groups
workplace design	workplace design

There is a convention that all entries starting with *Mac*, *Mc* or *M* are treated as though they were spelt *Mac*; *Mt* as *Mount*; and *St* as *Saint*. However, other indexers follow the principle that index entries should be sorted as they are, rather than as what they represent. Unless there is a fixed house style, either method is acceptable as long as it is used consistently. Where possible, it is preferable to use the same conventions as those used in the bibliography and other ordered lists in the same publication.

Alphabetical sections of the index are usually separated from each other either by an extra line of space or with an initial letter (A, B, C etc.), depending on the house style and the space available.

Spelling and capitalisation

The spelling of names and terms should follow the text, with cross-references made from alternative forms; for example, an entry under *Mao Zedong* might have cross-references from the non-preferred terms *Mao Tse-tung* and *Chairman Mao* (e.g. Chairman Mao *see* Mao Zedong).

For surnames preceded by articles and prepositions from foreign words, such as *de*, *von*, *el* and *la*, the form given by the author in the text should be used, with cross-references from non-preferred forms.

The first letter of each entry should be lowercase, unless it is a proper noun.

Page references

Page references should be given in sequence, in ascending order.

References to illustrations, by page, figure or plate number, may be given in bold or italics. If principal pages are indicated in an entry, these numbers are sometimes given in a bold font, and in that case, italics would be used for the illustrations.

Where a page reference is to information in a footnote or an endnote, the abbreviation 'n.' is added immediately after the number.

In some indexes the entries refer to paragraphs or item numbers rather than pages. A note at the beginning of the index will make clear which system is being used, if it is not self-evident.

If the subject of the entry runs over several consecutive pages, the form *87–94* is used. Sometimes editors will see *87 f.* or *87 ff.* used instead, with the 'f.' and 'ff.' meaning 'and the following page or pages', but this is no longer common; it is not very helpful for the reader and indicates lazy indexing.

Page ranges should be consistently expressed according to the house style; for example, either as *256–61* or as *256–261*, but not a mixture of the two.

If the subject occurs incidentally on pages in close sequence, the individual pages numbers are usually given (e.g. 87, 88, 90, 92, 94), although *passim* (in italics) meaning 'here and there', may also be used (e.g. 87–94 *passim*), but sparingly. Again, *passim* is no longer commonly used, mainly because most readers do not know what it means.

EDITING AND PROOFREADING AN INDEX

If the index has been created by a professional indexer (by whichever method), the editor can generally simply focus on proofreading the entries. Usually, a quick check of the word order, spelling of terms, consistency in the use of punctuation and capitalisation, and other indexing conventions is sufficient. A spot check of a random sample of page number references will also ensure that no inadvertent errors have occurred and that they do indeed point to the relevant parts of the text.

If the index has been created by the author or an inexperienced indexer, the editor will need to shoulder more of the burden of carefully checking every aspect of the index. In addition to a simple proofread, the editor must ensure that the index is structurally sound, including checking that the entries are appropriate and comprehensive, there are not too many or too few levels of subentries, and there are no missing, superfluous, circular or empty cross-references. Most, if not all, page references must be checked carefully, as well as punctuation, order of entries, expression of page ranges and other conventions.

The initial editing of the index will usually be done in a separate Word document, using a PDF or hard-copy proof as the reference. Use the same onscreen methods for editing the index as for editing the main text; suggested edits should be made using *Track Changes* and electronic styling should be applied or checked. Styles should be applied according to entry level (e.g. *index1*, *index2*), with character styles used for *see*, *see also* or references to specific elements such as maps or photos (often marked in bold or italic). Queries should be addressed to the author or indexer using the *Comment* function.

For details on working with Track Changes in Word, see chapter 6.

Editing an index—a checklist

- Are any entries over-analysed? If there are numerous subentries with only one page reference, consider simplifying or combining several entries.

- Are any entries under-analysed? If there is a long sequence of page numbers, ask the author or indexer to provide appropriate subentries.

- Do any entries seem trivial? Consider deleting them; but be cautious, as this may lead to more work than anticipated!

- Are the entries or subentries too wordy?

- Are entries and subentries in the correct order (either word by word or letter by letter)?

- Are subentries consistent in ordering; for example, alphabetical or chronological?

- Do all general entries begin with a lowercase letter? Only proper names, acronyms etc. should have capitals.

- Are all entries given in the same way as in the main text (capitalisation, punctuation, italics)?

- Is the punctuation correct and consistent?

- Are page references for illustrations and principal pages consistently presented (e.g. in bold or italics)?

- Do all entries have page numbers or cross-references?

- Are there any page entries such as *23344* (23–44 or 233–4) or *158–58* (157–8, 158–9 or 158–68)? Check the pages.

- Are the sequences of page numbers in ascending order?

- Are spans of numbers given consistently?

- Are all cross-references actually there, and given in identical form?

- Are all the *see also* cross-references really needed? If not, and there are only a few extra page references in one of the entries, combine the two using the preferred term and create a *see* cross-reference from the rejected term.

- Is the index too long? If so, ask the author or indexer to reduce it; or if time is short, suggest appropriate reductions or deletions for the author's approval.

- Have a number of entries been spot-checked—both from the index to the text, and from the text to the index?

PROOFREADING INDEXES

Once the index has been edited and finalised, it will be inserted into the typeset document according to the design specifications (often in two or more columns). Page proofs will then be generated, in either PDF or hard-copy format, and the editor (or sometimes a proofreader) will then do a final check to ensure that there are no further corrections to the index. Ensure that there are no widows or orphans in each column and that page ranges are not split over two lines. If an entry or subentry breaks over a page or column, check that a continuation line (e.g. sport, cont'd) has been inserted correctly. Column lengths must be even if possible. Pages should be marked up in the same way as marking up proofs for the main text. By this time, the production schedule will often be very tight and more detailed checking may not be possible.

Proofreading indexes—a checklist

- Check that alphabetical groups are separated by a line space or other device.

- Double-check that all general words begin with a lowercase letter.

- Check that punctuation is used consistently.

- Recheck the alphabetical order for main entries and subentries.

- Recheck the numerical order of page references, and the consistency of spans of numbers.

- Have all long or short columns been dealt with? Have adjustments been made so that the columns on the last page are equal in length?

- Recheck the indentations: usually one em for indented subentries, two ems for all turnovers; or one em for run-on subentry turnovers.

- Avoid widows at the top of any column, especially at the top of the first column of a verso, and orphans at the foot of a column.

- If a string of subentries runs over to one or more following pages, is there a continuation line above?

- Are *see* and *see also* always given in italics?

- Are the running heads correct?

Final stages and print production

Once the typeset document has been thoroughly proofread and the author has approved the pages, there remain the final stages of cleaning up any last-minute changes and preparing the material for printing or ebook production. Time should also be put aside for winding up and archiving all documentation for the project once the publication is completed. This chapter reviews these final steps.

REVISED PAGE PROOFS

The editor is responsible for checking the accuracy of any final corrections to the page proofs before the book is to be sent for printing or ebook production. Revised proofs are not read in full. Only the corrections marked on the previous proofs need to be checked to ensure that they have been made correctly and that no further errors have been introduced. For speed and convenience, it is easiest to compare proofs side by side; this will immediately show if there have been changes to paragraph or page lengths. This can be done whether the proofs are checked using hard-copy printouts or onscreen PDF files.

It is important to check that all the author's final corrections have been made, including any that may have cropped up during the indexing process, and to skim and spot check the cross-references to make sure they are correct and complete.

Check the running heads and folios for each chapter. It is easy to take these for granted. Check also that any changes to chapter or part titles have been incorporated in the running heads and contents.

Artwork

Skim through the final page proofs to ensure that all artwork has been placed correctly and is at an appropriate resolution for printing. Also check that all the artwork has been converted to the correct colour mode for printing (e.g. greyscale, two-colour or four-colour).

Prelims

Reread all prelims very carefully, and check all late copy (e.g. foreword, acknowledgements). Have any details on the half-title and title page changed—title, subtitle, author name(s), order of names if more than one author, descriptions? The cover and jacket and publicity materials must be consistent with the title page.

If there is a translator, compiler or editor, recheck the spelling of their names.

Imprint page

Recheck the following:

- Have there been any changes to the publishing organisation's name and address, or the addresses of subsidiary or associated organisations?

- In the copyright notice is the date correct? Is the wording for the name of the copyright holder correct? Recheck the file or contract. Has a copyright notice been added for the illustrator or translator?

- Has the publication date changed, especially for publications that were originally scheduled for release at the end of one year but have been pushed over to the next?

- Have any details in the CiP data changed? If so, the CiP Unit at the National Library should be advised and the details updated.

- Do the ISBN and EAN correspond with the ISBN and EAN on the jacket or cover? If a book is simultaneously published in different formats (such as hardback, paperback and ebook), each edition will have a unique number. Distinguish clearly which is which.

- Are there any changes to printing details (size and style of typeface, printer's name and location)?

- Have the names of the designer, photographer, typesetter and illustrator been included? Sometimes, by arrangement, a freelance editor or indexer will also be acknowledged.

Contents

Recheck the page numbers, especially of the prelims, in case pages have been backed up on previously blank pages, pages left blank to make even sections, or the order changed. Check that the index page number is correct. Check that any changes to chapter or part titles have been incorporated in the contents list.

If there are lists of numbered tables and figures, recheck both the page numbers and the table and figure numbers to ensure that they are listed in numerical order and that no numbering has been duplicated or is missing.

Acknowledgements

Check the permissions file for any last-minute changes to the acknowledgements, especially if any artwork has had to be replaced, added or removed at a late stage.

Page extent

Once the prelims, endmatter and index have been completed, the total number of pages must be rechecked.

If the extent is one or two pages less than an exact multiple, that is usually acceptable. For example, 24 × 16-page sections produces 384 pages; if the total number of pages is actually only 382 pages, then it is usually acceptable to leave the last two pages blank or fill them with review comments, advertisements or other extra material.

Using the same example, if the final number of pages goes *over* by two pages, this potentially forces the printer to print another section of 16 pages, thus wasting 14 pages. In practice, the editor would either liaise with the designer to reduce the extent by the required number of pages (for example, by removing the half-title page), or the printer could add a half or quarter of a section to reduce the number of blank pages, though this would not be as cost-efficient. Double-check that any adjustments do not interfere with the position of special inserts or wraps of artwork, or alter the page numbers in the contents, other lists in the prelims or the index.

Ideally, the editor would keep an eye on the page extent throughout the typesetting process in order to catch such pagination problems as early as possible.

OTHER PROOFS

Die copy and packaging

The copy to be stamped on the spine of a hardback publication includes the title, the author's name, possibly an ornament, and the publisher's name or logo. The editor and designer both check proofs of this copy, as well as copy for a slipcase or other packaging.

Jacket and cover proof

Check that the book title is correct. Confirm whether the subtitle is to be included or omitted. Proofread any copy line or flash.

Check the author name(s) and position(s) against the prelims. Double-check that the blurb is consistent with the text in spelling, capitalisation and general style. Has the caption and acknowledgement for the jacket or cover illustration or design been included?

Check the barcode (including the ISBN and EAN) and its position— for a hardback it usually appears only on the back of the jacket; for a paperback, on the back cover and sometimes on the spine.

If time permits, send a proof of the cover to the author.

A final checklist

- Reread any email correspondence to make sure all decisions made have been followed through.
- Have all queries been answered?
- Have all cross-references been completed?
- Have all problems with long or short pages been resolved?
- Is all endmatter in the correct order and complete?
- Are any postal and email addresses and telephone numbers included in the manuscript up to date?
- Have any headings or chapter titles been altered? Have they been double-checked against the contents and running heads?
- Is the publication's title still correct?
- Has the spelling of the author's name been rechecked?
- Has the final master set of page proofs been signed off and approved, either on hard copy or by email?
- Have all previous copy and proofs been archived and filed?

FINAL FILES

The production department or designer will generate the final files either as press-quality PDF proofs (the most common method) or as a packaged folder containing the raw typesetting and graphics files, which the printer will then use to create a pre-press PDF. The files will be sent either to the editor or production manager or directly to the printer. If the files are very large, they may need to be transferred via FTP (file transfer protocol) to the printer's server or via a USB stick, CD or DVD. Smaller files can be emailed.

Press-quality PDF files embed all high-resolution artwork and typefaces within the file. They should be identical in appearance to the way the final publication is expected to be printed, except that the pages are surrounded by printer's and bleed marks that are eventually trimmed from the final product.

The editor or production manager must ensure that the printer has been given instructions as to the page extent, finished size, type of binding, paper stock (for cover and text), colours to be used, number of copies to be printed, delivery address, delivery date, requirement for advance copies, and any special instructions regarding tip-in pages or other additions or requirements.

PREPRESS CHECK

Once files have been transmitted to the printer, the printer's prepress department will prepare the file for printing and ensure there are no errors in the file. For simpler jobs, it may be acceptable to receive a prepress PDF as confirmation that the material has been received correctly and that no technical errors have arisen. However, especially for substantial publications, it is better to receive digitally printed page proofs in order to check trapping, the backing up of pages, font production, transparency problems and other issues that may not be evident otherwise. These proofs should be checked by the production manager and the designer as well.

Two main types of printed proofs can be provided:

- large sheets (usually A1 or A2 size) with specially ordered page spreads arranged for printing, folding and trimming into sections (called imposition; see figure 14.1, overleaf); these are often printed in high resolution on heavy stock as they will be used as the reference master for the printer

- a set of folded printed sheets, in unbound sections, which show the order of pages of the book once it is printed.

FTP (file transfer protocol)
a means of transferring electronic files across an online network, especially useful for uploading large typesetting files to printers

DVD (digital video disc)
a compact disc storing digital video, audio or computer data

printer's marks
markings on page proofs used by printers to identify the file, check colours and registration, and indicate where to trim the page

tip-in
an extra page or pages printed separately and fixed in position in a book by being glued along its inner edge; for example, a fold-out map or a colour page in an otherwise single-colour book

trapping (printing)
making colours overlap slightly to avoid unintended gaps when printing is out of registration

Figure 14.1: page setup for printing in 16-up sections

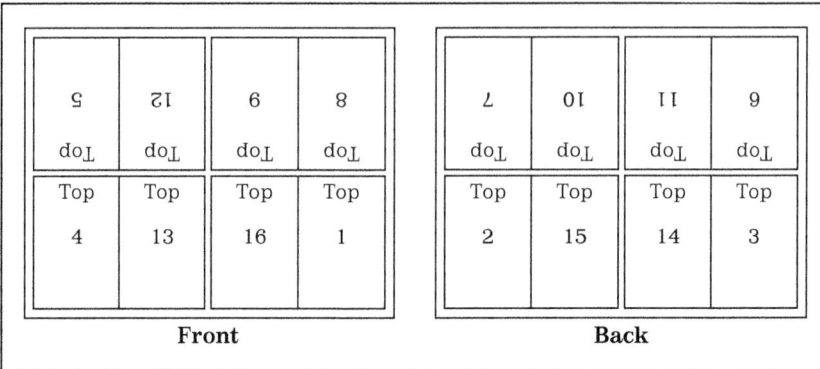

Some printers will provide both types of proofs. The imposed sheets allow the production manager or designer to assess whether colours, fonts, trapping and other technical aspects of reproduction have been correctly captured. The folded sections are more useful for the editor to check the text itself, pagination, backing up, numbering and other similar issues.

Editors should not re-read the proofs at this stage. Instead, they should carefully look through every page to identify any common printing errors that may occur. It is also useful to do a final check of the artwork, recheck the imprint page and any other last-minute changes that were made.

The cover proof is supplied separately. The editor needs to recheck that the title and author's name are spelt correctly and match those used in the book itself.

Printer's proofs—a checklist

- Check the page sequence to ensure that no pages are repeated or missing, and that all are in the correct order, especially between chapters or sections.

- Check that all folios and running heads, and page and chapter drops are correct and in alignment.

- Check that left and right margins remain consistent, and that the lines of text back up correctly on recto and verso pages.

- Check that all artwork has been correctly inserted and appears as high-resolution images.

- Look for any sections of artwork or text that may have become partially obscured by incorrectly placed artwork or from transparency problems (such as drop shadows).

- Check that all fonts used have been rendered correctly and have not been replaced inadvertently by a generic font.

- Check that any last-minute changes that were made are correct, including the imprint page.

- Check and recheck the spelling and accuracy of the title and author's name.

If changes are required, they need to be identified as either those resulting from a printer error (such as an incorrectly rendered font) or a publisher error (such as typos), as the latter will incur extra charges. Publisher's errors are better corrected by making the changes in the original typesetting files and regenerating the relevant pages as revised PDF files. This ensures accuracy and that the typeset files continue to match the final product exactly. It is also usually cheaper.

It is essential to check that any amendments do not lead to the text or other elements flowing onto or being brought back from the next page, as this potentially affects the contents page, index, cross-references and even several pages of the layout. If the changes are so extensive that this is unavoidable, then all affected pages must be checked, amended and regenerated accordingly, including any updated contents or index pages.

Most printers provide a form for signing off approval or listing any necessary corrections. If publisher's changes are required, it is best to note on this form which pages are affected and that revised PDF files for these pages will be submitted (usually by email). If printer's errors are detected, these should be marked directly on the hard-copy proofs and listed on the approval form. Even if no changes have been made, printed proofs usually need to be returned to the printer for their reference.

For the next stage, if amendments are not complicated, it may be acceptable for the editor and production manager simply to receive revised PDF proofs to confirm that the printer has incorporated the amended pages correctly. For more complex technical errors, it may be necessary to generate a new set of printed proofs.

Printer's proofs are approved by the editor or publisher, designer and production manager. They are not normally sent to the author.

Fortunately, as PDF technology improves and the digital publishing workflow matures, most potential problems (such as placement of artwork) can be sorted out before the file ever goes to the printer, and fewer technical errors occur between publisher's files and prepress output. However, the editor must continue to be on the lookout for the inevitable missed typos and unexpected last-minute changes.

OFFSET VERSUS DIGITAL PRINTING

digital printing
a process for printing
medium-quality,
low-volume jobs
from digital files by
transferring ink directly
to the page

Digital printing has improved greatly over the years, and for many types of publications (particularly text-heavy books) is virtually indistinguishable in terms of print quality from traditional offset printing. Digital printing also takes less time and is cheaper to set up. However, for books, digital printing is best suited to small jobs numbering in the hundreds, because the unit cost goes up as the print run increases. Offset printing is still the best, most flexible option for longer print runs (since unit costs go down as the print run goes up), and for jobs that require special colours, higher quality reproduction or unusual paper-stock types and sizes.

This does not mean that publishers are necessarily restricted to an either/or choice. For example, advance copies could be printed digitally while the longer print run is produced using offset. Another option is for the publisher to print a series of shorter digital runs to avoid printing too many copies that don't sell, or to save on warehouse storage costs.

Fortunately, once the decision is made about the type of printing to use, offset and digital printing prepress processes are similar, except that the printed proofs for digital printing may be supplied only in folded book form or as double-page spreads, and then only if requested.

ADVANCE COPIES

Advance copies, and run-on covers or sections are usually ordered for publicity or review purposes, and supplied by airmail if the publication has been printed offshore. As soon as advance stock is delivered, the editor should check a random copy to ensure that all is in order. Check especially for flaws in the printing and binding.

If a serious error is discovered (either a printer's error or a critical error that has been overlooked; for example, misspelling of the book title, or potential libel that requires rewriting to avoid litigation), all or part of a section, or even the cover, may have to be reprinted. If at all possible, avoid an errata slip; it is expensive to insert or tip in, and gives potential readers a poor impression of the reliability of the book.

Any insignificant typos or other errors discovered at this point should be noted in the publication file for attention in any future reprint or revised edition.

FILE, ARCHIVE AND DEPOSIT COPIES

When the final book has been printed and delivered, a reference copy is held and updated for future reprints or new editions. As corrections are notified or discovered, they are added to the file copy, which should be clearly labelled 'Correction copy'. A list of the pages to be corrected is usually included on the inside front cover or endpaper. This copy should be securely stored.

Alternatively, a new version of the typeset file may be created and any corrections made directly to the new copy. If the typesetting program has a facility to track changes, it is useful to turn on this function so that corrections can be found easily and reviewed before issuing a reprint or revised edition. This new file should be clearly labelled as being the corrected copy, and stored securely on the publisher's server.

A mint copy of each book is also archived, usually in a secure area. Copies are also sent to the National Library of Australia and other state and territory libraries as part of the Legal Deposit Scheme.

endpapers
a pair of leaves at the beginning and end of a book, one leaf of each pair being pasted to the inside cover to attach the binding to the book block

REPRINTS AND NEW EDITIONS

If a reprint or a new edition is being prepared, it is usually easier to regenerate the entire book as a new PDF, to ensure that any run-on effect of changes does not cause pagination problems. The editor must also check that any changes are reflected in the index, if there is one.

Check any new illustrations, labels and captions, as well as the acknowledgements. Check the proofs and advance copies as for new books.

Ebooks

An ebook (or electronic book) is a digital version of a book designed to be read using a device such as a personal computer, tablet or dedicated ebook reader. While ebooks are often based on a printed version of the book, increasingly many books exist only in electronic form.

This chapter looks at what ebooks are, and the role of editors in preparing ebooks for publication. Since ebook publishing is still in its infancy, numerous methods, technologies and workflows are still being tried out. The landscape is changing rapidly too, as new standards, formats and reader expectations develop. It will take time for all of these elements to develop into a more stable environment. It is therefore impossible to cover all aspects of ebooks in this brief overview, but it is hoped this chapter will provide a taste of what is possible. In the meantime, editors need to strap themselves in for the ride!

Ebooks versus EPUBs

Perhaps the greatest confusion in ebook terminology arises out of the difference between the terms *ebooks* and *EPUBs*.

- *EPUB* is a free and open international ebook standard that is not 'locked in' to any particular publisher or vendor. Other formats, such as AZW, KF8 and iBooks, are technically similar to EPUBs, but are 'closed' and require special software to read them. As a group, we will refer to both open and closed formats here as 'EPUB-like ebooks'.

(continued)

Ebooks versus EPUBs *(cont'd)*

- There are also stand-alone, usually multimedia, ebook applications that are not necessarily based on a particular standard and may run on only some devices. We'll refer to these as 'ebook apps'.

- *Ebook* is the generic term that applies to all electronic versions of books, including not only EPUB-like ebooks and ebook apps, but also text files, word processing files, books on websites and PDFs.

A LITTLE HISTORY

The idea of ebooks was first conceived many decades ago and the earliest ebooks were simply plain text documents that could be read only on the few computers available at the time. Today ebooks appear in many forms, ranging from simple text documents to website ebooks, PDFs, EPUBs and complex multimedia applications, and are offered on many different devices, either offline or online.

Over the last decade or so, publishers have increasingly sought to find a way to take advantage of digitised forms of the book. Indeed, for some time it has been common practice to provide PDF replicas as an added extra for some printed books, particularly textbooks, so that readers need not to carry around heavy printed volumes. It has also been increasingly common to provide non-commercial publications, such as government reports, in full, either as a set of web pages or as downloadable PDFs, thus broadening availability and cutting down on printing and distribution costs. However, none of these formats have adequate digital rights management (DRM) capabilities, which aim to protect the ebooks from being illegally copied and distributed. It was not until the introduction of the Kindle 'ecosystem' (a reading device and easy access to a wide range of low-priced ebooks) that ebooks — as they are currently popularly thought of — finally took off commercially.

In 2013 ebooks generated about one-quarter of trade publishing revenue, and even though the growth rate appears to be stabilising,[1] this is a format that editors cannot afford to ignore.

digital rights management (DRM) technologies that restrict and control the use of digital content by users

---

[1]www.digitalbookworld.com/2014/ebook-growth-slows-to-single-digits-in-u-s-in-2013/

WHY EBOOKS?

The increasing popularity of ebooks is due in no small part to several advantages they have over regular print books.

- For readers:

  — ebooks are both portable and disposable and do not take up space

  — ebooks are generally cheaper than the print version, sometimes significantly so

  — ebooks can be downloaded online in an instant

  — there are usually far more books available from an ebook store than a traditional bookstore, particularly for popular fiction, often with reviews and ratings attached

  — many out-of-print books are being made available again as ebooks, often free or at very low prices

  — in EPUB-like ebooks, text can be resized and will reflow accordingly

  — ebooks with fixed layouts (usually ebook apps) often have interactivity and multimedia built in

  — text can be linked to other parts of the book (internally) or to websites (externally)

  — the text is searchable by keyword

  — text can be highlighted or bookmarked without damaging the ebook

  — in some cases notes can be inserted and shared with others using social media

  — some devices can read the text aloud, improving accessibility for some readers.

- For publishers:

  — there are more spur-of-the-moment purchases because it is easy to buy ebooks online

  — with DRM limiting the ability to lend books, there may be more individual purchases made

  — actual sales (downloads) can potentially be tracked live rather than waiting for sales figures and book returns to come in

fixed layout (ebooks) technology that forces the elements on an ebook page to remain in the same relative position to each other

accessibility making electronic documents available in alternative publication formats to increase the ability of people with disabilities to view, listen to and/or understand the content

— providing the appropriate rights are negotiated, ebooks are potentially available to many more markets worldwide as they do not need to be physically shipped and distributed

— there are lower delivery costs

— no printing, warehousing or pulping is involved, saving considerable resources

— out-of-print books can be made available again as ebooks, potentially indefinitely

— mistakes can be more easily rectified and revised editions re-issued, without the need to reprint the whole volume

— it is technically possible to track reading habits (such as whether readers finish the book, where they stop and so on) when the reader is online

— ebooks can potentially take greater advantage of more graphics and multimedia content to make them more engaging.

As with all things, though, there are also several disadvantages to ebooks, including:

• For readers:

— earlier versions of e-readers cannot display colour

— interactivity is limited in some formats and on some readers

— navigation in stand-alone ebook apps can be confusing as no standard has been developed yet

— many ebooks are not published to a high standard, especially those that have been converted by scanning pre-digital printed books

— not all print books are available as ebooks

— ebooks are not suited for replicating many hard-copy formats, such as die-cut, popup or lavishly illustrated books

— DRM restricts the use and lending of ebooks

— ebooks bought from proprietary distributors such as Amazon (through the Kindle Store) or Apple (through the iBooks Store) may only be readable using specific devices and software

— there is a profusion of formats and devices, and often they are not interchangeable

- users need to buy a device in order to read the ebook, and keep it charged

- users need to figure out how to use the software and devices, especially for finding, buying and downloading ebooks

- some devices need access to the internet to download ebooks

- reading on some screens can be difficult, especially in direct sunlight or in the dark

- for many, ebooks lack the perhaps indefinable tactility and physical presence of printed books.

- For publishers:

  - customers expect much cheaper prices than for printed books, even though printing and distribution costs constitute only a small proportion of the whole cost of a book

  - there are different standards, devices and formats, which means having to produce different versions of each ebook

  - formatting and layout control can be limited compared with printed books

  - stand-alone ebook apps are expensive to produce to a high quality and need careful design to make them usable

  - there is a need for staff to skill-up for the new technologies

  - conversions cost money, so re-issuing backlisted ebooks does have associated costs, even if those are less than for re-issuing printed books

  - conversions that are done cheaply and quickly may sacrifice quality, especially when the ebook is scanned from printed books

  - it is difficult to create a usable index

  - customers don't like DRM

  - Amazon and Apple dominate distribution so publishers have fewer choices about the terms of sale and other conditions.

The pros and cons of ebooks possibly explain the current pattern of ebook reading; although a quarter of publishing revenue is generated by ebooks, a majority of readers are still purchasing printed books. Some of the disadvantages of ebooks remain significant enough to prevent many people from taking the leap at all, while others may be selective about which types of books they purchase as ebooks and which as printed books (e.g. readers might prefer to only buy light fiction in ebook format). These patterns may change as the technologies develop and distribution channels become less confusing.

EBOOK FORMATS AND DELIVERY

The proliferation of different ebook formats has made ebook publishing quite complex for publishers. As not all software or devices can read all the different formats, and each format has its own strengths and weaknesses, decisions have to be made as to which formats the publisher will use, given limited resources.

The EPUB format

So where does all this lead us? To the most important of the current ebook formats: EPUB. EPUB is an open ebook publishing standard developed by the International Digital Publishing Forum (IDPF). At the time of writing, EPUBs can be read using most reader programs and devices except for Kindle software and older Kindle devices.

International Digital Publishing Forum (IDPF) an independent organisation that develops and promotes the technical specifications for the EPUB standard

While the most common ebook formats on the market are currently those in the Kindle ecosystem, it is important to realise that Kindle's ebook formats (mobi/AZW/KF8) share a history with EPUBs and are therefore technically very similar in concept, construction, vocabulary and other rules. EPUBs can be converted to the Kindle format relatively simply, so it is common practice among established publishers to develop an EPUB version of an ebook first, as the standard, and then convert it to other formats as required. Note that other ebook stores, such as Apple iBooks Store and Nook, generally use EPUB as their standard format, with DRM attached.

Ideally, when the technologies are mature enough, they will merge into a single standard format so that publishers will only need to publish one version rather than a version for each of the various formats that they now need to consider.

The most commonly used EPUB version is currently EPUB 2, which is best for the creation of mainly text-based books. EPUB 3 is the more powerful version, allowing the insertion of multimedia and better control over the placement of elements, though it has yet to be widely adopted, not least because at the time of writing very few software programs or devices fully support it.

EPUB is based on standards that are also used in websites, so the two formats have similar functionality. However, EPUB-like ebooks are distinguished from websites in several ways that are more focused on book publishing requirements:

- Although EPUB-like ebooks are like mini-websites, comprising multiple text documents and graphic files, they are packaged into one compressed (zip) file.

- Being self-contained, they can easily be delivered through ebook stores and other sources as a single file, without fear of any components of the package being lost.

- Once they have been downloaded to a device, they are designed to be read offline.

- They are designed to adapt dynamically to the size and capabilities of the reading software and device and to (limited) customisation by the reader, with the content reflowing accordingly.

- Different formats also have varying capabilities to fix the layout of elements to ensure that text and graphics stay together when required.

- EPUB-like ebooks define the reading order of the pages and chapters. While this does not force the reader to progress through the book sequentially, it imposes a formal structure that is not necessarily present in websites.

- They are designed to include standard navigational elements (such as a table of contents) to assist the reader to find content.

- They have DRM capabilities, allowing publishers to provide some protection from illegal distribution.

- By default, they require the addition of standard publishing metadata to identify and describe the publication so that readers can discover the ebooks more easily.

- They provide a standard format for depicting book covers in an electronic library.

A key feature of EPUB-like ebooks is their ability to reflow the text when the typeface or font size is adjusted, to better suit the reader's requirements. Figure 15.1 (overleaf) illustrates how changing the typeface or font size results in the text reflowing accordingly to take up more or fewer pages. Note that in these examples, the number of pages remaining in the chapter, shown at bottom right of each spread, changed from 8 to 13 pages.

metadata
information about content (e.g. a book, ebook or photograph), such as descriptions of its subject, authorship, ownership and structure, that is not immediately visible in that content but can be used to identify, search and navigate it

Figure 15.1: the typeface or font size in EPUBs can be customised to some extent by the reader, which can lead to the text reflowing

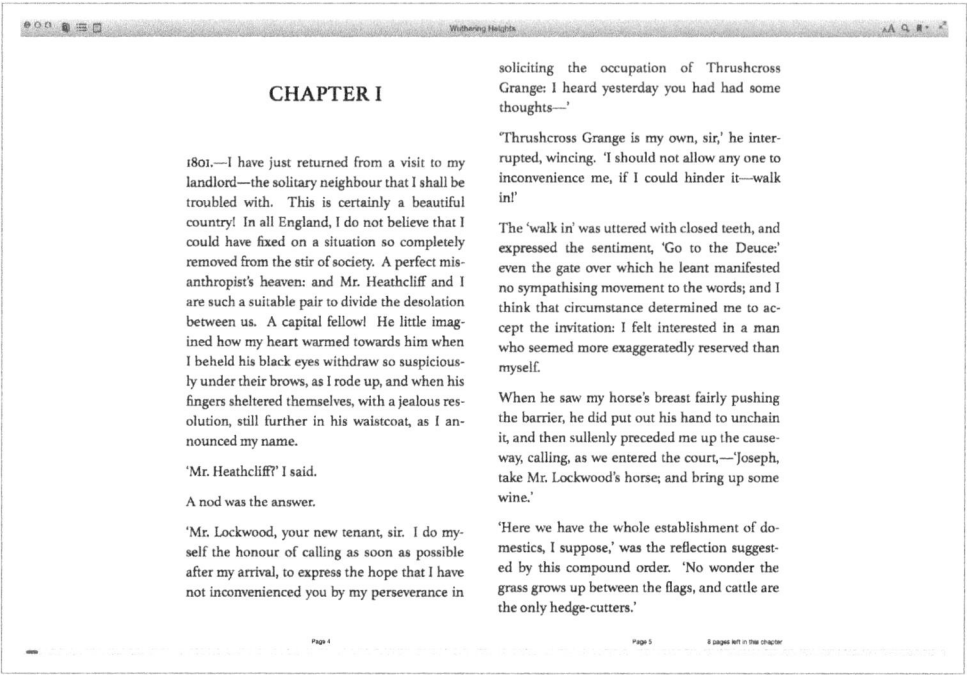

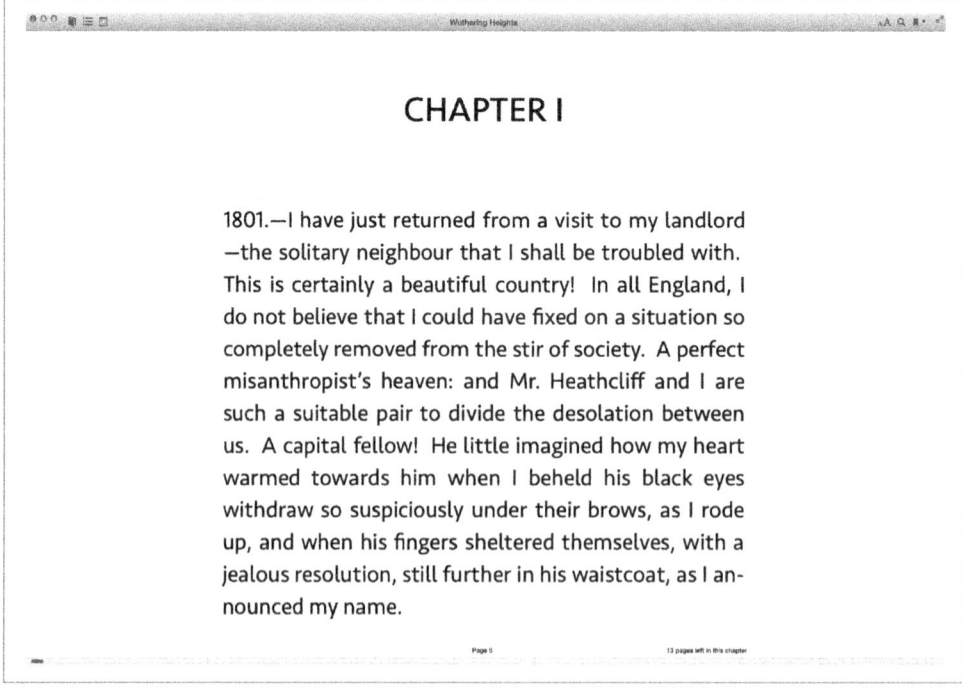

Other ebook formats

The other most common ebook formats are website ebooks, PDFs and ebook apps.

Websites are already familiar to most people. They are used for a wide range of communication purposes, including for publishing ebooks. They have the advantage of being easily updated; however, they can appear differently depending on the browser or device used and the user's own settings, making it difficult to ensure that all readers have the same experience. More recently, it has become possible to dynamically resize and rearrange page elements to suit the particular device or window being used to read them (also known as responsive web design), whether on a smartphone, tablet, or desktop or laptop computer.

Websites have limited DRM capabilities, so most publications on websites are non-commercial documents, such as reports produced by government agencies or not-for-profit organisations. In these cases, structural and navigational features usually match the publication's division by chapter and parts. Parts of the text can be hyperlinked to each other (for example, from one chapter to another) or to another website or document. While an ebook published on a website can in theory be downloaded as a set of pages and other files, in practice this is often unwieldy, especially for long publications, so most website ebooks are read online, downloaded as a PDF or printed in hard copy for offline reading.

PDF ebooks are usually virtual replicas of the printed version of the book, using exactly the same layout, typefaces, graphic elements and so on. Parts of the text can also be hyperlinked to each other or to an external website. They are easily produced once a book has been typeset and will appear the same, no matter what device is used to read them. This means, however, that on a tiny screen a full page may also appear tiny. Though the page can be enlarged onscreen, the text is not reflowable, so everything will be made bigger, not just the font size, and the reader will need to scroll around to view the whole page. Most often, therefore, users read PDFs on larger screens, such as a tablet, or desktop or laptop computer, or print them out for reading in hard copy.

Ebook apps are usually much more complex. They are self-contained programs that run only on specified software or devices, but usually contain multimedia features in addition to the text. For example, one of the earliest such apps, which was produced as a proof-of-concept ebook for the Apple iPad, was the ebook app version of the printed book *Our Choice*, by Al Gore. The original print book was repurposed for the app, using the same text but adding numerous videos, audio narration, animations, interactive graphs and links to maps. The layout is fixed so that typefaces, layout and graphic elements cannot be changed. The app is very engaging, but it only works on Apple mobile devices (such as the iPad) as a stand-alone app and is a very large file (55 MB) compared with most EPUB-like ebooks (usually less than 1 MB).

Reading ebooks

Ebook formats can often be read using a variety of software and reading devices. Table 15.1 lists three common ebook formats and shows that even if a particular format can only be read using specific software, that software may run on a range of devices.

Table 15.1: compatible ebook formats, software and reading devices

Format	Software	Reading devices
EPUB	Any ebook software except Kindle	Any ebook device except older Kindle reading devices
Kindle	Kindle software and, for ebooks without DRM, software such as FB Reader	Kindle devices and devices that can run Kindle software (such as iPads, Android devices, and desktop or laptop computers)
iBooks Author	Only iBooks software	Apple mobile devices and recent Mac computers

e-ink
low-powered electronic simulation of text used in many ebook reading devices

LCD (liquid crystal display)
digital screen technology widely used in computers, ebook reading devices and televisions

Two main types of screens are used in reading devices: those using e-ink technology (such as many Kindle, Kobo and Nook devices) and those using more traditional LCD (liquid crystal display) screens (most smartphones, tablets, and desktops and laptops). E-ink is ideal for reading greyscale text on a screen for long periods and in bright sunlight. It requires very little power and renders text sharply and smoothly, though reading e-ink in lowlight conditions can be a problem and colour e-ink is not widely used. E-ink devices are very popular, due to the dominance of the Kindle. As the ebook market matures, however, LCD-based smartphones and tablets are becoming increasingly popular for reading ebooks because they also offer email, web surfing, games and other functions, reducing the need to carry more than one device around. While LCD screens offer clear, sharp, colour-based ebooks, they can be difficult to read under bright lighting and consume far more power, requiring more frequent charging of devices.

The reading software for EPUB-like ebooks usually allows the user to adjust their reading experience in limited ways, including:

- changing the type size and, to some extent, the type

- changing the horizontal word and vertical line spacing

- turning hyphenation off or on

- adjusting the brightness and colour of the background and text

- reading in one- or two-column layout, in portrait or landscape mode

- setting the text block to be justified or left aligned

- being able to bookmark, highlight or annotate the text.

Not all ebook reading programs offer the same options.

Some common software and web-based ebook readers include:

- desktop and laptop computer software:

  — Adobe Digital Editions (Windows and Mac)

  — iBooks (Mac)

  — Kindle (Windows and Mac)

  — Kobo (Windows)

  — Nook (Windows)

- mobile device software:

  — iBooks (iOS—iPhone and iPad)

  — Inkling (iOS)

  — Kindle (Android, Blackberry, iOS, Kindle)

  — Kobo (Android, Blackberry, iOS)

  — Nook (Android, iOS)

- web-based e-readers:

  — Inkling

  — Kindle Cloud Reader

  — Nook.

The final brick in the ebook wall is distribution. By far the dominant distributor of ebooks is Amazon, followed by Apple, with the rest (such as Kobo, and Barnes and Noble) lagging far behind. Although an ebook bought in the Kindle Store or iBooks Store is locked in to being read on their proprietary software or devices, these channels have the advantage of offering near-to-one-stop shopping, with vast libraries of ebooks available at a single click. Readers do not even need to know their credit card details after the first purchase. It is no surprise therefore that publishers focus on Kindle and EPUB as the two major ebook formats to use.

WHICH EBOOK FORMAT?

Although most publishers will choose EPUB and Kindle as the formats for their ebooks, there may be other options. Some issues to consider when deciding what format to use include:

- Who are the likely readers?

  — What devices do they use?

  — Where and when are they likely to read the books?

  — What will they want to do with the content?

- What type of content is it?

  — Is it mainly text?

  — Would it be readable on a small screen?

  — Would the content need to be simplified for readability on a screen?

  — Are there a lot of tables and graphics?

  — Is a fixed layout required?

  — Is it better presented with animations, video or interactivity?

  — Is the book being published for sale or free distribution?

- What is the threshold for quality?

  — Is the aim just to get the publication out into the open?

  — Is it to have lavish production values?

  — Are high-resolution images required?

- What are the conversion options?

  — Is the current version in Word, PDF or InDesign?

  — Is the current version available only as printed pages that will need to be scanned?

  — Is the content in a database (such as for a dictionary)?

- What is the budget?

- What rights are held? Are they for print only? What about worldwide electronic rights?

The answers to these questions may lead the publisher to decide in the end that print alone is best, or perhaps that a website ebook or stand-alone multimedia app is warranted.

TYPICAL EBOOK WORKFLOWS

Most published books are commissioned, curated and managed by bodies such as trade publishers, government agencies and research organisations. Most of these use editors to assist in improving the manuscript and ensuring that the resulting publication meets professional standards, no matter the format in which it is released.

Even the increasing numbers of independently published authors and ebook conversion houses are recognising that a good editor can make a major difference to the quality (and therefore success) of their book. Freelance editors in particular may increasingly be called upon to work with independent authors and thus be operating outside the boundaries and supports provided by a more traditional publishing organisation. Being in command of a range of additional skills in these circumstances (including typesetting and ebook conversion) would be very useful.

ebook conversion house
an organisation that specialises in converting publications to ebook formats

With the widening range of publishing organisations and individuals releasing ebooks, there is an increasing range of ways in which ebooks can be created and of roles that editors can take in these processes. Some examples are discussed next, though these are by no means the only workflows possible.

Print to ebook

To create an ebook from a print book, common steps include:

1 The manuscript is written, edited and electronically styled as for a print book, but with a view to the multiple output formats being planned.

2   The book is typeset, paying particular attention to preparing
    the text, artwork and other elements for export to EPUB/
    Kindle or website formats.

3   The book is output (straight from the typesetting program) to
    the required formats: PDF (for printing or downloading), EPUB
    and/or website, and is manually tweaked to fix output errors
    and add metadata, as required. This is sometimes outsourced
    to specialist ebook conversion houses or website developers.

4   EPUBs may then be converted to Kindle and other related
    formats using Amazon's free Kindle conversion tools.

5   The ebook is proofread using programs such as calibre
    (free, Windows and Mac) or Adobe Dreamweaver or oXygen
    XML Editor (both paid, Windows and Mac), and checked in
    all formats, preferably using a range of reader programs
    and devices.

6   The Kindle or EPUB ebook is submitted to appropriate
    distributors, such as the Kindle Store and the iBooks Store.
    Website ebooks are uploaded to the appropriate website.

For more
information about
electronic styling,
see chapters 6
and 7.

In this workflow, the editor undertakes the usual tasks of editing
the manuscript, but may also assist with quality control once the
ebook versions are output, including proofreading and checking
the navigation, metadata and common outputting issues.

Books on the backlist

When re-publishing a backlist or out-of-print book, the following
steps might be followed:

1   If there is a digital version of the book, the files must be
    checked for readability and potential conversion issues. Older
    typeset documents, for example, are often not set up and
    styled correctly for clean output to ebook formats, or the book
    may only be available digitally as a PDF.

2   If there is no digital version, a printed copy of the book is
    scanned and put through optical character recognition (OCR)
    to digitise the text.

optical character
recognition (OCR)
a process of scanning
text as an image and
using software to
convert it to digital
text by recognising the
shapes of the letters

3   The editor or ebook conversion house cleans up and styles the
    digitised text in preparation for conversion to ebook formats.

4   The book is output to ebook format. This can be done using a
    typesetting or specialised conversion program, or a Word file
    can be converted to website format first and then output to
    EPUB using EPUB editing programs such as calibre or oXygen.

5 EPUBs may then be converted to Kindle and other related formats using Kindle's conversion tools.

6 The EPUB and website output is manually tweaked to correct output errors, if necessary.

7 The ebook is proofread and checked in all formats, preferably on a range of software programs and devices.

8 The ebook is submitted to distributors such as the Kindle Store and the iBooks Store. Website ebooks are uploaded to the appropriate website.

In this workflow, the editor potentially has a role both in cleaning up the text in preparation for outputting to ebook, as well as quality control checking once the ebook has been created.

Independent publishing straight to ebook

It is now technically relatively easy to write a text in a word processing program and convert it to an ebook for upload to a distribution channel such as Amazon without ever having to deal with an editor or publisher. Many authors have gone down this self-publishing route and a few of them, especially those in genre fiction such as romance, science fiction and fantasy, have been very successful—so much so that some independently published ebooks have since been bought by trade publishers for release as more traditional print books or re-packaged ebooks. Some publishers have also begun to explore publishing straight to ebooks themselves.

Authors who opt to publish independently may or may not have their manuscript professionally edited, though the more successful ones usually do. They may then submit the file to one of the many ebook conversion services or convert the file themselves to EPUB or Kindle format. The author, conversion service or editor proofreads and checks the ebook in all formats before submitting the file to an online store.

Multimedia ebooks

Multimedia ebooks can be published as separate ebook apps or as EPUB 3 ebooks. Ebook apps require publisher, author, editor and developer to work closely together to ensure that the text and multimedia elements are designed to work effectively together.

Multimedia EPUB 3 ebooks are not widely available yet, but there is great potential for growth in the education market in particular.

Tools such as iBooks Author and Inkling Habitat make the creation
of such ebooks much easier, though the ebooks produced are
locked into the iBooks and Inkling environments respectively.

While ebook app publishing is an exciting and interesting area of
ebook development, the landscape is set to change rapidly over
the coming years, and their development processes are beyond
the scope of this book. The rest of this chapter will therefore focus
on the most common ebook format used in publishing, EPUB-
like ebooks, though many of the principles are similar across
the formats.

THE EDITOR'S ROLE IN QUALITY CONTROL

The quality of EPUBs can be variable; it can be very low indeed
if the publication's production has been rushed through or
done cheaply, with poor quality control checks. The editor or
proofreader, therefore, can and should play an important role in
ebook production. Even if an ebook is created from a carefully
edited and proofread print book, close checking is still needed
because the conversion process itself can introduce new issues
that affect the readability of the publication.

Structure and content issues

Developers of EPUB-like ebooks, and the software and devices
that read them, have tried to make reading on a screen as similar
as possible to the print book experience. Thus, users turn pages
by tapping or swiping the screen, and can bookmark pages and
add notes to passages of text. They can also easily go to the table
of contents from anywhere in the book, and then resume reading
where they left off. However, not everything works the same way
on a screen and so an ebook does not always benefit from slavishly
following the print book format.

Some issues that might arise that the publisher and editor may
need to consider include:

- *Updating and moving elements to a different position.*
  Publication details for the ebook must, of course, be updated
  to reflect the different edition of the work (including having its
  own ISBN). It is also common practice to move the imprint and
  author information to the end of an ebook, because otherwise
  the reader may have to swipe through too many pages at the
  beginning to find where the first page starts, especially if the
  reader has chosen a large font size.

- *Setting the starting page.* Some ebook distributors may require that the EPUB be set to bypass the prelims altogether and open at the first page on first start-up. The prelim pages are still at the beginning of the book for reference, but the reader doesn't have to wade through them to find the beginning of the text.

- *Removing or replacing some elements.* Some purely graphical elements, such as a page border, may not work at all in a reflowable ebook, so these may need to be omitted. In addition, some elements, such as a dinkus used to mark a section break, may be included in the ebook as a graphic, but different coloured backgrounds in the ebook may spoil their appearance. It may be better in these cases to replace these with another separation device, such as characters from a standard typeface, that will work under all circumstances.

- *Repurposing the table of contents.* A good EPUB has a separate hyperlinked table of contents that is easily accessible from any point in the text. This often duplicates the contents list that normally appears in the prelims of a printed book. The publisher has the option to remove that list from the main text or use the space to provide a different type of contents page, perhaps to a greater or shallower depth, or with additional summary information to assist the reader.

- *Redesigning the cover.* Some cover designs work much better in thumbnail format than others. Print books can get away with having quite small text or graphical elements, but on a tablet or smartphone, much of that detail, including even the title itself, can become lost or unreadable.

- *Managing fixed layout requirements.* In some books it is important for graphical and textual elements to appear in the same relative position to each other (e.g. side-by-side or on the same page). This can present difficulties, especially in EPUB 2, where fixed layout controls are fairly basic. The editor will have to assess how such layout issues can be managed, including whether to even try to publish in the ebook format.

- *Dealing with tables and graphics.* Large tables and low-resolution graphics may be difficult to read in an EPUB. iBooks software allows large tables and graphics to be expanded to fill a tablet screen, assisting readability, but other reading software may be more limited in this regard.

- *Indexing.* Indexing a book that has no fixed page numbers presents problems. There are ways to include indexes in an ebook, but they involve varying levels of complexity to implement. Using InDesign's inbuilt indexing option offers the most efficient method of generating hyperlinked indexes that will allow a reader to link from the indexing term to the appropriate location in the text (though not the other way round), but most professional indexers do not use InDesign to index, as it has limited functionality. An alternative is to manually create hyperlinks between the index terms and the text, which is laborious. Another is to simply include the index as plain text (which would be searchable using keywords), so that readers will at least know what topics are covered. It may also be considered useful to include the page numbers from the print version, to indicate the relative position of their occurrence in the text (e.g. page 46 in a 288-page printed book, about 16 per cent of the way through, though this requires advising the reader how many pages were in the printed book in the first place).

Proofreading

Having sorted out any broad structural and content issues, the editor or proofreader then proofreads and checks the workability of the EPUB. While some or all of this work may be undertaken by the ebook conversion house, it is still important to understand what needs to be checked in order to manage the quality control process.

What can and cannot be changed

At this stage, as with regular proofreading, the text is checked for missing or duplicated text, typos, errors that were missed in earlier rounds, cross-referencing and layout issues. The issues are not, however, exactly the same as for print books because control of the layout is much more limited in EPUBs; for example:

- running heads and feet are not output to EPUBs from typesetting programs, as they are generated automatically by the reading software

- pagination, page drops, widows and orphans all change as text reflows

- there is limited control over where page breaks occur and what typefaces are used

- line, word, letter and punctuation spacing is controlled by the reading software

- paragraph alignment and indentation, and word breaks and hyphenation are controlled by the reading software and user preferences.

Some of these issues (such as word breaks) can be dealt with to a limited extent by using workarounds, but most cannot be controlled.

What to check

First, the proofreader should scan through the entire text on at least one of the target EPUB readers and devices. Viewing the text at different font sizes and with different backgrounds (if available), and in both portrait and landscape modes, using single-page scrolling or double-page spreads, will help the proofreader to see if any layout issues arise as a result of reflowing text, such as graphics being cut off, tables not fitting or elements that belong together being split over two or more pages.

Next, the entire text should be re-read to ensure that everything has been converted correctly. It is useful to know the origin of the text before starting. For example, if the text has been scanned in from a printed copy of the book, common OCR errors—such as misreading ligatures, confusing letters such as 'I' with '1' and 'l', and unnecessary hyphenation—can be targeted. If the text has been output from a typesetting program, such as InDesign, other distinctive errors might be generated—such as excessive CSS formatting or elements that are out of order—that the proofreader should look out for.

Another potential problem is where special characters or mathematical equations are required. These have to be carefully checked to ensure that they appear correctly, whatever typeface is used in the reading device. Workarounds include using substitute characters (e.g. an X instead of a tick mark) or converting the characters to images.

Simple textual errors may be corrected more efficiently by the proofreader, but this requires an understanding of how an EPUB is structured, and learning at least some coding and how to use an EPUB editor such as calibre (discussed further later). Layout and other more complex issues may best be fixed by the ebook developer, as these may require special workarounds. In any case, it is likely that the proofreader will need to liaise closely with the developer to decide how to deal with quality control issues.

Because there are usually no fixed page numbers to indicate location, the editor will need to discuss with the developer the best way to indicate where problems occur. One option is to use the inbuilt functionality of the ebook reader to bookmark the location, highlight the relevant text and add notes. However, such markings usually do not translate across devices unless the same account is used on the same reader software (e.g. using iBooks with one shared Apple ID), so this would need to be set up appropriately beforehand. Other options include opening the EPUB in an EPUB editing program and inserting queries directly into the text, taking a screenshot of the relevant page or copying and pasting the relevant text into another document together with notes about the problem.

The proofreader should also discuss with the publisher what to do if errors are found in the text that were missed and should also be fixed in other versions of the book. If the print version has not been printed yet, it may be possible to correct the errors in the original typeset document. Otherwise an erratum slip might need to be added or the error noted for fixing in a future edition or reprint (if there is one).

Proofreading EPUBs—a checklist

Content

- Has all the text been included? Has any of it been duplicated?

- Have lists been converted correctly—bullets to bullets, numbers to numbers?

- If there are sidebars, pullouts etc., are they all in the correct place? Do they move with the text when it is reflowed?

- Do any headings or captions break awkwardly? Is it worth fixing them?

- What do tables look like? Are they too large? How can this be avoided or fixed?

- How consistent is the format, layout, and readability with the print version? Is this what was planned?

- Are the imprint, author and other information to be moved to the end?

- Are there blank pages left in from the print version?
- Which page does the book start on?

Fonts and typography

- Does the EPUB contain embedded typefaces? If so, do they work? (They often don't in EPUB 2.)
- Have special characters carried over correctly?
- Have all font styles (bold, italic, small caps etc.) transferred correctly?
- Has all punctuation, such as em and en rules and typographic quotes, been converted correctly?
- If the EPUB has been created from scanned text, have ligatures and other common OCR errors been fixed?

Images

- Are the images in the right relative location and at the appropriate size? What happens at page breaks?
- Do they look OK in greyscale and in colour? If images are in greyscale, does the text still make sense?
- Are images with text still readable?
- Have images without copyright permission been removed and the text reworked?
- Has the cover image transferred properly? Is it readable at thumbnail size? Does it need to be? Does it appear as a thumbnail as well as in the book (if required)?

Interactivity

- Do all cross-reference and internal links (including footnotes) work?
- Do links to external resources work?
- Is the embedded table of contents accurate and complete, and does it link to the right parts of the ebook?
- If there is multimedia content (in an EPUB 3 ebook), do all the elements work correctly? If an internet connection is required, is this made clear?
- If there is an index, are the terms hyperlinked correctly to the text?

(continued)

Proofreading EPUBs—a checklist *(cont'd)*

Publishing

- Are the publication metadata (such as details about the publisher, author, title, ISBN) complete and accurate?
- Have all appropriate steps been taken to ensure that the EPUB is compatible with the targeted reading software and devices, and can be uploaded to various distribution channels?

WHAT'S IN AN EBOOK?

As mentioned earlier, an EPUB-like ebook is like a mini-website, comprising a set of pages, graphic files and other elements that are packaged so that the ebook appears to be a single file. When proofreading and checking such ebooks, it is useful for editors to understand their structure so they can learn how to make minor corrections, or at minimum know what common problems to look for or ask about when checking.

For simplicity's sake, the focus in this section is on EPUBs, but similar principles apply to other EPUB-like ebooks.

Cracking open an EPUB

It is relatively simple to open an EPUB and have a look the files inside because, although they have the file extension *.epub*, they are actually compressed using zip archiving technology. They can also be viewed and edited without having to unzip and zip them, but for now we will look at how to unzip them manually.

In Windows, EPUBs can be uncompressed by changing the *.epub* file extension to *.zip* and then extracting the archive (the method varies depending on the version of Windows being used). To compress the files again, use the standard method to zip the files and then change the file extension back to *.epub*. On the Mac, the process is a bit more complicated, as unzipping EPUBs requires a special (free) script, but once the script is installed, the EPUB file can simply be dragged onto the script. To re-create the EPUB, the folder of files just needs to be dragged onto the script again and the file extension is automatically compressed to the *.epub* extension.

For resources on unzipping EPUBs with a Mac, see the list of resources in appendix 11.

Once uncompressed, the EPUB appears as a folder of files. Figure 15.2 shows an example of the contents of an EPUB 2 folder. There are two main subfolders, *OEBPS* and *META-INF*, containing various text files, plus a text file called *mimetype*. The *OEBPS* (Open eBook Publication Structure) folder is the most important for editors and proofreaders, as the other files contain instructional information for the reading software that should not be changed.

Figure 15.2: typical contents of an unzipped EPUB 2 file

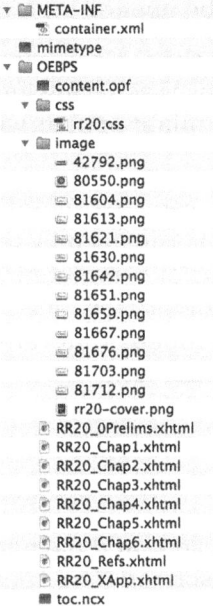

Within the OEBPS folder are a number of elements, all of which can be edited to ensure that the EPUB content is correct and that it passes validation checks:

- *content.opf*. This file contains tags that define the publishing metadata (such as date of publication, ISBN, keywords, description, language etc.), catalogue and locate all the text and graphics files in the EPUB, and determine the reading order of the files.

- *css* folder. This contains one or more CSS files describing the formatting of the text in the EPUB, including font type, size and style, colours and paragraph spacing.

- *image* folder. This contains all the image files in the EPUB. PNG and JPEG files are preferable, as these are compressed formats that keep the file sizes down.

- *.html* or *.xhtml* files. These files are similar to website pages and contain all the text content of the EPUB. There is usually one file for each chapter or division in the EPUB (each file forces the EPUB reader to start the content on a new page). Each of these files can be opened and the content edited.

- *toc.ncx* This file defines the table of contents navigation system in the EPUB. This is separate and can be different from a table of contents that might appear within the text of the EPUB itself.

In EPUB 3 the structure remains mainly the same, with some additions. The *toc.ncx* file is replaced by the *toc.xhtml* file (though the former is included in order to maintain compatibility with older readers) and additional folders for fonts, audio, video and other special materials can be added. This reflects the more powerful capabilities of the newer standard.

Naming conventions

Note that some of the folder and file names can be different from what has been described. The ones given here are those generated by InDesign, but different EPUB converters may use different conventions. So long as the EPUB works as expected and passes validation checks these differences are not usually important.

Coding basics

In order to make changes to the content of an EPUB, the files need to be opened in either a text editor or specialised EPUB editor such as calibre or oXygen. While it is possible to make textual changes without knowing any coding, it is important to have at least a basic understanding of coding in order to progress beyond simply adding or deleting letters or words.

HTML (hypertext markup language) the formatting language used on the World Wide Web, but also in EPUB-like ebooks

The text content is contained in HTML (hypertext markup language) files, which is the same format used in website pages. HTML uses tags to define and apply a standardised structure to parts of text. Table 15.2 lists some of the most commonly used tags in HTML.

XML, HTML and XHTML

Some readers will see the terms *XML* (extensible markup language) and *XHTML* (extensible hypertext markup language) used in reference to websites and EPUBs and might wonder how these relate to HTML. In short, they are all closely related and together form the basis of the latest HTML 5 specification, which allows greater interactivity and device responsiveness. To avoid confusion, the term *HTML* is used generically in this chapter to represent these specifications.

Table 15.2: common HTML tags used in website and EPUB-like ebooks

Tag	Semantic meaning
<h1> (<h2>, <h3> etc.)	level 1 heading (level 2, level 3 etc.)
<p>	paragraph
 	line break
<blockquote>	block quotation
<ul>	unordered (bulleted) list
<ol>	ordered (numbered) list
<a>	hyperlink
<em>	emphasised text
<strong>	strongly emphasised text
<img src="[filename]">	insert image called [filename]

HTML generally requires both an opening and closing tag, in the format *<tag>text</tag>*. For example:

```
<h1>Preface</h1>
<p>The author wishes to thank the many reviewers who
provided valuable feedback on chapters in this book.</p>
<p><img src="sig.png"/></p>
```

would make the word *Preface* appear as a level 1 heading and the rest of the text appear as normal paragraph text. The last line inserts an image with the file name of 'sig.png'.

CSS (cascading
style sheet)
a computer language
for formatting text in
electronic publications,
such as on websites and
EPUB-like ebooks

In addition, once the text has been conceptually marked up in this way, developers use CSS (cascading style sheets, currently at version 3) to define how each tag will appear (such as typeface, font size, spacing, italics and so on). For example, CSS formatting for an <h1> tag might look like this:

```
h1 {
        font-size: 1.8em;
        text-align: left;
        font-weight: bold;
        color: #590505;
        padding-bottom: 10px;
}
```

which would make all level 1 headings 1.8 em in height, left aligned, bold and a dark red colour, with 10 pixels of space below the text. Fortunately, while CSS is a coding language, it has specific vocabulary and punctuation rules that are also relatively easy to identify and can be fairly well understood by mere editorial mortals.

CSS coding can reside within the same file as the HTML document but, more commonly, a separate CSS file is created to which many different HTML pages can refer, thus ensuring consistency across documents.

Does all this talk of structure and formatting sound familiar? It should! Using HTML to define structure (such as with <h1> or <p>) is similar to applying electronic styles (such as *Heading 1* or *Body Text*) to text in Word or InDesign, while using CSS to define appearance is similar to formatting those styles with different typefaces, fonts, spacing and other features.

CSS is a very powerful means of displaying the same text in a different way. Figure 15.3 illustrates what can be done simply by applying different CSS coding to the same HTML file.

Figure 15.3: the same HTML page can be formatted with CSS to look very different

Middlemarch by George Eliot

Chapter I

"Since I can do no good because a woman,
Reach constantly at something that is near it." — The Maid's Tragedy: Beaumont and Fletcher.

Miss Brooke had that kind of beauty which seems to be thrown into relief by poor dress. Her hand and wrist were so finely formed that she could wear sleeves not less bare of style than those in which the Blessed Virgin appeared to Italian painters; and her profile as well as her stature and bearing seemed to gain the more dignity from her plain garments, which by the side of provincial fashion gave her the impressiveness of a fine quotation from the Bible,—or from one of our elder poets,—in a paragraph of to-day's newspaper. She was usually spoken of as being remarkably clever, but with the addition that her sister Celia had more common-sense. Nevertheless, Celia wore scarcely more trimmings; and it was only to close observers that her dress differed from her sister's, and had a shade of coquetry in its arrangements; for Miss Brooke's plain dressing was due to mixed conditions, in most of which her sister shared. The pride of being ladies had something to do with it: the Brooke connections, though not exactly aristocratic, were unquestionably "good:" if you inquired backward for a generation or two, you would not find any

Middlemarch by George Eliot

CHAPTER I

"Since I can do no good because a woman,
Reach constantly at something that is near it." — The Maid's Tragedy: Beaumont and Fletcher.

Miss Brooke had that kind of beauty which seems to be thrown into relief by poor dress. Her hand and wrist were so finely formed that she could wear sleeves not less bare of style than those in which the Blessed Virgin appeared to Italian painters; and her profile as well as her stature and bearing seemed to gain the more dignity from her plain garments, which by the side of provincial fashion gave her the impressiveness of a fine quotation from the Bible,—or from one of our elder poets,—in a paragraph of to-day's newspaper. She was usually spoken of as being remarkably clever, but with the addition that her sister Celia had more common-sense. Nevertheless, Celia wore scarcely more trimmings; and it was only to close observers that her dress differed from her sister's, and had a shade of coquetry in its arrangements; for Miss Brooke's plain dressing was due to mixed conditions, in most of which her sister shared. The pride of being ladies had something to do with it: the Brooke connections, though not exactly aristocratic, were unquestionably "good:" if you inquired backward for a generation or two, you would not find any yard-measuring or

'Noir' layout by Jeremy Cancenko http://cuporobots.com (top) and 'Wallpaper' layout by John McCoy http://mccoy.pair.com (bottom)

Ideally, it would be best for any editor working with ebooks to be familiar with both HTML and CSS, if not enough to actually construct a page from scratch in these languages, at least to recognise what the coding means and how changes might affect the text.

For resources for
learning more
about HTML
and CSS, see
appendix 11.

Note too that both HTML and CSS files are purely text files that can be read in any basic text reader. It is the coding in those documents and their respective file extensions (*.html*, *.xhtml*, *.css* or variants of these) that allow browsers and EPUB readers to identify how the files should be used and the content displayed.

AMENDING EPUBS

If the editor or proofreader is required to amend the EPUB, they will need to learn how to use a specific editing program to do so.

Once again, as with other aspects of ebooks, the field of EPUB editing and proofing is still in its infancy and an industry-standard workflow or professional software that is universally or even widely used is yet to emerge. The editor or proofreader must therefore remain flexible and be prepared to work with whatever appears to be the best option for the job in hand.

The most important skill to learn is HTML coding, as once this is mastered any EPUB can be edited in any program, even with a simple text editor.

Useful features of EPUB editing programs

A number of software programs can be used to edit EPUBs. Some are more mature than others and each has its strengths. The proofreader may not have a choice about which program to use, but if they do, obviously they should choose one that offers features that will make their job easier.

Not surprisingly, professional XML coding programs, such as Adobe Dreamweaver or oXygen XML Editor, have the most features and are the most standards-compliant. Dreamweaver, for example, provides live side-by-side editing of both the text and code of the EPUB, allows the development of powerful macro commands, and can also open and edit website ebook pages. However, both these programs are expensive and offer more features than most proofreaders need when making simple changes to EPUBs. At the other end of the spectrum are simple text editors. Because EPUB files are all just plain text (albeit with a lot of coding in them), any text editor can be used to create and edit them. Some text editors (such as Notepad++ for Windows or TextWrangler for Mac, both free) are even able to show the coding in colour, which makes it easier to distinguish the content from the coding. However, a proofreader would need to be comfortable with HTML and CSS coding in order to use such programs.

In between these extremes is a free, cross-platform program, calibre, which can be used to both read and edit EPUB-like ebooks. While not fully featured or bug free, this program offers enough functions to enable proofreaders to check and correct EPUB-like ebooks more easily.

Another free, cross-platform EPUB-editing program, Sigil, is more powerful and easier to use than calibre, but it is no longer being developed and so will eventually become out of date and unusable. For this reason, we do not cover it here. However, it is likely to continue to be available and remain usable for some time. See appendix 11 for download details.

It is beyond the scope of this book to describe in detail how to use calibre or any of the other programs to edit an EPUB. However, we will use calibre here to illustrate the major types of functions that a proofreader will find useful when checking EPUBs.

In calibre, the proofreader can view and edit the content without having to unzip and zip the EPUB file manually. The EPUB opens in a window with three panels, listing all the files in the EPUB on the left, the code version of the file in the middle and a preview of the content, roughly as it would appear in an ereader, on the right.

Unfortunately, textual corrections can only be made in the middle coding panel, so the proofreader must at least know how to make changes to the text without unnecessarily touching the coding. However, the coding is coloured so that it can be distinguished more easily, and any changes made in the coding panel are immediately reflected in the live preview in the right-hand panel, which helps the proofreader to check the corrections (see figure 15.4, overleaf). calibre also provides buttons and shortcuts for the most common changes, such as applying different heading levels or formatting text. A find and replace tool includes the use of regular expressions (similar to wildcards in Word) to create complex searches, and tools are available for creating links and inserting images.

Figure 15.4: calibre displays the EPUB file contents, coding and live preview panels side-by-side

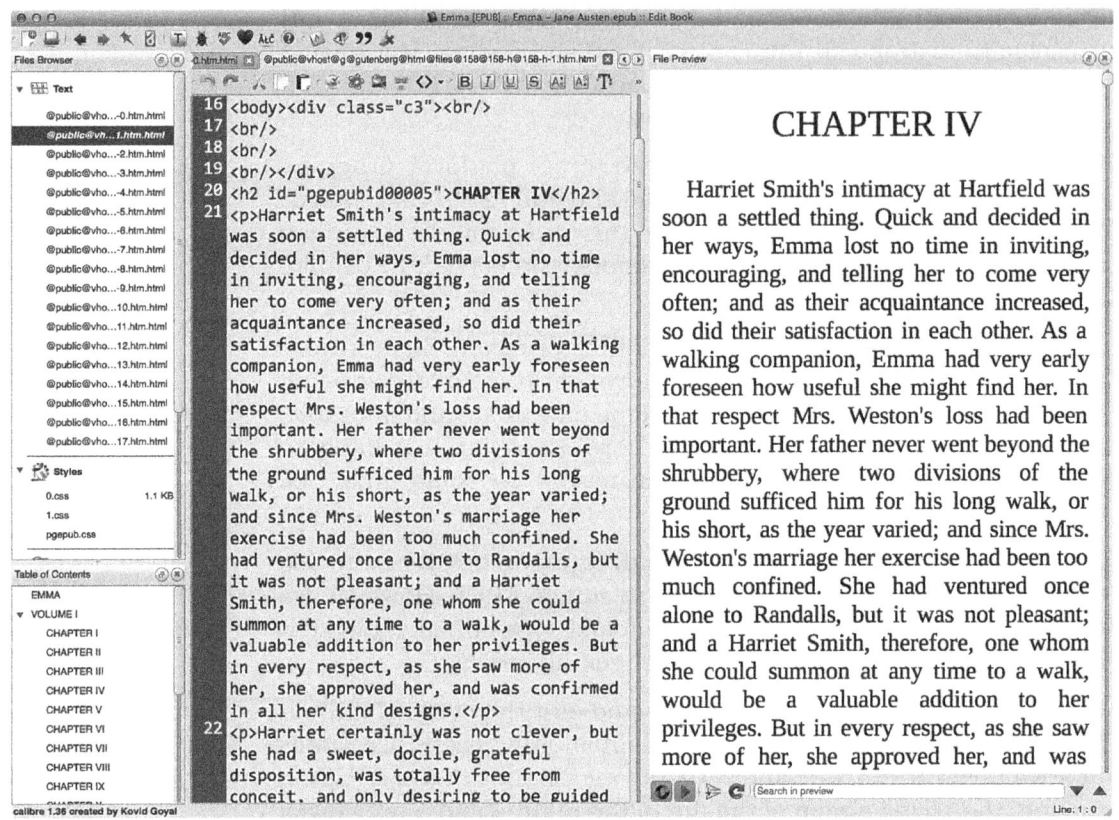

Making basic changes

If the editor or proofreader is using calibre, the workflow for amending an EPUB might look like this:

1 Make a copy of the EPUB to work on and save the original in a safe place.

2 Add the EPUB copy to the calibre library, using the *Add Books* option. Once the EPUB appears in the library, right-click on the book title and select *Edit Book* from the dropdown menu.

3 A new window will open. All the EPUB files will be listed in the left-hand panel, with the main text content (the HTML files) grouped in a folder called *Text*.

4   Open each HTML file in turn and proofread each one, using the live preview panel on the right, which will make the text appear as it would if the editor were using EPUB reading software.

5   Make simple text changes—such as fixing typos, punctuation errors and incorrect special characters—in the coding panel in the middle, carefully avoiding making unintentional changes to the coding in angled brackets. Any changes made are reflected in the live preview panel on the right.

Take great care when undertaking global find and replace searches on the text (e.g. to fix common OCR errors). Many EPUBs suffer from having had such global changes made without the results being carefully checked.

For more complex changes—such as layout or artwork issues—it may be necessary to mark up the problems for a developer to fix, using whatever system has been agreed for flagging errors.

6   Add or amend metadata if required (see later).

7   Save the EPUB regularly as proofreading proceeds.

8   Validate the EPUB when all corrections have been made (see later).

9   Amend the EPUB further if the validator flags any errors.

10 Test the EPUB again on a variety of reading programs and devices.

This workflow would be similar if using other EPUB editing programs.

Adding publication metadata

If the editor is required to add publication metadata to the EPUB, they will have to edit the *content.opf* file, in the coding panel only (there is no preview), and add information into the appropriate fields.

The metadata fields in an EPUB are mostly based on the international Dublin Core (DC) standard. They include fields for title, author, description, ebook ISBN and other publication information. It is particularly important to ensure that at least the title and author are included in the metadata, because the EPUB

Dublin Core (DC)
a metadata vocabulary for describing electronic resources, including websites and EPUB-like ebooks

reading software extracts this information to create the running heads, usually with the author on the left and the title on the right (when viewing the EPUB as a two-page spread).

Like HTML tags, the metadata tags appear within angled brackets and there should be an opening and closing tag for each instance. For example:

```
<dc : title>Emma</dc : title>
<dc : creator>Jane Austen</dc : creator>
<dc : description>The story of a woman with a very high
opinion of herself.</dc : description>
<dc : publisher>Austen Books</dc : publisher>
<dc : date>2013-11-14</dc : date>
<dc : language>en-GB</dc : language>
<dc : identifier id="bookid" opf:scheme="ISBN">urn :
isbn : 0521-096-308-X</dc : identifier>
```

Some of the DC metadata must be inserted using a specific, controlled vocabulary (such as *en-GB*, which means that the language is in British English). Nevertheless, like CSS coding, it can be seen that DC tags are fairly self-explanatory and it is actually not too difficult to figure out what type of metadata is to be inserted and where. Note too that programs such as InDesign may generate standard metadata tags in an EPUB even if there is no information to insert in them. Any unused metadata tags can be left blank or deleted.

For resources relating to Dublin Core metadata, see the list of resources in appendix 11.

Validating the EPUB

Once all the proofreading corrections have been addressed and there are no other problems that need to be fixed, the proofreader may be required to validate the EPUB to ensure that it meets the required technical specifications. Outlets such as Kindle Store and the iBooks Store will reject EPUBs that have failed validation.

A couple of open-source, cross-platform EPUB validators are available: EpubCheck and Flight Crew, which can check both EPUB 2 and EPUB 3 files. Both of these validators will check the EPUB and flag any errors that do not meet the specifications. For example, a line of coding might be missing a closing tag or an image listed in the *content.opf* file might not actually appear in the EPUB.

Open the EPUB in the validator and run the check. A list of errors, if any, will be produced that will identify in which line of the coding each error has occurred, making it relatively easy (in theory anyway) for it to be fixed.

Each validator has its strengths, but they can produce different results for the same EPUB. Using both will ensure that all errors are caught and fixed. Once again, it can be seen that this field is in flux and mature programs are yet to be developed to ensure a consistent and stable environment in which to work.

What does validation mean?

If an EPUB passes validation, this does not mean that it is completely free of errors. It just means that it has passed the technical tests for validity. A valid EPUB could be beautifully coded but still be full of typos, have the wrong images in place, have major layout problems and a host of other errors.

For resources relating to EPUB validation, see appendix 11.

Want to know more?

There is a great deal more to learn about ebooks that cannot be covered in this introductory chapter. Some other topics to explore further include:

- accessibility guidelines and techniques, such as the Web Content Accessibility Guidelines (WCAG)

- the EPUB 2 and 3 specifications

- HTML and CSS coding

- ebook development platforms such as iBooks Author and Inkling.

For resources that will provide starting points for these topics, see appendix 11.

Where to from here?

Editors who are starting out in their careers may feel somewhat daunted by the wide range of possible areas of work ahead of them. While the publishing areas discussed in this book are important sources of employment for editors, much work is also available in other spheres; for example, in editing magazines, publicity material, general websites and software products. And, no doubt, over the coming years, further fields will open up that we have not even thought of yet.

The personal keys to success, no matter what area of publishing an editor enters into, are to be flexible, respectful, rigorous and ready for lifelong learning.

Remember too that though rapid changes in technology are constantly driving editing and publishing to use new formats, techniques and processes, at the heart of editing will always remain a strong command and love of language, heavy doses of common sense and a continually questioning mind. Such skills will always hold the editor in good stead.

Glossary

accessibility making electronic documents available in alternative publication formats to increase the ability of people with disabilities to view, listen to and/or understand the content

AI the vector image file format created by the industry-standard vector software program, Adobe Illustrator

all caps all letters in a word, phrase or sentence are capitalised

appendix additional material, separate from the main text, that is added to the end of a publication, such as a glossary or list of resources

Arabic numerals the numbers 0 to 9

artwork graphic material, such as photographs, drawings or charts, prepared for reproduction

ascender the part of a letter that ascends above the x-height of the text (such as in 'b' or 'f')

author corrections changes made to proofs by the author(s)

AZW a software format for reading ebooks on Kindle devices

backing up (file management) regularly making and securely storing copies of electronic documents to avoid losing work

backing up (printing) when every line of text on the recto of a printed page aligns with the line of text behind it on the verso

backlist books already published by a company and kept in print

barcode a printed code for the ISBN and EAN, consisting of vertical lines of various thicknesses, to be read by an optical scanner

baseline an imaginary common line in type on which all capital letters, x-heights, Arabic numerals and ascenders rest

bibliography a detailed listing of books and articles related to the contents of a publication that may or may not have been referred to in the text (*see also* references)

bitmap *see* BMP (bitmap)

blad a version of a publication created for marketing purposes, containing sample chapters or sections and enclosed in a proof of the cover

bleed the part of an artwork or other element that runs out past the edge of a printed page; when the page is trimmed, there is no space between the edge of the page and the artwork

blind folio a folio counted in the numbering of the pages but not printed (e.g. on the title page and any blank pages)

block quote a separate paragraph containing a long quotation, set differently from the main text, such as indented and in a smaller font

blurb a description of the book to appear on the jacket or back cover, or in publicity material

BMP (bitmap) a type of raster image format

bold/boldface a heavy typeface used for contrast or emphasis; commonly used in headings

book block all the pages between the covers of a book, including the endpapers

CAL *see* Copyright Agency Limited (CAL)

call-out, pull-out or **pull quote** a short piece of text that is highlighted by placing it in the margin or setting it apart in a box or using a different design

caption the title or explanatory matter printed above, beside, below or even on artwork

caret an insertion mark

cascading style sheet *see* CSS

case (binding) the assembled front, back and spine covering material into which the book block is bound

case (capitalisation) the use of capital and non-capital letters in a word

cast-off an estimate of the number of printed pages a manuscript will make when set in a given typeface and measure, following a predetermined page design

cataloguing-in-publication data *see* CiP

CD-ROM (compact disc read-only memory) a compact disc used for storing digital data that can be read optically and processed by a computer

CiP (cataloguing-in-publication) data bibliographic description of a publication, obtained from the National Library of Australia

circular cross-reference a cross-reference, usually in an index, where two non-preferred terms refer only to each other (e.g. cats *see* felines; felines *see* cats), thus leading the reader nowhere

CMYK printing printing using the colours cyan (C), magenta (M), yellow (Y), and black (K)

comp (comprehensive) a low-resolution, watermarked version of an image that is used for drafting layouts

contents page or table of contents a listing of the major sections, chapters and headings in a book, usually following the imprint page

copy all material that is to be set in type

copy editing examining and correcting a written work according to an established editorial style; usually also involves electronic styling of a document in preparation for typesetting (*see also* substantive (structural) editing)

Copyright Agency Limited (CAL) a non-profit organisation representing artists and other content creators that provides information and advice on copyright issues

Creative Commons a copyright licensing system that encourages the free but responsible sharing of information, generally via the internet

cropping trimming or masking off unwanted portions of an artwork

cross-reference a pointer in a text or index to related material elsewhere in a publication, usually indicated using *see* or *see also* (*see also* hyperlink)

CSS (cascading style sheet) a computer language for formatting text in electronic publications, such as on websites and EPUB-like ebooks

curly quotes *see* typographic quotes

DC *see* Dublin Core

descender the part of a letter that descends below the x-height or baseline of the text (such as in 'p' or 'y')

desktop publishing (DTP) *see* typesetting

diacritic a typographic mark combined with a letter to indicate a change in pronunciation (e.g. à, ç, ñ)

die copy copy, such as author and title, printed on the spine and case of hardback books

digital printing a process for printing medium-quality, low-volume jobs from digital files by transferring ink directly to the page (*see also* offset printing)

digital proof a proof generated directly from electronic files and output on a laser printer or similar device

digital rights management (DRM) technologies that restrict and control the use of digital content by users

digital video disc *see* DVD

dinkus a typographic device (such as an asterisk, fleuron or other element) used to mark a break between text passages

dingbat an ornamental character used in typesetting, such as symbols, fleurons and bullet markers

discretionary hyphens *see* soft (discretionary) hyphens

DRM *see* digital rights management

drop the distance between elements on a page, such as from the top of the page or the baseline of the running head to the baseline of the first line of the type area

drop initial capital (drop cap) an initial capital at the beginning of a chapter or part set to drop down one or more lines in a larger point size than that of the main text, sometimes with additional decoration

DTP (desktop publishing) *see* typesetting

Dublin Core (DC) a metadata vocabulary for describing electronic resources, including websites and EPUB-like ebooks

dummy a set of blank pages made up to the specified size and format of a printed book

duotone a method of printing an image, such as a photograph, by combining two colours (usually overlaying black with a contrasting colour)

dust jacket the wrapper around a hardback book, giving publication information, and designed to protect the case and attract attention

DVD (digital video disc) a compact disc storing digital video, audio or computer data

EAN (European Article Number) an international product numbering convention consisting of a 13-digit barcode

ebook a digital version of a book, designed to be read using a device such as a personal computer, tablet or dedicated ebook reader

ebook application stand-alone, book application software, usually multimedia, that is not necessarily based on a particular standard and may run on only some devices

ebook conversion house an organisation that specialises in converting publications to ebook formats

edition a new publication; a changed and/or reset reprint; a publication produced in a different format (e.g. paperback or ebook)

editorial style editorial decisions made about the grammar, punctuation, usage and spelling of text

e-ink low-powered electronic simulation of text used in many ebook reading devices

electronic styling identifying the semantic role of paragraphs or characters in a text, which can then be used to control the consistent appearance (formatting) of all text during typesetting (not to be confused with editorial style)

ellipsis a mark of punctuation (three fixed-spaced dots), usually to indicate an omission

em (typesetting) the square of any type body, so named because the letter 'm' in early fonts was usually cast on a square body; a 10-point em is 10 points wide, a 12-point em is 12 points wide etc.

em rule or em dash a rule or dash taking up one em width

en half an em

en rule or en dash a rule or dash half the width of an em rule

encapsulated postscript *see* EPS

endmatter all material that follows the main text, such as appendixes, notes, bibliography and index

endnote a note that appears at the end of a chapter, section or whole work, rather than at the bottom of the page (*see also* footnotes)

endpapers a pair of leaves at the beginning and end of a book, one leaf of each pair being pasted to the inside cover to attach the binding to the book block

entry or headword the main term in an index or dictionary used for a concept, topic, name or other item, followed by the page number(s) where it appears in the book, and sometimes by subentries

epigraph a quotation that appears in the prelims or at the beginning of a part or chapter

EPS (encapsulated postscript) a commonly used vector image format

EPUB an open access ebook standard developed by the International Digital Publishing Forum

European Article Number *see* EAN

extensible hypertext markup language *see* XHTML

extensible markup language *see* XML

extent the length of a book: the number of pages or the number of words

file a set of digital information with a unique name and location in a computer system or external storage medium (such as a hard disk or file server)

file transfer protocol *see* FTP

fixed layout (ebooks) technology that forces the elements on an ebook page to remain in the same relative position to each other

fixed space a space between two characters that does not break when it falls at the end of a line

fixed-width or monospaced typeface a typeface in which every character takes up the same horizontal space

flash a design element added to a book cover to draw the reader's attention to a special aspect of the content, such as a new edition or map inserts

fleuron stylised form of flowers or leaves that serves as a typographic device, used, for instance, to mark a break in text

folio a single leaf of a manuscript; a printed page number

font a specific size, weight and style of a typeface

foot or feet the margin from the bottom of the type area (text block) to the bottom of the page

footnote a note that appears at the bottom of the page to which it relates, rather than at the end of the chapter, section or whole work (*see also* endnote)

foreword a short recommendation included in the prelims of a book that has been written by someone other than the author

format (artwork) the method of encoding a digital image to suit particular purposes (e.g. JPEG for raster images or AI for vector images)

format (book) the size, style, margins etc. for a publication; the trimmed page size; the medium of production, such as print, ebook or website

formatting (text) marking up text visually, often to express semantic meaning, such as by applying bold, italic, spacing and different typefaces

forme (die) cutting cutting or punching out paper or board to a required shape, such as to produce a book with rounded corners or with a hole in the middle

four-colour (CMYK) printing *see* CMYK

frontispiece an illustration facing the title page

FTP (file transfer protocol) a means of transferring electronic files across an online network, especially useful for uploading large typesetting files to printers

full out type that is set so that all lines in a paragraph are flush to the left and/or right margin; the first line is not indented

GIF (graphics interchange format) a low-resolution raster image format

glyph a graphical element used in a typeface alone or in combination with other glyphs to represent a letter or graphical symbol; for example, letters of the alphabet, diacritics, dingbats etc.

graphics interchange format *see* GIF

greyscale gradations of tints between black and white; sometimes simply called black and white

gutter the space between two columns or between two facing pages

half-title a page showing only the title of the publication

hanging indent type that is set so that all lines in a paragraph are more indented than the first line; the first line may be full out or indented

hard copy copy produced as a printout from a word processor or typesetting program; any computer printout

hard hyphen a hyphen that is required under all circumstances and is inserted manually

hard return or **paragraph break** a manually inserted break in text that creates a new paragraph (*see also* soft return)

hardback a book bound with stiff or rigid covers, usually cardboard covered with cloth or other material and often covered by a dust jacket; the spine is usually sewn rather than glued (*see also* paperback)

head the margin from the top of the page to the top of the type area (text block)

header, footer *see* running head, running foot

headword *see* entry

hierarchy of headings the arrangement of headings and subheadings according to their relative importance and place within a logical sequence

house style a publisher's guide to preferred spellings, punctuation, word usage, formatting and preparation of electronic files

HTML (hypertext markup language) the formatting language used on the World Wide Web, but also in EPUB-like ebooks

hyperlink a virtual link or reference between elements within an electronic document or from elements within a document to an external file (*see also* cross-reference)

hypertext markup language *see* HTML

IDPF *see* International Digital Publishing Forum

imposition arrangement of typeset page spreads on a large sheet to ensure pages appear in the proper sequence while maximising efficient printing

imprint page bibliographic, copyright and other publishing information printed in a work, usually on the reverse of the title page

indent (typesetting) a line or paragraph of type set so that it begins or ends inside the normal margin

index an alphabetical list of entries identifying where in a book significant topics, concepts, people and places are mentioned

International Digital Publishing Forum (IDPF) an independent organisation that develops and promotes the technical specifications for the EPUB standard

International Standard Book Number *see* ISBN

International Standard Serial Number *see* ISSN

ISBN (International Standard Book Number) an international book numbering system that identifies each publication, whether in book or electronic form, by a unique number

ISSN (International Standard Serial Number) an international numbering system that identifies each serial publication (newspaper, journal, magazine, newsletter etc.) by a unique number

italic sloping type, often used to denote emphasis, foreign words, defined terms, titles of book and journals and special uses such as statistical abbreviations (*see also* roman)

Joint Photographic Expert Group *see* JPEG

JPEG (Joint Photographic Expert Group) a compressed raster image format, which is not as high quality as an uncompressed format

justified text words and letters spaced to a given measure, producing vertical alignment at right, left or both margins

kern adjusting the spacing between two characters so that they are visually more readable

key in indicating the approximate position of artwork by inserting a note, comment or draft image in the manuscript

keyline the border around illustrations, boxes, maps and other text and artwork elements

KF8 (Kindle Fire 8) an ebook software format for reading ebooks on newer Kindle devices

Kindle Fire 8 *see* KF8

Kindle an ebook format, device and distribution service developed by Amazon.com Inc.

landscape the format of a page or illustration that is wider than it is deep

layout (design) a plan of a publication page, specifying the typeface and font styles and size, area of the text block, treatment of headings and other text elements, and position of illustrations

layout (typesetting) assembly of all the elements (text and artwork) to make up a page

LCD (liquid crystal display) digital screen technology widely used in computers, ebook reading devices and televisions

leading or **line spacing** the spacing between lines of type; not to be confused with paragraph spacing

Legal Deposit Scheme a requirement under the *Copyright Act 1968* for publishers to deposit a copy of any print work published in Australia with the National Library of Australia and the relevant state library

letter of transmittal a signed letter from the head of a reporting body to the responsible government minister, authority or client

ligature two or more letters joined together in a single matrix (e.g. 'fi' or 'fl')

line break *see* soft return

line spacing *see* leading

liquid crystal display *see* LCD (liquid crystal display)

literal or **typo** a misprint, such as the omission of letters, incorrect punctuation or the inclusion of incorrect letters in words

locator a page number or other device used in an index to pinpoint where a topic, concept, person or other issue is to be found in a book

lowercase small letters, as distinct from uppercase (capital) letters

macro a single-command shortcut for performing a string of operations in a software application; it can be created and customised by the user

macron a diacritic printed as a line above a letter, usually to indicate a long or stressed vowel

manuscript (MS, pl. MSS, typescript) originally handwritten copy, now used to describe an author's unpublished copy, whether in hard copy or electronic format

margins the space surrounding the type area at the top, bottom and sides of a page

maximal case *see* title (maximal) case

MB (megabyte) one million bytes of electronic data

megabyte *see* MB

metadata information about content (e.g. a book, ebook or photograph), such as descriptions of its subject, authorship, ownership and structure, that is not immediately visible in that content but can be used to identify, search and navigate it

minimal case *see* sentence (minimal) case

mock-up a model of a finished page or book to show how the elements will be combined

moiré unwanted patterns that appear in images in printed books due to the overlaying of printed dots during the printing process

monospaced typeface *see* fixed-width typeface

MS *see* manuscript

non-preferred term a synonym or alternative spelling of a preferred term; readers are directed from non-preferred to preferred terms using *see*

note a supporting comment or citation added to the text either at the bottom of the relevant page (footnote) or at the end of a chapter, section or the work (endnote); usually indicated in the text with a superscript symbol, number or letter

OCR *see* optical character recognition

offprint a printed copy of a single article or part from a book or journal

offset printing a process for printing high-quality, high-volume jobs by pressing large sheets over an inked rubber blanket; for colour printing, the printed sheet is repeatedly run through the printing press for each colour required (*see also* digital printing)

open access publication a system that provides unrestricted access to books and articles online, often under a Creative Commons licence

optical character recognition (OCR) a process of scanning text as an image and using software to convert it to digital text by recognising the shapes of the letters

orphan a single word or part of a word that sits on its own in the last line of a paragraph, or the first line of a paragraph that sits on its own at the bottom of a page

OSC (out, see copy) a markup made in the margin of page proofs to indicate when there is a large amount of missing copy to be inserted that is supplied separately; for example, in a Word document

out of registration *see* registration

out, see copy *see* OSC

overset or overrun text that does not fit into a text area in a typeset document; it exists in the file but does not appear on the page because the text area is too small, or the text too long or the font size too big

page spread two facing (verso and recto) pages of a book, presented on one sheet

paperback a book bound with flexible covers, usually heavy paper or thin cardboard; the spine is usually glued rather than sewn, and the cover printed directly with ink (*see also* hardback)

paragraph break *see* hard return

paragraph spacing the spacing between paragraphs; not to be confused with leading

PDF (Portable Document Format) an Adobe file format commonly used in print and ebook production to view, proofread and print the exact typeset layout of a book without having to have the software that created it

permissions agreement(s) obtained from the copyright owner to reproduce part or all of a copyrighted text or artwork in a publication

pixel a tiny digital block that combines with other pixels of different colours or greyscale tints to form a raster image

pixellation the unwanted visibility of individual pixels, rather than smooth gradations, in a raster image when it is reproduced at a larger size than the resolution allows

pixels per inch *see* PPI

placeholder text dummy text (e.g. XX) that is inserted in the early stages of editing and production to indicate where text needs to be updated

PNG (portable network graphics) a low-resolution raster image format, widely used in electronic books

point a printer's unit of measurement (approximately 0.35 mm), used principally when dealing with typefaces

Portable Document Format *see* PDF

portable network graphics *see* PNG

portrait the format of a page or illustration that is deeper than it is wide

PPI (pixels per inch) the density of pixels in an image; the higher the density the higher the resolution (quality) at which the image may be printed

preface a short description by the author about the publication, including changes from a previous edition, usually following the contents page

preferred term a word or phrase that is chosen to describe a particular topic, concept, person or other item (*see also* non-preferred term)

prelims (preliminary pages) all pages preceding the main text of a work, such as the title page, imprint page, preface and contents page

prepress preparation by a commercial printer of a digital file, such as a PDF or InDesign document, so that it is suitable for printing on specific equipment

print run the number of copies of a work to be printed

printer's marks markings on page proofs used by printers to identify the file, check colours and registration, and indicate where to trim the page

proof a trial reproduction of a typeset document or artwork for the purpose of checking and correction

proofreading checking typeset pages to ensure that they are free of errors, well laid out, accurate and complete

pullout or **pullquote** *see* callout

range to align elements either vertically (e.g. for line endings or a caption with an illustration) or horizontally (e.g. for table elements)

raster an image format consisting of tiny pixels of colour or shades of grey; low-resolution raster images may become pixellated when reproduced in print books and so are better suited to ebooks

recto the 'front' of a leaf of paper in a book, usually a right-hand (odd-numbered) page (*see also* verso)

references a detailed listing of books and articles that are referred to in a publication; related sources that are not mentioned in the text are not included (*see also* bibliography)

reflow (ebooks) technologies that allow ebook content to rearrange and resize elements according to user and device settings

registration (printing) aligning pages when they are printed offset in two or more colours (requiring two or more passes through the press); if the pages are misaligned (out of registration), the printing will be blurred

reprint printing more copies of a publication in exactly the same format or with only very minor corrections (*see also* edition)

responsive web design designing to allow websites to resize and rearrange page elements dynamically according to the size of the screen or window being used for reading

rich text format *see* RTF

rights-managed image artwork that is licensed for one-off, limited use, e.g. for a specified duration or location, with any further uses requiring the payment of additional royalty fees

river of white space a coincidence of word spacing occurring in successive lines that forms an unwanted eye trap or distraction

roman (numerals) numbers based on the ancient Roman system of letters (e.g. i, v, x or I, V, X, L, C, D, M)

roman (type) upright type (not italic)

rough an artist's or author's sketch or layout to be used as a guide for the illustrator or designer

royalty-free image artwork that is licensed with a one-off fee that allows reuse over an unlimited period without the need for the user to pay further royalties

RTF (rich text format) a widely accessible text file format that allows text to be styled and formatted

rule or dash a horizontal line used to link characters, words or numbers

run on to make sentences follow each other without starting a new paragraph; to start a new section, chapter or other text on the same page as the end of the last one, rather than on a fresh page

running head, running foot a title or brief descriptive heading printed at the head (top) or foot (bottom) of each page

sample setting a page design showing where and how text and graphic elements are to be presented

sans serif a typeface without serifs

section a printed sheet folded in multiples of four, usually consisting of 8, 16, 32 or 48 pages

sentence (minimal) case capitalising only the first word and any proper nouns in a heading, title or phrase

sepia a warm tone added (usually digitally) to a black-and-white photograph and printed using the duotone method

serif short cross-line or stroke at the end of the main vertical or horizontal stroke of a printed letter

set down set type in a smaller size

small caps (small capital letters) uppercase characters set at the x-height of the lowercase letters surrounding them (e.g. BCE and CE)

smart quotes *see* typographic quotes

soft copy copy produced as a digital version of a word processor or typesetting file

soft (discretionary) hyphens special hyphens inserted where words *could* be broken if they occur at the ends of lines, but otherwise are invisible; they can be inserted manually or calculated automatically by typesetting software

soft return or **line break** a break in text that creates a new line, but not a new paragraph; can be inserted manually or calculated automatically by typesetting software (*see also* hard return)

solidus an oblique stroke dividing alternatives or ratios; not to be confused with the forward slash on a typical computer keyboard

special character a character, such as a mathematical symbol foreign language diacritics or fractions, that may need to be treated separately

spine the binding edge of a book's cover or jacket; the outside of the spine is visible when the book is stored on a shelf

spot colour (printing) a coloured ink that is pre-mixed so that it can be printed in a single run rather than using CMYK or other colour combinations that require several runs (*see also* offset printing)

stet ('let it stand') used to mark where a written correction in page proofs is to be ignored

stock paper or other material (e.g. cloth, plastic) used for printing or binding

storyboard a rough layout of the text and artwork elements in a publication, provided to a designer

structural editing *see* substantive (structural) editing

subscript a character in a smaller font size that prints below the x-height; used, for example, in equations

subentry an indexing term for a sub-topic of the main entry

superscript a character in a smaller font size that prints above the x-height or at the top of a line; used, for example, in footnote references and equations

substantive (structural) editing examination and correction of a written work to ensure that its structure is sound, its order logical, its content complete, and the language clear and appropriate for its audience (*see also* copy editing)

table of contents *see* contents page

tagged image file format *see* TIFF

text block the lines of text that are bound by the margins on a page

thin space a space that is one-fifth or one-sixth of an em wide

thumbnail a smaller version of an image, such as a cover, that is used in publishing catalogues and on reading devices to more easily identify a book

TIFF (tagged image file format) a raster image format that is well suited to high-resolution reproduction in printed books

tip-in an extra page or pages printed separately and fixed in position in a book by being glued along its inner edge; for example, a fold-out map or a colour page in an otherwise single-colour book

title (maximal) case capitalising every significant word (excluding prepositions, articles and conjunctions unless they are the first word) in a heading, title or phrase

title page the page in the book appearing near the front that contains the title and subtitle of the book, the name of the author and other elements such as the publisher and place of publication (*see also* half-title)

tone (writing) the attitude that the author implies in a text about the content and the intended reader

Track Changes a system used in Microsoft Word for electronically recording changes in word processing documents

trapping (printing) making colours overlap slightly to avoid unintended gaps when printing is out of registration

trimming (printing) cutting the edges of printed pages after they are bound to create a smooth edge

turnovers the second and subsequent lines of a paragraph, bibliography or index entry

typeface a complete set of all the fonts sharing the same design features; also called a font family

typescript *see* manuscript

typesetting or desktop publishing (DTP) the use of specialist software, such as Adobe InDesign or QuarkXPress, to produce a print-ready and/or electronic copy of a publication

typo *see* literal

typographic quotes (smart or curly quotes) quotation marks that are curved rather than straight

typography arranging type to form a pleasing design and assist in communicating its content and meaning

unjustified type set with even word spacing so that successive lines are of irregular length, usually aligned on the left

uppercase capital letters, as distinct from lowercase letters

vector an image format based on mathematical formulas that can be scaled up or down to almost any size without losing reproduction quality

version control managing versions of an electronic file so that there is no confusion about which is the latest version; older copies are archived and only the current version is worked on for the next stage

verso the 'back' of a leaf of paper in a book, usually a left-hand (even-numbered) page (*see also* recto)

voice (grammar) the relationship between the verb and the subject to indicate whether the subject is the doer (active voice) or the receiver (passive voice) of the action

widow the last line or word of a paragraph that sits on its own at the top of a page

word break splitting (hyphenating) a word at the end of a line

wraparound a small group of pages (usually printed separately from the rest of the book, due to their different content or format) wrapped around a section, or part of a section, in the makeup of a book

x-height height of a lowercase letter without ascenders or descenders (such as 'x' or 'n')

XML (extensible markup language) the formatting language that is used as the basis for the World Wide Web, EPUB-like ebooks and many software programs, such as Word and InDesign

XHTML (extensible hypertext markup language) a formatting language combining XML and HTML that is used as the basis for the World Wide Web and EPUB-like ebooks

Appendixes

Appendix no.	Title
1	Publisher's brief
2	Page design brief
3	Artwork and permissions brief
4	Illustration brief
5	Editorial schedule and checklist
6	Example permissions letter
7	Author's questionnaire (educational publisher)
8	Sample style sheet and word list
9	Proofreading symbols
10	Useful contacts
11	Further reading and other resources

Appendix 1

Title	
	☐ Working title / ☐ Final title
Author(s)	
Publication date	
Publication date tied to	
Series	
ISBN	
Print run	
Suggested price	$
No. of pages (print)	
Finished size (print)	
Binding (print)	☐ Hardback / ☐ Paperback / ☐ Spiral / ☐ Other:
Ebook distribution	☐ Kindle / ☐ Nook / ☐ EPUB / ☐ Other

Marketing information

Subject	
	☐ General / ☐ Primary / ☐ Secondary / ☐ Tertiary, TAFE / ☐ Reference / ☐ Fiction, poetry, drama / ☐ Children's illus. book (age group:) ☐ Other:
Special features	
Main competition	
Other books by same author(s)	
Launch date	
Media release	

(continued)

Author(s) contact details

Address	Home:
	Work:
Telephone (tick preferred method of contact)	☐ Home: ( )
	☐ Work: ( )
	☐ Mobile:
Email	
Hours available	

Details of MS

Draft/final MS received	
Level of editing	☐ Structural / ☐ Copyediting
Text to come	☐ Draft blurb / ☐ © line / ☐ Foreword / ☐ Preface / ☐ Acknowledgements / ☐ Extracts
Artwork to come	☐ Author photo / ☐ Illustrations / ☐ Photographs
Permissions required	Author to request:
	Publisher to obtain:
Permissions budget	$

Design recommendations

No. colours	Cover:
	Text:
No. illustrations	
Section/wraparound/insert (no. of pages)	
Illustrator to be commissioned	

Signature (Publisher)	
Date	

Appendix 2

Title	
Author(s)	
Series	
Format	☐ Hardback / ☐ Paperback / ☐ Spiral / ☐ Other:
Audience	☐ General / ☐ Primary / ☐ Secondary / ☐ Tertiary, TAFE / ☐ Reference / ☐ Fiction, poetry, drama / ☐ Children (age group:) ☐ Other:
Style guide	☐ Attached
General page design requirements	

Parts of the MS

Prelims

	i
ii	iii
iv	v
vi	vii
viii	ix

Main text

Parts	
Chapters	
Headings	
Extracts	
Running heads	

(continued)

Running feet	
Illustrations	
Tables	
Special characters	
Equations/formulae	
Poetry	
Footnotes	☐ Bottom of page / ☐ End of chapter / ☐ End of book
Other	

Endmatter

Bibliography	
Glossary	
Appendixes	
Index supplied by	☐ Author / ☐ Indexer
Other	
Signature (Editor)	
Date	

Appendix 3

ARTWORK AND PERMISSIONS BRIEF

Title
Author(s)
Series
Colour or b/w
Date artwork required by
Market
Brief description of book

Figure number	Page of MS	Bitmap, line, extract	Supplied by author	Publisher to obtain	Publisher to create?	Description	Source	Permission needed?
1.1	7	Bitmap	✓	—	—	NASA rocket launch	The Age	Yes
1.2	13	Line	—	—	✓	Cartoon at tuckshop	See rough	
1.3	13	Line	—	—	✓	Cartoon at bus stop	See rough	
1.4	19	Bitmap	✓	—	—	Vietnam protesters	Sydney Morning Herald	Yes
2.1	27	Bitmap	—	✓	—	Gough Whitlam—It's Time	Try Sun-Herald?	Yes
2.2	33	Line	—	—	✓	Cartoon of dole queue	See rough	
etc.								

Appendix 4

Line illustrations to be supplied

Figure no.	Page of MS	Description
1.2	8	Young man putting down phone, looking frustrated.
1.3	23	Young woman standing aggressively with arms folded.
1.6	66	Young man introducing older man to older woman.
3.1	96	Father on bike with child in safety seat.
3.5	125	Children playing in sandpit.
5.1	153	Young woman driving forklift (see attached rough—note safety features).
5.2	162	Young man stocking supermarket shelves.

Notes   Please use a mix of ethnic backgrounds in these illustrations.

Appendix 5

EDITORIAL SCHEDULE AND CHECKLIST

Book details

Author(s)	
Title	
ISBN	
Editor	

Schedule

Item	Action		Date
MS files	PDF and Word files received from author	☐	
	Files checked for viruses	☐	
	PDF corresponds to Word file	☐	
	PDF & Word file discrepancies queried with author	☐	
	Corrected files (if required) received	☐	
	Original files stored securely	☐	
Editing	Structural and copy editing and electronic styling completed	☐	
	Queries to author	☐	
	Author responses due	☐	
	Author responses received	☐	
	Author corrections and responses incorporated	☐	

(continued)

Item	Action		Date
Editing *(cont'd)*	Final edited MS to author	☐	
	Final author responses due	☐	
	Final author responses received	☐	
	Final corrections incorporated	☐	
	MS sent to typesetter	☐	
Artwork	Artwork and permissions brief received or prepared	☐	
	Illustration brief prepared and sent to:	☐	
	Illustrations due	☐	
	Illustrations received	☐	
	Illustrations checked and edited	☐	
	Corrections to illustrator	☐	
	Corrected illustrations due	☐	
	Corrected illustrations received	☐	
	Final illustrations sent to typesetter	☐	
Permissions	Artwork and permissions brief checked against MS	☐	
	Text extracts: sources listed	☐	
	Text extracts: permission requested	☐	
	Text extracts: permission received	☐	
	Illustrations: sources listed	☐	
	Illustrations: permission requested	☐	
	Illustrations: permission received	☐	
	Acknowledgements prepared	☐	

Item	Action		Date
CiP data	Requested from National Library	☐	
	Received from National Library	☐	
Cover	Cover copy prepared	☐	
	Cover copy sent to designer	☐	
	Cover copy due from designer	☐	
	Cover copy received from designer	☐	
	Cover design approved	☐	
	Final title approved	☐	
Page design	Page design brief completed	☐	
	Page design brief sent to typesetter	☐	
First pages	First pages due from typesetter	☐	
	First pages sent to proofreader	☐	
	First pages due from proofreader	☐	
	Proofreading of first pages completed	☐	
	First pages corrections sent to typesetter	☐	
Second and subsequent pages	Second pages due from typesetter	☐	
	Second pages sent to proofreader	☐	
	Second pages due from proofreader	☐	
	Proofreading of second pages completed	☐	

(continued)

Item	Action		Date
Second and subsequent pages *(cont'd)*	Second pages corrections sent to typesetter	☐	
	Revised pages due from typesetter	☐	
	Revised pages checked and approved	☐	
	Revised pages sent to indexer	☐	
Index	Index copy due from indexer	☐	
	Index copy received	☐	
	Index copy edited and checked	☐	
	Index copy sent to typesetter	☐	
Final pages	Final pages checked and approved	☐	
	Final pages sent to printer	☐	
Printer's proofs	Printer's proofs received	☐	
	Printer's proofs checked and approved	☐	
Advance copies	Advance copies due	☐	
Ebook	Final pages sent for ebook conversion	☐	
	Converted ebook due	☐	
	Ebook proofread and checked	☐	
	Corrections sent to conversion house	☐	
	Corrected ebook due	☐	
	Corrected ebook checked and approved	☐	

Material to come

Material	Description	Date due
Text	☐ Blurb:	
	☐ Foreword:	
	☐ Preface:	
	☐ Acknowledgements:	
Artwork	☐ Author photo:	
	☐ Illustrations:	
	☐ Photographs:	

Appendix 6

Dear _____

We are preparing for publication an illustrated travel book for adults by Hemi Green entitled *Tramping the Milford Track*. It is to be published in Australia in 2015 as a paperback with a print run of 3000 copies, and as an ebook. The retail price for the printed book will be $45.95 and the ebook $39.99.

We request your permission to include in this text the material in the attached copy. Full acknowledgement will be given to the source. If you are prepared to grant permission, please return one signed copy of this letter. If you do not hold the copyright, please forward this letter to the copyright holder or advise us to whom we should write.

Yours sincerely

Christine Haapu
Editor
Enc.

I/we grant permission to reproduce the copyright material specified below.

_____

Description of material: _____

Desired form of acknowledgement: _____

_____

Fee (if any): $ _____

(to be paid on publication unless requested otherwise)

Name (please print): _____

Signed: _____

Date: _____

Address: _____

Appendix 7

AUTHOR'S QUESTIONNAIRE (EDUCATIONAL PUBLISHER)

Address	Home:
	Work:
Telephone (tick preferred method of contact)	☐ Home: ( )
	☐ Work: ( )
	☐ Mobile:
Email	
Hours available	
Title of book	
Author's name (used on cover and promotional material)	
Photograph of author	☐ Attached / ☐ To come
Current position held	
Previous publications	Title, publisher, place, date:
Biographical details	Qualifications, positions held, other professional details:
Draft blurb for cover (100–150 words)	
Why do you feel a new book is needed in this subject area?	

(continued)

At what level(s) do you expect your book to be used?	☐ Primary/secondary: ☐ 1 ☐ 2 ☐ 3 ☐ 4 ☐ 5 ☐ 6 ☐ 7 ☐ 8 ☐ 9 ☐ 10 ☐ 11 ☐ 12 ☐ TAFE ☐ College/university ☐ Postgraduate
For which course(s)/ readers is your book intended?	
What are the main competitors to the proposed book?	Author, title, latest edition, publisher, place, date, price:
How will this book be superior to its competitors?	
Do you know of any competing books in preparation?	
List any journals to which we could send a copy of this book for review	

Appendix 8

SAMPLE STYLE SHEET AND WORD LIST

Style sheet

Author(s)	Llewellyn & Edwards
Title	Africa by the Long Road
Editor	Leanna Rowe

Spelling

Australian spellings (-ise, -our)

Use first instance in *Macquarie Dictionary* (except proper names)

Capitalisation

In references: capitalise first letter and proper nouns in headings and titles of publications and articles

In text: capitalise all significant words for titles of publications and articles

Punctuation

Unspaced en rule between numbers

Unspaced em rule between clauses

Spaced ellipses

No Oxford (serial) comma

Quotes

Single quote marks for quotes and coined expressions

Use block quotes with no quote marks when more than about 30 words

Only use double quote marks when quoting within a quote surrounded by single quote marks

Numbers, measurement and dates

Spell out numbers one to nine, except for percentages and ages

Add comma in numbers with 5 digits or more (10,000, 3000)

Metric units of measurement, use numerals with abbreviated units (50 km)

Australian date format (Wednesday, 26 January 2012)

Time: 7.30 am

Acronyms and abbreviations

No full stops in acronyms (US, UK)

Full stops in abbreviations not ending in last letter (Vic., Dr)

Formatting

Italics for titles of books and journals, foreign words, for emphasis

No italics for names of programs, projects, conferences

No punctuation for bullet lists that comprise sentence fragments; full stop for last bullet point

Captions appear above tables, below figures

Data source appears below tables and figures (but above figure captions)

Word list

Author(s)	Llewellyn & Edwards
Title	Africa by the Long Road
Editor	Leanna Rowe

A
aardwolf
acknowledgement
among (*not* amongst)
Aughrabies Falls
B
Bangweulu (Lake)
birth rate
blaaubok
boyfriend
breakdown (noun)
C
cichlid
cross-cultural
D
diarrhoea
dibatag
drug-runner (adj)
drug runner (n)
duiker
E
Earth (the planet)
earth (the ground)
email
enrol
F
flamingos
fledgling
freshwater
G
girlfriend
grysbok
guerrilla

H
handwritten
hartebeest
heartbroken
heterogenous (biological)
Hluhluwe River
I
infrared
interrelationship
J
jail
judgement
K
Koran (*not* Qu'ran or Quran)
L
labelled
lifelong
longlasting
M
manoeuvre
micro-economy
microfibre
miniscule
multicultural
N
nerve-wracking
neverending
O
off-site
online
on-site

P
Paleolithic
prehistoric
pre-occupied
R
re-arrange
re-invent
resettle
revisit
rinderpest
S
sea shore
semi-automatic
subhuman
sub-tropical
Sudan (*not* the Sudan)
T
Tessaout Valley
travelled, traveller
U
Umfolozi River
underfoot
under way
V
verandah
W
wait-a-bit thorn
web page
website
whydah
X, Y, Z
x-ray

Word list in a grid

A	B	C	D
artwork acknowledgement age range appendixes	best-selling backup barcode bookshop book-back	copy editing cooperation cost effective co-production	decision-making (adj) decision making (n) database
E	**F**	**G**	**H**
ebook e-store EANs Earth em rule (en) e.g.	Fahrenheit footnote footers (not running feet)	graphics interchange format (GIF) greyscale gluing	hi-lo graphs half-title hypertext mark-up language (HTML) hyperlinks
I	**J**	**K**	**L**
italics ink-jet International Standard Book Number (ISBN)	jacketing jewel case	keyword Koori	layout letter-by-letter lowercase
M	**N**	**O**	**P**
manuscript (MS) mark-up marketing metadata	National Library of Australia (NLA) non-linear	offset old-style (numbers) optical character recognition (OCR) online	print run page proof password
Q	**R**	**S**	**T**
quality control queens (gen) Queen (spec)	reprints recommended retail price (RRP) run-on	SI units set-off subtitles sans serif	tag line timeline Torres Strait
U	**V**	**W**	**X,Y,Z**
uppercase up-to-date (adj)	variable-data printing	word-by-word workplace website word break	zoom lens

Appendix 9

PROOFREADING SYMBOLS

Instruction	Textual mark	Marginal mark*

*Marginal instructions in this table are circled, words in italics in this column are not part of the marginal mark.

Instruction	Textual mark	Marginal mark*
	___ ⬭	(ital)
	⬭ ___	(rom)
	~~ ⬭	(bold)
	~~ ⬭	(bold ital)
	⬭	(w/f)
	≡	(caps)
	/// ⬭	(l.c.)
	≡	(c/sc)
	≡ ⬭	(sc)
	⅄	#
	⅄	(thin #)
	| |	(eq. #)
	/	(less #) (close up)
	⌒	⌒
	///	(letter #)
	⌐___¬	(keep together)
	>	#
	( )	(less #) (close up)

Instruction	Textual mark	Marginal mark*

run
on   r/o

□   1
□□   2

f/o

centre

take   t/o
over

take   t/b
back

np

raise

lower

cross-   x-ref
ref

Appendix 10

Professional organisations

Editing

Institute of Professional Editors (IPEd): www.iped-editors.org

State and territory societies of editors

Canberra Society of Editors Inc.: www.editorscanberra.org

The Society of Editors (NSW) Inc.: www.editorsnsw.com

Society of Editors (Queensland) Inc.: www.editorsqld.com

The Society of Editors (SA) Inc.: www.editors-sa.org.au

The Society of Editors (Tasmania) Inc.: www.tas-editors.org.au

Editors Victoria: www.editorsvictoria.org

Society of Editors (WA) Inc.: www.editorswa.com

Media, Entertainment and Arts Alliance (MEAA):
www.alliance.org.au

Indexing

Australian and New Zealand Society of Indexers Inc. (ANZSI):
www.anzsi.org

ACT Region: www.anzsi.org/site/act_contacts.asp

New South Wales: www.anzsi.org/site/nsw_contacts.asp

New Zealand: www.anzsi.org/site/nz_contacts.asp

Northern Territory: www.anzsi.org/site/NT_contact.asp

Queensland: www.anzsi.org/site/qld_contacts.asp

South Australia: www.anzsi.org/site/sa_contacts.asp

Tasmania: www.anzsi.org/site/tas_contact.asp

Victoria: www.anzsi.org/site/vic_contacts.asp

Western Australia: www.anzsi.org/site/wa_contacts.asp

Publishing

Australian Publishers Association (APA): www.publishers.asn.au

Authors

Australian Society of Authors: www.asauthors.org

The NSW Writers' Centre: www.nswwc.org.au

Queensland Writers Centre: www.qwc.asn.au

SA Writers Centre Inc.: www.sawriters.org.au

Writers Victoria: www.writersvictoria.org.au

Copyright and other legal issues

Arts Law Centre of Australia: www.artslaw.com.au

Australasian Performing Right Association Ltd (APRA) | Australasian Mechanical Copyright Owners Society Ltd (AMCOS): www.apra-amcos.com.au

Australian Copyright Council: www.copyright.org.au

National Library of Australia: www.nla.gov.au

Viscopy: www.viscopy.org.au

Literature

Children's Book Council of Australia: www.cbc.org.au

Literature Board of the Australia Council: www.ozco.gov.au

The Wheeler Centre: www.wheelercentre.com

Appendix 11

FURTHER READING AND OTHER RESOURCES

General editing references

Copy editing

Butcher, J, Drake, C & Leach, M 2006, *Butcher's copy-editing: the Cambridge handbook for editors, copy-editors and proofreaders*, 4th edn, Cambridge University Press, Cambridge.

Einsohn, A 2011, *The copyeditor's handbook: a guide for book publishing and corporate communications*, 3rd edn, University of California Press, Berkeley, CA.

Institute of Professional Editors 2013, *Australian standards for editing practice*, 2nd edn, Institute of Professional Editors, Point Cook, Vic., www.iped-editors.org/About_editing/Editing_standards.aspx.

Mackenzie, J 2011, *The editor's companion*, 2nd edn, Cambridge University Press, Melbourne.

Saller, CF 2009, *The subversive copy editor: advice from Chicago (or, how to negotiate good relationships with your writers, your colleagues, and yourself)*, University of Chicago, Chicago.

Dictionaries

Delahunty, A (ed.) 2008, *The Oxford dictionary of foreign words and phrases*, 2nd edn, Oxford University Press, Oxford, 2000.

Isaacs, A, Daintith, J & Martin, E (eds) 2009, *New Oxford dictionary for scientific writers and editors*, 2nd edn, Oxford University Press, Oxford.

Macquarie Aboriginal words: words from Australian Aboriginal and Torres Strait Islander languages, 2005, Macquarie University, Sydney.

The Macquarie dictionary, 2013, 6th edn, Macquarie University, Sydney. (Also available by online subscription at www.macquariedictionary.com.au.)

Moore, B 2009, *The Australian concise Oxford dictionary*, 5th edn, Oxford University Press, Melbourne.

Oxford dictionaries, www.oxforddictionaries.com.

English-language usage

Burchfield, RW 1998, *The new Fowler's modern English usage*, rev. edn, Oxford University Press, Oxford.

Peters, P 2007, *The Cambridge guide to Australian English usage*, 2nd edn, Cambridge University Press, Sydney.

Ritter, RM 2005, *New Oxford dictionary for writers and editors: the essential A–Z guide to the written word*, 2nd edn, rev. A Stevenson & L Brown, Oxford University Press, Oxford.

Grammar

Arts, B, Chalker, S & Weiner, E 2014, *The Oxford dictionary of English grammar*, Oxford University Press, Oxford.

Carter, R & McCarthy, M 2006, *Cambridge grammar of English: a comprehensive guide*, Cambridge University Press, Cambridge.

Crystal, D 2004, *Rediscover grammar*, 3rd edn, Longman, London.

Trask, RL 2000, *The Penguin dictionary of English grammar*, Penguin, London.

University College London, 2013, *The Internet grammar of English*, University College London, London, www.ucl.ac.uk/internet-grammar. (Also available as an iOS or Android app.)

Style guides

AMA manual of style: a guide for authors and editors, 2007, 10th edn, Oxford University Press, New York.

The Chicago manual of style: the essential guide for writers, editors and publishers, 2010, 16th edn, University of Chicago, Chicago. (Also see *The Chicago manual of style online*: www.chicagomanualofstyle.org.)

The Economist 2014, 'Style guide', www.economist.com/styleguide/introduction.

Melbourne University Law Review Association & Melbourne Journal of International Law, 2010, *Australian guide to legal citation*, 3rd edn, Melbourne University Law Review Association, Melbourne.

Publication manual of the American Psychological Association, 2010, 6th edn, American Psychological Association, Washington, DC.

Ritter, R 2012, *New Oxford style manual*, 2nd edn, Oxford University Press, Oxford.

Smart, P, Maisonneuve, H & Polderman, AKS 2013, *Science editors' handbook*, European Association of Science Editors, Cornwall.

Style manual for authors, editors and printers, 2002, 6th edn, rev. Snooks & Co., John Wiley & Sons, Brisbane.

Thesauruses

Kipfer, BA 2010, *Roget's international thesaurus*, 7th edn, HarperCollins, New York.

Knight, A 2001, *The Australian Oxford paperback thesaurus*, Oxford University Press, Melbourne.

Macquarie Thesaurus, 2007, 2nd edn, Macquarie University, Sydney.

Oxford dictionaries, www.oxforddictionaries.com.

Writing and style issues

Fowler, HR & Aaron, JE 2011, *The Little, Brown handbook*, 12th edn, Longman, New York.

Gowers, E 1987, *The complete plain words*, 3rd edn, rev. S Greenbaum & J Whitcut, Penguin, London.

Queensland Department of Communities, Child Safety and Disability Services, 2012, *A way with words: guidelines for the portrayal of people with a disability*, Department of Communities, Child Safety and Disability Services, Brisbane.

Strunk, W Jr, White, EB 1999, *The elements of style*, 4th edn, Longman, New York, www.bartleby.com/141.

Swift, K 2001, *The handbook of nonsexist writing for writers, editors and speakers*, 2nd edn, iUniverse, Bloomington, IN.

Truss, L 2003, *Eats, shoots and leaves: the zero tolerance approach to punctuation*, Profile Books, London.

Watson, D 2004, *Death sentence: the decay of public language*, Vintage Australia, Melbourne.

Onscreen editing

Connor, N & MacDonald, M 2013, *Office 2013: the missing manual*, O'Reilly Media, Sebastopol, CA.

Goodwill Community Foundation 2014, 'Word 2013: Track Changes and Comments', www.gcflearnfree.org/word2013/26.

Grover, C 2010, *Office 2011 for Macintosh: the missing manual*, O'Reilly Media, Sebastopol, CA.

Hart, G 2010, *Effective onscreen editing: new tools for an old profession*, 2nd edn, Diaskeuasis Publishing, Pointe-Claire, Quebec, www.geoff-hart.com/books/eoe/onscreen-book.htm.

Lynda.com tutorials for using Word, www.lynda.com/Microsoft-training-tutorials/124-0.html?category=word_326&views=0.

Microsoft 2014, 'Track changes' (Word 2013), http://office.microsoft.com/en-us/word-help/track-changes-HA102840151.aspx?CTT=1.

Microsoft 2014, 'Use track changes' (Word for Mac 2011), http://office.microsoft.com/en-us/mac-word-help/use-tracked-changes-HA102928670.aspx?CTT=1.

Williams, R 1995, *The PC is not a typewriter*, Peachpit Press, San Francisco.

Williams, R 2003, *The Mac is not a typewriter*, 2nd edn, Peachpit Press, San Francisco.

Picture research

AP Images, www.apimages.com.

Australian War Memorial Collection, www.awm.gov.au/search/all.

Corbis Images, www.corbisimages.com.

fotolia, au.fotolia.com.

Fotosearch, www.fotosearch.com.

Getty Images, www.gettyimages.com.au.

iStockphoto, www.istockphoto.com.

National Library of Australia Trove pictures, photos, objects, http://trove.nla.gov.au/picture?q=.

Newspix, www.newspix.com.au.

Indexing

Browne, G & Jermey, J 2007, *The indexing companion*, Cambridge University Press, Port Melbourne, Vic.

Fetters, LK 2013, *Handbook of indexing techniques: a guide for beginning indexers*, 5th edn, Information Today, Metford, NJ.

Leise, F, Mertes, K & Badgett, N 2008, *Indexing for editors and authors: a practical guide to understanding indexes*, American Society of Indexers, Wheat Ridge, CO.

Ebooks

General and industry news

Digital Book World, www.digitalbookworld.com.

Pigs, Gourds and Wikis (ebook blog), www.pigsgourdsandwikis.com.

HTML and CSS

Codecademy 2014, 'HTML & CSS', www.codecademy.com/tracks/web.

Howe, S 2013, 'A beginner's guide to HTML & CSS', http://learn.shayhowe.com/html-css.

W3Schools, www.w3schools.com.

Creating ebooks and EPUBs

Castro, E 2011, 'EPUB straight to the point', www.elizabethcastro.com/epub.

Cunningham, C 2013, 'Resources: going from InDesign to ebook', www.digitalbookworld.com/resources-going-from-indesign-to-ebook.

EPUB Secrets, www.epubsecrets.com.

Garrish, M 2011, *What is EPUB3? an introduction to the EPUB specification for multimedia publishing*, O'Reilly Media, Sebastopol, CA.

InDesign Secrets, www.indesignsecrets.com.

EPUB validation and standards

Dublin Core Metadata Initiative, dublincore.org.

EPUBCheck: https://github.com/IDPF/epubcheck.

Flightcrew (EPUB validator) https://code.google.com/p/flightcrew.

International Digital Publishing Forum, www.idpf.org.

World Wide Web Consortium 2011, 'Getting started with web accessibility', www.w3.org/WAI/gettingstarted/Overview.html.

Ebook production processes

Australian and New Zealand Society of Indexers 2014, 'Ebooks', www.anzsi.org/site/ebooks.asp.

McKesson, N & Witwer, A 2012, *Publishing with iBooks Author: an introduction to creating ebooks for the iPad*, O'Reilly Media, Sebastopol, CA.

MobileRead 2014, 'E-book formats' (support forums), www.mobileread.com/forums/forumdisplay.php?f=177.

Nix, LK 2011, 'Ebook conversion: the basics', goldenorbcreative. wordpress.com/2011/07/10/ebook-conversion-the-basics.

Sturdivant, J 2012, 'Inside the e-book production process: 3 publishers give you a behind-the-scenes look into their e-book conversion workflows', www.bookbusinessmag.com/article /inside-e-book-production-process-3-publishers-show-you-do-it.

Software

Adobe Reader: http://get.adobe.com/reader (download); https:// helpx.adobe.com/acrobat.html (support and help).

calibre: www.calibre-ebook.com/download (download); manual. calibre-ebook.com/edit.html (help).

EPUB Zip-Unzip (Mac): www.mobileread.com/forums/attachment. php?attachmentid=95318&d=1351859908 (download).

oXygen XML Editor: www.oxygenxml.com (download and support).

Sigil: https://github.com/user-none/Sigil (download); wiki. mobileread.com/wiki/Sigil (support and help).

Index

Printed in Australia
20 Feb 2020
732188